luxury online

luxury online

styles, systems,
strategies

Uché Okonkwo

palgrave
macmillan

First published 2010 by
PALGRAVE MACMILLAN

Palgrave Macmillan in the UK is an imprint of Macmillan Publishers Limited,
registered in England, company number 785998, of Houndmills, Basingstoke,
Hampshire RG21 6XS.

Palgrave Macmillan in the US is a division of St Martin's Press LLC,
175 Fifth Avenue, New York, NY 10010.

Palgrave Macmillan is the global academic imprint of the above companies
and has companies and representatives throughout the world.

Palgrave® and Macmillan® are registered trademarks in the United States,
the United Kingdom, Europe and other countries.

ISBN 978–0–230–55536–5

This book is printed on paper suitable for recycling and made from fully
managed and sustained forest sources. Logging, pulping and manufacturing
processes are expected to conform to the environmental regulations of the
country of origin.

A catalogue record for this book is available from the British Library.

A catalog record for this book is available from the Library of Congress.

10 9 8 7 6 5 4 3 2 1
19 18 17 16 15 14 13 12 11 10

Printed and bound in China

This book is dedicated to the memory of my grandfather John Okonkwo, who left great impressions on me, even as a child

Contents

List of tables and figures

Tables

Figures

list of tables and figures

List of Case Analyses

Foreword

It was not too long ago that to suggest that the Internet had an important role to play in the rarefied world of luxury was either an act of misplaced bravery or an outright heresy, depending on your point of view. Today, however, all the major players in this sector are falling over themselves in a rush to embrace the online world.

Until recently, the wisdom of using an official company website for anything more than a few bland declarations and a limited online brochure was still being challenged in the boardrooms of luxury conglomerates. Now, after a stampede to set up transactional e-retail websites, luxury brands, often with the self-consciousness of a child arriving at a new school halfway through the term, are looking to attach themselves to every new online phenomenon, from blogging to Twittering via YouTube and Facebook.

So why has it taken so long for the world of luxury to embrace the Internet and new technologies? Blinkered by fears of 'channel conflict' – diverting business from their bricks and mortar stores and upsetting their wholesale customers – luxury brands had convinced themselves that luxury was 'different', that it could not be 'delivered' online without being debased and undermined. So the received wisdom was that at best the Internet was irrelevant, at worst an insidious threat. The leaders of the luxury fashion industry therefore either ignored the online world altogether or opted for a half-hearted level of agnostic semi-engagement which left observers from the real world scratching their heads in bemused disbelief.

Luxury brands, for so long dismissive of the need to listen to their customers, had this time been left far behind by these clients. It has taken them a while to realize this. Indeed, it has been left to the pioneering entrepreneurs of the industry, with the vision and self-belief to challenge the received wisdom of the industry heavyweights, to demonstrate this. Their example illustrated that the Internet can be as powerful a force for change and growth in the rarefied world of luxury as it has proved to be in all other sectors of the retail world. Of course, the luxury Internet trailblazers had the advantage of not being encumbered by the legacy of business structures that were preoccupying their established rivals. They also had the sense to look at the wealth of research about the evolution of e-retailing, all of which pointed to the fact that the twin obstacles to delivering a rich 'luxury' experience online – conservative consumer attitudes and technological limitations – had been melting away quicker than ice-cream on a summer's day.

The reticence of the established groups also helped create the opportunity for the new arrivals, of which Fabergé is one. The price of a piece of prime real estate on any prestigious luxury street or shopping mall around the world has become prohibitive to all but the wealthiest brands, even before factoring in the cost of building a retail temple grand enough to catch the attention of the passing customer. However, the cost of creating a presence to rival the same companies online is less intimidating. At the same time, the opportunity to offer a user experience and level of service superior to these established rivals has been very real.

These trailblazers have demonstrated, by wholeheartedly embracing the power of today's technology and combining it with traditional retailing skills, that it is possible to provide an online experience that offers a compelling alternative to the traditional location-bound and time-restricted alternative.

It was this opportunity that captivated my team when we set out to plan how to restore Fabergé to its rightful position at the pinnacle of luxury. We also saw the foot dragging of many established rivals as an opportunity. We identified the changes in consumer attitudes, accelerated by the early twenty-first-century economic crisis, and understood how these were enhancing the appeal of the Internet as the preferred primary point of interaction between the consumer and brand or retailer, irrespective of the category and price-point. We confirmed from research and practitioners that these trends were even more apparent among high net-worth audiences for whom discretion and convenience were becoming increasingly important considerations. We were excited by the opportunity that developments in software and imaging technology were providing to transform the online user experience into one that replicates the exclusive and intimate world of the high-jewellery salon. We were impressed by the scalability of an online flagship store open to the world 24 hours a day seven days a week from day one. We were attracted by the power of modern CRM software to nurture an enduring and personal relationship with our customers around the world and provide them with a level of service difficult to match with a black book and a telephone alone.

This significant and groundbreaking book explores all these elements and much more, for the first time. It provides invaluable insights to help all those looking to unlock the massive potential of the Internet and new technologies as an invaluable means of enhancing the luxury experience for the customer and the profit potential of its delivery for the provider. I intend to keep *Luxury Online* close to me for a long time, and I counsel you to do the same.

MARK DUNHILL
CEO, Fabergé

Acknowledgments

I may have offended some people by my refusal to discuss the contents of this book while I was writing it and so I will begin with a small explanation and apology hoping that they will understand (and still buy it!).

My main reason for being reluctant to discuss *Luxury Online* was because of the intention to present an extensive view of luxury e-business through a set of sound and objective strategies that are independent of any luxury company's direct influence. Although I interviewed several professionals and experts in the field, including academics, if I had allowed unsolicited opinions, unstructured viewpoints, invalid business models, not to mention incessant debates on the place of the Internet in the luxury world, my intentions would have been undermined. I also didn't want to appear to be in favor of any particular luxury brand or product and service category for that matter. As you can imagine this was tricky to manage, particularly when I had to crawl back to the same luxury companies that I refused to discuss the book with to double-check facts and figures (which was often) and to request for permission to use the images! I thank them for their support and for ensuring that our business relations and mutual respect have been sustained.

I also hope that the many people who wrote to ask for a peek into the book before its publication (including the American guy who was ready to fly to Paris for a surveilled reading of the manuscript for a few hours) understand that I was not in a position to oblige them, although my publisher put me in a corner by putting up the book's information online before I even completed the manuscript! This is however the beauty of the Internet – to create awareness and generate news!

I will begin by thanking the brilliant team at Palgrave Macmillan for all the work they have channeled towards putting this book together and getting it to the public – Stephen Rutt (for believing and being ever so patient), Alex Dawe (for being a super-woman who understands how to manage me), Paul Cooper (your enthusiasm is infectious!), Eleanor Davey Corrigan (for getting it), Adrian Scott (for your dedication to my work), Dylan Moulton (for being ever responsive), Regina Chan (for always thinking forward), Clare Hodder (for your creativity and flexibility) and my painstakingly meticulous editors Linda McGrory and Keith Povey and all at Palgrave Macmillan.

I'd like to thank especially Mark Dunhill not only for being so kind as to write the Foreword of the book, but also for being one of those who believe in my non-stop preaching of the power of digital media and technology. His support means a lot to me.

I'd like to give a big kiss and hug to Yaffa Assouline, my "Queen Mother" of luxury, for being my constant source of inspiration and support and for sharing my vision. And to André Kolasinski, the "coolest Internet guy in town". Avec mes sincères remerciemenents!

The luxury brands that form the membership body of Club e-Luxe – the luxury e-business executive club that we created several years ago – have acted as my sounding board in all manners and forms for every aspect of luxury e-business strategy and execution. I owe all the professionals, brands and companies that have been involved in the club a note of gratitude for sharing the passion and dedication towards luxury online advancement – Louis Vuitton, Gucci, Cartier, Coty Prestige, Hermès, Christian Dior Couture, Boucheron, Piaget, Fabergé, Sonia Rykiel, L'Oréal, Parfums Christian Dior, Daniele de Winter, Gottesman Paris, A Small World, Skywire, Gilt Groupe, Luxe.TV, Luxury Culture and so many others too numerous to mention. Thank you.

I also owe a big thanks to all the luxury brands and companies that kindly provided permission for me to reproduce their content, images and screen shots in this book – Louis Vuitton, Gucci, Cartier, Boucheron, Chloé, Adler, Fendi, Lancôme, Rolex, Christian Dior, Coach, Valentino, Raymond Weil, Maison Calavas, Jaubalet, Van Cleef & Arpels, Chaumet, Guerlain, Viktor & Rolf, Oscar de la Renta, Giorgio Armani, Karl Lagerfeld, Rémy Martin, Hôtel Le Bristol, Ritz-Carlton, Fauchon, and many others. I appreciate your confidence and belief in this book.

I'd also like to thank the several online magazines, e-retailers, bloggers, bloggees, social networks, forums, TV channels and all the websites in the social web movement that granted me the rights to reproduce their text and images in this book – Luxury Briefing, Luxury Culture, Browns, Vivre, A Small World, Gilt Groupe, Sac de Luxe, Vente Privée, Taaz, Portero, My Wardrobe, Sonodea, My Virtual Model, Mila & Eddie, Luxe.TV, Luxury Channel, Avelle, Portero, The Watch Avenue, Koodos, My Fab, 20 Ltd, Billionaire 500, Iconic Chic, Mrs O, 43 Things, Luxist, Style Bubble, Shoewawa, Interactive Luxury, Greek Tragedy, C Koi Ton Rêve and many more. These trailblazing websites have all contributed to the advancement of luxury online and I'm honored to have featured them in this book.

My thanks also go to the indomitable Luxe Corp team and my long suffering Assistant and Webmaster for constantly averting potential disasters and for always maintaining a smile and for keeping me in check in spite of the constant pressure. Thank you to Jessica Reyfish for diligently tracking all the copyrights, to Taka Okazaki-Leblanc for understanding and working around my pressure cycles especially related to the deadlines linked to this book. You all contributed to making *Luxury Online* possible.

acknowledgments

This book would not have been written without the support of my family to whom I owe my everlasting gratitude for keeping me solidly grounded – my mother whose well of love is endless, my sister Uju who understands "everything" and all my sisters and brothers as well as my father who are always there whenever, however and whatever. I may not say this enough but I'm really grateful to God for making me a part of the "Okonkwo" clan. I love you all and I thank you for believing in me.

Finally I would like to thank God for giving me the opportunity, resources and strength to write this book because, frankly speaking, I don't know how I did it.

UCHÉ OKONKWO

Author's Note

Luxury is online but is not yet in line. Did you notice? As an industry that is known for creativity and avant-gardism, it remains a surprise that luxury is playing catch-up to the rest of the world in embracing the e-culture and adopting digital technology. It is a well-known fact that luxury brands have been locked in a love–hate relationship with technology since it became apparent that the Internet is here to stay. But two decades after the arrival of the Internet, this scenario ought to have changed. The question of 'why' luxury should be online is no longer relevant but the current issue is 'how' luxury should present itself online, particularly as consumers take charge of their online experiences. The likes of Louis Vuitton, Gucci, Cartier and the Ritz-Carlton are paving the way and leading luxury brands to repent their anti-Internet stance but the journey remains a long and challenge-ridden one.

As the most powerful marketing tool that will drive luxury businesses forward in the next century, the Internet has become indispensable for luxury to reinforce brand presence, break into new territories, engage clients on a higher level and demonstrate overall value. This reality is both worrying and exciting. It is worrying because placing luxury, which is based on rarity and refinement, on a medium such as the Internet, which thrives on mass access and mass appeal, is logically paradoxical; and its excitement comes from applying the right mix of the relevant strategies, tools and techniques that will result in a powerful online presence for luxury brands and an enhanced experience for the clients.

The luxury consumer has been reborn after twenty years of interacting with the Internet. The shifts in their value systems and mind-sets have been heightened further by the global economic slowdown leading to a different luxury market climate. A new world order is in the process of emerging and the luxury market will never be the same again.

What does luxury require to excel in this new world? Luxury has to get its act together by embracing technology through an infused e-culture and adopting advanced strategies for e-communications, e-marketing, e-branding, e-commerce, client management, channel integration, social web marketing, website design, mobile marketing and applied technology in product development, merchandizing, retail, mobile and sustainable development. All of these have been addressed in this book.

Luxury Online is not about exalting or crucifying luxury brands, neither is it about providing magic formulas for $millions in sales without strategic vision. This is also not a technical book but one that addresses bottom-line business issues that luxury brands face in the context of the Internet, digital media and new technologies. It is an eye-opener that strives to reveal the approaches to overcoming the challenges of luxury online while meeting the requirements of business in the twenty-first century digital context. Its recommendations will lead to long-term client affiliation, business growth and sustainable brand value, even as luxury online strives to come of age.

UCHÉ OKONKWO

Introduction
Moving beyond slow motion

"A journey of a thousand miles begins with a single step."
—Lao Tzu, Chinese Philosopher

In April 2005, I wrote an article titled "Can the luxury fashion brand atmosphere be transferred to the Internet?" which was published on Brandchannel. com. Within days, my inbox was flooded with emails from people all over the world with comments, opinions and incessant questions about this new business area that had become crucial in luxury management. The emails were mostly from luxury brand executives, entrepreneurs, analysts, academics and students with the common interest of understanding how luxury can be successfully presented online. The majority of the messages revealed major concerns about e-branding and e-commerce and others questioned the challenges of understanding online luxury clients, and yet other messages expressed urgency in identifying a coherent manner of communicating online while preserving all the qualities of luxury. Some people also wrote to tell me that they thought I was nuts to believe that luxury should be placed online as the Internet was a mass medium that has nothing in common with luxury. One gentleman actually went as far as saying that I was living in a bubble of my own imagination. However, in general, the undertone of most of the messages was apprehension, perplexity and some disorientation towards luxury online.

Four years on, I am still receiving emails based on this article (unbelievable!) and although the luxury online situation has evolved, there remains a wide gap in the strategies, business applications and knowledge of every aspect of luxury online. This was proved in June 2007 at one of the luncheons for my previous book, *Luxury Fashion Branding,* where I had an interesting chat with a luxury marketing executive. It went along the lines of "So why did you write the book?" And I gave an answer along the lines of "I discovered that there was a real need for a book like this because no business texts existed on the topic and there is an important evolution taking place in the luxury industry... etc." He complimented several aspects of the book but also mentioned that he thought the chapter that analyzed luxury e-business could have been more extensive as this was one of the most challenging business areas for luxury companies (by the way, this is the second longest chapter of that book!) Anyway, I informed him that I was aware of the nightmarish nature of luxury e-business and that I was already working towards another book as a way to make my own small contribution towards the evolution of luxury online. The result is the book you now have in your hands.

I became interested in and began researching and experimenting in luxury e-business several years ago (in 2001, precisely) when most luxury brands viewed the Internet with suspicious eyes and several were still debating whether the Internet was worth their attention or not. At this time, only a handful of brands like Louis Vuitton and Gucci had websites while others like Versace had only a front page and yet others like Prada hadn't even thought of going a step further than their domain name registrations. During this period, two comments that I heard from two of the most respected French luxury companies left me appalled at how dismissive and undermining luxury brands were of the Internet – an indispensable business tool – but their comments also confirmed the state of luxury online at the time. One of them told me, "Uché, we're not interested in the Internet and we will never sell our products online." The second brand's response when I asked about their e-business strategy was, "Our CEO doesn't like the Internet and he doesn't use a computer. We don't need the Internet. The Internet is not luxury."

If you're guessing that these two brands have since "repented" from this somewhat outdated standpoint, you're right. These brands are also struggling while playing catch-up to the rest of the luxury industry – which is what happens to late adopters – even though the luxury sector as a whole is playing catch-up to the rest of the business world as the Internet continues to evolve. So imagine how far behind these two brands currently are.

The reality of the lateness of luxury online and the urgent need to address the strategic issues in luxury e-business has led luxury brands to realize the importance of establishing Internet divisions and creating an innovative corporate culture. It has also led to the creation of Club e-Luxe, the executive club for luxury e-business professionals which is dedicated to enabling the advancement of luxury practices in the context of the Internet, digital media, new technologies and innovation. Since its creation in 2006, the club has been meeting the objective of providing luxury companies with access to the cutting-edge strategies, applications, techniques, tactics, developments, systems and expert knowledge that is required to meet the inevitable challenges that luxury is currently facing in adopting new technologies. It has served as a unique platform for the advancement of the e-business practices of major international luxury brands who are also provided with access to the expert consultants and developers in the field. Club e-Luxe's creation brought about a turning point in luxury e-business practices and is one of the reasons that writing this book was possible.

As you may have guessed, this book didn't come about as an abstract idea or an accident. I decided to write it because of a real gap that was identified in my daily practice as a strategist and consultant for luxury companies. This gap is linked to the necessity for progression on both strategic and operational levels prevalent across all luxury categories irrespective of product or service type. Constant exchanges with my fellow luxury professionals confirmed the lack of a clear and reliable approach in e-business strategies, applications, operations and metrics attuned to the mechanics of luxury management. Some of them even confessed that their decisions related to the Internet and new technologies were based on intuition and instinct rather than on strategies that have been developed from sound knowledge and a clear understanding of the Internet and luxury market. They constantly asked all manners of questions about luxury online and very often I found myself having conversations along these lines.

Q: Do we really need to be online?
A: Without any doubt.

Q: We (finally) have a website. Isn't that sufficient?
A: Cyberspace exists beyond your website. You need to control your brand in the complete World Wide Web.

Q: How can we drive traffic to our website? Should we pay for Google ads?
A: Internet users and luxury consumers search for specific luxury brand names in Google and are not likely to use phrases like 'best luxury brand' except if they're journalists or researchers. So it is better to build your offline brand awareness to support your online searchability and complement this with online buzz marketing through the social web.

Q: Should we sell our products online because other brands are doing so?
A: Sell your products online if your clients expect you to (and in most cases they do).

Q: Are consumers likely to shop more online because of the slow economy?
A: The economic downturn will surely affect the way clients perceive the value of luxury goods and services. They will increasingly use the Internet both to search for and to purchase luxury. The rate of purchase however will depend on market specificities.

Q: But the Internet is for the masses and luxury is for the… well, the wealthy
A: The wealthy are all online, sorry.

Q: Is the Internet going to go away?
A: Make another wish, please.

And on and on it would go.

It may seem that luxury companies have been unnecessarily difficult in approaching the Internet and in adopting new interactive technologies but this is hardly surprising if we take into consideration the very core of the luxury business. Most luxury companies were built on the foundations of skill and craftsmanship, high creativity, relentless innovation, exclusivity, made-to-measure, a strong vision, a unique clientele and the kind of passion that often borders on insanity. This drove the development of products that are often described as "masterpieces", whether it is jewelry, fragrance, wine, spirits, gastronomy, watches, leathergoods, automobiles, fashion and accessories; and in the case of services, the best experiences and comfort from hotels, private residences, travel and concierge services. If you take these characteristics and merge them with the Internet, which thrives on mass appeal, accessibility, availability and in most cases a "one-formula-fits-all" approach, you will agree that these qualities are hardly compatible with luxury. This explains the original phase of suspicion, confusion and apprehension that most luxury companies went through with the Internet.

Thankfully, we have moved on. However, the luxury sector may not be moving as fast as its public expects it to be in adopting cutting-edge Internet applications. This is largely due to the reasons already mentioned and also discussed in *Luxury Fashion Branding*. For example, Prada, one of the most respectable Italian (and indeed international) luxury brands didn't have a website until 2007 – nearly twenty years after the invention of the Internet! And having a website is just one baby step in the journey towards real existence in cyberspace. If you add the adoption of interactive media through other channels like mobile technology and digital products, this will make website development far less than a baby step. Another brand, Azzedine Alaïa, which is a far cry from actually owning a website, leads the pack of luxury brands that demonstrate Internet aversion although news and information about the brand can be found randomly online, initiated, spread and controlled by consumers. Yet others like Mikimoto, Berluti and Christian Lacroix, which all have websites, have not yet strategically elevated their online presence to correspond to their offline brand positioning and values through their websites.

Beyond fashion, luxury hotels like the Plaza Athenée and the Jumeirah Emirates Towers have also under-utilized the Internet's potential as a powerful channel for brand reinforcement, communications and CRM and not only for reservations. Yet others like the Ritz-Carlton and the Four Seasons have developed websites that have sacrificed their unique brand experiences for features so identical that one could be mistaken for the other. The luxury car segment is also not left out in the Internet strategy under-utilization. Brands like Aston Martin and Ferrari have focused on functionality and e-commerce with the occasional video and flash animation on their websites while others are like Maserati, which actually provides the driving experience online and presents its cars as valuable symbolic objects rather than products, but has neglected to use the Internet to power its thriving Maserati Club.

To depart from this gloomy picture however, several initiatives have been recently launched as pointers in the direction of developing advanced e-business tools, strategies and applications that are suitable for luxury companies to adopt for best practices. In addition to Club e-Luxe, which congregates members annually in Paris through a summit where the latest luxury online strategies and applications are unveiled, there have also been e-business-themed conferences organized by bodies such as Luxury Briefing, the Walpole British Luxury Association, the Milano Fashion Global Summit and the *International Herald Tribune*. But what luxury e-business advancement requires today is more than seminars and conferences, which is one of the factors that convinced me that this book should be written.

In continuance with the progression of luxury in the digital age, this book has been written to provide an indication of practices required for the luxury business in the context of the Internet and technology. It contains information, data and analysis that have been collected over a six-year period as well as observations, strategies and applications that have been validated in ongoing practice. It includes conclusions that have been drawn from examining over five thousand websites and web elements during this period and practical insights garnered from consulting for several luxury brands worldwide.

This book is divided into two main parts – Getting It! and Doing It! The first part – Getting It! – serves to explain the progression and current state of luxury online and the second part – Doing It! – provides analysis, strategies and tools of different aspects of luxury online that may be used to enhance its role in luxury management and to ensure its continuous evolution.

References have also been made to the works of respectable luxury professionals like James Ogilvy, through the *Luxury Briefing* journal; Yaffa Assouline through *LuxuryCulture.Com* magazine and the multiple business leaders whose works have been published on Brandchannel.com, in addition to hundreds of websites, blogs, plogs, vlogs, mlogs, social networks, discussion platforms, online communities and virtual worlds. Notable researchers and academics like Kevin Keller and Elyette Roux and business writers like Mark Tungate, Larry Weber, Robert Scoble, Shel Israel and Eric Le Reste have also provided invaluable content through their publications that I have used to highlight the continuous evolution of the Internet and new technologies in the business of luxury.

To the best of my knowledge, the information provided in the following pages was correct at the time of writing (January 2008–July 2009). However, due to the fast pace of the Internet evolution and constant updating of

moving beyond slow motion

websites, you may find that some web contents may have changed between the time of writing and the time you acquired this book (or as a result of the existence of this book!). Although the Internet is in constant evolution, I have focused on ensuring that the analyses provided in this book are as timeless as possible, so that they may be applied progressively in different contexts, periods and across multiple product and services categories. Hopefully, you will agree so.

Some of the content of this book has also been translated into English from several languages particularly French, Italian, Spanish, Japanese, Chinese and Korean. In both cases where the translations were made by myself or by a professional translator, we have strived to remain as close to the original version as possible. However, if anyone feels that we may not have done justice to his or her text, I apologize in advance. I also send a note of apology and appreciation to my fellow luxury professionals, academics and others who were aware that I was writing this book and with whom I blatantly refused to discuss its contents. Thanks for understanding that my refusal of unsolicited opinions was not out of disrespect but purely because of the unstructured consensus and inconsistency of thoughts and practices of luxury e-business, as a result of the infancy of luxury online. In other words, I didn't want to be confused.

Finally, I can't resist adding that I'm excited to be a part of this generation where profound change is taking place in humankind's evolution through the digital revolution (I don't know about you). As the World Wide Web celebrates its twentieth anniversary this year, and reinforces its power to influence entire societies and shift the course of history – think the Obama Internet-powered campaign – it has become evident that this will be the most important business platform in the near future and that luxury needs to get its grip on it.

I have thoroughly enjoyed writing this book not only because of the passion I have for the subject, but also because I "lived" the online experience during the time that it took me to write. I wrote bits of this book in different places – Paris, Tokyo, New York, Shanghai, Sofia, London, Moscow, Montréal, Boston, Miami, Mumbai and the list would go on if I were to include several airports, airplanes, trains and waiting rooms (I hope my publisher appreciates this!). But it really didn't matter where I was because irrespective of location, I only needed to be "connected" and I was ready to go. This is the beauty of technology.

I hope you will find some value in this book and that you will agree with me that both the business of luxury and the luxury client have changed forever because of the Internet and digital technologies. If you do, then somehow my intention to make a contribution towards the development of luxury online would have paid off. And I had better stop here because I've been accused in the past of having the tendency to "go on forever" when I speak about the luxury business (that is, if I haven't already).

Figure I.1 *Club e-Luxe, the executive club for e-business professionals created by Luxe Corp, is playing a key role in the advancement of luxury online through providing luxury executives with access to the most advanced and cutting-edge strategies, applications, techniques, tactics, developments, systems and expert knowledge that is required to meet the inevitable challenges that luxury companies are currently facing in adopting new technologies*

Part One
Getting It!

Chapter 1
Is luxury (still) afraid of the Internet?

> "Every few hundred years in western history there occurs a sharp transformation. Within a few short decades, society rearranges itself: its worldview, its basic values, its social and political structures, its arts, its key institutions. Fifty years later there is a new world."
> —Peter Drucker, Business Guru

The world has changed because of the digital revolution and it will keep changing. This change is currently being felt by every society in all their facets and will continue to resound in every business sector whether technology-driven or unreceptive to transformation. It is a reality that can no longer be questioned or resisted, even by an industry that carries as much economic and socio-cultural clout as the luxury sector. The reverberation of this digital-driven revolution is echoing even louder in the face of the current global economic recession, which has encroached into the luxury arena and has led to the stalling of the uninterrupted growth that the luxury sector has known for several decades. The famous phrase "unsinkable luxury" has been challenged by the multiple issues that digital technology has brought to the luxury domain. To make matters worse, the arrival of the dreaded word, "recession" in the luxury vocabulary, mainly as a result of stalling growth in key markets, has thrown the entire sector into a pandemonium of sorts and magnified the challenge of the digital and interactive technology. Hopefully this scenario will be temporary.

This drastic transformation that is powered by technology is taking form in ways unexpected and interconnected. For starters, the challenges are not only in luxury e-retail – which has been an ongoing debate for over a decade – although as I write the industry as a whole continues in its struggle to get its act together and cover the gap of its lateness in adopting e-retail. In the meantime the social web movement has come along led by citizen journalists (otherwise known as bloggers) and social network addicts (otherwise known as cyber residents) who are affirming the power of independent thought and triggering a worldwide generation of opinionated consumers. Their spin-off sibling, the virtual world, which until now has been underestimated, is proving to lead the next wave of revolution in digital media. As if this is not enough, the advancement made in mobile technology and the advent of such applications as mobile recognition, location-based services, mobile ticketing, m-coupons and m-commerce is creating unprecedented expectations among mobile user-residents. And in case you're wondering, a large chunk of these users fall within the luxury consumer bracket even if we would like to think that they are a bunch of geeks who look like the types that wallow down long office corridors in over-sized black rimmed glasses.

With the rapid advancement of everything digital and mobile coupled with the challenging social order acting as catalysts, there is a current drastic transformation of the mind-set of consumers worldwide whether they are luxury clients or not. This movement which began several years ago will lead to the emergence of a new world, to quote Peter Drucker. Luxury clients will demand more meaning from luxury brands that transcend products, services and brand names. The way luxury presents itself will be challenged and its perceptions will be altered. Ideas, concepts, attitudes, behaviors, expectations and interpretations will evolve. All of these will be accelerated by the Internet and digital media. This era will be eventually marked by a *before* and *after* for both the Internet and the economic recession. The good news however is that in the current scenario of evolution, the Internet has become an indispensable medium for growth prospects through its multiple possibilities that enable understanding client psychology; reaching a wider international clientele in a cost-effective manner; and projecting a luxury brand's core essence and universe to a wider public.

A look at the other side of the coin and we may find it surprising that the immense opportunity of the Internet as both a business and creative tool has not been fully exploited by luxury brands. The luxury industry has been (rightly) decried for several years for being late in adopting the Internet and its accompanying interactive and digital technologies in marketing and overall business strategies. Main players in sectors like telecommunications and automobiles have even as much as sneered at the luxury sector's apparent lack of commitment to integrating advanced Internet practices in daily business functions. The consumer society has also been dismayed at first and later exasperated at how far behind the luxury industry seems to be in Internet offerings when compared with other industries. A quick tour of the luxury cyber-land where you may come across the hyperactivity of the Dior website or the ineffectual tools that Hermès has used to interpret online interactivity or the mass auto-style layout of the Mauboussin website and you won't blame these parties.

As an industry that is known for avant-gardism, innovation and creativity, it may not be immediately apparent why luxury brands and digital technology have been locked in a love–hate relationship since it became evident that the Internet is here to stay. But as with every case of reverse human behavior, this can be explained (although not necessarily excused), when we examine the meaning and core of luxury.

Luxury as we all know is related to pleasure and indulgence of the senses through objects or experiences that are more ostentatious than necessary. It may be expressed through objects that are rare, original, expensive and of the best quality or through services that are refined, exceptional and offer the best in comfort. Although in our modern context, the meaning of luxury is gearing towards individual interpretations, we may generally agree that luxury is synonymous with pure pleasure and indulgence. Coco Chanel, the madam of luxury definitions, was known to have repeated at every chance that "luxury is a necessity that begins where necessity ends" and that "luxury is not the opposite of poverty but that of vulgarity". Enough said.

Luxury has been built on the foundation of certain principles that can neither be ignored nor compromised. It is a culture that requires understanding prior to the adoption of business practices because its output is essentially different from daily consumer goods. Luxury's original function and *raison d'être* is also significantly different from those of other product or service sectors. This function is rooted in the social stratification of the past societies when royals, nobles and aristocrats used ostentatious consumption to stamp their superiority and maintain their distance from the lesser privileged. While this rigid structure has more or less disappeared from our current society, what has not changed is the deep-seated need of man to show his distinction, to be admired, recognized, appreciated and respected, through differentiating himself, in most cases with his possessions. This form of indirect stratification, which meets the innate desire of human beings to ascertain their place in society, remains a part of today's world. And this practice of distinction is prevalent in all cultures and societies irrespective of economic situation or geographical region. So we can say that the role of luxury has stayed basically unchanged although this role can now be created and controlled by each individual according to their dreams, goals and means. This new order means that luxury remains in a superior position as it acts as a pointer for defining the new codes of social stratification or, if you prefer, social separation. Consequently the consumer still looks up to the luxury brand in many ways and the relationship remains to a large extent "top-down".

If you take this relationship and place it in the context of the Internet where the consumer is in total control and expects to be looked up to, then the likely outcome will be "resistance, apprehension and anxiety" from the top (the luxury brand); and 'confusion, surprise and disappointment' from the bottom (the luxury client). This is exactly what has been happening in the context of luxury online in the last ten years and explains why it took brands like Prada until 2007 to have a website and why brands like Chanel and Hermès continue to resist integrated e-retail, leaving their clients at the mercy of fake luxury goods hawkers found on websites like eBay.com and BuyHighReplica.com among several others. Thankfully, the resistance of luxury brands towards e-retail and e-business in general is becoming a thing of the past, particularly as the economic recession has led to mandatory investment in e-retail and social web marketing strategies as sources of sustainability.

In addition to these factors that separate the world of luxury from the other "worlds", luxury has always had innate characteristics that are intrinsic to its very being and comprise elements that speak more to passion than to reason. These include originality and creativity in product and retail conceptualization; craftsmanship and precision in production; emotional appeal and an enhanced image in brand presentation; exclusivity and limit in access; and high quality and premium pricing, all for a niche clientele. The reproduction of all of these elements often requires an unwavering dedication to perfection that sometimes defies logic. This often means a rather narrow approach, which has consequences for business management. The natural reaction to any possibility of interrupting this approach and thought process would be "apprehension and resistance", which was the initial reaction of luxury to the advent of the Internet.

To illustrate this dedication to perfection that forms a core aspect of luxury let's take a look at the process that goes into making cognac. The drink known as cognac as you may know is made from what is called *l'eau de vie*, which translates literally as "the water of life". It is a blend of specific types of grapes mixed in exact proportions that are distilled twice through a meticulously precise process and subsequently aged in specific oak barrels which are stored over accurate periods, the least being two years, before they are bottled and sold. Some are stored for four or six years while the *grand crus* may be stored for as long as 20 years. In order to qualify to be used in making cognac, the grapes must be grown in a precise territory in the Cognac region of France (from where the drink took its name) because of the specific conditions of both the climate and the soil of the region. The entire creation process from the selection of the *terroir* or the soil, to the assortment of grape vines, their cultivation, harvesting, grouping, distillation, storage, dilution, blending, packaging and eventual retailing is strictly controlled by laws that demand a process that hasn't changed much in the last three hundred years. This ensures consistency in quality and the least likelihood of imperfection. If one of the multiple creation steps goes wrong, the entire harvest is completely destroyed. One of the world's best known cognacs, the Rémy Martin's Louis XIII is a blend of more than 1,200 *eau de-vie* aged between a minimum of 55 years and over 100 years in very old Limousin oak barrels that sometimes date back 200 years. Hennessy's Richard Hennessy Cognac comprises over 100 *eau de vie* aged for up to 200 years in a special blend that is both unique and rare. Suffice it to say that the creation of certain cognac blends begins with one generation and ends with another. The same applies to the dedication given to the care of the *terroir* – the soil – which sometimes involves investments with expected returns projected within a minimum of 50 years.

This dedication to perfection is similar across other luxury categories including timepieces, jewelry, fashion and fragrance. Christian Dior once said that the only time he was ever satisfied with his creations was when he looked at them and marveled at the fact that they were so perfect that they could not have possibly been made by man. He was known to destroy model after model of his creations because they were not at the level that evoked this feeling in him. Today this culture of luxury is ever present irrespective of the size of the luxury brand. French bespoke luxury furniture brand Gilles Nouailhac subscribes to the philosophy that taking one's time to meet the requirements and standards of high quality is not a luxury of the past, and the brand is known staunchly to defend its meticulous production approach and time-scale that may be perceived by some to be long.

How can you rationalize the Cognac heritage? Or the feeling described by Christian Dior? Or Gilles Nouaihac unwavering philosophy? They are totally illogical from both human and business perspectives but this is what the business of luxury is all about and this remains ever true today, irrespective of contrary claims (Figure 1.1).

Moreover, the non-corporate structure in which luxury has been operating over the previous centuries until the eighties and nineties, acted as a catalyst for the contracted view of the activities linked to luxury e-business. On the surface, the above-mentioned characteristics of luxury do not seem to be compatible with the main features of the Internet, which include mass access and mass appeal, hence the initial resistance to the Internet.

In addition to these factors that initially led luxury away from the Internet, when we throw in all of the misconceptions that originally surrounded the

Figure 1.1 *Luxury brands like Rémy Martin, whose Louis XIII cognac is shown here, and Christian Dior, who is seen here inspecting a piece on a model, have an unwavering dedication to perfection that sometimes defies logic, which has led to a precise business approach that is incompatible with the characteristics of the Internet*

Internet we may understand luxury's initial opposition to the Internet. These presumptions range from the credence that the Internet is a channel of retail for price-discounted mass products and damaged goods, or that online advertising over-exposes a brand's image and damages its equity, or yet again that luxury clients won't bother with making online purchases but would always prefer the sumptuous surroundings of the physical stores and the real human contact with the products. You and I both know that these assumptions are no longer valid.

Irrespective of the fact that luxury should adapt to a changing business world rather than remain inflexible and risk becoming obsolete, we have also to recognize that luxury thrives more on progressive evolution in both business and creation and would likely flourish less by jumping on the bandwagon of change without a sound strategy. This could also explain the visible struggle that the industry has been undergoing in its attempt to strike the right balance between satisfying the requirements of luxury in a changing market context and consumer orientation, driven by the Internet revolution.

Fortunately modern business applications have made it possible to develop, adapt and apply e-business strategies that will enable luxury to thrive on the Internet and the digital world without compromising its innate qualities. Exploring these strategies, styles, systems and applications is what this book is all about.

In recent years and particularly in the last year, the luxury sector has shown signs of commitment towards catching up with the other industries that are considered to be more advanced in e-business and regaining its position as a truly innovative industry in every sense of the word. For example, Louis Vuitton's launch of the Soundwalk (Figure 1.2), the first digital product by a luxury company, introduces a new chapter to the extension of luxury product categories beyond physical products to virtual products. Armani's reconstruction of its Milan flagship store in the virtual world, Second Life; Cartier's creation of Internet downloadable music and films; and Ritz-Carlton's launch of Internet-based short movie series (Figure 1.3) shot in its different hotel locations are all testimonies of the luxury industry's increased openness to the adoption of digital technologies. Luxury companies are also using the Internet as an essential channel for educating new clients and reinforcing their positioning in emerging markets such as China, India and Russia. A notable example is Lancôme's online community, Rose Beauty, which in less than a year has become one of the top references in online beauty portals in China, generating 550,000 message posts every month. While all these efforts demonstrate a movement in the right direction, there remains a lot to be done, particularly in customer experience and brand reinforcement through engaging the clients that now have control of the cyberspace. Luxury clients currently have high expectations from luxury brands in terms of online innovation even as this channel becomes a crucial source of growth for brands. If these expectations are not met, today's luxury clients will simply move on.

Figure 1.2 *Louis Vuitton's launch of the Soundwalk, the first luxury digital product, has heralded a new dawn in innovative approaches of luxury in the digital media context*

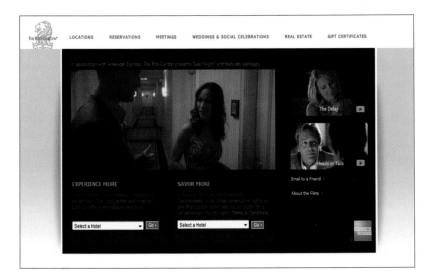

Figure 1.3 *The Ritz-Carlton's Internet-based short movie series shot at its different hotels around the world, has enhanced the online brand image and customer experience through interactivity and an invitation into the brand's universe*

But what opportunities does the Internet and digital technology really hold for the luxury industry and how may these be tapped?

If you were to ask this question to the average luxury brand executive two or three years ago, the answer you would have likely received would have been along the lines of "Well not much that we can't live without, but we currently don't have a choice about being online because all our competitors and clients are." Today, you will likely hear "The economic turmoil has driven a new type of consumption online therefore we are working towards optimizing our e-commerce." While not all brands share these viewpoints, until recently several luxury companies felt that there wasn't much more to do on the Internet and with digital technology beyond having an attractive website with as many images and flash animations as possible. The general consensus has also been that there isn't "much" going on in cyberspace that could possibly have a consequence for the luxury business. How wrong this is!

Personally, when I heard these or similar comments, or read about them in press articles, I was eager to dismiss them as unfounded generalizations by outside observers of the luxury sector but I was proved wrong when I mentioned to a highly respectable luxury executive that I was writing this book. His response was actually a question: "Is there really enough going on in luxury e-business to fill a book?" Well, I guess the response is here.

Luxury on the Internet has not come of age. In fact, luxury online, or what some prefer to call e-luxury, is still very much in its infancy and a far cry from the state of affairs in other industries. This is the reason for the general consensus that there isn't enough going on in the sphere of luxury on the Internet and that the digital world doesn't necessarily have much to offer luxury brands beyond their websites. It is also the reason that the benchmarks for best practices in several aspects of e-business cannot be found among luxury brands. The unfortunate reality is also that luxury online currently has no brand leader in a foremost position, making all brands followers and exposing them to the challenge of drawing benchmarks from other industries that don't necessarily have the culture, values and mechanics of luxury. For example, luxury brands have been looking up to independent e-retailers like Net-A-Porter.com and Amazon.com for e-merchandizing tools and rely on others like My-Wardrobe.com, MySpace.com and FaceBook.com for directions in social web techniques. This major drawback however will be overcome as luxury online evolves and benchmarks begin to emerge. One of the key factors that will drive this is the application of effective and meaningful metrics to measure the impact of digital tools in several aspects of the luxury e-business like communications, buzz marketing, social web referencing and so on.

As I write, the luxury industry still lacks standard feasible procedures for e-business ranging from the website design, choice of digital marketing techniques suitable for different products, brands and categories, the choice of websites for advert placements, the type of advertisements to run, the measurement of online advert effectiveness, approaches to social web marketing through blogs and online communities, the development of e-boutiques with effective e-merchandizing, webmosphere and e-CRM tools and other e-business dimensions. However, these challenges will eventually be overcome as several luxury brands no longer underestimate the powerful influence that the Internet wields, particularly in view of its increasing adoption in new markets.

The significance of the Internet is currently influencing behavior change in luxury brands, their clients and the wider public. The online consumer society, which has exhibited the highest shift in behavioral change, is currently driving the direction of luxury online although luxury brands have also understood the importance of steering the wheel of the online luxury experience. However, creating an online luxury experience first requires an understanding of the scope and extent of the digital world, which stretches from San Francisco to Tokyo.

It is no longer news that we now live in a world of hyper-interconnectivity thanks to Internet and digital platforms that go beyond the computer to include Smart Phones, PDAs, MP3 players and other peripheral devices. In several parts of the world, like South Korea and Scandinavia, the rate of Internet penetration is so high that the cyberworld is now as accessible as clean water. In countries like Japan, mobile banking and m-shopping is now standard practice and is so widespread that it is done at several feet underground by city commuters in the underground train. Several countries in Asia, Europe and the US, which represent the regions with the highest Internet penetration in the world, are also Internet playgrounds for millions of cyber-residents. In these societies, learning how to use the Internet begins at almost the same age as learning to read and write. With the advent of Smart Phones, notably the Blackberry and the iPhone, the average consumer is only a click away from being connected to the rest of the world. When a friend recently mentioned that she thought the inventor of the Blackberry should be punished for stealing away our peace of mind forever, I actually acknowledged the truth in her statement because although the Internet began with connections through PCs, we are now connected on a 360° level through multiple devices. Recent statistics from WikiAnswers indicate that a staggering 171 or more billion emails are sent daily. This is excluding the time spent browsing the more than 180 million websites that exist in cyberspace or reading the over 170 million existing blogs in practically every language you can think of, or simply connecting on social networks that are growing at a mind boggling rate. We are all a part of this change whether you view yourself as a victim or a victor in this success story of man's advancement.

The general consumer society has not only easily become a part of the Internet age but now has the power and clout to control marketing communications and messages from companies and to influence the way fellow consumers interpret them – something that several luxury brands are still struggling to accept.

So what are the main challenges that luxury brands are facing in adopting e-business practices?

First, let's get the definition of e-business right and understand its scope. e-Business is often wrongly thought to be the same as e-commerce which is in turn often thought to be different from e-retail. To clarify, e-business is not the same as e-commerce. e-Business is, rather, an integrated approach to every aspect of online business and features the continuous optimization of a company's value proposition through adopting digital technology and the Internet as channels of multiple business activities. This means that e-business includes online communications, client relationship management, consumer monitoring, Internet marketing, experiential marketing, branding, retail, logistics and their connected dimensions like merchandizing and after-sales support. e-Retail or e-commerce on the other hand uses the Internet and digital applications and systems to enable the buying and selling process and transactions.

With the arrival of e-business, the luxury business is currently facing both multiple challenges and as many opportunities, although these are not immediately apparent as their identification requires a strategic and organized approach. The Internet serves as an ample breeding ground for the evolution of luxury, both in the creative aspect as well as in communications and business. Before exploring these opportunities, let's first look at the main challenges.

The principal challenge and main drawback that luxury companies face in their move towards adopting Internet strategies is that of corporate orientation. As already mentioned, the intricate features of managing a luxury business means that luxury companies are structured to function in a manner that is unaccustomed to change. The arrival of the Internet has created an imperative need for a change of corporate orientation from rigidity to openness and flexibility. This doesn't mean completely changing a company's corporate strategy and culture or discarding the intricate codes of luxury, but simply acknowledging that communicating and, indeed, operating on the web platform requires a new way of thinking and re-thinking existing practices across all business aspects. Of course this is easier said than done, as it remains a well-known fact that some CEOs of luxury companies neither use the Internet nor have email addresses!

A change of orientation also means recognizing the important place of the Internet and new technologies in the overall corporate strategy, and allocating the appropriate position (and budgets!) to this channel in corporate planning. This means ensuring that a real Internet department exists and dispensing the multiple functions of the department to suitably qualified managers. It may not be news to you that several established luxury companies don't have Internet units and those that do have only webmasters in this department. This is a real dilemma because a webmaster may be skilled in systems integration and web traffic monitoring but they are in most cases ill-equipped to make strategic decisions linked to e-communications, e-commerce, e-branding, e-marketing and client management, and the social web to name just a few. The multi-faceted functions linked to these activities ought to be integrated in a department designed to function as a complement to the marketing, branding and communications business units and executed by specialists. The majority of both established and emerging luxury companies are still struggling to understand the scope of the Internet and how to allot a place for it within the internal organization. Others are trying to overcome the widespread (and unfounded) animosity that exists between the Internet retail and store retail teams as they compete for the same clients and sales revenues. The brands that will lead in luxury online are of course those that embrace the Internet as a complement to offline activities, instead of viewing it as a threat; those that integrate Internet activities with existing offline departments, instead of treating the Internet as an independent business unit; and those that apply Internet and digital tools in the full-range of their online marketing activities.

The second fundamental challenge facing luxury companies online is the somewhat unfounded belief that the Internet is simply a channel of communications or a channel of retail, in other words, advertising and selling. Several brands approach the Internet as another advertising medium that is evaluated in the same way as magazines, television and newspapers. This is appalling because there is simply no basis for viewing the Internet as a single channel. The Internet is not a channel that serves one (or even two) business purposes; rather, it is a multi-channel for communications, branding, client services, retailing, consumer analysis, client congregation, marketing, customization and product development, not to mention managing logistics, supply chain and operations. Digital technology enables the assembling of these multiple aspects for the optimization of efficiency and performance. It remains a surprise that some luxury companies have subscribed to the outrageous idea that the Internet exists only for communications through advertisements and that they need media buyers to execute this. Even if a brand has applied the most effective choice criteria for selecting suitable websites to advertise (for example A Small World and Café Mode), as Larry Weber appropriately writes in his book *Marketing to the Social Web*, "you don't just drop 30 ads into websites the way you have dropped 30 spots into television shows or a color spread into a magazine". Except if your plan is to look back two years down the line and ask, "What were we thinking?"

In order to communicate online effectively, a luxury brand must first separate advertising from communications because advertisements are one-way, and the Internet now requires two-way communications where the receiver is engaged in a 360° interaction with the brand, even on e-retail websites (see Figure 1.4). Understanding how to approach e-communications both through the brand's own website and other appropriate websites goes far beyond advertisements. Luxury brands currently need to comprehend how to "converse with" their publics because the Internet is now a real "world" that includes the social web where consumers also congregate, connect and exchange dialogue in an independent way that excludes both the luxury brands' direct participation and the influence of the mainstream media. As much as I recognize the importance of advertising, I have to emphasize that the Internet is not a channel of

Figure 1.4 *ASmallWorld.com (1), BrownsFashion.com (2) and CaféMode.com (3) all represent an integration of a 360° communications approach with luxury clients through a combination of advertisements (1 & 3), editorials (1 & 2) and user exchanges (1, 2 & 3)*

communications; neither is it a channel of retail or a channel comprising only both of these. Some have even contended that the Internet is not a channel at all.

The third challenge luxury e-business executives are facing is the issue of understanding how to *represent* a luxury brand's core essence online from its own website. In other words, how to bring about the effective translation of the brand's fundamental identity, personality and image on its website. So far, the pattern of website creation has been to concentrate on creating "pretty" and "flashy" websites or on copying those of competitors or, worse still, just putting everything in a black background (as if there was a secret convention where it was pronounced that black is synonymous with luxury online). In many cases, the emphasis has been on ensuring as many flash animations, product images, videos and as much music as possible and, more recently, providing downloads on as many pages as possible. Although all of these are important design elements of website creation, they are insufficient in brand image projection and they cannot exist in isolation without an integrated website design approach. Luxury website design doesn't begin and end with featuring a video of the latest runway show or the latest store opening but includes a balanced approach towards key aspects like usability and functionality, content and relevance, design and aesthetics, as well as creating a luxurious webmosphere (web plus atmosphere) or, as I prefer to use, our newly coined term the *Luxemosphere*. This is why on some websites, like Van Cleef & Arpels, we may find that the webmosphere is highly represented at the expense of content; other websites like Dolce & Gabbana, the content may be more developed than the usability, and yet others, like Prada, may have a strong visual impact while lacking in rich content.

With regards to website design, at *Luxe Corp* we are constantly asked by luxury brands to recommend web agencies or website designers to overhaul their websites. We often discover in most cases that it is not the websites that need overhauling but the entire e-business strategy (which of course includes the website) and although several web agencies are generally effective in design, unfortunately, I have yet to come across one that is also equipped to provide an integrated e-business strategy plan for a luxury company and actually execute it to the letter (as much as I respect and enjoy working with web agencies). This is one of the reasons for writing this book and for the existence of *Club e-Luxe* (see Introduction).

Fourth, the luxury sector is struggling with understanding that the *cyberspace* means a whole universe comprising an entire virtual world that exists beyond a company's website. As I previously mentioned, having a website is now a given and the reality is that the development of a brand's own website is just a short baby step towards existing in the cyberspace. Every luxury brand needs to be appropriately *positioned* in the cyberspace beyond its own website and this is where the challenge lies, as cyberspace positioning means sharing control of the brands' image projection with cyber-residents or online consumers. The brands that will succeed in achieving this are those that understand not only the vast scope and immense potential of the Internet, but also its ability to change the behavior of millions of people in a matter of seconds and positively to orientate them towards particular brands. These are also the brands that understand that the Internet is a multi-dimensional channel that comprises many segments.

The fifth area of challenge for luxury companies as they navigate their way in the virtual world is linked to the luxury clients who are apparently the reason why luxury brands were forced to go online in the first place. As mentioned in the early part of this section, the majority of luxury companies were initially reluctant to adopt the Internet until they realized that the wealthy segment of the consumer population were mostly online and were also using the Internet beyond information search to actually shop! This was back at the beginning of the noughties when the frenzy of registering domain names and developing websites was in full swing. What many brands however mistakenly took for granted was that their consumers would stay the same after over a decade of being exposed to the Internet. The truth is that the Internet has changed the orientation, behaviors, attitudes and interests of luxury clients worldwide. Luxury clients have moved on from the discovery stage of the cyberspace to the control stage of the virtual world. Their behavior change is reflected in the way they interact with one another and subsequently with luxury brands both online and offline. They have become demanding of instant rewards and do not hesitate to relegate the brands unable to deliver.

In addition, the vastness of the cyberspace and the prolific way that luxury clients use the Internet has also resulted in an additional challenge of segmenting and profiling them online (quantitative) to further understand how their online attitudes are reflected in their offline relationships with the brands (qualitative). There are incessant questions linked to this challenge, such as "Where and how do we find luxury clients online beyond the shopping websites?", "How can we segment them?", "How can we evaluate their attitudes and interests?", "How can we monitor their presence online?" All of these are valid questions and their answers are required in order to develop the appropriate marketing and retail strategies both online and offline. Therefore the brands that have raised these questions are already on the right path towards finding the solution for obtaining competitive advantage both online and offline.

Then there is the big question of e-commerce, which is directly connected to revenues and one of the measures of the success of a luxury brand's online presence. Two fundamental questions linked to luxury e-retail (I prefer this term to "e-commerce", sorry Americans!) are "What to sell?" and "How to sell?" The former is related to understanding whether all of the product range in each category should be displayed in the e-boutique or not, and, if so, whether their their prices should also be placed online or not. If not, then there is the additional question of whether the choice of the appropriate products should be based on price, product category, geographical market, client segment, demand, competition, logistics and so on. There is also the issue of catering to different geographical markets and possibly different languages and prices, as well as managing the distribution and logistics systems from different warehouse locations. The second fundamental question of "how to sell" is linked to the development of the e-boutique and in designing the selling space beyond strong aesthetic elements, but also to feature an enhanced webmosphere and optimized e-merchandizing and e-CRM. This is applicable to both luxury companies selling products and those selling services online. Understanding how to re-create the store design and atmosphere online and presenting the products in such a way that the person in front of the computer screen forgets that they're staring at a screen as they become immersed in the brand's virtual universe is a definite challenge. But is it possible? Of course it is, thanks to digital technology and e-business strategy.

Finally we arrive at the hot topic *du jour*, the so-called Web 2.0 or the social web, which encompasses the phenomenal changes taking place through all manner of user-to-user communities such as blogs, vlogs, plogs, mlogs, chat groups, social networks, virtual worlds and other 2-D and 3-D platforms that congregate consumers. The arrival of the social media and the blogosphere has put the phrase "the consumer is king" permanently in e-marketing vocabulary. In this world, the consumer is in total control of not just receiving and interpreting messages from luxury companies, but also of deciding their legitimacy, endorsing them (or not), spreading this endorsement (or worse still, condemning the brand) and generating debates about the brand while influencing millions around the world in a matter of minutes. This phenomenon also shows that the Internet is rapidly becoming the most important and critical marketing medium, and this will be even more prevalent in the near future as the social web goes into full bloom. But the challenge for luxury companies remains how to approach the social web and engage luxury clients in a strong dialogue at this critical early stage before the clients settle into the inevitable life pattern on their chosen online social communities.

All of these highlighted challenges are addressed in this book. *Luxury Online* is not about raising further questions and challenges in luxury e-business but about providing answers, pointers, indicators, strategies and general guidelines that will enable anyone interested in the subject of luxury e-business to understand how to approach the Internet and digital technology in the current challenging economic climate and competitive market context. These strategies have been identified and developed through both extensive research and continuous practice in luxury strategy and management consultancy. They have been tested and confirmed in practice through luxury e-business consultancy and involvement with Club e-Luxe, the executive club for luxury e-business professionals, which has the principal objective of providing the luxury industry with access to the latest developments, techniques, applications, systems, strategies and resources in e-business. These methods will serve to position luxury companies on a vantage point to take advantage of the Internet both in its present state and in the course of its continuous evolution.

Chapter 2
Connected luxury

"Everything we use now online … blogs, etc, was what we did in 1990. There's no difference. That was how we started."
— Robert Cailliau, Co-Founder of the World Wide Web

Suzy Brian's typical day begins at 7am. She usually starts off by scanning through her emails while sipping her morning coffee. On this morning, she opens her mailbox and observes that about twelve new messages have come through overnight, mainly from the several newsletters she had subscribed to, from luxury brands and other related websites. The first was an alert for a blog post from *The Wealth Report*, a blog by the *Wall Street Journal*, saying that the word *luxury* is dead. A quick read of the post and reader comments reveals that several people think that the term *luxury* is currently "slapped on everything from cellphones to toilet paper" and has therefore been rendered banal. She thinks that the word has even become more over-used since the beginning of the credit crunch by retailers and brands who desperately present every product as luxury in a bid to make a sale. At least this is the case in the home interiors market which she is quite familiar with. Anyhow, she isn't convinced that luxury is dead because she knows that true luxury still stimulates the senses, evokes desire and inspires respect. People just didn't seem to understand luxury anymore.

The second email is from LuxuryCulture.com, where she reads that the spaceship-like museum, the Mobile Art created by Chanel, has been withdrawn from its world tour as a result of the global financial crisis. It was supposed to be headed to London after the New York stop. She makes a note to include this information on her blog and to jump-start a discussion about it hopefully beginning from her Tokyo, Hong Kong and New York-based readers, where the museum has recently showcased. She thinks the viewpoints of those that visited the museum will give an idea of the influence of art in luxury fashion and also if the exhibition provided a form of distraction from the gloomy economy. She quickly clicks on the link in the newsletter which re-directs her to the Luxury Culture website from where she downloads the article in PDF and at the same time links to the Chanel website where she is able to obtain an image of the Mobile Art in high resolution, which she will later post on her blog.

Her third email is from Larry King via Twitter who she's following ardently. He says that Tyra Banks will be on his show the following week and that Suzy may tweet him questions for her! Aha! After a scratch of her head, she types frantically "Can you ask Tyra when Michelle Obama will be on her show and which designer will be dressing her?" With a click the message is gone to Larry King as well as her 2,780 followers! While still on Twitter she spots a new entry by Karl Lagerfeld who she's also following "I'm open to everything. When you start to criticize the times you live in, your time is over." "Typically Karl Lagerfeld", she muses.

Next email is from Fendi, inviting her to visit their website to view the latest collection and to watch a video of the launch party of the re-interpreted *Baguette* handbag and also participate in the *Design Your Dream Baguette* competition. She is curious to see what the bag looks like but also to know what others think about it as well as personal design initiative (see Figure 2.1). She decides to skip the Fendi website but instead logs on to PurseBlog.com where she quickly finds a blog post about the handbag. From the post, which details the bag's style, versatility, materials, colors and the inspiration for its creation, Suzy sees that the blogger seems to like it and she couldn't agree more – the bag looks gorgeous but what draws her even more to it is the approval of the blogger whose independent judgment Suzy trusts. She notices that there have been about 70 comments about the bag and she quickly scans through them. Some of the comments mention the aesthetics of the bag and others are applauding its *"Made in Italy"* tag while yet others are asking for information about the price. She spots a response to the price question. The bag costs $1,290 and is already released in Fendi stores across the country. Suzy's appetite for the bag increases and her brain goes into twists and turns on how she could obtain it. Maybe she could find the bag at a cheaper price online and save a few precious dollars. She logs on to Gilt.com in the hope that by some miracle it would be on the list of sample sale items but a quick search reveals that it isn't yet in stock. Then she types Net-A-Porter.com into her browser and she finds it on display and even in three different colors. She checks the price and it's the same as on PurseBlog but Net-A-Porter has price quotes in several currencies so she quickly checks the price in euros and pounds and does some quick calculations and finds to her delight that she can purchase it for up to $50 less if she pays in euros. How sweet! She can put that $50 savings towards renting the Bvlgari necklace she has been dying to have from Avelle.com later in the week for a cocktail party. Or maybe she should borrow the Fendi bag directly from Avelle.com instead of buying it or better still wait for her next trip to Paris and borrow it from SacDeLuxe.com for her entire stay in the city? And if she was satisfied after using it, then she could think of purchasing it. Yes, that seems like a better idea. She puts her name on the borrowing waiting list on both websites – she'll make the choice later.

Next email is from one of her social network members on aSmallWorld. net. She's just informing Suzy that she has an exclusive VIP invitation to shop the entire Valentino collection at sample prices on Gilt.com

(1)

(2)

(3)

(4)

Figure 2.1 *Previously a luxury client like Suzy Brian would have been content to visit only Fendi.com (1) for information on the Baguette handbag and subsequently to purchase it either from the brand's own website or from its physical store. Today, she is likely to search for information related to the brand from independent websites like the blog PurseBlog.com (2), bag renting companies like SacDeLuxe.com (3) and bidding websites like Portero.com (4)* and would like to know if Suzy is interested in the sale as it will last for only 72 hours. And oh, by the way, the friend also sent a link to purchase the Chopard diamond necklace that Suzy has been longing for, which has finally shown up on Portero.com with a current bid at a bargain price of $170, which is 70 percent less than the original price. Suzy clicks on the link and bids for $195 hoping that it would be hers at the end of the auction period. Her friend also reminded her to sign up to be invited to the Mercedes Benz fashion event in New York, to support the movie *Sex & the City*. The invitations are exclusive to the members of the aSmallWorld community and were limited. She immediately signs up.

Next email is from online magazine Luxe-Mag.Com, where she learns about the group of ten designers that are currently considered to be the "New League" of the Parisian fashion scene. She has only heard of three of them and she makes a note to investigate the rest for her blog posting later in the week and also to find out whether the videos of any of their latest runway shows have been posted on YouTube.com. She must also not forget to "Tweet" the link to her "followers" on Twitter.com.

The rest of her emails are a mix of newsletters from luxury brands or information sent from her RSS news feed software which redirects news on the fashion and luxury industry to her mailbox from publications like the *WWD* and the *New York Times*. She discovers new store openings, advertising campaigns, product launches etc. and makes notes of what interests her.

By the time she's done with her coffee, it is 7:45am and she gets up to prepare for the business of the day – her job as a partner at one of the leading corporate and home interiors suppliers in New York City. She feels informed, empowered and totally in tune with the world. Surprised that Suzy is not just another privileged fashionista or worse still one of the clueless bloggers popping up all over the cyberspace? Well, you're in for more surprises. In the space of forty-five minutes, Suzy digested about fourteen emails, was linked to an additional twenty websites, made several downloads, posted comments on four blogs and an online forum, scanned shopping websites, reserved handbags on two websites, bid for a necklace, signed up for an online private shopping event, enlisted for a fashion show and saved information to be uploaded to her own blog and Twitter page. During this short exercise, she was exposed to nineteen luxury brands in seven products and services categories but she only fleetingly visited one of the luxury brands' own websites although she had the latest information about these brands at her fingertips. Wondering what is going on? Welcome to the new age of luxury online where the client controls her own online universe and can literally navigate the luxury cyberspace while shutting luxury brands' direct influence out. This is the new e-culture and the consumer is at the centre of it.

Meanwhile, as Suzy is preparing to leave for work, on the other side of the Atlantic in Paris, it's 1pm and Jacques Durand is sitting in his cosy office in the La Defense district, ready to dash out for lunch with his colleagues from the oil services company where he is a Director. He decides to spend a few minutes online to finalize his travel plans for his next holiday, which he will be spending sailing along the Mediterranean Sea. His entire travel itinery had been made through his connections on the online exclusive travel social network, ZeroTwoNine.com, which he has recently joined (by invitation). Thanks to the exclusive offers to members, he is able to obtain a private villa in Corsica for his family and arrange a private yacht cruise at reduced prices. Since he is passionate about sailing and yachts, he also wants to use his two-week break to explore the possibility of buying one. His network members have already put him in contact with Millennium Super Yachts, a company that builds customized yachts and has worked with Versace in interior fittings. He has also got more information from SailingNetworks.com especially about the techniques and fittings of sailing and has even enlisted in the yacht network on ZeroTwoNine.com, which is full of tips about sailing, valuable to an amateur sailor like himself. While browsing YachtingMagazine.com, he reminds himself that he must not forget to buy sailing essentials – a flashlight and compass for himself and a cashmere sweater and jacket for his wife. Since he is a man of little time but great taste, he prefers custom-made items and unique pieces to avoid being seen wearing the same outfit as some of those "hippies" that parade the city in leggings-like trousers.

He remembers reading about an online retailer that sells only unique luxury pieces but can't quite remember the name. A quick Google search and he finds it and logs on to CoutureLab.com and within five minutes he has found a travel throw and cushion set by Missoni which sells for €300, a cashmere sweater by Kris Van Asche at the price of €325, and a dress by Duro Olowu. Apart from Missoni, he has no idea who the other designers are but the product descriptions show their excellent quality and inform that they are unique pieces made in limited quantities. They are also well presented so he makes the purchases anyway and even sends a link of the website to his wife.

He also makes a mental note to recommend this website to his network members on ZeroTwoNine if he is satisfied with the goods when they arrive. While browsing CoutureLab.com, he notices a nice weekend bag by Valextra and is attracted not just by the purity of its design but also by the fact that it was made in just twenty pieces. He hesitates purchasing it immediately even though he knows that he needs new luggage for this trip. On a whim, he decides to find out if there have been any online discussions about the brand or the bag, and logs into his account on aSmallWorld where he searches for a discussion among luggage enthusiasts. And there, he finds a thread of discussions based on the topic *"What does your luggage say about you?"* This was posted six months ago and has been viewed by more than 5,000 people and responded to by 358 people. Wow! He is impressed at the number of people commenting on just luggage. He finds out that the majority of them think that Valextra is modern, that Louis Vuitton luggage is classic, that Lancel's is contemporary (he didn't even know they had a luggage range) and that a lot of people think Samsonite is passé. He also discovers new brands in the discussion, which he plans to check out later as he has to leave for lunch. Just as he has finalized double-checking his travel plans and is about to sign off, he receives an incoming message beep. A quick look and it is his wife, asking him what he thinks about the Mauboussin cocktail ring she is about to purchase from the sample sale website VentePrivée.com. It has been marked down from €3,950 to €990. What a coincidence that they were both shopping at the same time. He takes a quick look and sends her a quick "Yes, it's beautiful" and silently thanks God that she isn't spending the original amount.

Meanwhile, Jacques' wife Mirielle, a freelance journalist, also receives his link to the Valextra bag and loves it so much that she decides to snoop around the web for more information on the bag and possibly a lower price. Her search takes her to My-Wardrobe.com where she doesn't find the bag but however finds a pair of Louboutins at half price; Koodos.com where she also doesn't find the bag but is able to sign up for a Gucci sale in two days that promises up to 70 percent off original prices; and finally to Ideeli.com where she not only finds the bag but discovers to her delight that it is the item of a giveaway promotion through a draw that will be made at the end of the month. What a lucky discovery! She enlists to be alerted for the draw and notices that there is a discussion thread on the bag and that more than 200 people have posted comments. She reads through a few of them and sees that they are all hopefuls like herself that wish to win the bag. She will wait for the draw and if she doesn't win, then tough luck. However, she ensures that all these are in her "favorites" folder of web addresses.

Meanwhile, it is nearly 8pm and Yu-Chieh Chan, a retail consultant living in Shanghai, has just finished her business of the day and is about to join friends for dinner. Just before logging off her work PC, she decides to take a sneak peak at RoseBeauty.com.cn, the online beauty community of Lancôme fans, which allows the expression of 100 percent independent opinion while learning more about the brand and beauty products in general. Upon browsing through for moisturizers, which she needs badly, she discovers the new UV Expert Neuroshield that is being previewed on the website. Upon reading the feedback comments posted by people that have tested the product, she discovers that it has been created through a new technique of innovative UV protection, which is great for preserving clear skin. She might just need this product but she isn't sure if it is suitable for her skin type so she decides to post a message describing her skin condition and lifestyle to get some feedback from someone with a similar condition. Within five minutes, she receives seven responses, all with glowing feedback on the product. Some of them even offer to allow her try their own moisturizer but she decides to find out if she may purchase it online. To her delight, upon clicking on the product she is redirected to the Lancôme's official website where she is able to view the price and to save it in her favorites. She will read more of the 400 message posts linked to the product and then maybe pass by the store for a test before purchasing.

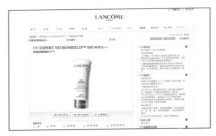

Figure 2.2 *Websites like RoseBeauty.com.cn (left), the online beauty community based on enabling people to exchange independent opinions while educating clients on the brand's offerings, is a successful initiative by Lancôme for the Chinese market. The brand recognized early on the influence of online user-to-user communities in buyer behavior, particularly in emerging markets. This online community is responsible for the majority of the user traffic and online sales on the Lancôme website in China*

Suzy, Jacques, Mirielle and Yu-Chieh are hardworking, legitimately wealthy, high net-worth individuals who have normal passions. In the case of Suzy, it is fashion and luxury living; in the case of Jacques, it is luxury travel and sailing; and Yu-chieh is attracted to beauty and appearance. They are all young – in their thirties, have cultivated tastes, are aware of brands' offerings and curious to discover more, but are also mindful of where and how they spend their money. They represent the typical luxury client of the noughties and their lifestyles, both online and offline, are not abnormal. Apart from her day job, Suzy writes a luxury blog in her spare time and has 40,000 readers per week, while Jacques spends at least three hours a week in exchanges and dialogues on his sailing social network with "virtual" friends and Yu-Chieh regularly consults online beauty portals for the latest products and is one of the active users of RoseBeauty (Figure 2.2) who post an average of 500,000 messages per month. Mind you, three hours on the Internet is equivalent to three days in the real world and 500,000 messages on a Chinese online portal have the potential of influencing millions of Chinese around the world.

Scary isn't it? Or exciting? Well, take your pick, but the bottom line is that the current e-culture is significantly different from that of the previous decade. Although consumers are using the Internet for the same purposes, they are interacting with this medium in ways that are different from what was the norm in the first ten years of the Internet's existence. A look at the origins of the Internet shows that the web was designed to be a collaborative space where people can interact with each other. This was the case in the early stages of the Internet, when this interaction was based on email exchanges; is still the case today, as conversations move to social networks; and will remain the case in the future when we move to 360° virtual worlds.

However, what has changed and will continue to evolve as digital technology advances is the way users interact with the medium. For example, instead of only visiting the corporate website of a luxury brand for information about a new product, the user is likely to seek additional independent opinion of that product from blogs, social networks and other interactive platforms online. The user is also likely to engage in discussions about the product to express their opinion or at least form their own impressions of the product and brand based on the comments of others. This was not the case in the past when Internet users depended on luxury companies to "feed" them with information about products and services. Today, the table has been turned and the online luxury consumers are writing their own rules of the game and in the process driving the brands to the point of "freaking out" – excuse my language – and influencing hundreds of thousands in their tow. If you're on the aSmallWorld social network, take a look at several forum discussions linked to luxury brands and you'll be amazed at how much time and passion people devote to these discussions, which sometimes generate in excess of 10,000 responses and comments, both positive and negative.

Does this mean that consumers don't trust luxury brands anymore? No. This change is taking place because luxury clients are no longer just looking for one-way information from brands; they also want a two-way interaction that comes in the form of dialogue, exchanges, sharing, entertainment and engagement. They want these exchanges to be based on recognition and respect. Most luxury brands have not been able to provide the means for online interaction with clients; neither have they been able to meet this apparent need for acknowledgment and participation. But even if they do provide platforms for participation, the brands will likely not be able to meet up with the level of dialogue that goes on among luxury clients on a one-on-one basis. So what should luxury brands do in this case? And what lies in stock for the consumers themselves in the future *vis-à-vis* the brands? Well, read on to find out.

The Internet is currently entering its fifth phase in its evolutionary cycle. Since the first Internet-based information exchanges were made in 1973 and the World Wide Web was invented in 1989, with the first web pages created in 1990, the cyberworld has come a long way. Today, there are more than 180 million existing websites and over a staggering 1.4 billion (1,407,724,920, precisely, as I write) Internet users around the world, more than half of them in the 15 years to 34 years age bracket. This statistic changes several times per minute so assume that this number has increased substantially since this sentence was written. In 2005, the Internet user number surpassed the 1 billion mark and it has been forecast that the next billion will be reached by 2015. What this means is that cyberspace is growing at an astonishing rate even as Internet penetration reaches the four corners of the earth. Now when I say Internet users, I don't mean those using the Internet only to send and receive emails or read the occasional news and make one or two transactions. I mean those cyber-residents that actively have a parallel life on the Internet as they have in the real world. This means people that use the Internet to search for and obtain information, compare products and services, evaluate brand offerings, purchase items, access services, conduct financial transactions, exchange information, dialogue with fellow users, participate in online communities, upload content to express themselves, find long-lost family and friends, partake in online dating (and even marriage!), exist in virtual worlds through avatars, participate in e-learning programs, conduct surveys, test concepts and use e-health facilities. This is a long way from the email exchanges that was the principal role of the Internet when it first appeared on our radar. These are the members of the e-culture, who spend an average of 21 hours online every week and make hundreds of thousands of transactions on the Internet every month.

A substantial number of these online users are high net-worth individuals like Suzy and Jacques. These wealthy (*nouveau riche* or not) individuals who are active online are estimated to number 9.5 million, a mere 0.6 percent of the cyberspace population but who generate annual transactions totalling 76.5 million. Their usage of the Internet is no longer in question but you may be surprised to know that they are also active participants in social networks and all other forms of user-to-user communities. In fact, recent statistics have shown that one in four affluent consumers belong to at least one online community and approximately 38 percent of them log in at least once a week to participate in the life of the online community. In the US, it is estimated that 60 percent of wealthy clients belong to an online community and more than 38 percent of these people belong to at least three social networking websites. Another surprise is that 10 percent of them publish their own blogs. This shows that current usage of the Internet as a medium for participation and engagement is as applicable for the wealthy as for everyone else and shatters any notion that wealth and technical skills are somehow mutually exclusive.

Predictably, younger wealthy consumers are the most avid participants of online user platforms but adoption rates even among those older than 55 years of age are surprisingly high, having quadrupled between 2007 and 2008. The case is no more different in the US than in Europe and Asia because wealthy clients can currently be found on every continent and even in the most remote of places. Location has been rendered insignificant because you only need to be "connected" to be virtually active.

Although the Internet has been in constant evolution and online behavior has been in constant transformation, the core purpose of the Internet, which is to converse, remains constant even as the technology, attitudes and behavior evolve. It began with email exchanges, which is a form of conversation, and then moved on to information dissemination and now we're back to conversing through the participation platforms brought about by the social web. This full circle will eventually take us to a 360° virtual world existence where the conversation will continue through "living" experiences in virtual worlds such as Second Life and Cyworld.

The crucial questions for luxury brands to ask at this critical moment are:

- How has the Internet evolved to this point where the consumer has taken the lead in online brand perceptions and relationships?
- What are the real challenges and opportunities that this evolution has brought to the luxury sphere?
- How is this remarkable online and economic revolution going to re-define luxury management practices?
- What impact could it have on the perception that future consumers will have of luxury?
- And what can be done about all of these?

As the dot com era recedes fast into our memories it is noteworthy to revisit the past in order to understand how to tackle the future. Anyone who remembers the early days of the Internet will agree that those were the days when the Internet was viewed as a channel for dishing out press releases and corporate information, addresses and phone numbers in addition to image-enhancing photos. In this first phase of the Internet evolution between 1989 and 1993, also known as the era of the *World Wide Web* (see Figure 2.3 on p. 40), websites were developed mostly by companies and not by individuals. During this time, most companies were still trying to get to grips with what the Internet represented for them and what objectives their investment in the Internet could serve. While industries like telecommunications and technology quickly adopted the Internet, it was unthinkable for luxury brands to even venture near this new platform. This was because during this era most major luxury companies were still family-owned and family-run in a traditional way. The modern luxury industry as we know it today, with a corporate set-up and structured business consensus, didn't exist at this time. The creation of the pioneer luxury conglomerates LVMH and Richemont at the end of the eighties and early nineties would later act as a backdrop for the inclusion of innovative business practices in luxury management including the Internet. In the meantime, the entire consumer population were moving at the same pace as companies in discovering the Internet and its uses. This period of discovery, which lasted for about five years, was the period that defined the Internet as a channel of information because this was principally what the Internet was used for. Companies created websites mainly to provide corporate information, in most cases comprising a list of their products and services, their location and press information, while consumers used the Internet mostly to access this information, send emails and exchange general information.

Since this period, the Internet has evolved beyond being a channel for information exchanges to becoming a multi-channel and multi-platform that is proving to be the most important marketing medium in the history of modern business. So far, the Internet has progressively moved from information provision to communications and exchanges, then to commerce and eventually to participation through all the 2-D and 3-D interactive applications (or, if you like, web 2.0 platforms) discussed throughout this book. All of these have been propelled by both the technological developments that have enabled web applications as well as the progression of the competence and interest levels of web users.

The first phase of the World Wide Web was driven by *curiosity* and the need for both consumers and luxury brands to discover the Internet. Both parties were assimilating the scope and extent of this new channel but while the brands remained somewhat hesitant and suspicious of the Internet, consumers took up the web with much enthusiasm, leaving the brands behind. The result was that by the time the Internet moved to its second phase of content generation, luxury consumers had become visibly more advanced in using the Internet than the luxury brands that were supposed to be providing the content.

The second phase of the Internet evolution, which we witnessed between 1993 and 2000, was the period of the Internet *Boom and Bust* and then revival that was based mainly on commerce. This period began with much fervor and zest for retail and other multiple purposes as the discovery stage gave way to a new kind of knowledge on advanced uses. Web portals like Yahoo, Hotmail and AOL began to emerge between introducing search engines, albeit in a limited form. Internet users were already hooked on emails and were searching for more offerings while Internet providers were at the same time looking to tap the opportunities within this expanded and growing market. As a result, online shopping websites began to emerge, introducing products at low prices to encourage shoppers to spend online without being suspicious of security issues. Others also introduced end of season products and goods that could not be sold online. The Internet got its first taste of commercial activities while generating a reputation of being a channel for the retailing of low price, low quality, low involvement goods. The popularity of the bidding website eBay, which was founded in 1995, solidified this position as the website became a standard in "low prices for all" and "price independence" through its involvement of users themselves. Others like Amazon.com which focused on retailing fast-moving mass market goods like books, CDs and DVDs also enabled the Internet's reputation as a low price retail channel. The Internet climate towards the end of the nineties was similar to a "gold rush" and several people made a bid to launch Internet-based businesses, many of them with unfeasible business plans and operational models. The nature and fast rate of these business launches however eventually led to a bust in 2000 famously termed the "dotcom crash" and websites like Boo.com became the references for this dramatic episode in the history of the Internet. In the case of Boo.com, an estimated capital investment of $130 million was lost. For several luxury brands like Hermès, Chanel, Ferrari and Prada who were already skeptical about the Internet, this was confirmation that the Internet was a no-go area.

During this period, Internet businesses were trying to do everything to gain the trust of the public, hence the low-price context, while online users were trying to understand the viability of shopping online. Internet providers on the other hand were striving to improve connectivity through broadband and wi-fi versus telephone dial-up. And all of these had to match in terms of progression.

The second phase which focused on *content* (Figure 2.3 on p. 40) took place between 2001 and 2005 and was the period of the Internet revival from suspicion to establishing trust. It was during this period that luxury e-retail showed signs of taking off, pioneered by the likes of Net-A-Porter as well as the bold moves of brands like Louis Vuitton and Gucci, which were the first luxury brands in fashion and accessories to take the path of online retail. The former was already retailing its products on e-Luxury.com and was therefore in a position to transfer synergies and e-retail mechanisms. The second phase of the Internet luxury evolution was also the period that interactivity on luxury websites began to appear through flash animations, videos, slide-shows, sound and movement features which became popularly adopted. With the introduction of e-retail on several websites, elements like zoom, spin, flip, drop and drag were used more on luxury websites. At this time, luxury brands were focused on providing interactivity through downloads and trying to outdo one another in the integration of the most interactive web elements using these tools. The key driver among luxury companies during this phase was the instinct to follow, which explains the rampant copying of website design that reigned supreme. This was the period where questions like "Is our website now better than brand X?" was a daily mantra. At the same time the consumers were driven by curiosity and affiliation for the Internet and were seeking extensive information on websites through rich content as well as interaction with luxury brands – beyond downloading images – and enhanced experiences that would compensate for the lack of human presence online. This was also the period that the client's affinity for websites over luxury brands emerged. Clients began to decide and choose the websites that "delivered" over those that lacked essence. Consumers began to link website impressions to brand perceptions, and the enablement of a higher level of interactivity through commerce or otherwise formed key aspects of defining online relations with clients. As a consequence the "website loyalist" emerged among luxury consumers contrary to the expected "brand loyalist".

The third phase of the Internet evolution is what we are currently experiencing in full-force and it is the age of *participation* (Figure 2.3), driven mainly by the need of consumers to congregate, share and collaborate. This phase that is completely controlled by clients has introduced a new chapter in online relations between companies and clients, irrespective of sector. It is the phase of input through creating, contributing and editing that focuses on uploads rather than downloads. It has brought to the forefront unexpected features and attitudes that encourage consumer-generated content (CGC) and is influencing the way millions view luxury brands through online conversations and dialogue. This phase had led the online client to expect a 360° interaction with luxury brands through endless possibilities for interactions, collaborations, exchanges and feedback. The level of web experience and impact of this phase is currently high and includes the expectation of clients to be able to personalize products, services, web pages and online experiences. Consumers are in total control of the *participation* phase and are showing no signs of letting go, and therefore brands must catch up with them or risk becoming forgotten. Just take a look at Twitter where individuals have taken it upon themselves to create "luxury branded" pages and feed their "followers" with information and content about the brands, some of which they have created by themselves without the influence of the brands! Log on to Twitter.com and type in "Gucci", "Louis Vuitton" or "Chanel" and you'll discover several surprises. There is even a "Fake Karl", as in a counterfeit Karl Lagerfeld, in there.

The reaction of the luxury industry to the *participation* phase is reminiscent of the landscape of the early days of the Internet when brands were apprehensive of this new medium. Since the arrival of the social web, it's been apparent that the general feeling among luxury brands has been that of fear and suspicion arising from the possibility of losing control over the brand image online. But the reality is that the control has already been passed on from the brands to the clients, and luxury brands currently have no choice but to get in the game of the social web – through the right approach – rather than pretending that it will go away. However, several luxury brands have started to integrate online features that encourage the two-way exchanges that clients are currently seeking. These have appeared mainly in the forms of uploads (Prada), online events (Guerlain) and personalization and buzz (Louis Vuitton). Other luxury brands like Christian Dior, Giorgio Armani and Hublot are using the social web mainly for publicity and buzz marketing, particularly linked to new product launches.

While the brands remain suspicious of the *participation* phase, luxury consumers are currently driven by confidence garnered from controlling online discussions and knowledge obtained from exposure to others' input, opinions and influences. They have been empowered by the opportunity to generate content (CGC) and adverts (CGA) as well as to create (think YouTube and Second Life) and to co-create. The dialogues they are having online indicate that they are passionate about luxury and seek to be connected with those that share the same passion, without direct corporate or media influence. The *participation* phase is a period of online exchanges and collaborations and as a result client expectations from luxury brands include a high level of brand intimacy that is derived from two-way exchanges on a one-to-one basis.

The fourth phase of the evolution of the Internet and luxury online is the Virtual Life (Figure 2.3 on p. 40). This phase is characterized by a 360° total web experience which goes beyond the current 2-D exchange format to feature a complete virtual existence through human-replica avatars. In this world, the user is in complete control and determines every aspect of their web experiences. It is driven by activities that enable people to interact in the way they would normally do in the real world including eating, drinking, socializing, shopping and interacting with others. The phase of the Virtual Life which has already been introduced by virtual worlds like Second Life and CyWorld feature a mixture of several of the characteristics of the content phase and additional elements that include input through creating and editing, consumer-generated products (CGP), and convergence through the assembling of avatars for exchanges, sharing, connecting and conversing. The current form of Virtual Life will eventually lead to a complete virtual existence where users will be able to develop personal avatars which will be transported to several websites and online destinations. Companies like My Virtual Model are already pioneering the creation and integration of personal avatars used in e-retail and online communities. These applications will make way for the full emergence of the phase of the virtual world, where 3-D human avatars will be integrated through several portals for the same user. The level of control and influence will become even higher when this time comes.

As you may have guessed, luxury brands are as apprehensive of the virtual world as they are of the social web. Users are meanwhile currently driven by boldness and energy in their use of the virtual world applications. In addition to 360° web interaction, they are also using, and will continue to use, virtual world platforms as a means of connecting, conversing, influencing, creating and belonging to a distinct and unique group.

The fifth phase of the Internet evolution is right around the corner and will be about the meshing all digital and Internet applications with new media platforms such as mobile technology and other applied technologies that power peripheral devices. This phase will be punctuated by users – rather than technology – as the central point of the digital experience. In this world, the user will be able to live seamlessly in a 360° virtual world and will be able to carry out such activities as conducting business transactions, shopping, networking, entertaining and generally carrying on with life online through a single ID and multiple platforms and devices. The route to the virtual experience will become the lesser factor and the individual user-experience will become the higher factor. This will be the age of the re-definition of the World Wide Web that will touch on consumers in ways unimagined and will further affect the way companies relate with clients, particularly in the luxury field.

It is pretty much clear that the Internet is here to stay. And this intention to stay includes a permanent position in the luxury sphere. This is not a call to have a panic attack but a declaration that the Internet presents tremendous opportunities for luxury companies to establish more intimate bonds with clients and garner additional clients in the process. The Internet also provides a unique platform for young and emerging luxury brands to stand on the same

luxury online

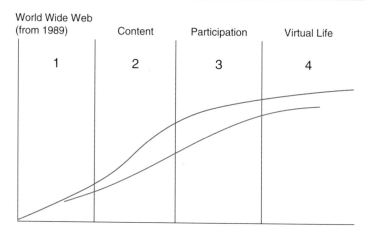

Figure 2.3 *The web evolutionary phases and its relationship to the progression of luxury online indicate that luxury brands have been evolving online at a pace that is slower than luxury clients, and the connecting lines of the two groups are yet to meet in the twenty years of the existence of the World Wide Web. The Internet has gone through four key phases in its evolution and is gearing to enter its fifth phase in the near future. Luxury brands are therefore required more than ever to keep up with the pace of the evolution of the Internet*

par with established brands without risking being drowned or relegated to the level of invisibility by the dinosaurs of the luxury world. In addition, the eternal nature of the Internet also means that users like you and I have a unique opportunity to enhance our satisfaction level with luxury brands by making our voices heard and steering the brands in the direction of improved services in enhancing relationships and experiences. The beauty of the Internet is that it's a multi-channel with multiple opportunities for successfully minimizing the potential risks that it also presents.

The World Wide Web is celebrating twenty years since its creation in 2009 and, although the Internet has been in active existence in this period, companies are still battling with turning its opportunities into business success, particularly in the luxury field. Most of the challenging issues facing luxury brands online go beyond creating beautiful and flashy websites or identifying the key to a successful website design. Well, there is no key as it is an individual matter that depends on the brand and its unique personality. If there were a key, it would be too easy: the wealthy brands would buy the key and all their e-business worries would be over; the smaller brands would struggle to allocate a budget to obtain the key; and I will be out of a job!

Luxury is all about surprising through desire, creativity, innovation and experience. It is about making a statement and there is no better place to make a powerful statement than online. The Internet moves at a speed one hundred times faster than the real world, therefore there is no reason to wait for the right time to develop a successful online presence. Luxury is already wired up and now needs to ensure that this online connection is in line with the client.

Chapter 3
Web 2.0, the social web (or whatever you prefer to call it) is real!

"I suddenly notice a strange object, with a screen and a keyboard, connected – marvel of marvels – by a high-speed line. I know that the moment I press a button on that machine, the world will come to me."
—Paolo Coelho, writer and poet

A great elderly Japanese Zen master (let's call him Makoto) owned a cat that was the love of his life and was by his side always, including during meditation classes. When the Zen master died, his disciples decided to keep the cat because they were so used to it. When the cat died, the current master and the monks agreed to buy another cat because they were so used to having a cat in the temple. Other monasteries found this intriguing and concluded that the greatness of Makoto's monastery came from some mysterious powers or effects from the cat. And so monasteries all over the region began introducing cats in their meditation classes. This practice went on for generations and even led to the publication of theses and treatises on the importance of the cat in increasing human concentration and eliminating negative energy. It took one century and a master who was allergic to cat hair for the first temple to refuse a cat in the monastery. When nothing happened to the master and the monastery apart from continuous progress in their meditations, other monasteries also began withdrawing cats – in the process saving money from feeding so many cats! Within a few decades, new theses and treatises appeared highlighting the power of the human mind and the importance of meditation without the aid of animals. Within a century, the cat vanished entirely from the Zen meditation in that region. But it took two hundred years for this behavioral circle to run its course.

After reading this story in Paolo Coelho's *Like The Flowing River* I couldn't help but draw an analogy to the phenomenon of the social web, or "web 2.0" as it is famously called. The similarity lies in the fact that sometimes human behavior has no logic or meaningful explanation, particularly in a case of a lack of direct pre-reference, as we currently see on the social web. Although there are several useful blogs providing relevant information, there are however hundreds of thousands of pointless messages on other blogs and conversations on social networks sometimes written by attention-seekers who unfortunately have the power to influence hundreds of thousands others. To make matters worse, we are also likely, as humans, to jump on the bandwagon of change in whatever form it comes and baptize it with a scientifically coined and improvable name (web 2.0) and condemn anyone who comes close to even questioning or analyzing the purpose of this baptized "out-of-the-ordinary" occurrence that is taking place. Let's take what is currently happening on Twitter as an example. This new and exciting messaging tool has been turned into a mandatory "update machine" by millions of individuals, brands, companies, organizations and bodies, many of whom haven't taken a second to understand if they need to be on this bandwagon. Think of the cat and the monastery for a moment and try to imagine how much time, energy and money each of those Zen masters and monks could have saved if they hadn't been caught up with the bandwagon effect of the cat. But then again, perhaps this evolution was necessary to force them to think and rethink in a different way and eventually become better at the art of meditating or understand that their original method was and remains superior.

So what am I saying here? The social web (I prefer this term to web 2.0 because no one has managed to convince me that web 2.0 is not meaningless jargon) is a real phenomenon that marks an important phase in the evolution of the digital media and human psychology and behavior. Every aspect of the social web beginning from blogs, peer-to-peer networking, podcasts, online social networks, wikis, discussion platforms, messaging platforms and various user-to-user communities, and virtual worlds have triggered a series of activities that have been shaped into behavioral patterns and actions that are changing the consumer mind-set and influencing the wider society. This change currently taking place is as sure as the clouds up in the sky. What is yet to be clarified today is where this change will take the luxury industry and how it will transform the public's attitudes, interests and perceptions of luxury itself. What has also been unclear is how luxury brands should approach the social web and take advantage of its opportunities while avoiding the "cat effect" and the bandwagon pattern and consequences. If you're conversant with luxury, you may be wondering what sense it makes for brands like Lanvin, Chloé, Cartier and Dolce & Gabbana to have official groups and communities on social networks like Facebook and MySpace. Is this the bandwagon effect? An output of the confusion surrounding the relationship between luxury and the social web? Or a reaction to public expectations?

In recent years, multiple fingers of condemnation have been pointed at luxury brands with screaming messages along the lines of "Why don't you have a blog yet?", "You should have an online community", "You need to be on Facebook", "Your clients are discussing your brand on forums, why don't you create yours?", "You must advertise on MySpace" and so on. The general press and those affiliated with the industry are at the forefront of these charges and while it is justifiable to raise questions and ponder on the lack of social media powered by luxury brands, it is even more important to ask what use the social web currently serves or could serve luxury brands and, further, what purpose a blog or social forum manned by a luxury brand would serve both the consumers and the brand itself. These are exactly the indications that should be addressed in the luxury sector today.

As an advocate of the Internet and a believer in the evolution of the digital media, including the social web, I am aware of the tremendous impact and transformation that has been brought about by the social web and its potential for being responsible for behavior change in consumers, its consequences and future evolution, which I will share later in this chapter. Also, as an even stronger advocate of the luxury business, I am aware of the consequences that the social web can have on the way luxury is perceived but before we delve into the topic, let's get some definitions straight.

Web 2.0, the magic term that sends everyone linked to digital media into a frenzy of excited discussions and reflections, has been around for over half a decade but its powers and influence have been drawn to the forefront in the last three years. But what does the term web 2.0 really mean and where did the name actually come from? It seems that nobody knows (I've been asking around for years!). When web 2.0 came about, we were already in the third phase of the Internet evolution so we cannot even say that the name came from its evolutionary phase on the web. Nonetheless, what most people seem to agree on is that this term is generally used to refer to the actions that bring people together to connect with others online, most of them through social activities that have elements of sharing, exchanging and influencing. But wasn't this what the Internet was supposed to be doing in the first place – to act as a platform for exchanges, interactions and collaborations? Yes, but although the Internet was first created as a collaborative platform through the exchange of information, the social web goes beyond this and has become a barometer of influence in consumer behavior worldwide through multiple platforms that enable them to generate conversations, share interests and engage in causes that often lead to real actions.

The social web may be defined as the use of the digital and interactive media to congregate users with common interests and goals in a collaborative community that thrives on dialogue, participation, sharing and influencing. It features a new way of communicating and reaching out to a sizeable audience in the digital environment. It provides an unprecedented and powerful opportunity to be heard, seen, felt, engage, influence and be influenced. In short, the social web gives a voice to anyone who desires one through which to spread a message, create awareness, ignite action, vent out frustrations or just banter about nothing. This possibility has led to an empowerment of the individual and a power-shift in the relationship between luxury companies and the online consumer base. It has changed the rules of the game by putting the consumer in charge of their own online experiences for the first time. They can now choose, interpret, accept or reject brand messages while influencing thousands and, in some cases, millions of others as they go along. They hold the cards and decide when and how to play the game; and if they decide to play in favor of a brand, the results are positively rewarding but when they decide to turn the tables, the consequences could be fatal. The result? Luxury brands no longer control their existence in cyberspace. The control today is limited only to each brand's own website, which unfortunately is one of millions of other websites existing in cyberspace. Beyond a luxury brand's own website, the consumer is in control. Accept it or reject it, this is the new order.

The social web places the individual at the centre of its universe and finally fulfills the online consumer's craving to be seen and heard. *Time* magazine recognized this in 2006 when it voted "You", the consumer, as the *Person of the Year* instead of the line-up of politicians, entertainers and other opinion leaders in different fields. The consumer was recognized as the one that controls the information age because when it comes to the Internet and new technologies, they now decide, create, control, contribute and influence not only web content but also their web experiences and those of millions of others around the world. They now have the key and the power, and possess the skills, tools and know-how to navigate around the cyberworld and craft their place in it. This opportunity has given the consumer an unprecedented level of confidence and audacity, and they are no longer in an acquiescent position of accepting information from luxury brands without questioning. The online luxury consumer is the one who converges, connects, creates, edits, contributes, personalizes, shares, controls, influences and interacts. They have turned the plate of content from "downloads" to "uploads" and have ensured that online interaction has moved from a "two-way" to a 360° web interaction.

What this means is that it's time for luxury brands to make a critical assessment of the new opportunities brought about by the social web and how they may be applied (or not) to the luxury business. This means approaching the relationship with clients in a more intimate way and understanding that the online business calls for flexibility in the way of thinking. More than that, luxury brands must constantly observe, track and monitor the social web as a guide to understanding the evolution of the consumer mind-set and how the social web is influencing its shifts. Luxury brands must listen to the multiple voices and dialogues about not only themselves, but also about competitors, collaborators and affiliates in multi-product and services categories. It is not enough for a brand to breathe a sigh of relief if they haven't yet been "attacked" on a blog, or for a brand to be jubilant if they have been given kudos by the members of an online community. Luxury brands will not get far by trying to influence bloggers through offering gifts and other perks. It is as important for a luxury brand to monitor its path vigilantly on the social web as well as those of its competitors. Why? Because luxury brands share the same client base and these clients have collective experiences and assimilate information on social forums on a collective basis. For example, a conversation on a social network on the topic "the death of the IT handbag" or "where can I buy a Chloé bag?" will affect Chloe as much as Chanel, Gucci or Louis Vuitton.

The advantage of the social web lies in its transparency and independence of thought, but these also pose its biggest challenges. It is the responsibility of luxury brands to understand these intricacies and how to tackle them before jumping onto the bandwagon of creating blogs and social networks. Key issues linked to the position that luxury should take on the social web should be assessed, including whether luxury brands should be aggregators as opposed to dispersers on the social web. Should luxury brands be observers instead of participants? Should the brands be news broadcasters or news respondents? Should they watch, wait and see for the moment or should they plainly ignore the social web in the belief that it will run its course and go away? The issues are multiple and the approaches for tackling them are even more complex due to the relatively early stage of the social web in luxury coupled with the intricate nature of the luxury business. But they must be tackled.

The seeds of the social web were sown in the early days of the Internet when software companies used "user-groups" to test-run systems and programs. These groups were also used to enable people to come together to master the new technologies and also to connect with like-minded people. In addition to this early period, the social web of today came about as an offshoot of the chat rooms and message boards that previously existed. If you remember the early days of MSN chat and Yahoo Messenger, there was a strong fascination among people about chatting to others whom they didn't know but had the chance to discover and connect with (or not). This period was however marked with anonymity as people preferred to hide behind the mask of pseudo names and identities even though they influenced one another's thoughts and actions through private conversations. The early part of the noughties also brought websites like Amazon which promoted (and still promotes) participation through product reviews, feedbacks and ratings. Again, the purpose remains to influence others with a shared interest.

Today, these elements have been reproduced in the social web but the individual is no longer anonymous. If you log on to FaceBook, MySpace, LinkedIn and Twitter, you will be amazed at how much information people are willing to share publicly about themselves, ranging from how many children, dogs and cats they have to how they bagged a million-dollar deal, not to mention their holiday photos, family portraits and even modelling wannabe photos. People no longer only want a voice online, they also want a face. They don't only want to be heard, they also want to be seen. The social web provides an outlet for expressing people's ideas, interests, emotions and even obsessions. As a result, individuals have become bold and many are so involved in the social media that one may wonder if their lives depended on it. I recently came across a blog that has been in existence for three years with daily updates which no one has ever responded to or commented on and I wondered why the blogger is still determined to inform and convince the world that there is an artistic concept behind the sky's blueness and that a movie should be made about it. But this may be his only outlet for expressing himself and obtaining the reward of feeling that there are thousands of people who silently agree with him and that one day he will own the rights to a blockbuster movie. This takes us back to the "me" idea and to the fact that the social web and media empowers the individual to show that they are at the centre of web interactions and that they have unprecedented importance online. Looking at the well-known social websites like YouTube (watch me), Twitter (follow me), The Sartorialist (see me), Facebook (hear me), A Small World (admire me), Chic in Paris (love me) and Greek Tragedy (listen to me), it's apparent that the focus on "me" is not just an idea but the reality of the social web.

With over 170 million blogs existing in cyberspace, the majority of which are updated weekly, and the daily creation of more blogs and online communities at a mind-boggling pace, the flow of personal information in online public forums is unmatched by any other phenomenon that has taken place on the Internet or offline. The social web today serves multiple purposes including finding and connecting, conversing and influencing, participating and sharing, all for more effective communications. In addition, the social web also enables consumers to shop better, look better, learn better, complain better and generally feel better.

There is no more going back to the way things were before the social web. The mind-set of consumers and the general society has changed forever and this includes the group of wealthy people that make up the luxury consumer market. And don't be falsely led to believe that wealthy people are not active on the social web because that would be the first mis-step.

To begin with, recent research indicates that one in four affluent consumers in North America belongs to a social networking website and nearly 40 percent of them log in daily to see what's happening with the people and organizations on their list or in their network. Also, 38 percent of these people belong to at least three social networking websites although, in general, they have one or two in which they are active participants. Not surprisingly, 10 percent of them publish their own blogs – and these are individuals with an annual net income of at least $300,000. For those that don't have the time to log in, daily updates are sent to their email boxes in the form of e-newsletters and activity updates from the social networks. And North America is not even the world's first blogging region.

Another indication is from A Small World, the online social network for the world's wealthy and successful "happy few". The social network, whose value is derived more from the quality rather than the quantity of member profiles, has over 300,000 members with an average household income of $330,000 from all the world's regions, with Europeans topping the list even though the company is New York based. With profiles ranging from billionaire and millionaire businessmen, senior executives, entertainment moguls, and sportsmen and women, A Small World has a strong focus on building a community based on trust and monitors behavior through a strict code of conduct and etiquette. This means that the community is for the serious-minded who wish to connect on professional and personal levels. This unique

Figure 3.1 *The world's affluent are active users of social networks such as A Small World, where they seek opinions, connections, information and exchanges with like-minded people. Their exchanges include luxury-related topics*

group, however, comprises active users of the network with 60 percent logging in regularly every month, during which they view an average of eight pages per visit and spend an average of 8.5 minutes on each page. These wealthy people are using social networks like A Small World (Figure 3.1) to obtain advice and information on everything from luxury living tips, luxury brands, private jets, holiday resorts, wealth management, real estate, events and sports. They also use the network to stay connected with friends for pleasure and linked with contacts for business purposes.

On the blogging front, indications show that wealthy people are active blog readers and recent research has also shown that nearly 40 percent of all bloggers themselves are affluent individuals who make up the luxury consumer market. Not surprisingly, they are more likely to purchase luxury online than non-bloggers or blog readers. These wealthy people are also using blogs for the exchange of opinions, information, news and entertainment. The opinion exchanges are geared towards current affairs and lifestyle topics, including discussions about luxury brands and products. The majority of them consider blogs to be a more reliable source of honest information about luxury brands and products than mainstream magazines. This is evident from the more than 75 percent of wealthy blog readers who consult a blog before making a purchase for a luxury item whether online or offline, while 87 percent seek brand opinion from fellow blog readers. Of course, they do not follow the recommendations made on blogs to the letter but the advice obtained from blogs goes a long way in influencing their immediate purchase decisions and long-term perceptions of the luxury brands and products.

As I write, the luxury sector is yet to define a clear consensus for the adoption and integration of the social web's collaborative tools in a clear-cut strategy. Due to the lack of sufficient capabilities at the majority of the luxury companies and their associated agencies (see the Introduction and Chapter 4), the common practice today is either to "watch, wait and see" or to "join the bandwagon" either by advertising on as many social websites as possible, without defining a marketing objective and the metrics to measure their impact and effectiveness, or by creating social web platforms like blogs and social networks, without necessarily understanding their rudiments and potential impact. Several luxury brands have gone ahead to create what I would call mostly "half-baked" corporate blogs and social networks in a bid to demonstrate an innovative spirit or in fear that their competitors will do so before them. These haphazard efforts have however led to a general feeling of dissatisfaction among luxury brands because despite several efforts the social web, which was expected to generate positive change in everything, literally, is yet to prove its ground-breaking results in sales turnover and market share gain.

As a medium whose appeal comes from its staggering numbers of users (175 million monthly users of FaceBook, 200 million monthly users of Qzone, 140 million tracked blogs etc.), the social web has been presented and is viewed as a destination for the masses and everything that appeals to them, which is innately different from that which luxury represents. Ironically, the luxury sector like many other industries has been expecting the social web to result in extraordinary sales revenues that equal the social web's mass-based appeal but, somehow, luxury brands have expected this to happen without sacrificing the innate luxury qualities of exclusivity and superiority. And this brings me to the key issue of the suitability of the social web to luxury; the approaches that may be adopted in integrating the social web in the context of luxury online; and to what extent luxury brands should be exposed and represented on the social web. Before delving into these issues, it's most relevant to clarify the confusion of the terms associated with the social web, particularly those grouped under 2-D platforms (blogs, forums, social networks, e-zines and discussion boards) and 3-D platforms (virtual worlds and game worlds), as well as to explore their major aspects, benefits and challenges.

2-D platforms are essentially the social web networks that allow for a one-to-one interaction in a public or private medium in a manner that is two-way. This means that the interaction could be between two people, say in a conversation, although as many people as possible may join in the discussion. In most cases the people participating in these discussions are known to, or at least can be seen by, others through their profiles and photos, which give them a face. And most importantly, they are united by a common interest. Examples are blogs that are themed around people or specific interests such as luxury, fashion, travel and aviation like Café Mode, Luxist and Le Blog Luxe, as well as social networks that may be exclusive to a specific group or aimed at the masses. Other types of 2-D networks are online forums, which act as messaging platforms like Twitter, discussion boards or debate platforms that are integrated in online magazines such as Luxe-Mag.Com's "Opinion" section; and e-zines featuring interactive elements where readers can comment and debate on published articles, for example the *Wall Street Journal*'s online magazine. They often feature rich and insightful content, which allows for the analysis of the topics and messages, the usage patterns and user influence.

3-D platforms, on the other hand, are virtual worlds, also known as metaverses, where people have a 360° existence through avatars that have been re-created to represent them. These avatars exist in real time in a virtual world that has a close resemblance to the real world and partake in activities that a human being would normally be involved in, like shopping, partying and gardening. In most cases, the avatars are also able to walk, run, talk and perform other extraordinary feats like flying and teleporting. Since the avatars exist in a community that is within a wider virtual society, 3-D platforms naturally have social web features that enable participating, connecting and sharing because the avatars live in the way that the people who created them wish them to exist. Virtual worlds, also known as Virtual Immersive Environments like Second Life, Kaneva and Activeworlds, as well as game worlds like World of Witchcraft and Everquest, represent 3-D platforms that have a dedicated cult user following.

Both 2-D and 3-D platforms provide luxury brands with a unique opportunity to track the progression and evolution of the online consumer mindset, particularly the consumer group that may be classified as early adopters. The change in consumer mentality that has arisen as a result of 2-D and 3-D platforms signals a progression in human consciousness that is taking place at a rapid pace and is centred on the "me" universe.

Features and functions of the social web

The social web attracts people because it's a medium created by real people for real folks and, better still, its contents are all about giving individuals an opportunity to have some recognition and attention. Since it is an inborn human trait to be attracted to anything that allows us to be the centre of focus, the social web is a natural winner in connecting with people. It's no wonder that there are bazillions of people on social networks like FaceBook, MySpace and YouTube and that newcomers like Twitter have taken off in such a short time. In addition to being concentrated on the individual, the social web also has several core characteristics that separate it from other digital mediums serving similar purposes. These features underlie the hidden rules that must be respected in strategically approaching the social web as well as the specific tactics that luxury brands could adopt in overcoming the challenges of the social web. Unlike other online media, the social web is hardly static and is also not controlled by a structured operational model but derives its own mechanism from the manner of its usage. These mechanisms feature the following characteristics, which are quite obvious but which could well be worth highlighting.

Transparency

The most apparent feature of the social web is its transparency, or what many have called its "naked" nature. The first rule of thumb is that the owners, founders or moderators of the social networks must be known to the participants. Whether it is an individual, association, company, group of friends, a family or whoever, they must show their face and tell their story. People will not participate in an online forum if it is not clear who is behind it. This may explain why blogs like *Gucci Space* (www.guccispace.com) and *Prada Handbags* (www.pradahandbags101.com) hardly generate any conversations or participation from people despite their many posts.

Secondly, the dialogues and exchanges that take place on blogs, social networks and other user-to-user platforms are conversations that can be seen, read, heard and discussed by anyone with even a remote interest or with an active mouse. This means that there is nothing hidden on the social web and that the activities on the platforms are exactly as they appear. Also the fact that the social web exists in real time makes the content relevant and the topics being discussed most appropriate. The open nature of the social web also makes it accepting of criticism and negative input. This means that users and participants have signed up to be exposed to both praise and ridicule because negative comments are not lacking on online forums. Fortunately, most social web platforms keep the negativity objective because the moderators also have a reputation to protect. The upside of the transparency trait is that for luxury brands, it is easy to identify the brands and products that consumers have an affinity for or the brands, products or even adverts that the public detest. And the downside is that if it happens to be your brand or product that is the scapegoat, then the world will find out at the same time as you do, if not before.

Independence

Online social forums are often the products of individuals or groups with varying motivations that are in most cases linked to a specific area of interest or relevance. These social media founders and moderators are often independent of corporate influence and manipulations. Most of their credibility is derived from the public's perception of their impartiality in presenting the contents and their detachment from the corporate world. This is the core source of their attraction. Let's take Stephanie Tara Klein, the blogger behind Greek Tragedy, as an example. Although she has been blogging about her life as a New York social girl with the occasional dropping of brand names and product tips, her audience expects that when she mentions brands in her blog posts, it should be in reference to her personal viewpoints or linked to her social lifestyle and not because a brand is behind it.

In the case of luxury-themed social forums, the importance of independence is even higher because luxury consumers are highly sensitive to the idea of luxury brands "bribing" social networks to portray them positively. This is the reason that several blogs and social networks do not hesitate to discuss luxury brands who try to influence the moderators directly or indirectly. In most cases, it is the moderators themselves who go online and post comments along the lines of "So I got a call from brand X and can you believe that they offered me their new bag in exchange for writing a glowing piece about them?" And the discussion that would normally follow will be the inevitable bashing.

Passion

In general, when people engage in discussion with friends, family, colleagues or anyone that happens to be present, it is often about the things that interest them. Online dialogues on social forums are no different. In fact, the level of interest for subjects expressed on the social web is even more elevated as these discussions take place in forums that often comprise thousands of people who hardly know each other in real life but are brought together by their common interest and passion for a specific issue. In most cases, it is also passion that drives the moderators of the online social forums to create the networks in the first place and to make them active. As the saying goes, "No one lights a lamp in order to hide it behind the door. The purpose of light is to create more light, to open people's eyes…" It's therefore no surprise that the levels of activity on some blogs and social forums are so high that the time both the moderators and participants spend on them may be equated with the time spent on full-time jobs. But when a blogger is passionate and the readers are likewise, time becomes a secondary issue.

Accessibility

The social web, being a core aspect of cyberspace, is easily accessible to anyone anywhere, anytime who is connected to the Internet. The beauty of this accessibility is that there are no geographical, social or income barriers. Anyone with an interest in the central theme of the online forum is welcome to participate as long as they have Internet access and something to say (or in some cases, nothing really to say). Online forums themed around luxury, fashion or lifestyle are particularly attractive for both clients and non-clients of luxury. The social forums not only provide access to information on luxury brands but also enable aspiring luxury clients to rub shoulders with those already accustomed to the world of luxury.

Informality

The social web may be viewed as a series of online social diaries developed by citizen journalists. Since they involve conversations touching on issues that people are interested in and passionate about, most of these are presented in an informal format to demonstrate spontaneity and invite participation. A look at the Twitter entries of a parade of high-powered celebrities and politicians will confirm this. Also several people who blog or are involved in social networks have no formal training in writing and lack advanced skill in articulate expressions, therefore the informal nature of the social web enables them to overcome the intimidation factor and puts everyone on par. This is why it's no surprise to see rampant text errors in online social forums, which are mostly forgiven by readers and participants. This, however, is forgiven because most active participants on social networks are suspicious of the smooth and refined language that generally accompany official text originating from companies or the flowing journalistic language from news publications seeking to buy the attention of the public. When the language is too smooth it is easy to conclude that there is some corporate ghost behind the website. Generally, social network residents seek "agenda-less" independent thoughts and opinions and not the kind of indirect manipulation and influence that companies employ in order to sell more products or that magazines use in order to sell more copies and more advert space. So the more informal, the better.

Interactivity

The social web is built on exchanges and thrives on interactivity. Its nature as a social medium means that its main element of functioning is community, which is based on person-to-person relations. This means that one of the key factors that attracts people to social networks is the opportunity to connect with other users who may have similar viewpoints, interests, passions and values. Several luxury brands have the simplistic idea of viewing the interactivity factor on social networks as comprising exchanges which may not necessarily be on a person-to-person level but could be interaction with products or product elements. For example, Hermès, which is one of the luxury brands that may be considered as a latecomer to the Internet, have demonstrated the brand's interpretation of online interactivity through the provision of a remake of the brand's famous Kelly bag in paper form. The paper version of the bag may look cute but online consumers have evolved from meaningless activity, such as interacting with paper, to interacting with real people for meaningful exchanges.

Thematic

The main attraction of social websites for their users is the fact that they often have a central and unifying theme. The themes are frequently in areas of high interest and relevance to the people that participate on the forums. Whether it is linked to lifestyle, sports, politics, fashion, a destination, a hobby or even a person, social media like blogs and discussion forums often have a central idea to which its participants can relate. The blog Mrs-o.org draws hundreds of comments from readers worldwide, just minutes following each message post only because the readers are fascinated with (and some have even said addicted to) Mrs Obama and her fashion style.

Objectivity

The moderators of social websites draw their credibility from their objectivity. As mentioned, participants of social forums like blogs expect the moderators to be unbiased and fair in presenting facts and opinions, particularly when it involves existing brands, products, services or people. Blog readers and participants on social networks are generally quick to point fingers at both bloggers and fellow participants if they feel that the message of a blog is biased or disfavors a party unfairly. This explains the reason that bloggers are fiercely protective of their individual and collective reputations. When someone recently posted a message on A Small World with negative comments about Louis Vuitton, several members of the social network were quick to jump in and vindicate the brand as well as set the record straight about some of the factually wrong content of the post.

Trust

In the real world, most social groups are based on trust and this is no different on online social forums. It's a well-known fact that consumers trust the opinion of fellow consumers more than they trust companies and the press. In fact, 63 percent of online shoppers in North America make purchase decisions following reviews and product recommendations by fellow online users. This trust is based on connecting with real people whose identities are verified and who can be related to without suspicion of a hidden agenda, unlike companies who have the goal of profitability. However, when the trust is broken on an online social forum, it spells death for the community, particularly if the source is linked to the moderators. Social web enthusiasts trust the moderators and we all know what happens when trust is broken. Typically, the active users of social networks belong to two or more online forums and if one of the forums happens to disappoint their expectations of trust, they tend to slip away and focus on the other communities.

Communal

Although the social web involves individuals that exist in clusters on different forums, they are innately interlinked through the connections and relationships they share. The social web is a community and therefore its activities are on a collective rather than on an individual level. Although when we interact with other people on online forums, we are in reality mostly alone with our computers or mobile phones, the experiences we have are collective and shared. This is the reason that most active users of social networks with a large network base complain that when they see their friends in real life, they lack topics of conversations because everything has already been said online.

Ownership

The social web brings people together on collaborative platforms to connect, interact, converse, influence and entertain. All these involve exchanging information, opinions and other forms of content on a mass scale. These contents are discussed, debated, lauded, enjoyed, forwarded and shared within and outside the online communities. These activities evoke not just a sense of belonging to a group with common interests, but also the feeling of ownership of the contents and other aspects of the online forum. When people contribute to an online discussion, they are most often giving their opinion and viewpoints on a subject and their ownership of this opinion is extended to the entire contents of the social website. This explains why members of the A Small World social network have an affinity to the network and many feel like part-owners of the site.

Interconnectivity

Blogs are interconnected and linked to one another. It is normal to find blogs in different categories with a directory of other blogs featuring their web links. The blogosphere is highly networked and blogs depend on other blogs for their visibility and validation. Since blogs do not exist in an exclusive format and are reliant on others for their longevity, the influence of blogs is vast and the blogosphere has collective values for companies including luxury brands.

The upside of the social web

The mass adoption of the social web is mainly due to the solution it offers rather than the technology that drives it. This means that for users, the social web's benefits derive from its multiple opportunities for interaction rather than its enablement of the mastering of the web application tools.

Learning and understanding how the tools of the social web function is not perceived as challenging for today's online user but simply as a necessary step towards the benefits of this new medium. Since the social web has put the individual at the center of its universe and relegated corporate bodies, the online user has even more motivation to be active on the social web. The more active they are, the easier the collaborative tools will seem to them and the quicker they will evolve. This means that luxury companies must also master the tricks of the social web and its technical tools in order to evolve at the same pace as consumers. This is particularly important, as parallel evolution will provide better insight into the change in the psychology of the luxury client.

The social web provides an exceptional avenue for luxury brands not only to track consumer tastes, but also to get into their minds through a level of transparency and openness that has never been seen before. The conversations and exchanges that take place on the social web are naked and conclusive interpretations may be drawn from their topics, content, tone, passion, involvement and even structure. Through the social web, luxury brands now have the opportunity to see, feel, perceive and anticipate the psychological evolution of the wealthy online whether they are clients, potential clients or the wider public. Although not every luxury brand has recognized the multiple direct and indirect benefits of the social web, people actively converse about luxury brands on the social web and they will keep talking whether the brands listen or not.

The benefits of the social web go beyond monitoring the evolution of the consumer psychology but also include multi-faceted communications, client management and retail aspects that could contribute to the optimization of the performance of luxury companies and a more intimate relationship with clients. Here are a few of the most crucial benefits of the social web for luxury companies:

1. The social web is an important tool for building brand awareness and reinforcing brand identity. Brands that enjoy positive brand equity among luxury consumers are generally more likely to be discussed or mentioned in online forums. Luxury brands are also mentioned in a negative context

if they have somehow failed to fulfill client expectations. Since social web forums easily draw millions of participants from around the world who participate in real time, the content of discussions about luxury brands have far-reaching effects.

In addition, the social web provides an opportunity for targeted online communications and advertisements. Unlike the common practice by luxury brands sometimes to blindly place advertisements on any media website that claims "+100,000 unique visitors per week", etc., the social web offers an opportunity for luxury brands actually to communicate on web pages that will generate not only a glance, but also a click and perhaps an online purchase. For example, advertising Louis Vuitton's travel trunks on A Small World's "Travel Forum" would likely yield better follow-up results than placing the same advert on the homepage of a major newspaper's website.

Also for young and emerging luxury brands, the possibilities are endless. Imagine the level of awareness a new luxury brand would generate if they manage to strike the right chord and spark an ongoing positive discussion among thousands of people in an online social forum. I've lost count of the number of remarkable new luxury brands that I've discovered through online social forums that I may not have come across otherwise. Also, let's not forget that today's online consumer trusts the social web more than the mass media and therefore the brands that other "real" people recommend are more likely to be accepted than the brands that the mainstream press impose on consumers.

2. The social web reveals the weaknesses of competitors. As previously mentioned, it is the responsibility of every luxury brand to monitor the contents of social websites and to follow not only what is being said about the brands, but also what conversations are taking place about their competitors, related product categories and service standards. The content of these discussions is a real source of information capital for brands as they not only provide insight into the way consumers perceive the brand's competitors, but they could also be a source of ideas generation for the improvement of brand image, products, services and other multi-polar aspects of the brand's universe. It is therefore not enough for a luxury brand to heave a sigh of relief if their competitors have become the subjects of negative commentary on blogs and social networks. There are no exceptions or immunity to the brands that are discussed, meaning that luxury brands ought to be prepared for what some believe is inevitable.

3. The social web helps to identify thought-leaders and influencers in the consumer market. It is no longer news that there are millions of blogs in every possible language existing today in the cyberspace. Recent research from the *New York Times* as reported by the book *Naked Conversations* (Scoble and Israel, 2008) indicates that these days a blog is created almost every second and that most of these blogs are updated upwards of three times per week. This may seem mind-boggling but the reality is that not all blogs and social networks have a dedicated cult following. In fact, only a handful of social

media forums in specific areas of interest constantly generate content from participants. These active blogs and social networks are those that are led by influencers and opinion leaders who have the clout to change the perceptions of their audience worldwide. These influencers can affect the way the public perceive luxury brands and products and are important not only to be watched, but also to enable the spread of a brand's true values through feeding them with real and up-to-date information and enabling them to reach a wider audience. The influencers could come from any background and generation. A example is the fashion blog Style Rookie, written by 13-year-old Tavi Gevinson, who has become somewhat of a darling in the fashion world.

4. The social web provides an intersection between online communications and commerce. One of the key benefits of the social web is that it is a medium that has circumvented the conventional approach of several independent aspects of e-business like e-communications, e-commerce and e-marketing. The social web integrates multiple e-functions on a single platform and provides varied benefits. For example, numerous luxury e-retail websites like Brownsfashion, Net-A-Porter and My Wardrobe have integrated social web elements suitable for both e-communications and e-commerce like blogs, videos, discussion forums and other interactive platforms in their e-Boutiques to enable interaction and exchanges in the shopping environment. These have been done in the form of editorial e-retail that provides rich content, entertainment, interactivity as well as commerce. This level of participation promotes a sense of belonging and enhances affinity between the shoppers and the website while increasing purchase probability. As earlier indicated, online consumers trust fellow community members and shoppers more than the brands and journalists, and therefore shopping blogs and forums are likely to generate more sales than information coming from the brands or the e-retail websites and the press.

5. The social web helps to monitor consumer psychology, mind-set evolution and value-shifts in response to societal evolution. This is particularly crucial in the current context of globalization, culture convergence, market expansion, global warming, digital communications and global economic slowdown. The luxury industry is undergoing an important revolution as a result of these factors and their impact on the sector will be both quantitative, in terms of financial performance, and qualitative, in terms of the changes in consumer psychology. The social web is one of the most important media for understanding the impact of all these changes in the psychological make-up of consumers. Because people say what they think, literally, on social networks and blogs, it is quite easy to follow their thought processes through tracking the relevant dialogues and conversations.

6. The social web helps to improve client relations. As a medium that enables the understanding of the desires, interests, attitudes, needs and expectations of consumers, the social web leads to enhanced relations with clients. When consumers are better understood, then it is easier for luxury brands to

fine-tune the approach in relating to them by speaking to them in the manner and language that they desire. The social web could also be an avenue for luxury brands to interact with clients on a creative level. For example, the members of a social network could be reached out to for a product co-creation project or a concept-testing exercise or even ideas generation, which would eventually produce satisfaction among them through the feeling of being recognized and invited into a more intimate relationship with the brands. The social web could also provide a means of channeling customization or personalization of products and services to the members of a specific online network who may appreciate this offering. Improving client relations doesn't simply end with the better understanding of client needs, but using this understanding and the social web platform to enable more intimate relations with clients. In addition, the social web allows luxury brands instantly to inform clients or potential clients of the latest developments and events in the world of the brand. Twitter is a typical example of this instant communication mode that enables consumers to be in tune with the brand in real-time.

7. The social web enables creativity in products and services. Since the social web is a platform for collaborative interactions, it is one of the most suitable media for brands to experiment in product concepts or even go as far as collaborating on co-creation and entire design of products with clients. This could be through interactive contests with members of social web platforms or simply by drawing inspiration from the content of exchanges and discussions of the members of online communities.

8. The social web is also useful for gauging public opinion on various issues and determining how they would react to a certain matter. This could be particularly relevant for luxury brands in trend analysis and product design. A closer look at the conversations about luxury that take place on websites like Facebook, My Space or even the short 140-character updates on Twitter could provide luxury brands with insights that a trends analyst may not be able to.

The dark side of the social web

As much as the social web has substantial benefits, it also exposes luxury brands and consumers to several risks and disadvantages that could have far-reaching adverse effects on both brand performance and perceptions. Several of these risks are linked to the structure of the social web and others have emerged as a result of the behavioral patterns that have borne out of usage by consumers. Yet other risks are directly linked to the manner in which the luxury business operates, including the need to maintain a certain distance from the public. In addition, the high expectations of the social web to change everything since its emergence has also led to dashed hopes since this has yet to happen. Several parties and companies viewed the social web as the channel that will change their business performances but have been disappointed, particularly since luxury brands are currently operating in an era of accountability in a challenging economic context. The dark side of the social web include several challenges:

1. The first challenge is that of moderation and control of the contents of online social forums. The transparent nature of the social web and its transmission in real time poses a challenge for controlling overall content, particularly negative comments that could potentially damage brand image and perceptions. Since the participants of social websites have the freedom of expression, they are well aware that they have a high degree of liberty to show both positive and negative viewpoints and they don't hesitate to express themselves on this basis. When a brand becomes the subject of downbeat conversations on a social platform, it is quite challenging to curb the pattern.

2. The second challenge is linked to the verification of the credibility of the authors, moderators and participants. Anyone can start a blog or online social forum and draw thousands of followers irrespective of their motivation or agenda. In addition, the social web is littered with all manner of profiles that sometimes call the integrity of the social media into question, from teenage diarists to the politically obsessed, celebrity wannabes, ambitious self-promoters, emotional blackmailers and so on. As a result, companies are quite cautious before sending off their business development people into the social media world to connect with people.

3. In the early days of the Internet and e-retail, one of the major concerns of online users were issues related to the protection of personal data and the respect of the privacy of users to avoid unsolicited information and intrusion. Although these concerns have been addressed by most e-retailers and search engines such as Yahoo! and Microsoft, they remain a key issue on social networks. Since the social web is currently thriving and draws millions of enthusiastic participants worldwide, the mass of information that is transmitted through these online platforms and stored on the websites' servers is enormous. Although the familiarity level that regulars of the social web or "cyber residents" currently have with the Internet is high, hence the rampant transfer of the most personal of information on social networks, online socialites are beginning to call into question the way this mass of information is stored and used. Recently, Facebook, one of the most popular online social networks, came under extreme criticism and scrutiny when its users realized that the website retained a copy of all messages, exchanges, content, actions, updates and information of both members and previous members on its server, even after people had left the network. Typically, this means that social websites own all such information and have the liberty to use, transfer, sell and store it. Such social websites that maintain an indefinite right to retain user information and use this to their advantage have led cyber residents to be conscious of the level of exposure and control that social websites have on their users.

4. Time consumption is another main negative issue that has been linked to the social web. Cyber residents or active online socialites devote substantial time to their participation in online forums and, in the case where this is not a full-time job, it can be problematic to find equilibrium between the thrill of being a part of the online social scene and having a parallel life in the real world. Many tales have been told of jobs lost, marriages ended, relationships threatened and projects abandoned due to "addiction" to the social web.

5. In addition to privacy issues, the social web has also been wrought with problems linked to legal rights of the hosts and moderators of the social web and consumer rights of the users. For example, several social websites are known to use the content of information exchanges and personal profiles to target paid advertising messages to social web users. For example, the users that actively engage in conversations linked to aviation are more likely to see advertisements from private jet companies on their profile pages of social websites than those that discuss jewelry. Consumers are increasingly aware of this indirect manipulation from the owners of online social platforms who provide access to user information to companies in exchange for revenues generated from advertisements. Consumer rights groups have raised concerns on this issue.

   The members of social networks are also increasingly under surveillance on another level. Law enforcement agencies and legal authorities are also using social webs to track offenders such as drug traffickers, gangsters, paedophiles and other manners of law breakers. Even companies currently use the social web for information verification on employees and candidates seeking employment.

6. Another dark side of the social web is the potential damage it could cause companies if it happens to be the medium through which competitive information about a company is leaked. Since the social web has the potential of spreading information like wildfire, any company information that is unintended to be divulged in the public domain and which happens to find itself on the social web risks a point of no return.

7. The social web also steals the real-life social life of its most ardent users. One of the downsides of addiction to websites like Facebook and MySpace is that friends who spend substantial hours on these networks daily end up discussing everything online and when they meet in real life, they have nothing more to say to one another. Talk of reverse advantage effects.

8. The social web could also pose a challenge in managing conflicts that may arise as a result of the communications and PR plans within luxury companies. For example, most luxury companies are structured in a way that separates the online communications service from that of offline, likewise their budgetary allocations and implementations. In the case of the social web, which is a relatively new area for several luxury brands, there is the challenge of understanding how to approach the marketing initiatives

in a manner that doesn't conflict with both the conventional marketing plan and the e-marketing program.

Blogging your life away

Mrs O was in Strasbourg, France on 3 April 2009 where she visited Rohan Palace with another equally well-known Mrs, to the delight of photographers whose cameras didn't stop snapping. Later that night, she had dinner with her husband and several other equally famous couples and again camera flashes popped in her face. Mrs O wore an elegant black dress by Azzedine Alaïa to the dinner and raised frenzy because, as an American with great influence, this choice of designer was unexpected. Within minutes of her arrival for the dinner and while she was still dining, pictures of her in the AA dress showed up on the Internet and one of the destinations of its debut was the blog Mrs.O (www.mrs-o.org), an independent blog dedicated entirely to tracking Mrs O's every public move and reporting particularly on her personal fashion choices and her status as a style icon (see Figure 3.2). Within minutes of the blog post, whose text was as short as 160 words, comments from the blog's readers appeared on the website and votes for her outfit began to be cast. By less than half a day and while Mrs O might have still been sleeping following a busy evening, the blog post had generated up to 273 comments and 251 votes had been cast, giving her outfit a 4.5 star rating out of 5 stars.

The ensuing conversations by the blog readers included more images of Mrs O which they had forwarded, linked and shared while the discussion went on. Meanwhile, Azzedine Alaïa's name had been mentioned a few hundred times and questions about him had been asked and answered as the readers conversed among themselves. Someone even asked why he didn't have a website if he was such an iconic designer. Also within minutes, the store where the dress was bought was revealed and the model of the dress was divulged as well as its price. The undertone of the conversations was admiration and adulation while the enthusiasm that the commentators had for discussing Mrs O was very much apparent.

By now you have probably guessed who Mrs O is and why a blog has been consecrated to her. Since the US President Barack Obama assumed office in January 2009, the media has been in an over-drive frenzy reporting on his and his wife's every move. On the Internet, most of the news about Mr Obama has been of course on news publications' websites but the online discussions about Mrs Obama have been more on blogs linked to politics, fashion, lifestyle and women than on standard news media websites, even those that allow people to comment on articles. And now that a blog has been dedicated to Mrs Obama, a destination has been born not only for her admirers, but also for those keen on following the fashion and style that Mrs O embodies including the luxury brands that she endorses through wearing their collections. This may look like a simple website but my inkling is that this blog will act as a propagator of high fashion designers worldwide *à la* Mrs O. It will also be a breeding ground for those in the know of fashion and luxury to publish their commentary and influence thousands of enthusiasts worldwide while changing perceptions, ideas and values linked to luxury brands and fashion in general. It will also not be surprising to see advertisements from major luxury brands on this website in the near future. Mark this page and we will come back to this topic in the near future.

Blogging is, however, not about stalking first ladies or celebrities, neither is it about endless conversations among people who have little to do. It is, rather, an important phenomenon of the social web that is proving to be one of the most influential marketing channels in the history of modern business. It is a revolution that is transforming the way companies and clients relate to each other and how their communication pattern is evolving. It is a powerful tool that has altered the traditional rules of marketing and has contributed to reinforcing the client's position as the "king" of the world of consumerism. The blogging phenomenon has crept into every sphere of business and its level of impact on different sectors remains substantial. Blogs have given consumers a voice and an outlet to make themselves heard and recognized. Blogs have ensured that companies are no longer able to ignore clients at will or diffuse unwanted messages to them but must observe, inform, converse and listen to them always. The luxury segment is not excluded from this revolution and, although luxury brands have traditionally dictated tastes to clients and have always controlled the communications with the public, blogs are challenging this position because the client is now firmly seated on the throne of power in the relationship with companies, including those in the luxury segment.

You most likely know the meaning of blogs and perhaps you are even one of the moderators of the more than 70 million blogs that exist in cyberspace, so I may not need to define a blog to you. However, it may be useful to jog your memory a bit before we get to the core of the blogging phenomenon and its place in the luxury sector. Blogs, which derive the name from web logs, are essentially web journals mostly created and controlled by independent users who offer principally genuine and non-judgmental views on specific topics, which are frequently updated and debated. Blogs are designed to offer authentic viewpoints on several issues and foster participation and exchanges among interested parties with frequent updates featuring relevant information. Wikipedia defines a blog as "a website, usually maintained by an individual with regular entries of commentary, descriptions of events, or other material such as graphics or video". A typical blog uses text, images, links and sometimes videos to send their message to the public. The entries made on blogs are commonly displayed in reverse-chronological order.

But blogs are nothing new. They have existed as online diaries and journals since 1994 and the first real blog was created in 1999. Contrary to the widespread viewpoint in the early days of the social web that blogs are personal diaries published by clueless people and therefore are not worth any attention from luxury companies, blogs have become congregation and reference points for most luxury categories. It draws both luxury clients and those aspiring towards luxury. In fact, the word 'blogger' is now an official job title and currently features as a professional category in several formal listings. The relevance of this new metier is increasing to such an extent that several companies, including those in luxury, regularly draw insights and inspiration from bloggers for better business strategies. Even politicians and presidents have been caught on the blogging bandwagon, including US President Barack Obama, whose campaign and current presidency is actively boosted by his 'Organizing for America' blog; and Russian President Dmitry Medvedev, who made his first live blog post in April 2009 on LiveJournal.com, Russia's most popular blogging and social networking website with 19.2 million subscribers worldwide.

Bloggers themselves are basically citizen journalists who, although mostly informally trained in writing, have become expert in engaging conversations and technology. Blogs such as Luxist, Luxury Business and Le Blog Luxe, which are centrally themed around luxury, are written and moderated by passionate citizen journalists and constantly draw commentary from equally passionate readers. These bloggers generally enjoy a high level of credibility as a result of their passion and dedication, while blogs that are written by those seeking an outlet for baseless discussions or some attention often add limited real value to the readers and therefore are unable to draw a large and dedicated audience. However, most blogs have a certain degree of influence on consumers whatever their theme and this has consequences for companies, particularly those in the luxury sector.

Figure 3.2 *Blogs such as Mrs O, which is dedicated to following the fashion style of America's First Lady Michelle Obama including the luxury brands that she endorses by donning their products, have a powerful influence on both luxury clients and the public. When Mrs Obama recently attended an official dinner wearing a dress by Azzedine Alaïa, the cyberspace went into a frenzy of online discussions and information search on the designer. Many were surprised to discover that the brand doesn't have an official website*

Blogs, plogs, mlogs and vlogs

Blogs are, however, not only about journal-style texts and text-based conversations with a few images to spice up the mix. What are generally referred to as blogs are actually a collection of interactive and discussion platforms that come in varying formats in addition to text. This includes videos, images and music formats and they are generally termed as blogs, plogs, mlogs and vlogs.

Plogs are web journals that are based mainly on pictures (hence the "p") and minimal text. The principle of plogs is the use of strong and often emotionally charged images to pass a message and generate conversations. Several plogs have come into existence in the cyberspace but plogs were popularized by the website The Sartorialist (www.thesartorialist. blogspot.com), which is based on demonstrating street fashion through published images of real people snapped on the streets of cities worldwide. The emphasis here is, of course, on style, fashion, accessories and luxury but the influence of these images is so high that they generate passionate conversations that go beyond the styles of those in the images to include debates on the brands, designs, colors, expressions and all manners of related issues linked to the photographs. This plog has gone on to become one of the influencers of luxury clients in addition to being named one of *Time Magazine*'s Top 100 Design Influencers. An image post can generate as many as 500 comments and debates in wide-ranging inter-connected areas. And the website is based only on images!

Mlogs are interactive web journals that are based on music rather than text and pictures. The evolution towards creating websites dedicated to music was particularly initiated by the likes of Deezer (www.deezer.com) (Figure 3.3), which has built an active community of over seven million members brought together by their love for music. Luxury brands that have a heritage connected to music have a definite audience on this mlog.

Vlogs are simply blogs that are based on videos and animations rather than text, pictures and music. Videos and movement generally have a high visual impact and, in the case of vlogs like 8h22 and C'est Quoi Ton Reve, which often feature videos that are linked to a specific theme, the impact level is even higher as there is an emotional link. Although vlogs themed around luxury are yet to become commonplace online, several communities connected to luxury, fashion and lifestyle may be found on YouTube and Daily Candy, the foremost video broadcasting websites. Some videos on these vlogs, such as a parody of the Clinton–Obama primaries campaign, which attracted more than 8 million views within a few months, make strong social and political statements.

In addition to these blog types, several other forms of blogs exist with a focus on luxury including product-themed blogs, brand-themed blogs, service blogs, category blogs and lifestyle blogs. Blogs that are centered on specific

Figure 3.3   *Blogs, plogs, mlogs and vlogs like Luxist (1), and Deezer (2) have established themselves as online destinations for those seeking to interact, converse and connect with people sharing passions linked to the world of luxury, through text, images, music and videos*

luxury products and service categories like fashion, leather goods, jewelry, watches, luxury palaces or private jets, are essentially important for the luxury sector due to the specific dynamics of different luxury products and services. For example, the blog Purse Blog (www.purseblog.com), which has a thriving community that has congregated over 165,000 lovers of luxury handbags, has also generated more than nine million conversation threads since the website began in 2005. These handbag enthusiasts are mostly young women who follow fashion to the letter and use the website to stay up-to-date with trends in the handbag and leather goods worlds. More than anything, they rely on their fellow community members for information and tips on everything about handbags starting from the latest designs, popular brands, worst designs, store locations, service experiences within the stores, the materials used for the bags' manufacture, their prices and so on. When a post was made on 9 March about Chanel's Essential bag, launched for the spring-summer 2009 collection, the blog's participants debated on every aspect of this bag, from the choice of leather, its processing, the timing of its release *vis-à-vis* the economy, the justification for its over-priced selling point and its lack of fulfillment of any aesthetic pleasure. Reading such conversations without even participating in them would certainly influence one's decision to purchase the bag and one's perception of Chanel. Other blogs like Shoewawa (www.shoewawa.com), which is dedicated to shoes, also fulfill similar purposes for shoe lovers while shaping their perceptions towards shoe brands (see Figure 3.4).

Brand-themed blogs are also not lacking in the luxury sector. Louis Vuitton appears to be a favorite for bloggers dedicated to luxury brands. Several

Figure 3.4 *Product-themed blogs such as Purse Blog and Shoewawa, which congregate enthusiasts of luxury bags and designer shoes, represent the online destinations of luxury clients seeking to stay informed as well as share independent opinions and participate in the life of a thriving community among people with common interests*

independent LV-based blogs exist all over the cyberspace in different languages, reuniting all the Louis Vuitton aficionados worldwide. Websites like In Love With Louis Vuitton (www.louisvuittonlover.blogspot.com) and Louis Vuitton Addict (www.louis-vuitton01.skyrock.com) are some of the thriving blogs devoted to the brand and those that have an affinity for it. Other luxury brands like Gucci, Prada and Tiffany & Co all have their brand-themed independent blogs that have been created by the brands' cult followers with the goal of attracting those that have an attraction to the brands and desire to share their common passion for the brands. The level of activity and the dedication of the participants of these blogs however vary, and are affected by both the actions that the brands take offline and the evolution of the consumer perceptions. As mentioned earlier in this chapter, online luxury clients belong to at least two social forums and therefore bring their collective and transferred experiences to every blog or social network they participate in.

Luxury services have also garnered a number of blogs, particularly in the area of the retail store service received by clients and the overall shopping experience provided by luxury brands. These blogs, which discuss the service experience in the stores of luxury brands like Louis Vuitton and Gucci, are cropping up all over the cyberspace. A Japanese blog even asks participants and the public to vote for the best and worst employee of Louis Vuitton's stores around Japan and encourages people to openly recount their shopping experiences at Louis Vuitton stores, whether positive or negative. Such information, of course, goes a long way in shaping the perceived service approach of Louis Vuitton and subsequently the relationship between the brand and its clients as well as the public's perception of the brand. This is the nature and power of blogging.

Services also extend to luxury living, particularly in the hotels and gastronomy segments, and blogs that are connected to these areas are not lacking. Luxury lifestyle blogs such as Travel Horizons (travelhorizons.blogspot.com) and A Luxury Travel Blog (www.aluxurytravelblog.com) (see Figure 3.5), focus on evoking critical review of the world's best hotels, restaurants and travel destinations including special offers, packages and travel tips and for those that have an interest in travel and luxury living. Discussions have ranged from the luxury hotels and stores that provide the best services to the cities that offer the best shopping experiences. When someone mentioned that New York and London offered the best in luxury shopping, several participants were quick to step in to outline the reasons why, in their opinion, Paris is the best destination for luxury shopping.

Others such as The World of Luxury (www.world-of-luxury.blogspot. com) and the destination blog New York City Luxury Living (www.nycluxurylivingblog.com) are all key influencers of online luxury consumer perceptions. Online consumers are more prone to consulting these blogs than official websites of hotels, restaurants and tour operators before embarking on a trip or moving to a new city.

Figure 3.5 *Blogs that are dedicated to luxury services and lifestyle including hotels, restaurants and destinations like Travel Horizons contribute to shaping the public's perceptions of luxury experiences around the world as consumers trust their independent viewpoints more than official travel websites*

In addition to blogs that touch directly on the consumer, there are luxury blogs that are themed on several aspects of the luxury business and which provide insight to key management issues in the luxury sector. Such blogs as Interactive Luxury (www.interactiveluxury.com) (Figure 3.6), which is centered on luxury and the Internet and Luxury News (www.luxurynews.com) (Figure 3.6), which focuses on approaches to luxury CRM, have a wide-ranging audience including professionals, students and the wider public.

The majority of existing blogs are private and moderated by individuals who have taken the obligation of bringing commentary, news, debate topics and general information to the readers that share a common passion for a subject. Millions of blogs in cyberspace have become successful in attracting a dedicated and active audience, mainly as a result of the factors already outlined in the early part of this chapter. Their success is not solely linked to the theme of the blogs or the topics discussed, neither is it as a result of their articulate manner of expression or their geographical location. The blogs that thrive are those that are created by real people who have no ulterior agenda, for real people who congregate to meet, connect, share and co-exist virtually.

Professional blogs that allow the advancement of consultants, researchers, analysts, freelance journalists, artists, photographers, writers and all manners of other professionals have also emerged by the million in the blogosphere. Blogs give these self-publishers an opportunity to aggregate their visibility, credibility and authority in their fields. They enable them to build businesses and also congregate an audience as a sounding board for developing their expertise.

Several corporate bodies, like Coca Cola and The Four Seasons, have tried to emulate successful blogs by reproducing their perceived winning formula. They fail to realize that when a blog is operated by the employees of a company, it has already lost a large chunk of its appeal without even trying. First, companies are not people. No matter how much the company tries to

Figure 3.6   *Several luxury-themed blogs such as Interactive Luxury and Luxury News focus on management issues in the luxury business rather than products and services*

show that it has a heart, soul, mind and body, we still refer to companies as "it" and not as "he" or "she", which should tell us something. Participants want their bloggers to be people and not a logo, symbol or brand name. In the case where a company decides to attach a name and face to the blog, as in the case of Coca Cola on its Coca Cola Conversations blog (www.coca-colaconversations.com), it still doesn't alter the perception that Coca Cola's objective is to make money and the blog is yet another publicity move.

In addition to putting a name and face to a blog, the topics, input and general content as well as their manner of presentation and choice of words and language are extremely crucial for a corporate blog that seeks to sound a bell of genuineness among the public. If you take a look at Coca Cola Conversations, you'll notice that the blog is written by Phil Mooney who has been the historian and archivist for Coca-Cola for the last 30 years, which gives him real credibility as a blogger even though he is still employed by the company and will of course do as the company says. However, a quick look through the blog and you will probably wonder why there are few comments and responses to the posts and why very few real conversations are taking place on a blog that has "conversations" in its name. But if you take your time to read through the blog postings, you'll probably notice what I did – it sounds like somewhere between a pure marketing advertorial and a university lecture on Coca Cola 101! Blogs are dialogues and when we want to chat with people, we have to say something interesting to capture their attention and retain their interest and not tell them in advance that the discussion will "only work if there is a two-way dialogue", to quote from Phil Mooney's introduction. It's like meeting someone at a dinner party and the first thing you tell them is that you intend to have a conversation with them but the conversation can only take place if they speak back to you. The person is likely to walk away with the conclusion that you are either crazy or need stress therapy. Conversations just flow if they're right. It's as simple as that. And what will make them right is engaging the audience with content that is informative (not educational) and entertaining (not tasking). Coca Cola Conversations is full of direct marketing information from the company's archives and initiatives on competitions, recipes and so on, which I have to admit is rich content. But these are presented in a teacher–scholar manner that gives the impression that the company is seeking to inundate the public with the richness of its past. No wonder people are not responding – sorry Phil but people are not looking to be "educated" about Coca Cola; they want the "experience" of Coca Cola to be extended to the blog to enable them to show their passion and love for the brand. This fact is also applicable to all the corporate blogs that litter the cyberspace.

In the case of My Years With Four Seasons, the blog that is written by someone who calls himself "Christian" (no last name and no photo), the offense is even worse. Christian claims to be German and to have been working at Four Seasons Hotels for the last 10 years in different positions including Assistant Director of Rooms at the hotel in Shanghai. His reason for starting the blog is to share his experiences within Four Seasons and his tales of living and working in China (even if we all know that starting the blog was decided by the marketing department). He goes on to give a glowing report of the excellence of the Four Seasons culture which he experienced working for the hotel in Berlin, San Francisco and currently in China. No details are given apart from the message that the Four Seasons is a great place to work with a great corporate culture. Christian, however, promised to share more experiences in his next post. The problem is that two months after Christian's (first) blog post on 11 February 2009, there was not yet a follow-up post or message and therefore no activity on the blog. Well, I'm sure you're thinking the same thing as I am – the Marketing Director hasn't yet found time to update his blog à la Christian. And this is in the age of supersonic hyper-connectivity and instant online messages in real time, where the average number of times a blog is updated is at least once a day.

The majority of companies that set up corporate blogs seem to be doomed from the start, especially since their efforts are far from the dramatic success they sought to achieve by creating the blogs in the first place. But the key for companies to benefit from the blogging phenomenon and the social web as a whole is not in "having" blogs but in understanding the dynamics of blogs and the extent of the opportunities they present for companies whether they're in the luxury sphere or not.

The blogosphere

The cyberspace is a universe that has no geographical, gender, cultural and, in most cases, age boundaries. The blogosphere has been elevated to this accessibility by its ability not only to arouse interest, but also curiosity and a desire to be a part of this world. Since location, gender and age don't matter in the blogosphere and since the participants of blogs are united by their interest in an area or issue, it is no wonder that blogs have gained an enormous global appeal and adoption. However, in order to assimilate the magnitude of the blogosphere and the potential it holds for luxury brands, let's take a look at the extent of this collective community of all blogs.

Recent statistics from Universal McCann (March 2008) indicates that there are 184 million blogs worldwide with 26.4 million of these in the US alone, which attract 60.3 million readers. They also indicate that 346 million people read blogs worldwide, representing 77 percent of active Internet users. In 2005, there were already an estimated 3 million people or nearly 5 percent of the population of France who have their own blogs, the highest proportion of blogs versus a country's population in Europe. Technorati, the blogging research company, put the number of tracked blogs at 70 million in April 2007 with expected doubling of the total number of blogs every five months. They also stipulate that 120,000 new blogs are created worldwide each day. That's about 1.4 blogs created every second of every day! The futuristic science and technology magazine, *Discover*, puts this number at 175,000 blogs created every day, which means about two new blogs every second!

Of this number, nearly three million blogs are updated every week, including nearly one million daily entries by bloggers and millions of posts by the participants every day. This may seem mind-boggling until we put into context that the blogosphere is the most explosive social media platform that ever existed. Although several blogs end up being either abandoned or inactive, several millions of others are interlinked with one another, making the blogosphere hyperactive.

You may be wondering where these blogs are, in what languages they exist and what factors influence their creation. Well, for starters, blogs exist everywhere (I'm pretty sure someone is blogging from Antarctica or the North Pole) and they also exist in practically every language in which we can find a computer keyboard configuration. As I write, the number one blogging geographical zones are Asia and Europe followed by North America, principally the US. Until 2008, English was the foremost blogging language but it has currently been overtaken by Japanese, which has become the

Table 3.1   A snapshot of the global blogosphere

Demographics	US Bloggers (N=550)	European Bloggers (N=350)	Asian Bloggers (N=173)
Male	57%	73%	73%
18–34 years old	42%	48%	73%
35+ years	58%	52%	27%
Single	26%	31%	57%
Employed full-time	56%	53%	45%
Household income >$75,000	51%	34%	9%
College graduate	74%	67%	69%
Average blogging tenure (months)	35	33	30
Median Annual Investment	$80	$15	$30
Median Annual Revenue	$200	$200	$120
Blogs with advertising	52%	50%	60%
Average Monthly Unique Visitors	18,000	24,000	26,000

Source: Technorati

language in which most blog entries are made – and this is just one tiny island of a country – which tells us that size doesn't matter in the blogosphere. Also, about 10 percent of all blog entries are made in Chinese, 3 percent in Spanish while French, Portuguese, Russian and Italian each have 2 percent, and German represents 1 percent of the blogosphere languages.

It may also be surprising to learn that bloggers are mostly well-educated people with steady incomes, and a large proportion of them are quite affluent. In fact, in the US, 74 percent of bloggers have a college degree and more than half of them have a household income of more than $75,000. This indicates that the stereotype that depicts bloggers as clueless teenagers is unfounded.

Table 3.1 and Figure 3.7 provide a snapshot of the global blogosphere in 2008 according to Technorati, the blog index and research company; and the top blogging languages as published in the *Club e-Luxe Quarterly*.

Figure 3.7   *The top languages of blogs*
Source: Club e-Luxe Quarterly, 2008

Blogs do not exist in isolation but are interlinked. Each active blog is connected to thousands of other websites and the more linked a blog is, the higher its chances of popularity and activity. This interconnectivity also enables the identification of the most active and densely populated parts of the blogosphere, which aids in tracking the most popular topics of data exchange on the blogs, for corporate use.

The practices in traditional Internet marketing, particularly among luxury brands, has been information dissemination in a vertical format, while blogs provide a lateral form of communications in an interconnected mode. The blogosphere is, however, different as is seen from Figure 3.8, which provides a snapshot view of the blogosphere in a geographical region. It gives an idea of the multiplicity of the nodes and outlinks of the connectivity in the blogosphere and confirms that the blogosphere is distinct from the cyberspace. The size of the nodes represents the number of inlinks to a blog and the colors represent the URL or the hosting of the blogs. Blogs hosted at the same domain have the same color. What this substantiates is the density of the interconnectivity of blogs and also that geographical location and domain hosting types of blogs are unlikely to affect the ability to link to other blogs. It is also interesting to note that the nodes of the largest sizes are found in the most concentrated areas of the diagram.

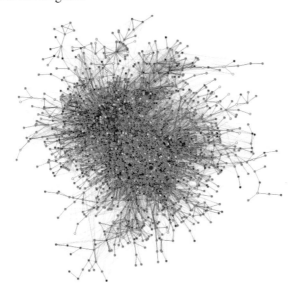

Figure 3.8 *A snapshot of the blogosphere's nodes, indicating the density and interconnectivity of blogs in cyberspace*
Source: Image courtesy of Datamining: datamining.typepad.com

As the blogosphere grows in size and scale, its level of influence will increase and its scope of activities will encroach more and more within mainstream websites. This is already happening, as can be seen in several media, professional, corporate and e-retail websites where it is now common to see a blog link on the sites' homepages. Fortunately, this integration is present to a lesser extent in the luxury domain (read on to understand the "fortunately"). Interestingly, blogs are also beginning to incorporate elements and formats of mainstream websites such as advertisements, in a bid to ensure richer content and more engagement with readers. This will eventually translate into the transformation of the interactive media and publishing as discussed later in this chapter.

Bloggers and bloggees

Blogs exist today because of people and they also thrive because of people. The technology that makes blogs possible remains important but in the blogosphere, what counts more than the technology, systems and process that power the websites are the moderators and participants that keep the blogs alive. This elite group of influencers is also becoming trusted information partners to their audience, particularly to a whole new generation of people who are digital-minded. Blogs now exist on a par with news publications and are viewed as complements to information, entertainment and opinions. This fact elevates the blogger to a position of authority, responsibility and influence.

Mastering the technology that supports blogs is now a given for bloggers and their audiences. Those seeking to understand their worlds, including luxury brands, must look beyond the technicalities and dig deep into the profiles, motivations, interests and attitudes of bloggers and their audiences.

Although blogs generally have a specific area of interest or style which draws their participants, bloggers are not a homogeneous group. They are, in reality, driven by varying motivations and as a result cover a range of interlinked topics. Statistics from Technorati indicate that, on average, five topics are covered in each standard blog. In addition, bloggers are able to identify relevant issues and present them in an engaging manner that is inviting to the reader to participate in the ensuing conversations.

Bloggers are not all the same of course, but in general they exhibit the following characteristics:

1. Bloggers are knowledgeable. They make it their business to be informed in order to keep their audiences intrigued by the dimensions of their information entries and their objective commentary. Their sources are vast, ranging from media to street research, interviews and panels, as well as tapping into the discussion entries of their participants.
2. Bloggers are savvy with technology and the cyberspace. They know how to use keywords, images and content to arouse the interest of their readers and understand how to navigate their way through cyberspace to make themselves seen, heard and discussed. They understand the tricks of the collaborative Internet world and how to ensure that their websites are referenced, linked, tagged, forwarded, shared and generally kept flowing in the virtual

world. Recent research indicates that they're using an average of seven publishing tools on their blogs and four distinct metrics for measuring success.

3. Bloggers are passionate about blogging and particularly about their choice topic area. Their core motivation is the pleasure they derive from discussing their interest area and influencing millions of people in the process. Their passion also gives them credibility as this is apparent to the readers. After all, when people are in love, they most often don't need to say that they're in love. It just shows.

4. Bloggers are champions of opinions and expressions. They want to be heard and increasingly to be seen. At the outset of the social web, bloggers were content only to be heard but with the evolution of social networks, which broke the barriers of identity and recognition online, bloggers are increasing sharing personal and even intimate details of their lives with the entire world and exposing themselves to both praise and ridicule. Take a look at Greek Tragedy (see Figure 3.9) and you'll understand what I mean.

5. Bloggers are devoted to their audience. They influence them but will also protect them and fight for them if the need arises. They provide feedback, opinions, advice, corrections and even act as counselors and, in the case of fashion and luxury, as style connoisseurs. This emanates from the dedication they have for their chosen metier and the fact that they recognize that their blogging activity has an incredible impact on people's lives.

6. Bloggers are ambitious multi-taskers that use the blogosphere to boost their careers and self images. Many bloggers have climbed up the corporate ladder or built a professional career as a result of their blogs. Many who acquire a credible reputation go on to become public speakers and recognized authorities in their fields. Others have written books, appeared on TV shows and even launched careers in music and cinema, while keeping their audiences intrigued by their rise and sowing the seed of admiration and emulation in their followers. Geraldine Dormoy (blogger of Café Mode) is now an animator for L'Express Styles Magazine, constantly visiting showrooms of fashion designers to interview them, and Scott Sculman (blogger of The Sartorialist) has not only contributed to magazines like Vogue and Esquire but is now also the official photographer of the fashion advert shoots of major luxury brands including Donna Karan as well as being the author of a recently published book. Mary Tomer, who writes the blog Mrs-O, is also on the author roll with a recent book version of the blog and its main subject, Mrs Obama.

7. Bloggers like to think that they're experts in their fields. While there are several million blogs existing, only a handful of bloggers can claim true expertise in their domains. The truth is also that several bloggers can be as clueless as their readers, creating what can be referred to as the confusion effect. However expert or non-expert, bloggers influence millions of people around the world and this is both advantageous and disastrous, especially for luxury brands whose appeal stems from the desire that their propagators are able to arouse in the public.

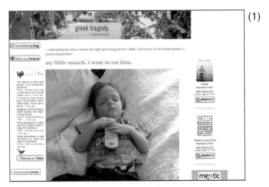

Figure 3.9 *The phenomenon of blogging is such that blogs like Greek Tragedy (1) have broken the boundaries of sharing personal and intimate information with the world. Also blogs like Dr Vino (2) and Susie Bubble (3) show that both expert and non-expert bloggers exert phenomenal influence on the public's opinions, perceptions and beliefs in specific areas*

8. Bloggers have a strong interest in lifestyle issues and many of these, of course, are linked to luxury living, whether it is the appreciation of fine objects, art, design, architecture, fashion, accessories, healthy living or beauty. Some bloggers may pretend that blogging about luxury may seem trivial but the rate of adoption of luxury-themed blogs remains high on both the blogger and bloggee fronts.

9. Bloggers are united and are interlinked with one another. They read each other's blogs, give tips to other bloggers and link other blogs from theirs. Recent research indicates that 96 percent of bloggers regularly read one or more blogs and nearly half of all bloggers read more than 50 blogs a week and a quarter of them read 100 blogs a week. They are bound together by trust and respect and they will not hesitate to defend one another if the case arises. They are a community with a strong affinity that allows one blogger to influence several others. This means that, for luxury brands, access to one blog could mean the opportunity to penetrate several others. It also means that when a company crosses the line of fire with a blog, the ensuing result could be disastrous.

Blog readers or bloggees are as active (if not more so) than the bloggers themselves. The blogging fever seems to be spreading at an alarmingly fast rate and blog adoption is now as common as having an email account. Bloggees, however, are not devoted to single blogs but tend to have a number of blogs that they visit regularly. In general, blog readers use blogs for varying purposes: information, opinions, and products and services insights top the list. According to the recent research, 75 percent of online shoppers consult a blog prior to making a purchase for luxury products, whether they intend to buy online or offline. Of them, 65 percent use blogs to seek other people's viewpoints and opinions on luxury-related issues while 48 percent click on blogs for light entertainment and 39 percent use blogs to keep themselves updated on news and general information on their areas of interest. For blog readers, regularly updated blogs are also a crucial source of information on the latest products and services from luxury brands as well as insights into brand histories, heritage and production techniques, materials and more recently the corporate responsibility acts of the companies and their initiatives towards charity, environmental protection and giving back to the community.

Bloggees are also more likely to shop online for luxury and other kinds of products than non-blog readers. The current state of luxury online is such that there are hardly any luxury brands that provide the kind of online experience that luxury consumers currently seek, therefore the clients resort to consulting other consumers through blogs before shopping both online and offline. Blog readers also care about the opinion of bloggers. They consider blogs as honest and reliable and will even overlook errors in text and expressions on blogs. However, they expect bloggers to be transparent and loyal to them. More importantly, they stay with the blogs that demonstrate independence of thought and are unsusceptible to marketing manipulations by companies, particularly in the luxury field.

The wealthy are also active bloggers. Reports have shown that social web adoption, including blogs, rises sharply at higher levels of wealth and income, shattering any notion that wealth, social interaction and technical skills are somehow all mutually exclusive. Predictably, younger wealthy consumers are the most avid users of blogs and other social media but adoption rates even among those older than 55 years of age are surprisingly high, having

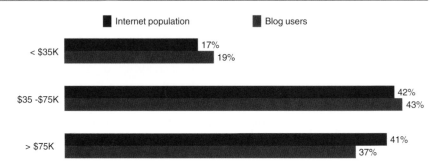

Figure 3.10 *Bloggers and bloggees may be found among the wealthy segment of the online luxury population*

quintupled between 2007 and 2008. The case is no more different in the US than in Europe or Asia. In the US, almost 10 percent of the wealthy, earning at least US$300,000 a year, have a blog, meaning they're not only readers but also writers and influencers. Figure 3.10 gives a glimpse of this.

Case Analysis 3.1
Bringing the wine experience to the world, Dr Vino style

Tyler Coleman is a doctor who drinks constantly. He tastes about 2,000 different types of wine a year and spreads the word on their quality and credibility to an audience comprising millions of people around the world. He is the type of doctor that prescribes wines instead of drugs as he lives, breathes, talks and teaches about wine.

Tyler Coleman is one of the millions of professional bloggers that exist in the blogosphere but what sets him apart is not only the expertise and authority that he exerts in the domain of wine economics (he has a PhD on the subject!) but his ability to congregate wine lovers worldwide. He has used the power of the blogosphere to amass a core base audience that shares his passion and enthusiasm for wine. His blog posts generate hundreds of comments, his entries and opinions have been lauded, his published books on wine have been bought by millions of people, his wine tasting events are popular and his press features abound in global publications like the *New York Times* and *The Guardian*.

So how does Tyler do it and what role has his blog, Dr Vino, played in all this?

First, his blog approaches wine criticism in an amicable manner albeit through the eyes of a true expert. Its focus on being a social media for quite a serious subject area has meant that even those who have little knowledge about wine feel at ease in his blog community. His choice of topics, style of expression and wealth of resources on the blog all add to the mix of his success factors. From wine policies to wine stores in New York, Paris and Chicago and to wine quizzes, wine events and wine-making tips, Dr Vino is a blog that is not only an online journal, but also a resource centre. The way Tyler Coleman approaches his interaction with his blog readers is also crucial. He offers himself at the disposal of his audience and responds to even the most elementary of questions.

This openness and confidence has created trust, credibility and affinity. He has also shown that he is fully independent and not affiliated with any wine company, chateau or domain – a crucial factor in the blogophere.

As a blog that is apparently independent of any interest groups, Dr Vino has also received a higher score among its public. Dr Vino confirms some crucial characteristics of blogs, bloggers and bloggees, which will serve luxury brands well as the reflection on whether luxury brands should create blogs or not continues.

What should luxury brands be doing about blogs?

In 2005, when both the blogging frenzy and its associated confusion were at a peak, several luxury brands were raising questions of the suitability of creating corporate blogs or seemingly independent blogs manned by the employees of luxury companies. Vichy, the French skincare brand, opted for an independent blog although this was a guise, as the blog was actually managed by the company's marketing team and their advertising agency. The blog was intended to promote a new anti-wrinkle cream and featured Claire, a young Parisian party-girl (who in reality was a fictitious character) who made regular entries on the improvement of her skin since she began using the product. She constantly whined of her lack of sleep due to too many soirées, her advancing age and the loss of firmness of her skin until she discovered the Vichy "magic" product.

The blog initially attracted high interest and as much as 12,000 views per page. This changed however when readers and other bloggers became suspicious of Claire's glowing posts and endless praise for Vichy and its new product. In addition, the set-up of the blog, the overtly polished language and the fact that so little was known about Claire, apart from the fact that she looked like a supermodel, didn't help matters. Blog readers began to send comments on Claire's postings that reflected their suspicions and to their dismay discovered that their comments were filtered and some of them weren't published. In no time, the website was inundated with postings from angry and suspicious readers reproaching the brand for not allowing real women to test the product if it were that fantastic. At the same time, snooping bloggers discovered the real story, which is that Vichy and their advertising agency had contrived the fake Claire as a way of extending the marketing communications strategy for the new product.

Bloggers were furious, clients were stunned at the blatant deceit and the business press had a field day, using Vichy as the scapegoat and case study for "what not to do in the digital marketing world". The brand received much bashing from all parties for lying, misleading and manipulating the public and there was a call to boycott both the blog and the brand. Vichy had to eat humble pie by apologizing to the blogosphere and the public but bloggers were not having it. They demanded that the culprits behind this scheme be exposed in the blogosphere and a photo of the marketing team was subsequently published online. Although the blog was completely revamped and re-launched, the seeds of mistrust had already been sewn and Vichy had to invest further efforts and resources in rebuilding confidence among its clients online and offline.

We could perhaps say that Vichy was a beginner in the blogosphere and therefore lacked an understanding of the rules of the blogging game, or that they took on an ad agency that also demonstrated as little understanding of the social web. However, the Vichy story reveals that more than respecting the core workings of the blogging world, the place of blogging in the beauty, fashion and luxury spheres is quite specific and should be thoroughly examined before being incorporated in an online marketing strategy.

The main questions that have arisen among luxury brands in relation to creating or participating in blogs have been "Should we?" or "Should we not?" and, if we should, "How should we approach the blogosphere?", "What strategies should we deploy?", "How do we find the specialists that understand this domain?" The quest to find answers to these questions has led luxury brands like Chanel to invite bloggers to visit their ateliers, boutiques and workrooms and have led other brands like Louis Vuitton to go as far as having breakfast with a group of bloggers. These initiatives, which in themselves are not wrong, have however not shed the light that luxury brands were seeking on several unclear blog-related business issues. Also, the internal organizational set-up of several luxury brands doesn't help matters much (see the Introduction and Chapter 5 of this book). This is because of the relative newness of the luxury blogosphere, which means that both bloggers and bloggees are still getting to grips with the key aspects of its evolution. In addition, not many bloggers know why they even blog and there are only a handful of people involved in the blogging world that can claim true expertise in both the workings of blogging and the mechanics of the luxury business. So it's no wonder that luxury brands have been asking questions about blogging while at the same time responding to much criticism that the sector has received on the lack of integration of blogging within the web strategy of luxury brands.

Now to the golden questions and my viewpoints:

Q.   Should luxury brands blog or not?
A.   My answer is a straight and clear no.

Q.   Should luxury brands have a corporate blog integrated on their websites?
A.   Again I would say no.

Q.   Should luxury brands have a separate independent blog?
A.   No no no.

Q. Should luxury brands team up with existing blogs in providing content?
A. Not at all.

Q. Should luxury brands have co-branding partnerships with blogs?
A. What?!?

Q. Should luxury brands create an independent blog?
A. Not unless they want to pull a Vichy.

So what should luxury brands be doing online then? What else is left for them to do if they cannot take advantage of the obvious? First, I would say that a luxury brand that purposely ignores the blogosphere is on its way back to the eighteenth century. Luxury brands ought to be in tune with the blogosphere. The brands that seek advancement in the twenty-first century market scene must partake in the world of blogs. They are required not only to observe or be up-to-date in tracking blog conversations, but also to be very much present in the blogosphere. This may be achieved in different tactical ways that don't require the creation of a blog by a luxury brand. One way of being linked to the blogosphere is to follow in the path of brands like Louis Vuitton, which invited six bloggers from different parts of the world to Hong Kong in June 2008 to discover and experience its digital product, the Soundwalk (see Figure 3.11). For four days, the bloggers followed the footsteps of the Soundwalk narrator Shu Qi whose voice guided them on a journey of the discovery of Hong Kong. This opportunity enabled the bloggers to have a unique first-hand experience in the brand's universe. Following this, bloggers have widely shared their impressions with their readers in their articles, photos and videos. The most important aspect of this exercise is that the bloggers are able to offer their commentary to their readers based on experiences that have been lived. There are also other multiple approches that luxury brands could take to exploit the opportunities brought by blogs.

Companies in different domains are reaching out to blogs to promote their products and services, as discussions on brands and retail experiences litter several blog postings. In fact, one third of bloggers have been approached to be brand advocates by both luxury and non-luxury brands. Other luxury brands have opted for their own blogs. But my question is "What are the brands going to blog about?" Luxury is rooted in creating a desire, respecting a tradition, nurturing a culture and bowing to a philosophy that leads to pleasurable experiences. This is translated through beautiful products that are objects of desire and through services that lead to positive sensations. But they are all a part of a universe made up of a brand and all that it represents. This cannot be expressed only in words or reproduced only in conversations but must be felt and experienced. And that is where the problem begins with blogging. Since most blogs linked to luxury are based on texts and images and on the often vivacious conversations that ensue, it is best for luxury brands to allow the clients to do the talking while they use the contents of such conversations to fuel the experience that is crafted within the universe of the brand.

Whether or not a luxury brand has a social web strategy (which is most unlikely at this stage), most luxury brands are already present in the blogosphere. Statistics from Technorati estimate that four in every five bloggers post brand or product reviews, with 37 percent posting them frequently and about 90 percent of bloggers make entries on only the brands that they love (or hate). Blog readers also love to discuss luxury brands, particularly as a result of the often emotional accord they have with luxury brands. When Michelle Obama wore a dress from Azzedine Alaïa to the G20 dinner in April 2009, it generated 282 comments within the first two days from more than 200 different people and most of the discussions were as much about the US First Lady as about the designer. So imagine the level of traffic that would have been drawn to Alaïa's website following the post had the brand given much thought to having a website – you may be surprised but yes, Azzedine Alaïa didn't have a website at the time of writing (but this is another issue that has been further addressed in Chapter 7).

If you look at blogs like Dream Yacht Blog (dreamyachtblog.com), Purse Blog (purseblog.com), Style Bubble (stylebubble.typepad.com) and Style Rookie (www.tavithenewgirlintown.blogspot.com) you may be surprised at the extent of conversations taking place among customers on products and services of luxury brands. The consumer has taken the lead in the conversation and wants to be in absolute control. Luxury brands have therefore become non-participants and been relegated to the role of watchers and observers because if luxury brands simply show up, announce themselves and expect the audience to be gleefully receptive, they are likely to fail. The bottom line is that luxury clients learn a lot about luxury brands through the social web so brands should learn about where their clients are getting this information and how they are sharing their stories. The role of the luxury brand in the social web is to influence the participants towards adopting their brands without seeming intrusive, manipulative and controlling. How can this be handled by luxury companies? Here are a few crucial Q and As and a seven-point guideline on how in my opinion luxury brands could approach the social web:

Q. Should luxury brands inform bloggers of the brand's initiatives?
A. Yes, of course.

Q. Should luxury brands monitor the blogosphere?
A. Definitely.

Q. Should luxury brands participate in blog discussions?
A. Yes, through reps that are real people with a name and a face.

1. Luxury brands ought to understand the scope of the social web and identify the blogs that are most relevant to their brand identity and product categories.

2. Luxury brands should identify blogs and social media platforms that have the right demographics of a brand's consumer segments(s). Not all social networks are relevant for luxury.

3. Luxury brands should observe blogs through both the postings and the comments of the readers and the responses to these comments by other readers. This will help to understand how consumers perceive the brand's products and services. It will also be useful in product development, brand strategy and communications approaches both online and offline.

4. Luxury brands should understand what specific aspects of the brand's entire offerings are suitable for each type of blog or social web platform and how to communicate these through the blog whether by advertising, special events, exclusive previews or other initiatives.

5. Luxury brands should incentivize employees to monitor and participate in blogs as brand ambassadors. Every luxury brand should have at least one dedicated human blog monitor – and the right software or application – who permanently navigates the blogosphere to get the scoop on what is being said about the brand, its competitors and its products or service categories. This employee should also step in and speak up for the brand, particularly in cases where untrue or distorted information is being spread about a brand (and this is frequent). This will influence other blog users to give honest and knowledgeable information and opinions about brands while enhancing their respect for those brands. The brand monitors should, of course, be honest and transparent about their status with the luxury companies and participate in the blogs as individuals (with a name and a face) rather than as corporations. In addition, there are existing softwares and applications that track blog features and conversations about luxury brands by the second. The brands ought to use this to converge and assess the status of their brands in the blogosphere.

6. Luxury brands should advertise on pre-selected blogs. The blogs don't necessarily have to be the most popular in the field but the most relevant in terms of the brand's identity, product portfolio and client base. Also the appropriate products should be advertised in the suitable blogs as each blog type has its core strengths. A brand may be better off placing product ads on product blogs and luggage ads on lifestyle blogs or hotel blogs. The trap of being stuck with pre-selected blogs should however be avoided at all costs. As you are well aware, a new blog shows up in the cyberspace every minute so being stuck with already tried and tested blogs is like using the dial-up telephone boxes today just because they are able to make and receive calls.

7. Luxury brands should generate an online buzz through word-of-mouth and word-of-mouse. The good old verbal information style is still applicable and efficient in today's luxury scene and is complemented and reinforced by viral marketing. This may be done by giving privileged information to bloggers that the public would normally not have access to. It could also

include invitations to special events like store openings, product launches, fashion shows and wine tastings, service concept presentations and even product trials. This will be effective because bloggers who have a direct first experience with brands are likely to give an honest and unbiased opinion of the brand and will draw their readers to the brand, if all goes well.

I guess you now see why I think that luxury brands shouldn't have blogs, at least in the current context of blogging. The case could however be different in the future if technology evolves in a different direction.

Figure 3.11 *Louis Vuitton, one of the luxury brands that continuously seeks interaction with bloggers, invited six renowned bloggers to Hong Kong in June 2008 to test its Soundwalk digital product and potentially give positive reviews and generate discussions about it on their blogs. Such initiatives that enable bloggers to experience a direct relation with the brand's universe are more likely to lead to exchanges about the brands based on factual information rather than perceptions*

A look at how blogs will evolve

As the blogosphere advances, blogs will become more specialized. Bloggers will look for more resources as sources of credibility. They will become media and communications experts and will eventually pose a real threat and competition for the media and publishing sectors. This will happen once the wheat is separated from the chaff and the blogs that add real value to readers will be sustained while the weaker blogs will disappear.

Today, blogs are all over the cyberspace. Everyone seems to have a blog including politicians and celebrities, and they are right to do so as blogs have changed the way the online media, communications and publishing works forever. Their influence on the wider society is also on the high radar. It has been said that blogging and the social web contributed to the popularity and influence of the US President Barak Obama during his campaign. The question today is no longer linked to whether blogs are widely adopted but rather their relevance to different parties, including luxury companies.

Everyone who blogs believes they have something to say until they are put on the blog pedestal where they have to say it. Then it becomes clear that perhaps not many people are interested in what they have to say or the way that they say it. This reality has led to the disappearance of more than 200 million blogs according to Technorati. It has also led to the diminishing of activities on several blogs as today as much as 45 percent of blogs are updated every three months on average, which is very low in comparison with the average weekly updates of blogs in general.

This filtering process will continue as the credible professionals with expert knowledge in different domains emerge as the leaders in the blogosphere. The non-expert bloggers who are passionate enough to be involved in key issues in their domains will also prevail even if they are not necessarily literary experts. These are the people that will obtain the most visibility and authority in their domains. Blog readers will also become experts in scanning blogs and deciphering the core value of every blog. What will happen for sure is that the category of blogs that are self-promotional stunts or plain jokes will disappear as their irresponsibility becomes unacceptable to readers.

Although blogs are unlikely to replace traditional media, they will be strong contenders for the attention and influence of the wider public. The blogosphere will propel the strongest blogs towards brand status and on this pedestal they will be able to compete with the *New York Times*, the *Herald Tribune*s, the *BusinessWeek*s, the *Le Monde*s, the *Vogue*s and the *Harper's Baazar*s of the media world. Several blogs like Beauty Addict, Café Mode and Who What Wear are well on their way to attaining this status. These blogs have their readers also as their editors and fact verifiers and they will remain accountable to them, making their roles dual and dependent. This is a unique and positive relationship dynamic which the traditional media will not be able to attain. However, the traditional media will be forced to recognize and quote the credible blogs in their editorial features. Blogs will also challenge the distribution of print media such as newspapers and magazines as they draw millions to their websites while print media readers decline. Already, people first check fashion news on blogs instead of magazines and this will be even further adopted in the future in other categories.

By now, you will likely agree that the idea of blogging will never disappear. What will continue to evolve is its process and structure. Blogs will undergo fundamental changes as more interactive media elements like videos, animations and widgets are incorporated in them to drive home the messages that the text and images are doing today. There will also likely be the evolution of microblogging, which will be seen more in mainstream

web 2.0, the social web is real!

websites such as online magazines and online retailers. These factors will also lead to the rise of micro-communities within blogs. All these parties will collectively form an important social and economic force in multiple domains.

As bloggers get smarter and blog readers learn to read both the lines and between the lines, the definition of a blog itself will be brought into question. Bloggers will also understand the value of blogging in several languages and how cultural orientation influences the response and content of blogs. Also, as vlogs, plogs and mlogs become more popular, the value of the raw data that they generate will be even more relevant for companies including luxury brands.

But a key issue for luxury brands to address is whether bloggers and blog-gees have less regard for luxury brands just because all the information about the brands are divulged for all to see online. If bloggers visit a brand's atelier and subsequently broadcast all the information, images and videos on the design and production approach, will the magic appeal that the brand has be gone forever? These are some of the issues that luxury brands ought to review before allowing bloggers to peruse the inner workings of the brands or before breakfasting, lunching or dining with bloggers. However, it is relevant for luxury brands not to be too far off the blogosphere.

The online world of social networks

When 27-year-old Vivian moved from New York to Paris, she didn't have any friends in the city, she couldn't speak French and she wasn't conversant in the French culture and way of life. She was somewhat lost and wondered how she could avoid that feeling of isolation that is familiar to strangers in big cities. So Vivian did what most people in her generation would do. She went online. It didn't take her long to find different Paris-themed groups on MySpace and Facebook, where she introduced herself. Within a few days she had received numerous messages with information, tips and advice on how to settle down to life in Paris. Someone even offered her lunch and someone else invited her for a countryside weekend visit with her family. She also found other "expats" of different nationalities who were more than pleased to share the pleasures and horrors of living in Paris with her. She got tips on administrative matters, language schools, references for restaurants, museums, stores, clubs and associations. She even found a house cleaner and a plumber from the networks. Facebook and MySpace became her resource centers and she was thrilled. Within a few weeks she had more than one hundred people on her private network and friendship lists on the two social networks. They chatted constantly about several topics and she was often surprised at how freely the people she met online discussed their private lives. She exchanged photos, videos and even began an informal advisory on how to best enjoy a visit to New York. She also met up with some of her "virtual" friends in real life and discovered that they were a bunch of really interesting people and she could envision long-lasting friendships with them. The feeling of loneliness was over for good. Within her first two months in Paris, she had become a real Parisian.

The world of online social networks is a reality of our society today. Apart from being a world where people "virtually" congregate, it is also fast becoming a bridge connecting our "real" and the "virtual" existence. It is also a world where the boundaries between the sources of influence of consumers are stretched. Online social networks have challenged the way human beings relate to one another and particularly the way they form perceptions, ideas, opinions and viewpoints when it comes to issues that they're interested in. This includes products and services, and is a real challenge for luxury brands.

Social networks are places where people are drawn together by a shared interest, which they discuss, share and also vent. They are online communities that serve the core purposes of congregating, engaging, educating and influencing people of varying age groups, social status, educational backgrounds, religious beliefs, cultural orientations and sexual preferences. These parties are often brought together because of that innate human need to connect with other human beings, particularly those that share common interests, values and passions.

To go for a more scientific definition, according to Wikipedia, "a social network is a social structure made of nodes – which are generally individuals or organizations – that are tied by one or more specific types of interdependency, such as values, visions, ideas, financial exchange, friends, kinship, dislikes, conflicts, trade, web links, sexual relations, disease transmission or airline routes. The resulting structures are quite complex". Like blogs, online social networks belong to the broader phenomenon of the social web, which also includes chat rooms, discussion platforms, virtual worlds and other user-to-user communities.

Social networks are a worldwide phenomenon and are becoming prolific with the likes of iVillage, MySpace, Flickr, Twitter, Facebook, LinkedIn, Asian Avenue and Diamond Lounge as the most adopted, while others like Qzone, Rose Beauty and Mixi have become references in online congregation in China and Japan. As I write, there are more than 175 million active monthly users on Facebook and more than 125 million on MySpace. Twitter, which had drawn over 17 million users by April 2009, is currently growing at a phenomenal rate of more than 1,000 percent. You may however be surprised to know that the social networks with the highest number of monthly users in the world are not in the US but in China. The Chinese social networking website QQ has more than 300 million monthly users while the Qzone community has attracted over 200 million monthly users, representing 50 percent more than the number of Internet users in China (see Figure 3.12). In Japan, the use of online social networks has also been on a constant rise. The social website Mixi, which has more than 10 million monthly users, has become an important destination for the digital media-obsessed Japanese. South Korea

Figure 3.12 *Qzone and Facebook, two of the online social networks that are at the forefront of attracting the highest number of members, with over 200 million community members on the former and 175 million members on the latter*

is not far off the radar either. Online social websites like Cyworld, which has drawn 90 percent of the country's population in their twenties and 25 percent of the entire population, is a popular destination for the digital generation of Koreans. The level of activity and information exchanged on social websites is also mind-boggling. MySpace has more than 20 billion mails and 14 billion comments on its website and 1.5 billion images, with approximately 800 million being uploaded daily. Facebook has more than 65 billion page views per month and more than 14 million photos uploaded daily, while the number of active users doubles every six months.

Social networks have thrived on numbers and quantity because of their ease of accessibility and their ability to draw millions in a short time space. Also, the companies behind the websites draw their income from the value added by the monumental figures that represent the users of the websites. In other words, the more people that are attracted to the forums, the better for the social websites. This means that, in general, social networks are essentially for the masses, an approach that is quite the opposite of what luxury represents or strives to offer. And this brings me to the issue of the suitability of mass-focused social networks for the luxury industry. Should luxury brands participate in social networks and, if so, how? Or should they just stay away and observe the public discussions about them and their competitors hoping that they would be portrayed positively and the competitors negatively. Before answering these questions, let's take a quick look at some of the main conceptions and misconceptions of social networks.

Conceptions and misconceptions of social networks

Although social networks are nothing new in the real world, they remain a relatively recent phenomenon online. Not surprisingly several conceptions and misconceptions have been formed about this medium, particularly in the luxury industry. Some of the most popular are the following:

1. Social networks are for people that have nothing to do
   This must be a joke. Online social networks are thriving communities that bring people of all walks of life together. They are as much for people who have ample free time as for those who have little time. The beauty of social networks and online communities is that the core value or interest area is often pre-determined and therefore people are drawn to participate in discussions and exchanges without feeling that they are losing their time. Also, the average time spent on social networks per visit is 8.5 minutes, which is quite minimal because people can jump in and out of conversations within seconds and it takes half a second to click on a mouse.

   Social networks like LinkedIn and A Small World are known for drawing highly educated and successful groups of people that range from senior-level company executives to record-setting sports personalities, award-winning artists and renowned politicians.

2. Social networks are for opportunists
   Well, there are surely opportunists on social networks but this is not the core group that form the very fabric of online social networks. Online communities are for congregating, connecting, engaging and exchanging, and these features are more to do with sharing and giving and less to do with exploiting, extracting or manipulating. Anyhow, the members of online communities are smart enough to know when they're being exploited and they will not hesitate to expose and boycott the exploiters whether it is on a corporate level or not.

3. Social networks are for the masses
   It is true that several social networks admit anyone and everyone with a computer and a mouse but there are online networks whose core values are drawn from their exclusivity. Even though the Chinese (Qzone etc.) and the Americans (Facebook etc.) are competing for the largest number of users in

terms of numbers on their online communities, others like A Small World and ZeroTwoNine have distinguished themselves not by the quantity of the users but by the quality of the members of the communities. A Small World, whose members are 90 percent employed with an average income of $330,000 (the other 10 percent range from millionaire philanthropists to aristocratic inheritors), is one of the few online communities with the highest concentration of the world's wealthy on a single platform. As you may already know, A Small World doesn't admit everyone and those that are admitted have to respect very strict guidelines to avoid being thrown out. Those that contend that a social network that doesn't have at least one million users is not relevant are evaluating the social web in terms of quantity rather than quality. As we know, quality matters more than quantity in luxury.

4. People on social networks shop more online than offline

Social networkers are more likely to shop online than non-users of social networks but it doesn't necessarily mean that they are likely to shop more online than offline. People on several social networks like A Small World often seek other people's advice, opinions and suggestions on brands, products, services, hotels, travel destinations and so on and, more often than not, these messages become public discussion forums. It's not uncommon to see a thread of discussion on topics such as "Which brand's luggage collection defines endless style?" attracting as many as 1,000 participants, each one naming their preferred brands and outlining their differential qualities. Such conversations inform, educate and influence both the participants and observers and go a long way in shaping perceptions towards brands and changing the mind-set and even value systems of people. All of these will eventually translate to a purchase decision at some point and the brand choice could very well be as a result of the discussion in the online community. In fact, 63 percent of people that spend time online consider product and brand reviews from other consumers to be as credible as the reviews made by experts. Also, 87 percent of members of online communities seek brand opinion from fellow members whether it is for purchase or information purposes.

5. Wealthy people do not use online social networks

This assumption sounds like a real joke. Recent research from the Luxury Institute indicates that 60 percent of wealthy Americans belong to at least one social network. This scenario isn't far from the reality in other markets. Apart from being active on social networks like LinkedIn, A Small World and even the likes of Twitter and MySpace, wealthy people also enjoy blogging and conversing with virtual friends. They are particularly active in discussions on their areas of interest like sailing, flying, photography and the good old shopping. A case in point is the online community A Small World with more than 300,000 members whose average household income is $330,000, not counting millionaires like Tiger Woods and Ivanka Trump. Also, user platforms like Twitter allow everyone to communicate with their "followers" through short but frequent messages that

---

Case Analysis 3.2
Qzone's way of changing the rules of social networking

On 31 January 2009, the Chinese online social network Qzone, which has become somewhat of a cult destination, welcomed its 200 millionth member for the month. This feat crowned Qzone the online social network with the greatest number of users in the world as they stole the title from Facebook which until then had 175 million users per month.

Qzone has become a meeting zone for the vast and active population of China's youth segment and those that may be classified as the nouveau riche, the understaters and the mature generations. They not only join the network for the sake of being on it but they are also prolific users who share not only words, but also their faces and lifestyles. The social network has more than 60 million pictures on its server uploaded by the members who post more than 150 million daily commentaries. Also, 4 million users add at least one picture on the network every day. That means more than 28 million photos every week, a number hardly to be ignored.

In addition, Qzone has set several records in the social web including attracting 50 million people who used its instant messaging service QQ in one day, a world record for an instant messaging service.

So how does Qzone do it?

First, there is the Chinese consumer market size, which is larger than any single market in the world. With a vast base of luxury consumers originating from both the middle-class and the nouveau riche segments, the number of Chinese who have caught the social network buzz is continuously on the rise. Second, there is the current thirst for knowledge and progression in China following years of communism and market closure. Third, there is the excitement of the Internet and the freedom it provides to users while exposing them to the entire world. And, finally, there is the youth generation that seeks to establish its own way of life empowered by new technologies.

These factors have led Qzone to the height of the summit of social networks, at least for the moment.

---

place greater emphasis on the connection made than the wealth or social level. The likes of Ashton Kutcher, Larry King and Britney Spears can surely not be categorized as "not wealthy".

How are people using social networks?

Social networks are built on community and trust. Unlike blogs where people can choose to remain anonymous or use pseudo names and opt out of uploading their pictures, social networks are actually built for people to have both a voice and a face. These people are active, smart, curious, responsive and bold with a highly independent viewpoint on several issues although flexible enough to be influenced by other community members whom they trust. Social networks offer people a sense of belonging and affiliation and, as we know, where there is affinity, there is naturally trust.

Their key reasons for using social networks range from gathering information and keeping themselves up-to-date, to entertaining themselves and others, exchanging opinions on several issues including preferred luxury brands, educating themselves and others, sharing everything from news to personal contacts, as well as influencing others on several levels whether it is to adopt the same hobbies, sports or brand. Like bloggers and bloggees, social network members exhibit a high level of passion for different areas but the fundamental difference between a social network and a blog is that unlike blogs, social networks are not necessarily created around a specific theme or interest area but instead act as platforms for bringing people from a wide range of backgrounds together. These people then go on to create mini-groups, micro-communities, online clubs, user groups and all other forms of communities within the main social network platforms. There are several thousands of user groups on social networks like MySpace and LinkedIn in addition to the millions of personal networks that exist on each of these social networks.

A new phenomenon that has been brought about by Twitter is the use of social networks as a pointing device through short and instant messaging. Twitter, which is based on building a network (through acquiring followers), allows people to keep their followers updated on their activities, thoughts, discoveries, news, events or whatever it is that catches their fancy as long as it can fit into 140 characters. This somewhat online SMS-like communications style enables sharing in a social community without getting into the time-tasking intricacies of standard online social networks like Facebook and MySpace or the energy that is required on virtual worlds like Second Life. Twitter simply lets people say things as they happen in a short and concise manner and this information appears on their followers' pages instantly. Its set-up means that the message comes to the users and not the other way round. Its concise nature also means that it can serve as a perfect pointing device for links to longer discussions, articles, videos, blog pots or whatever else one may find on the other side of a link.

The social web has equipped and empowered the ordinary citizen with online tools to create, manage and adapt their identities and to make themselves seen and heard. This has been translated to a change in the way marketing functions forever, and particularly the way the Internet has evolved from vertical to lateral interactivity. The way that products and services are evaluated by consumers has also changed. Users of social networks are currently more likely to seek the opinion of community members before making an online purchase of high-ticket items like luxury handbags in exotic skin, watches and luggage from well-known luxury brands. It is no longer a question of obtaining information disseminated by a luxury brand through its website but of obtaining validation of the brand's credibility and value from fellow luxury clients. It is now common to find conversations like *"Am I over Louboutin?", and "What is your favourite perfume?"* on social networks like

Figure 3.13 *The exclusive online social network A Small World not only provides one of the Internet's highest concentrations of the world's wealthy, but also enables the multitude of luxury brand enthusiasts in the community to have brand-themed dialogues such as the one shown, sometimes surpassing 10,000 posted responses. The high involvement in these dialogues indicates the level of passion the members have for luxury brands, even when the conversations have a negative undertone*

A Small World (see Figure 3.13). These kinds of conversations often attract thousands of views and participants who either validate or renounce the brands in question.

In addition to conversing about luxury brands, several participants of social networks subscribe to these communities in order to meet new people, reconnect with old acquaintances or be connected in some way to a community. This allows for the fostering of relationships or the creation of new ones.

Other uses of social networks include promoting a business or an area of expertise as is often seen on LinkedIn and A Small World, which some business developers and consultants have made extensions of their offices. Other members of social networks use them as platforms for the congregation and mobilization of people to promote a cause such as issues linked to environmental protection, human rights, gender equality and ethical business practices. One such network is the Authentic Luxury Network, created to foster sustainable practices in the luxury industry. These communities, which have a purpose, are often the propagators of social consciousness on certain issues.

The social web allows individuality and collective experiences at the same time. Social networks have enabled people to co-exist online even if in reality their interaction with the web is on an individual basis as they are often alone in front of a computer screen. The beauty of this dual manner of functioning is that users are still able to make independent choices while drawing some of their references from online social networks.

Social networks like Twitter, 43 Things and C Koi Ton Reve (short for *c'est quoi ton rêve*, meaning "What is your dream?") (Figure 3.14), which enable people to "do" specific things online like following other people

Figure 3.14 *As the scope of social networks continues to evolve from simply gathering people together towards enabling them to create and fulfill a purpose, there will be more communities like C Koi Ton Rêve, which features people's recorded narration of their lifetime dreams; and 43 Things which encourages people to share their goals and strive to achieve them. These purpose-based communities will transcend moral intentions to include luxury-themed purposes*

Case Analysis 3.3
It's A Small World for the wealthy online

A Small World, the online social network founded by Erik Wacthmeister in New York in 2004, is the only online community dedicated to the world's wealthy and elite. With members ranging from business moguls like Ivanka Trump and Hiro Nishida, actors and artists like Diane Kruger and Joshua Bell, designers and writers like Sang A and Caprice Cane, socialites and philanthropists like Naomi Campbell and Sanjay Rawal, as well as sportsmen like Mark Beaumont and Johan Nilson, A Small World's member list reads like a roll call of a first-class-only flight.

The website, which unites more than 300,000 members from every world region, has used two factors to craft its very essence – trust and community. Membership is upon invitation by another member if they have been given the privilege of inviting others (as decided by the managers of the website). Members are encouraged to participate in forums which range from aviation, sailing, fashion, style, beauty, motoring and so on, most of which feature passionate conversations, debates and events. People may also congregate for business purposes including participating in mini-clubs for investments, real estate and business modeling. The website has strived to overcome the issue of privacy and intrusion – one of the fundamental concerns of wealthy people online. It is governed by a strict code of conduct, which results in expulsion if not adhered to. Members may only connect to people they know and those that wish to get in touch with people they don't know have to follow the "network thread" which will enable them to identify people in their network or the networks of those in their network to make the necessary introductions. Pretty tough huh? Wait until you discover also that if you attempt to add someone to your network and the person declines, you will be expelled from the community. Also, if someone happens to dismiss you from their network, you're out. Rampantly emailing people who don't know you or haven't solicited your friendship could also attract expulsion.

A Small World is, however, a healthy breeding ground for business advancement, networking and entertainment. Investment capital of up to $10 million has been raised on the business forums, properties worth $millions have been bought and sold on the real-estate forums, sporting events tickets have been exchanged on the sports forums and private jets have even been swapped on the travel forums. Market research analysts have also found it to be a gold mine for tracking the behavior of the wealthy while event organizers use the community to reach people at the top-end of the wealth spectrum. Several events have also been organized exclusively for members by luxury brands like Moët & Chandon and Mercedes Benz and, when Nelson Mandela celebrated his 90th birthday in London, members had privileged places.

Since the wealthy are quite sensitive to privacy and personal information access, but at the same time seek to connect and interact with like-minded people, they are only likely to congregate on websites that they trust will both protect them and add value to their online experience. A Small World fulfills this. The online community enables connection with people within the same level of accomplishment, maturity, income bracket, educational background and international orientation. The average age of the members is 32 years, their household income averages at $330,000 while 95 percent of them have a university degree, 50 percent a masters degree and 90 percent are employed with the other 10 percent ranging from business owners to philanthropists. Their professional backgrounds range from finance, consulting, law, marketing, fashion, luxury, arts and other industries. They are international (only 16 percent are based full-time in the US), with Europe (Italy, the UK, France and Germany) having the highest density of members.

This online community embodies the key elements that luxury brands need to be well-represented in the social web, whether through advertisements, special events, communications campaigns, market research or client identification. In contrast with the "big worlds" like Facebook, MySpace, Cyworld and Miki, the marketing communications initiatives made on A Small World are viewed as useful and appropriate by members. Most of the members (84 percent) trust the advice they receive from fellow members and more than half of them view A Small World as the only online community they trust.

This proves that social networks are relevant as much for their qualities and not only for their numbers. It is clear from A Small World that the wealthy have also caught the social web bug.

(Twitter), setting goals and accomplishing them (43 Things) and connecting people who could realize life-long dreams (Ckoitonreve.fr) are also becoming popular online destinations for their positive experiences and reference points.

What should luxury brands be doing about social networks?

The social web has confirmed that consumers worldwide not only want attention from companies but they are also currently demanding to be more engaged in a way that no longer follows the old top-down marketing dissemination but instead functions through a bottom-up and lateral collaboration where the consumer is in charge or at least is well recognized. The mass marketing model of one-formula-fits-all, which marketers have applied since the industrial revolution, is no longer appropriate. Consumers are saturated with an over-supply of information and choices and they have decided to take the reigns of control and they LOVE it. This is why devices like TiVo that enable people to skip adverts are so successful. Companies are no longer in the position where they disseminate information into the market to connect consumers with their products and service; they must now connect with the consumers to be in tune with their tastes and preferences in order to influence their choices. This means building and nurturing relationships with clients through penetrating online communities and social networks. The days of "buy now" and "call now" are over, particularly in the luxury sphere.

The core challenge for companies is how to approach consumer groups in such a way that they will accept the company and become the propagators of their message. This is a particularly daunting task for luxury brands as the luxury segment's approach to client interactions has always been somewhat to maintain a respectable distance between the client and the brand. In the meantime, the clients themselves are becoming harder to reach as they are no longer loyal to single brands but are more prone to experimenting, mixing and even individualizing brands according to their tastes. And, of course, brands have the additional issue of justifying and evaluating the return on investment of initiatives taken in marketing through online communities. How can it be demonstrated to the executive committee of a luxury brand that monitoring conversations on hundreds of social networks like Twitter, A Small World, Facebook and MySpace will be useful in product development and brand image communications? What metrics would be used to measure the return on such activities in order to justify the budget allocated to it? And from which section can the budget itself be extracted? From the marketing intelligence budget or from the marketing research budget or the digital media allocation? The lack of a preceding reference model for social web marketing definitely doesn't make it an easy task for luxury brands.

But when dealing with the social web, particularly online communities, luxury brands must think less in terms of costs and more in terms of return on investment linked directly to the value that each client brings to the brand through their level of influence on others. This may be through their referrals, opinions, suggestions, network size, elevated position and clout. For example, on social networks like A Small World, people will be more likely to adhere to the suggestions of a luxury personal shopper with a network of 2,000 people than they would to those of a real-estate agent, no matter how wealthy and stylish the latter is.

So how should luxury brands approach online communities and social networks?

First, a luxury brand must have a real social media vision translated through a long-term strategy with clearly defined objectives for the company's entire online presence. This should naturally feature communicating through social networks and online communities. However, the luxury brand must first understand the dynamics of the social web and the evolution of the consumer mind-set in order to craft an integrated social web strategy. This means developing a best practice approach to Internet marketing and teaching, coaching and inculcating an online culture among employees internally. The Internet must be viewed as a multi-channel support system for reaching new clients, enhancing the relationship with current clients, reinforcing the brand image, selling online and providing services and enhancing the overall brand experience. For example, it must be well understood that although Facebook and Twitter are both online social media platforms, their dynamics and potential value for luxury brands are different and therefore luxury's approach to them must also be different.

Secondly, luxury brands have to align their Internet strategies to touch on the various communities that concern the wealthy and in which they want to participate. Identifying the online social network that suits the demographics of the brand is no longer sufficient, neither is it enough to blast all the members of the community with endless advertisements and offers of exclusive deals and events. Each luxury brand must take a further step into the social network and identify the micro-communities and interest groups that may be relevant for the brand, and understand how they function in order to design the appropriate marketing approach to adopt for them. Or better still, the brand should let the people come to them but when this happens there ought to be real value-adding interaction and enrichment. Luxury brands must also take advantage of the advanced tracking applications that have been developed to track social media conversations in real time.

Social networks provide luxury brands with the opportunity to monitor both the evolution of consumers (qualitative) and the returns on marketing initiatives (quantitative). In the case of consumer evolution, questions that should be asked include: How often has the brand been mentioned in online communities?, Which networks and why these?, What are people saying about the brand?, Who is saying it?, How influential is their voice?, How many people do they influence?, Have these conversations had any impact on sales and market share? These questions will help brands to clarify the dimensions of other assessments of the community members including evaluating their attitudes, behaviors and interests. In terms of quantitative monitoring exercises, these may include establishing the referral websites that are drawing traffic to the brand's website, which is relatively easy to do with the right technology. It provides the opportunity of knowing where the visitors to the website are coming from and if they are being driven from links provided in online communities and discussions or from other destinations. One of the beauties of the Internet is that it provides measurability on multiple levels. The most important metrics, however, have to be identified in order to measure the ROI as accurately as possible.

Monitoring exercises must be used in segmenting, not only through the usual demographics of age, gender, location and lifestyles, but also by what people do, feel, perceive and believe. And this may be determined by observing how people act (behavior), which groups they belong to and forums they participate in (interest) and how they respond to the multiple conversations that take place in the social web (attitudes). This approach enables grouping people according to what is important to them and what they value, like, dislike, think, believe, say and ignore. Once a luxury brand reaches the point of understanding online community members well enough to conduct a constructive segmentation process, the brand is well on its way to executing a social web marketing strategy that is focused on giving luxury clients what they expect in a meaningful and valuable way.

Social networks are excellent platforms for targeted advertisements if the core make-up population is understood. Exclusive social networks like A Small World and ZeroTwoNine provide luxury brands with access to a wealthy segment of the online consumer population. These websites provide the right environment for luxury advertisements without the risk of the brands appearing in the same advert space that was previously occupied by

Coca Cola or McDonald's and may be next taken up by Colgate or Starbucks. The approach of every luxury brand seeking to advertise on social websites is first to identify the right community (not the largest) and then to ensure that the website befits the brand (not because the competitors are advertising on it). This should be followed by ensuring that the right approach to compensation is adopted.

It has been the norm for luxury brands to adopt the cost per thousand (CPM) advertisement model both offline and online. Some websites have also created the cost per click (CPC) or cost per unique visitor approach. These metrics have been used to justify the advertisement expenditure but do they make any real sense as the metrics for luxury brands on the social web? I don't think so. Luxury brands could approach social web marketing in a different way. For example, instead of depending on web traffic statistics (which are sometimes too good to be true), luxury brands wishing to advertise on online communities could take the customer lifetime value (CLV) approach. This will enable the use of the qualitative information gathered on the clients in the community to measure the potential value that each client could bring to the brand if they were to stay with the brand over a lifetime or in the long term. Let's not forget that luxury clients have collective experiences which they transfer from one channel to another, so evaluating the relationship between the real-life and online behavioral patterns is essential in CLV-based advertisement assessments.

Online communities can also be used to build a desire around a brand through viral marketing, buzz marketing and word-of-mouth marketing. Recently the social web has also provided the opportunity for stealth marketing, which involves a company hiring active people on online communities to act as consumers in order to recommend a brand, its products or services to others in online discussions. There are several brands on A Small World which I suspect are the masters of this tactic as the names of these brands come up in every conversation about luxury. This approach is, however, not considered to be ethical and the users of online social communities are becoming more cynical and expert in fishing out the culprits in the game of deceit and manipulation – two characteristics that the social web opposes.

Online communities give luxury brands the opportunity to communicate on their moral purpose and responsible practices in ethics and corporate responsibility. This could also include educating the public on the adverse effects of brand counterfeiting as well as aspects linked to the transparent way that the company conducts its business, and its sustainable development practices. Sustainability, of course, must be in the core values and genes of the company otherwise it will come off as a PR-stunt. The moral purpose could include environmental responsibility, diversity in employment, respect for human rights, gender equality and appropriate working conditions. Luxury brands must act responsibly on the social web and this includes being sincere and transparent in presentations and communications. I have been appalled to see several employees of luxury brands trying to promote their brands on online social forums while pretending to be ordinary consumers interested in the brand. Online consumers, especially the wealthy, are smart and savvy and will not tolerate brands that insult their intelligence through clearly manipulative messages.

Luxury brands may also draw clients to themselves or retain existing clients by creating and fostering communities around the brand. I don't mean creating official communities on Facebook or MySpace but creating a unique community that will congregate those interested in the brand or curious about it. Luxury brand-based communities must however be very carefully executed. In order to do so, there must be a strategic purpose behind the community, with defined objectives and benefits. The central point of the community must be clearly apparent to the members. Also the members should be given the freedom of expression and direct interaction with the brand. If there is no real value or benefit, people will just come, look and then go away and the brand will lose its cachet. The community may be created to provide privileges to the existing clients like the Very Dior club created by Parfums Christian Dior and the Raymond Weil club (Figure 3.15); or it could be based on providing specific information on performance, functionality and maintenance of its products like the Aston Martin club. These communities, which are not based on open invitations but on recruiting members among clients who have made purchases, ensure that luxury brands stay close to existing clients while offering an appeal to non-clients to be a part of these private communities. However, private online clubs developed by brands should also include interactive features and content that is beyond products and services or the usual top-down information dissemination. This will enable sharing and connecting with other members of the community, which is also beneficial to the brand.

Another approach to online communities built around a luxury brand is through creating market-specific communities based on geographical location or cultural factors. This means identifying the luxury markets in which people "need" to be congregated for a specific purpose linked to luxury. For example, China, one of the fastest growing luxury markets, is in the introductory phase of luxury consumption and a large proportion of the wealthy and upper middle-class members need to be educated about luxury. This market is not yet at the stage where consumers make decisions based only on brand information and advertisements. The products have to be presented, demonstrated, discussed and shared before they are bought and used. This involves a kind of educational process that should be ongoing even after the purchase has been made. This is because it is essential to continue to reinforce the belief of the client in the product, the brand and their manner of usage of the product. Since the Chinese market is highly populated and has cultural features that are grounded in collectivism rather than individualism, one of the best ways of sustaining this education is through creating online communities around a luxury brand.

One company that understood these factors and effectively crafted a successful online community strategy is Lancôme (Figure 3.15), which created

Figure 3.15   *Luxury brands have approached social networks in different ways. While the likes of Cartier, Chloé and Dolce & Gabbana have created official communities in mass social networks like My Space and Facebook, which makes little strategic sense, others like Raymond Weil and Lancôme have approached corporate online communities more intelligently by incorporating core values and benefits for the members as well as interactive features to foster sharing and brand affiliation*

Rose Beauty, its online community for the Chinese beauty and cosmetics enthusiasts. The website, which records traffic of more than 500,000 message posts per month, has become an online destination for Chinese women of all ages seeking beauty tips, product trials and connecting with others. One of the key success factors of Rose Beauty is that the all conversations are published and presented in a clear and transparent manner, even if the people are discussing other brands or comparing Lancôme's products to that of its competitors. Another factor is that Rose Beauty links to the e-commerce portal of Lancôme in China from whence instant purchases may be made following the exchanges and education on the use of skincare obtained from Rose Beauty.

Luxury brands may also use social networks to provide a means for people to participate in the creative life of the brand. This could be through creative competitions or co-creation initiatives in controlled environments that do not sacrifice the brand's exclusivity. This doesn't mean that the public should be invited to design the brand's products or that the co-creation exercises should be on a recurring basis but has to be carefully managed to endear clients to the brand. This will also make clients feel recognized and respected and the news will spread, attracting more clients.

It is clear that the wealthy have moved beyond gulping down information from luxury brands but are instead seeking to be engaged by the brands online. Their expectation of engagement is not only connected with marketing and communications but also with online shopping. This is because they have been experiencing 360° web interactivity from websites like MyWardrobe. com where they can browse products, watch the videos of the collections, blog about them and exchange opinions before selecting and purchasing – all from the same website. These collective experiences that foster community are easily transferred by the clients to what they expect from luxury brands.

Investing in the social web costs only a fraction of what several luxury brands spend on offline marketing initiatives that sometimes yield little and unmeasurable results. The key for luxury brands on the social web is to influence rather than control; inform instead of manipulate; find instead of recruit; observe instead of post; and watch instead of ignore. In addition, luxury brands should also learn, research, apply, optimize and see the bigger picture of the opportunities of social networks before jumping on the bandwagon just because competitors are doing so.

e-communities

These are essentially several forms of user-to-user communities that serve similar purposes as blogs and social networks but appear in different formats online. They range from discussion forums and platforms, e-zines with interactive features, reputation aggregators, chat rooms, product networks to fan websites. These e-communities are able to draw people together either through the content of the websites or through the central area of interest of the communities. Like blogs and social networks, their roles include influencing consumer perceptions, raising consciousness about a core issue and generally shaping the evolution of consumer mind-sets and the society in general.

e-communities comprise discussion forums similar to those found within several user-group websites and websites that serve as meeting points for people with the purpose of exchanging viewpoints on issues of interest and concern. It often means that the people "virtually" know each other, or at least can recognize other members of the community from their participation in the discussion within the communities.

Online communities also include reputation aggregators like Google, Yahoo!, Ask and MSN, which are used for rankings and web references for searchability and findability. However, they continuously feature elements that enable interactivity and dialogue among users such as Google Talk, MSN Chat and Google Groups.

Another type of e-community platform is e-zines which are online magazines that include interactive features that enable sharing and discussions such as comment posts, ratings and forwarding. Some other e-zines like Luxe-Mag. Com (Figure 3.16) have discussion forums integrated in the website. Fan websites are the websites that are created around specific brands by independent users who wish to share their love for the brand with others. The website Fanpop's "Quintessentially for Louis Vuitton" which was created by Louis Vuitton's fans is one such. Other types of e-communities include non-social websites that have interactive features such as American Express and CNET.

The lines that separate these communities and websites seem to be blurring, particularly as mainstream websites are continuously integrating interactive features supported by compelling content that are required to maintain a high traffic stream to a website. The parameters of these features and the way they should be applied on the different kinds of websites currently appear to be haphazard and unclear in terms of form and structure. This is because the social web is currently growing rampantly in different directions. The social web will eventually self-organize and when this happens, it will become the most critical marketing medium for both luxury brands and others. In this scenario, the social web will become the primary center of activity for consumers worldwide whether they are seeking to shop, plan, learn, be informed, be entertained, communicate or play. This will reinforce the change that is already taking place in Internet marketing where the consumer

Figure 3.16 *Online luxury business magazine Luxe-Mag.Com uses its integrated discussion platform to highlight relevant issues affecting the luxury sector and encourage its readers to share their viewpoints in an environment that fosters community, trust and independence*

is not only in total control but is defining their influence through qualitatives rather than quantitatives. The effectiveness of the marketing approach will then depend on dynamic measures like client recommendations rather than brand recognition or brand recall. The place of luxury on the social web will also eventually become more apparent as luxury brands realize that it is not about the information from the brand to the clients but about the dialogue among the clients independent of the brands. The luxury brands will also understand by this time that they ought to influence (not control or manipulate) these dialogues if they want to remain in favor with the participants.

Virtual immersive worlds

In January 2008, the company behind the 3-D virtual world Second Life, announced that its registered residents had exceeded 10 million globally. These users are not only a part of simple statistics but are considered to be active members because, to be a user of Second Life, you have to create an avatar, buy a resident space and develop it by building a house with furnishings and equipping it with what your avatar needs to live. You also need to have some form of activity to make yourself more interesting to people and increase your chance of making friends and connecting with others. Some residents own stores, hotels, gyms, garages, PR agencies and several other forms of commerce and activities. To do this, the user must have a high level of commitment and invest substantial time to their "life" in this virtual space. It is not a question of scanning a blog posting or social network forum for five minutes, posting a comment and disappearing for months. Each visit to virtual worlds requires several hours of full immersion and participation. This makes a difference between this "world" and other social networks that exist online.

Virtual immersive worlds like Second Life and World of Witchcraft allow people to have a 360° existence by enabling them to engage in activities that they are accustomed to in real life or the activities they dream of or fantasize about. Virtual worlds have been described as fantasylands where dreams come true but they are more than that. They enable people to stretch their imaginations, foster creativity and provide a level of empowerment surpassing that obtained from blogs and online communities. Virtual worlds are fully immersive and require a high level of time and resource commitment for the full potential of the platform to be enjoyed. The participants of virtual worlds are seeking more fulfillment than connecting with others and sharing opinions. Their primary goal is self-expression through their avatar characters, which could be replicas of their real selves or creations that represent their ideal and desired selves. They are also curious, bold, skilled, smart, independent, active and increasingly multiple. Contrary to the initial pre-conceptions of virtual immersive worlds which people believed to be congregation points for psychos looking for victims or people seeking to live out their transversal aspirations, this platform has proved to be a pioneer in the next phase of the Internet evolution.

Virtual worlds like Second Life are global applications where anyone can become a resident. It means that they have a strong element of appeal to the mass market which is disparate from the exclusivity and control that luxury requires to thrive, especially on the Internet. It is, however, essential for luxury brands to understand what is going on in this virtual world and how it could be utilized as an online marketing tool.

Features of virtual worlds

- The activities on virtual worlds are based on avatars, which can be either male or female. These avatars take part in several activities as in real life, like shopping, dining, partying and even sleeping. The principal activity, however, is interacting and meeting people.
- Virtual worlds are global and residents can be in any geographical location and operate their avatars from anywhere in the world.
- Although virtual worlds like Second Life were created in the US, the adoption rate in Europe has been astronomical. Currently, 44.6 percent of Second Lifers are in Europe versus 32.3 percent in the US and 7.4 percent in Asia.
- The users of Second Life are not only those from the popular "Innovator" consumer segment but also from the "Early Adopter" demographic. These consumers are the trendsetters in adopting new technologies and are tech-savvy. They are also highly educated and have intellectual and cultural exposure. They are also brand sensitive and opinion leaders, which makes them a relevant group for luxury brands to watch.
- Virtual world users don't have avatar gender or age restrictions. This means that a male user can have a female avatar and vice versa; and anyone can create an avatar of any age. This makes it challenging to match the avatar gender and age group statistics to the real users behind the avatars. However, it has been reported that the average age of a Second Life user is 32 years, a figure that is substantially higher than users of other types of virtual worlds like MMOGs (Massive Multiplayer Online Games).
- A large proportion of virtual world users also belong to social networks in the real world. They transfer their collective experiences from the other forms of social web platforms to virtual immersive worlds and this plays a role in shaping their attitudes and comportments. It also increases their chances of influencing others through recommending brands, products and services.

Challenges for luxury brands

One key factor that virtual immersive worlds have precedented is the place of real-time 3-D in viewing web pages. Until now, products and services have been viewed on web pages either in static images, interactive flash format, slide shows or 2-D movement forms. The few websites that have offered a 360° view of their products have done so for limited sections or products. This has often been powered mainly through grouping static images and not through fully integrated applications. Virtual immersive worlds have changed this forever. As people get used to the idea of creating and using avatars for several purposes online, they will transfer this expectation to the websites of brands that are both product and service-based, whether in an e-retail environment or not. They will expect to view products in 3-D in real time and they will demand brands to provide them with applications that enable the trial of products on a personalized avatar in e-commerce websites. For service oriented luxury brands like retailers, hotels and resorts, consumer expectations will include viewing the locations in panoramic form and not in the standard boring slide-show format that is common today. These expectations will also be transferred to the offline brand interaction. As an industry that is known for avant-gardism and innovation, luxury brands will naturally be expected to lead in this evolution.

In approaching virtual immersive environments such as Second Life and World of Witchcraft, luxury brands have to first understand how this world functions rather than pretend that it doesn't exist. It is also essential to understand the demographics of both the user profiles (avatars) and the user controllers (the creators of the avatars). This will provide some insight into the key drivers of the participants and their motivations, behavioral patterns and desired expectations both online and in the real world. With this understanding, luxury brands will be ready for the next step.

In addition, luxury brands should view virtual immersive worlds as the vital environments for researching and experimenting in a wide range of areas including future trends, social evolution, brand perceptions, product design and service generation. These virtual platforms could be used as the place for discovery, inspiration, imagination and perhaps realization of multi-dimensional projects including design concepts and future trends analysis. This is particularly appropriate as the participants of virtual immersive environments are accustomed to stretching their imaginations.

Several parties have derided luxury brands for their minimal presence on virtual immersive environments. Apart from Giorgio Armani which rebuilt its Milan flagship store in Second Life, Hublot which held a press conference and product presentation, and Christian Dior which placed a teaser campaign for its jewelry collection on Second Life, other examples of luxury brands' initiatives in virtual worlds are scarce. This is, however, not a crime. Again, to avoid the cat effect (see the beginning of this chapter in case you missed that) or the bandwagon consequence, virtual worlds provide enormous opportunities for engaging luxury brands with the future through the eyes of the virtual world residents. Varying aspects like socio-dynamics, foresight analysis, creative groups, demos, cultural innovations, collaborative and inclusive research, and social entrepreneurship can all be fostered in virtual immersive communities. This could also lead to co-creation or dual collaboration opportunities with creative minds. The result for the brands that have included virtual worlds in an integrated online strategy will be continued innovation and a clearly envisaged future that will be defined by a clear path to success and leadership in their category.

Other business opportunities for luxury brands in virtual immersive environments include using it as a collaborative space for internal events such as trainings, seminars (or, rather, webinars) and meetings. This will also foster the orientation towards web-based applications and an e-culture within the internal organization. In addition, product co-creation, particularly in the aspect of customization and product experience, may be effectively achieved through virtual worlds. Brand experiences that lead to buzz marketing and integrative launch events could also be a winner for luxury brands in virtual environments if executed strategically.

Finally, luxury brands could benefit from virtual immersive environments in consumer-generated content (CGC) and consumer-generated adverts (CGA). CGCs and CGAs are already prolific online and consumers are generating these contents on their own initiative as a result of their affinity for the brand. Inviting them to generate these contents in an inclusive manner (perhaps only for experimenting) will yield a brand far better results than sitting and watching while consumers take over the brand image projection of luxury brands through uploaded self-made videos.

Beyond the social web: what will happen after the frenzy?

The social web is currently a-buzz with blogs, wikis, social networks, virtual worlds and all manners of online communities that make up the social web. This revolution has changed the rules of marketing forever. However, the social web will keep on evolving and will eventually organize itself in such a way that clear parameters for each of its segments will be set. This will follow through a filtering process where the wheat will be separated from the chaff and only those blogs and networks that provide real value in terms of content will be sustained in the long term. The emphasis will also move away from quantity (100 million unique visitors per day) to quality (length of time spent on pages). Interactive features such as videos and 3-D will also become increasingly important to convey complex messages that are often lost in text and static images. On-demand Internet videos will become more popular with the advent of vlogs and live video events will become the norm, further fragmenting client attention. Video clips will also be incorporated within text that will be amassed through search engines like Google and MSN Live. Other extended forms of instant social media platforms like Twitter (which allows people to follow you to know what you're doing at the moment) and Friendfeed (which allows people to build a customized feed of their desired content on their friends and family) will continue to emerge and intensify the nature of the conversations currently being held on blogs.

The impact of the social web will not only be felt on people's online behavior, but also on their offline behavior. The social web has enabled people to participate in communities in several ways and this has empowered them to be more individualistic, confident, savvy and unique in their tastes, style selections and brand preferences. This evolution will continue and will further challenge the way luxury is perceived through social web references.

The key elements for brands, however, are maintaining the brand's DNA and understanding that the social web is a collaborative space created by independent users and not brands. Luxury brands have enormous opportunities to steer social web elements in their favor if the rules of the game are followed. The most important factor is that all the social media elements must tell a unified story and each of them should be interlinked with the others.

As the Internet celebrates 20 years of its existence as a collaborative tool in 2009, it is time for both clients and luxury brands to get past the notion that luxury brands are confused online and, as the English are fond of saying, "get on with it" – unless the brands prefer to have the Zen-master cat syndrome.

Part Two
Doing It!

Chapter 4
The e-experience: creating more than a luxury website

"Sensory information flowing into the brain fuels our perceptions, memories, intentions and actions."

—Michael O'Shea, Writer

It's not just about having a website

Anyone who has ever driven a Porsche, say the Cayman or the Boxster, knows that there are a hundred reasons to fall in love with a Porsche. From the commanding beauty of its appearance, the delicate contouring of its form, the clean lines of its color, the ergonomics and comfort of its interior, the clarity and illumination of its lights, the smoothness and safety of its wheels, the agility and gravity of its engine and the multi-function of its communications, a Porsche is a teaser and pleaser through and through. But if you only get the chance to drive a Porsche once every few years, what you would remember may not be the characteristics listed. You will likely remember the power of the smooth motion against you, the inner firing of your spirit, the powerful unleashed force of freedom and the sheer reward of being in a special space. These are all linked to the experience of driving a Porsche. The experience, of course, derives from the sensations, feelings, moods, perceptions and emotions aroused during the entire activity of driving. This is what stays in the memory and this is why you will go back to drive a Porsche again and again.

The same principle applies to the way luxury is represented online. It is not only a question of being present on the Internet through having a website, or of developing the prettiest website or of providing the richest content. It is about creating an exceptional online experience for every person visiting and revisiting the website. It is about appealing to the senses and arousing a profound desire to be associated with the brand through enveloping every website visitor in an immersive environment that makes up the brand's universe online. It is about keeping a focus on ensuring the best possible web experience and perfecting this as the one and only mission of the luxury online strategy. This rich experience will eventually translate into sales and loyalty.

It is a well-known fact that luxury brands are fanatical about perfection (I mean the truly luxurious brands not the multitude of brands claiming to be luxury). This obsession with perfection is not only linked to product creation, but also to providing an optimal experience to clients through services. Through the in-store design, atmosphere and product merchandizing, packaging and sales interaction (which sometimes leads to ceremonial demonstrations of products) the experience is supposed to be the winning component in the luxury mix. The same applies to luxury services across hotels, private transport and concierge offerings. If you remember Rufus the jewelry salesman played by Rowan Atkinson in the 2003 British hit movie *Love Actually*, who epitomized this obsession with providing an impeccable experience in a luxurious environment, then you very well know what I'm talking about. This level of perfection in providing the best experience is essential as much offline as online.

As we may imagine, providing an exceptional experience in the physical environment is played out through human contact and supported by the features that influence the atmosphere and enhance the ambience in the immediate surroundings. When a client is in the lobby of a luxury hotel like the Ritz-Carlton and is immersed in the delightful world that has been enhanced by the style, colors and forms of the art works and decorations on display not to forget the lighting and scent, his mood is likely to be influenced by this unique environment (see Figure 4.1). This forms a crucial aspect of the Ritz experience and is likely to be further elevated by the outstanding attention of the hotel staff who ensure that the client's needs are met and their wishes granted sometimes even before they ask. The goal is quite simple – to make the client's experience positive through creating sensations that ensure that they feel good and that they continue to associate the Ritz-Carlton with these good feelings, which will likely lead them to return to the hotel. The same concept may be applied to luxury stores, restaurants and services points.

Now, if creating an exceptional experience is supposed to be a core ingredient in the luxury mix, it is time to wonder why this factor has not been represented and made a central point of a luxury brand's presence online. A quick tour of the cyberspace shows that the websites of major luxury companies are either content-free and flash-heavy or are information- and retail-focused in a bland form. The majority look like endless pages of online catalogues. This approach has been adopted as a result of the widely adhered to consensus that luxury clients are invulnerable to online experiences and that their major drive to the Internet is to save time. This is far from the reality. As a result, luxury brands have concentrated over the last ten years on developing websites in order to say that they are "online" and most of these websites are based on disseminating information and the occasional e-retail. But the issue is no

Figure 4.1 *The Ritz Hotel Paris is often described as the epitome of luxury that has the ability to subdue anyone. The special experience of the hotel, created through the harmony of the atmosphere, the decoration and the attention of the staff, forms a part of the expectations of the clients from the hotel's website. The Shopping Gallery, otherwise known as the "Hall of Temptation," shown here is well known as a whispering zone as a result of the sumptuous nature of the products displayed in the glass showcases*

longer having a website, whether it features e-retail or not. What rules online today is the experience that a brand is able to provide on its website and its ability to monitor its presence in the cyberspace and positively influence the public's perceptions towards everything that the brand represents. These are the main factors that affect the luxury brands' equity both online and offline as consumers transfer their collective experiences from the Internet to their offline expectations and vice versa.

In the current digital luxury context, having a web presence, whether through the brand's own website or in the social web, is now a given. Web presence is also no longer the factor that will assure the continuous relationship between luxury brands and clients. The mere existence of a luxury brand's website does not guarantee that clients will be interested in the brand, neither will it ensure frequent visits, no matter how "flashy" and "pretty" the website is. The reality is that the Internet has been around for two decades and consumers have become used to the basics and are now demanding more. Their level of expectation has increased dramatically and they are likely to lose patience with websites that don't offer an optimal package of benefits, values and experiences, including luxury websites.

With the multiplication of websites by the hour, Internet users have also become increasingly diverted by new sites, offerings, substitutes, deals and promises from thousands of brands on a daily basis. They have become masters of scanning websites for value and filtering out those that have little to offer. The bottom line: they're looking for an experience. And this is just no ordinary experience but an exceptional one that will appeal to their senses, enhance their mood, recognize their presence, engage their minds, capture their imagination and, in short, simply blow their minds away. This is what a luxury brand's website should offer to Internet users today. Whether this is currently the case is another question.

Often, when I speak about creating luxury experiences in luxury circles, I get a lot of debates because many disagree with this notion and believe that creating a virtual luxury experience is a mission impossible. I don't blame them as there are endless questions linked to luxury online, many of which are yet to be addressed. The classic questions, "How can a luxurious experience be created online?, Is it even possible?" lead the pack. Others include, "Why is it that some brands seem to get it right so easily online and others don't?", "What is the secret?", "The golden rules?", "The key to a successful website?"

Well, there is no key. It is matter of an integrated online–offline strategy that supports a brand's core identity and this depends largely on each luxury brand and the dimensions of their brand universe. If there were a key, it would be too easy, the wealthy brands would buy the key and all their e-business worries would be over; the smaller brands would struggle to allocate a budget to obtain the key; and I would be out of a job!

However, creating an online experience could be both easy and challenging depending on how a luxury brand chose to approach it. For the brands that are only interested in catching up to their competitors in terms of designing websites that feature more flash animations, more sound variety, more videos, more micro-sites and more content, it would seem fairly easy to develop an online experience because they're playing the copy-cat game. The result is that, in most cases, this approach contributes more to a negative online experience than a positive one as it leads to simply "too much" going on in the website. Also, in most cases the "flashy" concept is incoherent with the core essence that brand represents. One may get this impression when looking at websites like Dior.com or Chanel.com which have sections that are incoherent with others in terms of brand image, design, navigation, content and atmosphere. And Dior is not the only culprit in this area!

For the luxury companies that depend on web agencies and interactive media companies to create their website concepts and provide strategic e-business advice, it would also seem easy. However, the result is often that the web agency stamps their own style on the website instead of interpreting the brand's identity and creating an experience around the brand's universe. Whenever I come across a newly launched luxury website these days, I can almost tell which web agency developed it or, in the worst cases, how many web agencies and which particular ones developed it because all of their "styles" are on the website! The explanation is not that web agencies are dumb (most of those that work with luxury brands are actually extremely smart, skilled and competent in web design), but developing a luxury website requires a deep understanding of multi-faceted elements and not only web applications. This includes grasping the dynamics of the world of luxury; having a strong aesthetic appreciation; understanding the brand's DNA; the corporate goals; the online clients; the offline audience; the competitors; the Internet environment; and the brand's core e-business strategy, including online communications, e-retail and e-CRM and, of course, all the back-office applications, systems and tools. All of these make luxury online multi-dimensional and the task of creating a luxury brand's website one that requires first to be addressed on a strategic level. This may not necessarily be the interest or competence area of a web agency that just wants to develop websites. In the case where the luxury brand doesn't have an e-business strategy (and this is common), the web agency receives more responsibilities than they may be able to deliver. And the result? Websites that resemble one another because they all feature the same advanced technological applications (think flash and 3-D). These websites although closely resembling one another have nothing to do with each other's brand identity, core essence and DNA but everything to do with the style of the web agency that developed it.

Finally, for the luxury brands that understand the importance of having an enhanced online presence beginning with a high-impact website as a part of an integrated e-business strategy, the issue becomes a corporate challenge. And like most challenges, there is a solution as long as the focus remains on developing and implementing an integrated e-business strategy, which of course includes website design.

As already mentioned in the introduction of this book, e-business strategy is not only about e-retail or e-commerce, but also involves an integration of multiple "e" elements including the e-experience, e-branding, e-communications, e-consumer analysis, e-commerce, e-CRM, e-logistics, e-merchandizing, e-marketing, e-customization, website design and the all too important social media. All of these ensure that a luxury brand is on the right track towards concretely adopting the Internet and all the opportunities that it has to offer. The success of an e-business strategy is, however, reflected through the experience that each visitor "lives" during their stay on the website. This is what defines their perceptions and impressions of the brand during and after the visit and will ultimately influence their expectations at every touch-point with the brand.

Living the luxury e-experience

Imagine that a wealthy Arab princess called Laila is planning a shopping trip to Europe, with possible stops in Paris, Milan and London to purchase jewelry, clothes, accessories and gifts. She has been shopping at the stores of her favourite brands Valentino, Dior, Armani and Louis Vuitton for years but she is eager to discover new brands in addition to yearning for something new from the "old league". After looking through current issues of several fashion magazines and identifying some models of clothes and accessories that she likes, she decides to use the Internet to find out their availability and obtain more information about colors and sizes. She also intends to investigate the current collections of her favorite brands and at the same time find other designers and trends. Her goal is to have an idea of what her wardrobe would look like upon her return.

She logs on to the websites of the brands she is familiar with and after a few clicks she is disappointed that she couldn't find many of the models she had chosen in the magazine on the brands' websites. The few websites that had her preferences however didn't provide any information about the colors, sizes, prices and store availability of the products. In addition, the websites she visited all looked similar, presenting endless videos and slide shows of the runway shows, product photos, some flash animation and sound. She was unable to find any information about the products and how they could be worn, combined, styled or cleaned. Although she didn't care so much about the price, it would also have been helpful to obtain their prices online.

By the time she clicks on the fifth website she has become bored with the similarity of the websites and she decides to switch to media websites like Vogue or Elle – at least they would offer variety in content if nothing else. She discovers from an editorial feature in one of the magazines that Christian Lacroix has recently launched a new collection for La Redoute. She had never heard of La Redoute and decides to check out the collection through the web link, www.christianlacroixpourlaredoute.com. The website concept and design, which is based on a virtual fantasyland, immediately captivates her so much that she didn't realize that she had spent nearly an hour browsing the entire collection and taking notes of the pieces she would buy in Paris. At the end of her visit, she had two pages of product references and she was one step closer to being a fulfilled customer in Paris. Her preshopping was finished for the day. Mission accomplished.

What Laila was looking for was more than information. She wanted an experience that would reinforce her belief in these brands and ensure that she remains loyal to them. She was as much interested in the content (new collections and information) as the brand universe created through the ambience of the website or what I prefer to call the luxemosphere (see next section). Laila wanted an experience from the luxury brands' websites and she only got this from Christian Lacroix's special collection website. Even Lacroix's own independent website failed to provide this experience, as did that of La Redoute, although the latter is not a luxury brand. But Laila was already hooked on the collaboration website and she surely planned to revisit. Let's not forget that online consumers are more website loyal than brand loyal.

What does the online luxury experience entail?

An online luxury experience is exactly what it says. There are no hidden meanings. To illustrate this, let's look at what the two terms stand for. Some of the synonyms of the word "experience" are *encounter, incident* and *event.* Take these and add them to some of the synonyms of "luxury", which are *magnificent, indulgence* and *extra,* and you will come up with the following, directly from the dictionary. It's as simple as that:

- Magnificent encounter
- Indulging incident
- Extra event

These descriptions should pretty much clarify the luxury experience. So, down to the questions luxury brands ought to be asking: "Does our website embody a *magnificent encounter?*", "Does it represent an *indulging incident?*", in other words a pleasurable affair. "Is it an *extra event?*", meaning added value for the client. If the answers to these questions are not clear then read on but if they are, then we should probably have a chat as I have yet to find a luxury company that has a "yes" answer to all of the three questions.

Another way of looking at luxury online experience is through a simple communications approach. If you've ever come across the notion that only about 40 percent of communications is based on speech and text while the rest is a matter of experience, then you'll understand what I mean. The other 60 percent is about experience. In the luxury segment, the only factor that will determine an ongoing relationship with a brand is continuous reinforcement of positive experiences across all touch-points, particularly through the website. This is not only because luxury online is cost effective (it really is), but also because long after the price of a product or service is forgotten, it is the good feelings (positive experiences) that will always be remembered and associated with the brand. The same applies for the negative experiences.

And how does a luxury brand go about the business of creating an exceptional experience through its website?

First, it is important to understand the keywords that are linked to experience and then identify how to approach applying the web elements correlated to each of them in a balanced and integrated form.

- Mood
- Feeling
- Character
- Interaction
- Ambience
- Desire
- Emotion
- Atmosphere

The common point of these terms is that they express intangible qualities that are associated with the mind. This confirms the obvious certainty that experiences are associated with thoughts and feelings, which all emanate from the mind. It also confirms that the mind is the key aspect that ought to be influenced and affected by luxury brands both in the online and offline brand universe. Therefore, developing a luxury website should include a focus on integrating elements that will enhance the mood and influence the mind, leading to extraordinary experiences.

In order to have positive influence on the mind of the luxury client in the virtual world, it is important to ensure that they have a "brand" experience instead of a "person-to-screen" experience. In other words, they should be so deeply immersed in the virtual universe of the brand that they should forget that they are staring at a computer screen. It is only at this point that a luxury client would have attained a "high-impact" online experience.

> How may the elements outlined guide the creation of an outstanding online experience?

Before we analyze the tactical requirements of creating a positive online experience, let's experiment with a short scenario. If you're close to a computer, take a quick look at Rolex.com (Figure 4.2). You will likely notice a giant size Oyster Perpetual Datejust watch or similar model on the homepage, featuring the current date and accurate time. The high visual impact of the watch's precise engineering, design, features, movement, materials and even angular reflections are so clear-cut visually that you may feel that you are holding the watch right in your hands or at least that you're almost touching it. This feeling will likely arouse your curiosity to discover the brand's universe by clicking your way through the website. The demonstration of precision, skill and depth on the homepage ensures that there is a strong message and a real promise of value to be discovered beyond the homepage. The impact of this homepage on your mind has likely been positively high.

Now skip to Dolcegabbana.com and you will notice that the homepage is divided into multiple categories and sections that feature Dolce & Gabbana, the parent brand; the sub-brands D&G Dolce & Gabbana and D&G Junior; as well as other initiatives and activities of the brand like fashion shows, special projects, product extensions etc. The display of the different sections on the homepage gives an indication of the extent of the brand's universe and the richness of its world but the homepage hardly inspires the feelings that will arouse a strong curiosity to discover the world of the brand, unlike Rolex.com. At the time of writing, the homepage of Dolcegabbana.com featured twenty sections, represented by images linked to the brand's activity in each section. Looking at the homepage, a web savvy user is likely to understand immediately that each of these twenty sections would likely lead to other sub-sections, mini-sites, micro-sites and perhaps shopping sites. This would mean an endless stream of web pages linked to each of the twenty sections. If this user is enthusiastic about the brand or knows exactly what they are looking for, they may go ahead to visit the website but web-savvy users making an initial contact with the website may hesitate. On the other hand, a not-so-savvy web user may become utterly confused with the multiple possibilities presented and may easily get lost after a few clicks or worse still, may not bother venturing into the website for fear of becoming lost during the visit. Although not all web users will be deterred by the home page presentation, the notion of a high impact and a promise of an elevated experience have already been brought into question from the home page.

Figure 4.2 *The visual impact of the accuracy, movement and precision of Rolex's real-time Oyster Perpetual watch shown on its homepage contributes to a positive online experience through arousing the curiosity to discover the brand's universe online*

Although both Rolex.com and Dolcegabbana.com have extensive content on their websites, Rolex's website demonstrates a strong focus on driving the discovery of its world through a focal point on the online experience, while Dolce & Gabbana's website focuses on its content as a key driver of the discovery process, at least on the home page.

To ensure an enhanced and positive online experience, it is essential to create the right virtual environment on the website. The main influential component of this online environment is its atmosphere, through which a specific mood is generated and an overall ambience is derived. Creating a specific atmosphere in the virtual world, although a challenging feat, is possible through the application of specific tactics that are discussed in the next section. These tactics are linked to *webmospherics*, the strategy of creating a unique atmosphere in the online virtual space with the aim of influencing the mind and gearing the subconscious of the online user towards a positive experience that ensures that it remains an extension of the offline experience and vice versa.

Moving beyond the webmosphere to the luxemosphere

You probably know the importance of drinking at least three liters of water every day. Our mothers tell us from childhood, our doctors reaffirm this constantly, and our dieticians and trainers impose drinking water on us if they have to. But how many of us view water drinking as a pleasurable experience? I mean as an activity that we covet and desire so much that we cannot wait to experience it. When you drink water, do you immediately start dreaming of your next water-drinking experience? I'm pretty sure that you don't, just like me. That is, until I came across a Spanish company called Water Way of Life, which has eighteen prestigious water brands in their portfolio that grace the tables of several luxury restaurants around the world. A quick visit to the company's website revealed why they are successful. They have masterfully created an entire universe around water and turned the simple activity of water drinking into an art and a lifestyle. Their challenge to the conventional view of bottled water has led them to create a unique atmosphere on their website that uses visuals, colors, images, sound, movement and other interactive features to create a distinctive online ambience that generates positive vibes and sensations in the website visitor which arouse the desire to drink water. A look at this website will change your perception of water (unless you're a Koala bear or something) and will provide you with a glimpse into what I'm about to discuss here.

You may have come across the Internet marketing term webmosphere, a word that is derived from the combination of "web" and "atmosphere", which was highlighted in my previous book, *Luxury Fashion Branding*. As a reminder, it refers to the atmosphere on a website and is particularly used in the context where a website has a distinctive ambience. As we all know, the store atmosphere has been recognized as one of the key elements of successful retailing, particularly in luxury, which explains why a lot of attention is given to "atmospherics". In the physical context, the majority of luxury brands with retail points or client access locations are able to recreate their store atmosphere to exude the feelings that they aim to be associated with and to arouse certain desired effects in shoppers, in order to enhance purchase probability. The common features that are used to manipulate the atmosphere are colors, shapes, music, displays, layout, scents and aromas, temperature and tactile feelings. Atmosphere appeals to the psychology and emotions of shoppers through their subconscious, influences buying decisions and enhances the relationships with brands and products.

In the virtual Internet context, the strategy of developing a specific atmosphere, i.e. the webmosphere, is known as webmospherics. The concept of webmospherics, first brought into prominence by Lorna Chicksand of the Birmingham Business School and Rachel Knowles of Brandscape during the IBM e-business conference in 2002, became actively adopted during the second phase of the Internet evolution when content was a main ingredient of website creation. Webmospherics has itself evolved to become a crucial aspect of website design strategy, particularly in the creation of an overall online brand experience.

Webmospherics is directly linked to the five human senses of sight, hearing, smell, touch and taste through elements that are adapted to stimulating positive sensations directly linked to these senses and subsequently leading to positive experiences. Ensuring that a website has a unique webmosphere is currently essential as the expectations of web users continue to increase with their acquaintance with the web advances.

Luxemosphere® on the other hand is an extended Internet marketing concept coined by Luxe Corp's analysts, which describes the prestigious atmosphere that every luxury brand's website aims to attain both online and offline. It is the combination of the words "luxe" (luxury, in French) and "atmosphere" and has been extensively assessed in several articles on luxury e-business published on the online luxury business magazine Luxe-Mag.Com. The concept of luxemosphere was first unveiled at the Club e-Luxe Annual Summit held in Paris in June 2007 and has since formed an aspect of integrated online luxury assessment by several luxury brands piloted by Luxe Corp.

The aim of the luxemosphere is to recreate a truly splendid universe within the virtual environment of a brand mainly through replicating the unique identity, style, signature and codes that the brand uses in its offline existence. For example, when we click on the website of the Four Seasons Hotels and Resorts, we should expect to be ushered into a virtual world where the ambience is enhanced by the strong contemporary visual identity of the brand often expressed in its hotels through art, interior design, music and cuisine. Also, the brand's renowned focus on excellence through anticipation ought to be sensed from the luxemosphere of the website. At the time of writing, this was not yet the case since the website's focus is more on functionality than on user experience.

Luxemosphere uses elements that influence the senses, stimulate the mood and enhance the emotions through sensory technologies ranging from visual animation, movement, olfactory emissions devices and audio elements, including music and speech synthesis and several others.

The luxemosphere of a luxury brand's website plays multiple roles in luxury Internet marketing. First, it enables brand image reinforcement through a high-impact web experience. Brand perceptions are in the mind of the consumer and therefore a brand's strength emanates from the sum of what people "feel" about the brand rather than only what they "see", although what they see should validate what they feel and vice versa. The website of a luxury brand should reinforce the brand perceptions through generating the "feelings" that are unique to the brand and one of the most effective means of ensuring this is through the luxemosphere. A look at Van Cleef & Arpels' website (see Figure 4.5) will confirm that its luxemosphere corresponds to the brand's identity and its offline store ambience.

Second, luxemosphere is a strategy for sensory communications that speaks to the consumer's subconscious through a seamless online experience. As mentioned earlier in this chapter, if a website targets the "mind" rather than the "eyes", it is halfway down the journey of creating an enhanced web experience. Overall, our senses, including the sight, aural and tactile senses, play a holistic role in shaping the web experience and making shopping online enjoyable. Sensory communication is a powerful tool for influencing consumers as it leads to affiliation with

the e-experience: creating more than a luxury website

a brand and is likely to elevate the relationship with a brand from awareness to intimacy. After all, when someone makes you feel good, you're likely to want to be with that person as often as possible. A look at Chanel's website will confirm what I mean by a website that focuses on the "eyes" and as previously mentioned, Van Cleef & Arpel's website confirms what I mean by focusing on the "mind". Boucheron on the other hand uses an indirect approach to influence the mind through a strong play on the "eyes" through visuals (Figure 4.3) (except if these websites are re-designed before you read these lines!).

Figure 4.3 *Van Cleef & Arpels and Boucheron, two high-jewelry brands with extensive website content, have approached the luxemosphere differently on their websites. The former focuses on arousing feelings in the "mind"while the latter emphasizes influencing the website visitor through the "eyes", i.e. visuals*

Third, luxemosphere ensures a high stickiness level (the intensity of a website's attractiveness and the level to which it retains the web user on the website) and higher purchase probability in the case of e-retail. If a luxury brand's website features harmonized elements in its design, navigation and content that lead to an enhanced ambience, the website visitor is likely to be immersed in the experience both consciously and, more importantly, subconsciously. When this happens, they are likely to spend considerable time on the website in their discovery or re-discovery of the brand's universe and we can then say that the stickiness level of the website is high. In this case, we can also say that the website generates positive vibes in the visitor. When a client feels good on a website, they will remember this experience and return for more of these vibes, leading to brand affinity, website affiliation and higher purchase probability. More importantly, online users are more website loyal than brand loyal and this goes to say that the website is an important channel of drawing new clients to a brand and validating what the brand represents for old clients. Luxemosphere is a tool for ensuring an enhanced relationship and an intimate bond that only the right sensations can create.

Finally, the role of luxemosphere also includes ensuring memory recall. The environment of a luxury brand's website will ensure that we remember the website or that we don't. If you take a moment to imagine the number of websites that you have visited in the last five years, you'll most likely conclude that they run into thousands. Now, how many of these websites stand out in your memory? They will likely be a handful. And why do they stand out? Was it because of their content? Their visual impact? Their functions? Or the overall experience they provided and the feelings you had while browsing through the website? If you're able to answer these questions, then we understand each other. Let's also not forget that experiences could be negative but this is not the point of discussion here, as luxemosphere is linked only to positive brand experiences.

How can a luxury brand integrate the luxemosphere on its website?

Attaining a seamless luxemosphere was previously perceived to be impossible but several approaches and tactics now make it achievable through multi-sensory elements that directly stimulate the main human senses and ultimately lead to the immersion of the subconscious in a superior online experience. The web elements that should be incorporated online using available technologies that will ensure an enhanced luxemosphere are shown and analyzed. Some of these elements also feature extensively in the analysis of website design strategies in the next section. Before we analyze these elements, take a note of the keywords associated with luxemosphere: *senses, mood, ambience, emotions, sensations, desires, feelings, atmosphere, character, interaction, impression* and *experience.*

- Visuals
- Sound
- Scent
- Movement
- Flavor

Visuals

The visual luxemospheric element is linked to the human sense of sight. As we know, sight is one of the most important senses that attract and steer consumers towards a brand. In the physical store, sight may be maneuvered through colors, shapes, displays and layouts to create the desired store effects. This is more challenging to achieve online, particularly on a website that has an integrated e-boutique. To ensure a strong visual impact on a website, similar elements in the physical store should be applied in a modified manner tailored to the peculiarities and requirements of the Internet. The core luxemospheric visual aids are images, colors, text, graphics and shapes, and the aspects of the website that require the highest attention in terms of visuals are the welcome page, the homepage, design concept and the display of the visual elements.

Images are one of a brand's strongest visual essentials and their influence cannot be underestimated. They validate a brand's personality, its signature, its style and render its products or services visible and valuable. Images are one of the visual elements in the luxemospherics mix whose influence may be felt without direct dependence on the other sensory elements on a website. Images render support to other sensory elements like sound and movement which form part of the online brand experience and are inseparable from the memories, knowledge and emotions a person links to the brand during and after the website visit. It may seem obvious to say this but images on a website ought to be in high resolution and presented in such a way that the message is understood and the brand well represented. Images of products featuring text on the product or on the packaging should also be sharp enough to be legible and viewing options should be provided where possible. For example, the skincare and cosmetics section of Chanel.com has a low visual impact as a result of the low quality of the images displayed. This is particularly critical for brands in the beauty and fragrance categories as these products are susceptible to scrutiny by consumers and they expect to be able to read the text on products. Appropriate images such as product photos, store interiors, advertisements and other visuals should be suitably placed on different web pages and these must be updated accordingly. In addition, the use of images rather than text in the placeholder of navigational menus ought to be a strategic choice.

Colors, when appropriately used, provide a powerful first impression and validate a brand's visual identity and signature. For example, it is natural to expect to see a strong use of the color orange on Hermès' website as well as red on Cartier's, green on Rolex's and sea blue on Tiffany's. In general, color indicators also point towards the effect of certain colors on the brain, particularly in an isolated environment such as on a website. Colors such as light blue and green are perceived to be "intelligent" and aid in memory recall while others like purple and pink are emotional and are therefore likely to influence brand affiliation. Suffice it to say that color adoption on a website should be strategically linked to the brand's signature colors and that maintaining color scheme consistency throughout the website is essential. It is also important to ensure the presence of some background white space where possible as this has a calming effect on the brain and ensures a harmonized online visual experience. The target audience should also be considered in color adoption as well as the ease of the color on the eyes, particularly while being viewed on a screen. In addition, since color may be displayed differently on computer screens according to the screen resolution, it is essential to ensure that the effect of the color scheme chosen for a website remains the same irrespective of screen resolution.

Text on a website has two dimensions: the size and the style. It's common practice for websites to feature text in minuscule text sizes, which in most cases are illegible. Luxury brands are no exception to this practice and several have justified this by the fact that they have little text on their websites. In reality, however, text ought to be legible. In the case where a website prefers to feature small-size text to harmonize the look of the visual elements, it is suggested that a text control tool which aids in increasing and decreasing text sizes is integrated. Where possible, dark text color should be applied against a clear background, particularly for sections with extensive text, in order to increase legibility. In addition, the choice of words, clarity of language and consistency of tone should be in line with the brand's essence and should also suit the tastes and expectations of the clients. The language of the website should also be clear, concise and consistent in its tone through all the pages and should be in line with the manner in which the brand expresses itself.

Graphics include drawings, traces, pictures, charts and tables. They not only give clarity to the message of a website, but also contribute to memory recall of the products, features and information provided on the website. Graphics also aid in improving the feeling of human presence online through giving the impression of interactivity and exchanges. For example, animated pictures may be used to introduce special collections and sections of a website as Louis Vuitton has done in the past with several new product launches. Coach.com also uses graphics to show the size of the leather goods against the human form, through one dimensional avatars of various sizes. Graphics are most efficient when used to reflect interactivity and not necessarily when left dormant. Graphics may also be used as the theme for a website's design concept but when this is done the graphical representation must serve a strategic purpose, which could be either to reinforce the brand identity and brand spirit or to act as a tool for the repositioning of a luxury brand. Upon looking at Hermes.com, which has themed its website with playful graphics, one cannot help but wonder about the strategic purpose because the public's interpretation of the brand's identity as a classic, contemporary and timeless brand with a strong French heritage is in contrast with the brand image represented by the choice of its online graphics, which are youthful and vigorous.

Shapes also form a part of the visual elements of luxemospherics as they play an important role in validating a brand's visual identity. Shapes may be used to portray navigational menu links, sections and sub-sections, frames and overall format of web pages. The choice of shapes on a luxury brand's website should be linked to the brand's perceived identity. Some luxury brands may be perceived as "soft", for example Chloé, Valentino, Laurent Perrier or Stella McCartney, while others may be perceived as "hard", for example Boucheron, Rémy Martin, Yves Saint Laurent or Karl Lagerfeld. Such perceptions are linked to the interpretations from the sum of the brand's messages across several touch-points including advertisements, store concepts, service style, products and communications. These perceptions are also transferred to the expectations on the brands' websites and therefore we may not be so surprised if the shapes in the design concept of Yves Saint Laurent are square and those of Chloé are rounded. The link of shapes to brand perceptions should however not be the sole reason for the adoption of specific shapes on a luxury brand's website because important factors like usability, legibility and visual impact have to be harmonized with shapes. For example, Brazilian luxury fashion brand Carlos Miele's website (Figure 4.6) features a design concept based on the same abstract shapes that form the underlying visual concept of its stores. While these shapes have greatly contributed to giving the brand's physical store a unique and spacious feel, on its website the same shapes give a feeling of restriction and reduces its visual impact. Carlos Miele may have integrated soft shapes on its website without necessarily duplicating its offline shapes since what is suitable offline may not necessarily be suitable online and vice versa.

In addition to the visual elements that support the luxemosphere, several sections of a luxury brand's website require particular attention in the integration of visuals. These are the welcome page, the home page, the design concept and the display of the visual elements.

The welcome page is often mistaken for the home page, although they're starkly different in function and influence. To begin with, any luxury brand worth its salt ought to have a welcome page on its website. Why? Because the welcome page acts as the golden door that ushers a client or a potential client into the world of the brand. It is the point from which the online experience is defined. After all, in the physical world the door of a luxury store or showroom is never left wide open for passers-by to enter at will. The door is often closed but the store uses the window displays and the visible store decoration to invite the visitor to come in. The welcome page serves the same purpose. First, it reinforces the web visitor's arrival at the brand's territory through visual displays such as the logo, colors, symbols, images etc; then it validates the brand's identity using the brand's signature codes in the page concept; then it invites the user to come in and experience the world of the brand through the ambience evoked on the page; and finally the visitor is ushered into the world of the brand through a personalized experience promise from the choices given for location, languages and content. I've seen too many luxury brand websites that present the welcome page as if it were an unnecessary page or a make-do page for language and location choices. In this case, the brands use this page to plaster their logo and provide a list of a few language options without considering the brand identity, the evoked atmosphere or creating the desire to explore the website. What a wrong approach! Other websites portray the welcome page as an excuse for presenting heavy (and often long) flash animations without providing control tools. The welcome page serves both symbolic and functional objectives and should therefore have a high visual impact through images and other visual elements. It should make the right first impression and also emanate a specific ambience linked to the brand's core identity and should evoke the desire to explore the brand's world. Saying that there should be a balanced integration of both the functional and symbolic elements that support these objectives would be stating the obvious. A luxury website that has integrated an effective welcome page without "overdoing" or "underdoing" it is Swiss jewelry brand Adler (Figure 4.4).

Figure 4.4 *Swiss luxury jewelry brand Adler is one of the few brands that have effectively incorporated the visual elements that support both the requirements of the luxemosphere and functionality on its welcome page, without 'overdoing' or 'underdoing' it*

The home page is indispensable. It is the space where the website visitor understands if they are going to have an enjoyable experience visiting the website or not. The home page may be likened to the main floor space of a luxury store or the lobby of a five-star hotel, which provides an idea of the visual map of the environment. The home page should have a clear indication of how the visitor may navigate their way around the website. Above all, it should have a high visual impact and reinforce the brand's visual codes already felt on the welcome page. The home page is also where the visitor should be aware of the latest developments in the brand's world in terms of products, services, offerings and other highlights, and should therefore be frequently updated. A strong home page introduction is also essential both to capture the attention and to arouse the desire for e-shopping. It should present the navigational menu and the sections and sub-sections in a clear manner.

You may be wondering whether having a home page is mandatory. Well, to a large extent it is important to have a main page from where the navigational journey begins. Although the appearance of this page may vary depending on the design concept, the presence of a home page or "a point of departure" is essential. The benchmark that luxury brands may draw for the effective and consistent use of the home page in making both a visual and functional statement is from Apple.com (see Figure 4.5). Although not a luxury brand, Apple has demonstrated the importance of using images and well-structured home pages of product sections to ascertain a high impact over time. Luxury brands that come close to demonstrating high-impact home pages consistently over time are Louis Vuitton, Cartier and, more recently, Rolex.

Figure 4.5 *Cartier has demonstrated vision in creating high impact home pages in the recent past*

The design concept of a luxury brand's website is also an important visual dimension that supports a brand's luxemosphere. As has been emphasized throughout this section, the identity of a brand should be reflected in its website design concept and this, of course, should emphasize elements that produce a pleasing effect on both the eyes and the mind. Design concepts of several luxury websites tend to be ill-defined and inconsistent across the multiple sections and pages and, in most cases, they also lack a direct link with the brand's visual style. My observation is that, often, the web agency or interactive media company that developed the website produces a design concept that is in line with the agency's style and not the brand's spirit. In other cases where different companies or teams have been involved in the design concept, each of these groups leave their "stamp" on the website's sections that they have developed, creating a "mish-mash" effect and low impact.

The display of the visual elements is crucial to enhancing the visual impact and elevating a luxury website's luxemosphere. Having beautiful images in high resolution isn't enough; these images have to be placed in the right context to ensure that their value is optimized. This is similar to creating well-crafted products and displaying them in an environment that is nothing but exceptional. Can you imagine the Hermès Birkin bag or the Fabergé egg displayed in a steel cage at a street market? You may find this analogy ridiculous but a look at how some luxury brands display their products online could be likened to placing a precious object in a bird's cage. Online display of products and demonstration of services are linked not only to how products are placed or integrated within web pages, but also to how they may be viewed. Are there sufficient tools to manipulate product views? Can the screen display be placed in a full-screen mode? Can the products be "played with" in terms of spinning and flipping? These are the questions luxury brands should be asking.

Sound

Shakespeare was famously known to have said, "Look with your ears" (King Lear, IV). Can sound help us see? Feel? Understand? Experience? Change? When we open our consciousness to sound it is possible to gain a whole new meaning to particular sensations in our being. It is also possible to attain results that could never have been imagined. If you've heard of the mobile phone ringtone, invented by Japanese scientist Dr Tomobechi, which has been confirmed to increase breast size, you will understand what I mean. Within an environment, the appropriate sound contributes to the creation of a specific ambience and influences the mood. Sounds form part of an experience and are often inseparable from memories, knowledge and emotions. In the virtual world, sound is the anecdote that stimulates the other human senses of sight, smell and touch, and ensures that the online experience is not dominated by vision. Sound could also go a long way in creating a specific ambience as well as compensating for the lack of human presence online, and acts as a bridge to creating an emotional bond with a brand.

But does sound really help online visitors hear what their eyes cannot enable them to see? Yes, I believe so. Imagine for one second that you are blind and that your online experience is not dominated by vision. The sounds that you hear from a website enable you to build representations of unseen places in the universe of the brand. Nearly every luxury brand's website currently has a form of sound in all or parts of the website. If you visit one of these websites, take a moment to close your eyes and empty your mind and try to imagine that you're walking into a new arena guided by the sound you're hearing. Based on what you've heard, you should be able to form certain expectations of what you may visually discover in this arena. Now open your eyes and wander through the website with a few clicks. Does what you see correspond to what you expected to see when you were being guided by the sound? Have the sounds integrated with the visuals and other sensory elements of the website? If yes, then the brand is on the right track to providing a seamless web experience but if not, well read on.

In the physical retail environment, sound is used to stimulate different feelings in the subconscious of the shopper through music type, volume, pitch, tempo and other sound manifestations. For example, fast music is used to generate high shopping traffic inflow and spending; loud and funky music is used to encourage impulse purchases and quick departure while soft music such as jazz and classical are used to prolong the length of time that customers spend in a store. Slow tempo music on the other hand reduces the pace of human traffic flow and increases sales volume. Research has also shown that familiar and nostalgic sounds such as waterfalls, chirping birds and Christmas songs also stimulate spending. This strategy can equally be transferred to the Internet virtual environment and is effective when applied appropriately. As stated previously, it is imperative to maintain a focus on the brand identity and the target audience's expectations, and to apply the sound elements that best address these.

Alone, a sound can perhaps be appreciated or considered to be revolting, but when put within a specific context, it becomes more meaningful. More importantly, a sound heard in the context of an online experience enables understanding in an emotional and intellectual way. For this reason, the sound on a luxury brand's website should directly "reflect" the world of the brand, meaning its identity, personality, image, heritage, language and, in short, all of the brand's codes.

In the online sale of sensory products such as luxury objects, the use of appropriate sound elements ensures that the luxemosphere is rich and encourages stickiness and memory recall. However, it is important to apply the sound element appropriately and where possible to avoid featuring sound on all the pages of the website as this could become irritating especially if the sound type and effect is inconsistent, like we find on websites like Mauboussin's and Paul & Joe's. This means that the sound must have a function. Whether it is through music, melodies, voice narratives, nature evocations or clicks and tones, sound is innately linked to the website's atmosphere and therein lies its function. Some of the essential sound dimensions are music (melodies or sung), voice narratives, clicks, tones, nature, controls and options.

So how does a luxury brand ensure the appropriate integration of sound on its website?

Well, the first step would be to decide what kind of sound would be the most suitable for the brand. If it is music, then a further step would be identifying the type of music. Is it pop, rock, mid-tempo, classical, jazz etc? Assuming it is mid-tempo music, then it should be determined if the type of mid-tempo music required is only the melody or if it should be sung i.e. featuring a voice. If it is sung, then a further step would be to determine whether it should be an already existing sung mid-tempo piece of music or one specially composed for the brand. If it already exists, then the music, artist, language, awareness, impact, nostalgia and effect have to be universal and, more importantly, the music has to reflect the spirit of the brand. If it is specially composed music, then the composition should be directly linked to the brand personality traits and must reflect the brand identity and essence. Luxury websites deserve brand-specific sound online and where possible this sound should be specially composed for the brand. The specificity of luxury brands and the unique identity of every brand requires that the spirit of each brand should be distinctively reflected through its sound associations. Identifying the appropriate sound of a luxury brand should, of course, be done by experts with specific systems for corporate character testing and sound composition. Several companies provide sound composition services to luxury companies but one company approaches sound incantation through integrated brand soul assessment. Trupta uses the Corporate Archetype Music System to identify a luxury brand's character and draws on sound codes innately linked to this character to compose brand-specific music by experts, many of whom have been groomed at the Vienna opera. Another company, Sonodea (Figure 4.6), specializes in interpreting luxury brand codes and curating existing sounds in line with the DNA of each brand. The general practice however is that several luxury brands go the easy way and obtain the rights to incorporate existing music on their websites, in some cases without strategic evaluations resulting in incoherent effects.

Following the choice of the type of sound that best reflects a luxury brand online, then it is important to place the sound in the appropriate manner on the website. This includes the choice of the web pages for sound placement, in other words identifying the sections of the website where sound effects are required for an optimal experience. This may be on the welcome page, the home page, the catalogue pages or the e-boutique section and so on but the most important factor is to determine the role that the sound is expected to play in each section. There are distinctions between audio that aims to enhance the online shopping environment and consequently stimulate

luxury online

Figure 4.6 *Sonodea, one of the few companies that provide customized sound for luxury brands, specializes in interpreting brand codes and subsequently curating and compiling sounds to match the brand's unique DNA*

expenditure and audio that aims to improve the richness of the information and general content on the website. For example, would you rather feature James Brown's famous song *"I feel good"* in the reservations section of a five-star hotel's website or in the e-boutique section of a lingerie brand's website; or would you feature Bob Marley's *"No woman no cry"* in the catalogue section of a high-jewelry brand's website? Or would you compose music specifically for these sections? Well, you know the answers as well as I do.

An additional crucial factor in website sound placement is determining the variety or the mix of sound that is featured on the pages, in other words deciding if uniform sound should be placed on all the web pages where sound is featured or if these audio types should be different. Choosing the music type is one thing but determining if a single or several songs and melodies should be featured is another issue. If a brand decides to go for multiple songs or sound melodies on different pages of the website, then the challenge of ensuring that the sounds are collectively harmonious; that the functions of the sounds are met; and that the effect on the website visitor is coherent should be overcome. Multiple sound options could also be provided on the same web page, allowing the visitor to make their sound choice according to their mood. Roberto Cavalli has taken this approach on its home page in the past by featuring four options of very different sound types including "no sound" as a way to allow the visitor to the website to pre-determine the ambience according to their mood. This approach is however challenging, as it is imperative to ensure that all other sensory elements are in congruence with the multiple sound options to ensure a uniform luxemosphere and a seamless experience irrespective of the sound choice made.

Other types of audio manifestations such as voice narratives, background speeches, natural sound reproductions, click sounds, beep sounds, text listening options and text voice translations should all be considered as options for sound integration in website design. For example, in terms of speech, words should not be viewed as strings of data to be processed but exchanges of meaning and foundations of interaction. *What* we hear is important, but equally relevant is *how* we hear it and how it is expressed by the speaker. This is an important factor in speech and voice narration within websites. It should also be understood that the function and impact of voice narration is quite different from that of natural sound reproductions. The same applies to advanced audio applications such as the ability to listen to text as well as the ability to listen to voice translations of text in different languages.

Following the choice of sound variety, a luxury website must also provide sound control tools featuring the standard "play", "pause", "forward", "rewind" and "stop". In addition, there should also be a "skip" option and where possible a "variety" option. This is particularly relevant, as a substantial segment of the current online luxury consumer population are busy professionals seeking to enjoy the convenience of fitting online shopping within their hectic schedules. Therefore, they desire a relaxed atmosphere and sound and music satisfies this need, although this segment would prefer to control their audio choices on a luxury website. The sound control menu also provides an opportunity to feature information related to the sound type, whether it is existing music or specially composed sound.

Finally, the sound that is chosen for a luxury website should be the same or at least coherent with and complementary to the sound of the brand on both offline and online platforms. This means that where possible, there should be similar sound across all touch-points of the brand including the website, e-boutique, telephone lines, store, events and other initiatives and avenues that bring the brand into direct contact with its clients and targeted publics. In the integration of audio features into online platforms and storefronts, the strategic issues linked to collective consumer experiences at every touch-point of the brand should be continuously assessed. Although several luxury brands remain quite far from integrating uniform audio at every touch-point of the brand, one of the few luxury companies that has effectively mastered the use of uniform sound on both its digital platforms – website and mobile portals, as well as its offline touch-points – telephone lines, lobby, bar and restaurant, is the Parisian Palace hotel, Hôtel Le Bristol (Figure 4.7). The hotel has a specially composed melody that has become a part of the DNA of the brand and is the background theme heard in the hotel's lobby, restaurant, bar and telephone line as well as on its website. This harmonious sound forms the bedrock of the sensory character of the brand and is the uniting point of the collective experiences that clients have with the brand. In addition, Hôtel Le Bristol has ensured that its thematic melody reflects its brand personality and heritage while at the same time remaining balanced. As previously emphasized, audio features are important elements of the multisensory mix of luxury websites and are expected to be balanced in type, pitch, tone and melody and, above all, must be linked to the brand's core identity.

Figure 4.7 *Hôtel Le Bristol, one of Paris's Palace hotels, is one of the few luxury hotel brands that have a specially composed soundtrack that incarnates the spirit of their brand. This sound has been integrated in all the client touch-points with the brand including the hotel lobby, bar, rooms, telephone systems and the website*

Case Analysis 4.1
Sounding off the mind to breasts, hair and love

Believe it or not, a new discovery means that women can now increase their breast size without tortuous plastic surgery and men will soon be able to wave goodbye to baldness without resorting to hair implants. Everyone else will also be able to enjoy better memory and even get a chance to fall in love at first sight, thanks to this invention. And it doesn't involve a complicated exercise in patience and will-power but only calls for a few minutes of enjoyment per day. Sounds too good? Then wait until you hear the sounds, literally.

A scientific breakthrough has discovered that the power of sound on the mind not only can influence emotions, perceptions and behavior but can also lead to the physical development of the human body. Yes, the body! And how? Sound that is heard by anyone is sent to the brain, which decodes its messages that are both functional and subliminal and diffuses its understanding of these messages to the sensory nodes that instruct the body's organs on how to perform. If the sound is mixed correctly and the brain gets the right message, the instructions sent to the body organs could lead it to perform differently. But, of course, getting the right sound mix and the subliminal message to the brain is the toughest part. But it has been done!

For years, Japanese scientist Dr Hideto Tomabechi has been convinced that the power of sound can influence both the mind and the body, and for over fifteen years has been experimenting with different functional and subliminal sound mixes, to get the body to act, literally. He obtained his first proven result in 2008, with the development of a ring-tone in which he embedded a subliminal sound of a baby crying. Of course, you cannot hear the baby crying but the brain receives the message of the baby crying, which is hidden in the functional sounds, and then goes into full action to ensure that the breast increases as it gets ready to feed the "supposed" baby. His tests on women showed a 3 cm breast increase after they had listened to the ring-tone at least twenty times a day for three days. Women all over the world are falling over themselves to testify to its effectiveness. And Dr Tomabechi's next sound move will be for hair growth, memory enhancement and falling in love!

And what do these have to do with luxury online? This breakthrough gives a small glimpse of the enormous possibilities that luxury brands have in gaining substantial "mind share" of the consumer both online and offline. Just as it is possible to influence the mind and body using subliminal sound, it is also possible to create emotions, perceptions and actions in favor (and also disfavor) of a luxury brand!

Scent

Scent, fragrance, odor or however you may prefer to qualify that which is assimilated through the sense of smell is innately personal. It is linked to an individual's preferences, personality, mood, feelings and emotions. These factors already pre-exist before the scent choices are made although scent can also influence mood, feelings and emotions. Scent is also one of the human senses that have the strongest emotional and nostalgic effect on people. Have you ever walked down the street and perceived a scent that triggered a memory in your mind? Or met someone whose scent reminded you of someone else? Or worse still perceived an odor that you associate with an unpleasant past experience? Well, if you have then you must know what I'm talking about. The fact is that the human sense of smell is often underestimated although it is the sensory element with the strongest element of pre-determination. For example, if your preferred scent is musk or vanilla, you are more likely to purchase a musk or vanilla-based fragrance than one made with scent notes of lavender. Scent also has a strong nostalgic factor, which makes it the human sense that triggers the highest probability of repeat purchases.

In offline retail, scent is used to evoke specific feelings that ultimately lead to probable purchase because scent can easily be recalled. For example, the scent of fig trees in a retail store during the Christmas season is a reminder of the need to shop for presents. Retail stores also use certain fragrances that are aimed at calming the mind and subsequently relaxing the body to encourage lingering in the store for long periods, at crucial times. Scents that accelerate adrenalin, like ginseng, could also be used to get shoppers excited, particularly in relation to in-store events or new product launches. For example, a shot of camomile or violet in a store could induce either calmness or enthusiasm.

In the online environment, it may seem impossible to take advantage of the sensory elements linked to scent but scent-based products such as perfumes and fragrances actually belong to the group of luxury products that are the most frequently purchased sensory goods online. This is because scent can also be easily recalled and the affiliation with a particular scent is hardly outgrown. Selling scent online, however, remains challenging. The transfer of the scent element to the online environment may seem impossible but the advancement of digital and information technology, has introduced applications that enable overcoming these challenges. One such development is a digital scent software called the iSmell developed by the company Digiscents Inc. This application may be integrated in websites to emit scent notes which are then perceived from computers through external peripherical plug-in devices that function much in the same way as a computer's external speakers. Of course, the scent software has to be installed in computers in order for the device to function. iSmell makes it possible to perceive scents from websites in the same way that speakers make it possible to hear the music from websites. Imagine the potential and impact of this development on clients who will no longer be obliged to rely on store visits to be introduced to new fragrances. It has also been said that Nokia is experimenting in the area of creating the first mobile phone to emit scent through scent nodes.

Luxury brands with products which rely heavily on the sense of smell, such as perfumes and cosmetics, can also overcome the absence of smell online through offering samples of their products from their website to interested e-shoppers. This will give the shopper the opportunity to test the product and ascertain their like or dislike for the scent and make a decision regarding future purchases. This strategy is also a powerful tool for collecting customer data through permission marketing and subsequently manipulating

---

Case Analysis 4.2
Innovation highlight – the virtual science of scent

An innovative company called Digiscents is in the process of revolutionizing the way we think of the sense of smell. Digiscents has been conducting research to recreate the sense of smell mechanically. They have recently teamed up with Quest International, one of the world's leading fragrance, flavor and food ingredients manufacturers, with particular strengths in sensory design and consumer understanding. Together, the two companies envisage a vast array of new opportunities in making this new technology accessible as well as a profitability tool.

The result of the collaboration is the introduction of the iSmell device, which empowers an online browser to smell products that they see online. They see the convergence of the gap that currently limits the way consumers can experience things through the computer. Online shoppers are able to see, hear, and to some extent touch what is presented on the monitor. However, no computer simulation has been able to recreate the smell of the sea or freshly baked bread. With the iSmell device, this is now possible. The device works in a similar way to how digitalized music is downloaded and played through speakers attached to a computer. Online scents data can now be acquired through odor encoding and stored as digital data and played back as smells though this little gadget attached to a computer monitor in the same way that speakers are attached.

The digitalization and broadcast of scent will enable consumers to send scented emails, smell products before shopping, watch scented DVDs, and play scented games. There are many pluses to being able to smell flowers or fragrances before buying them. Apart from adding value to the online shopping experience, this element of luxemospherics will serve as an innovation to the digital-products world. The digiscent device, also referred to as "scentography", has the potential to launch the next web revolution, particularly in e-commerce.

the data for segmentation and targeting of the customer base and positioning of the brand. As we all know, a first purchase of a scent-based product following a sample testing usually leads to regular future purchases as a result of affiliation with the scent. This should ring a bell.

Another strategy for the sale of scent-based products in the virtual environment is through providing a strong and thorough scent description using precise and emotion-evoking words. As I previously mentioned, what we hear is interesting but how we hear it is often what has the most effect. To get an idea of what I'm talking about, read and compare these two phrases that are the description of the same newly launched fragrance by Valentino

> A soft and soothing scent that oozes energetic vanilla, with a base of calming lavender and a hint of powdery rose, for all day joie de vivre

> This perfume has been created with a special blend of vanilla, lavender and rose and lasts all day

Which of these two phrases would most likely influence a positive purchase decision? Your answer is as good as mine.

Movement

Movement is the luxemospheric element that is linked to the tactile sense of touch. It is clear that the sense of touch cannot realistically be reproduced in the virtual online environment but it can be simulated through the integration of certain elements that psychologically evoke the sense of touch and help the website visitor to forget that they are staring at a computer screen. These elements are mostly linked to movement because motion provokes a sense of progression, action and interaction that is often linked to physical touch and feel. If we take a simple example of watching a movie in a cinema or even in a home cinema setting, you will mostly agree that it is quite easy to become immersed in the scenes of a good movie to the extent that we feel that we're part of the action taking place in the movie. If we take this experience even to the elevated plane of the 3-D screen viewing of movies, the impact is even higher. In this case, we can almost swear that we can touch and feel the people and objects in the movie. If these feelings can be evoked through our interactions with television or cinema screens then why not a computer screen?

Reproducing movement online is fairly easy through videos, interactive flash, animations, zoom, 3-D, slide shows, flips, demos, avatars, navigational tools etc., but the challenge for a luxury brand lies in integrating these elements in a balanced form on its website. I'm often appalled at how simplistic luxury brands' approach to their website design is in terms of integrating interactive elements aimed at producing the sense of touch. The widespread practice has been to inundate the luxury website with flash animations on multiple pages, throwing in a mix of videos both in the main website and in linked micro-sites and presenting products through an inconsistent use of zoom, 3-D, flash animations, slide shows, full-screen, flip catalogues and any other kind of interactive feature you can think of. The result in most cases is inconsistent in visual identity and an unbalanced luxemosphere, and the impact on the client is, of course, low and in some cases quite repulsive. To draw from my own experience, I have refrained from revisiting several luxury websites as a result of the presence of a mish-mash of these interactive features that have resulted in "too much" movement on the websites – and these are mostly brands whose products I actually find appealing! What happens in this type of environment is that the real value of the products – both symbolic and functional – is not enhanced and optimized. Websites that have been overwhelmed with heavy flash and interactive animations actually devalue luxury products and the brands they represent, contrary to popular consensus. Of course, it is essential to ensure that there is a sense of movement on the luxury website but this has to be approached so as to ensure an optimization of the luxemosphere and not be to the detriment of the brand.

How may a luxury website feature elements that enhance movement and the sense of touch?

As you may already be aware, one of the most important movement elements is the video. The feature of short and relevant video clips on a luxury website will not only enhance the luxemosphere and generate interest, but also will aid in achieving a high level of stickiness, repeat visits, memory recall of the brand and the website as well as ensure a higher purchase probability. In this age of Internet content and participation, website videos have become rampant and therefore the video on a luxury website ought to be relevant to the target audience and have content that is compelling enough to be watched and remembered. It is obvious that client expectations in terms of videos have increased dramatically and the reason is obvious – they have seen it all and they are even making their own videos, and in some cases they have enough imagination and creativity to produce videos that surpass the output of luxury brands. A quick search on YouTube using luxury keywords will validate what I'm talking about. While it is always interesting to watch video clips from a brand's fashion shows and product launch events or the blatant display of their products on red carpet events by celebrities, all of these are *déjà vu* and no longer have the ability to blow the mind of the website visitor away – not even when entire videos are uploaded on the homepage in a desperate bid to compel each website visitor to watch it.

The important rule, if there are any, for videos is to make them short and compelling, with a strong message that is easy to understand and fast to download. Also imperative are control options to play, pause, stop, rewind, fast forward and skip the videos at will. This cannot be over-emphasized. Today's online consumer doesn't have time to wait for ages for a website to load just because of the presence of a heavy video file (think Chanel) and online users simply want to be empowered to maneuver their online experience according to their desire. And let's not forget that it takes only one click and a fraction of a second to switch from one website to another. The choice of the video and where to feature it on a luxury brand's website are key issues and questions that every brand ought to answer before rampantly placing videos on multiple pages. Videos that feature products, locations, services or demos should include close shots that linger on main features, as these will enhance the tactile sensory response. One website whose demo video captures the attention is H&M, which is definitely not a luxury brand but has one or two lessons to teach luxury brands about incorporating demo videos in relevant sections of its website. Although H&M is known more for apparel and accessories, they also have a make-up line and to demonstrate the different applications of make-up they have incorporated a full-screen close-shot video online, which not only shows effects of different colors but also traces the brush strokes during applications. One would have expected such a high-impact video from a luxury brand renowned for its cosmetics range like Chanel or Estee Lauder but this is not (yet) the case. Rather, another cosmetics brand that has come close to reproducing the tactile sense online is La Maison Calavas (see Figures 4.8 and 4.9).

Interactive flash animation is another movement feature that has become popular on luxury websites. While animation that is based on flash media technology could add excitement to a luxury website and also bridges the

Figure 4.8 *French cosmetics brand La Maison Calavas uses close-shot images to reproduce the sense of touch on its website and compensate for the lack of online human presence*

Figure 4.9 *Swedish mass fashion brand H&M (yes, it is not luxury) has a lesson or two to teach luxury cosmetics and skincare brands in incorporating close-shot video demos of product application and care as a means of reproducing the sense of touch online*

gap of the lack of human contact, a website that is flash-heavy for the sake of featuring interactivity serves no purpose. Like video, flash animation should be short and compelling with a specific and relevant purpose. It must also be in harmony with the rest of the website and, above all, be linked to the brand personality. As Internet users continue to evolve and to become more savvy with technology, they are also becoming more demanding and more difficult to please and incessantly "flashing" them in a bid to please them will lead nowhere. They require a coherent experience from a luxury brand both online and offline, and this is directly linked to sensory experiences through the luxemosphere. A well-integrated interactive flash animation is a strong brand enhancement and communications tool, and enhances the web experience to lead to impulse purchase, stickiness and repeat visits and consequently increased web and store traffic and higher revenues. Again, the purpose should justify the element and applied technology.

In addition to video and flash, movement may also be simulated on a luxury website through the integration of applications that allow the viewing of products in zoom and three-dimensional modes. These are most effective in the e-boutique and product presentation sections of websites. Although zoom has become commonplace, what is still lacking on most luxury websites is the ability to control specific parts of visuals powered by zoom. For example, although it is expected that a product featured in the e-boutique should be viewed in zoom modes, the products should not only be viewed in their entirety or in the universal mode but specific features of the products should also be viewed through enabling selecting and zooming in on product parts of the image, up to 2x or 3x their original sizes. This means that the images should be in high-resolution format for clarity and sharpness. The zoom facility should also be aligned with the 3-D features that enable the interactive view of products in a 360° format. Enabling image views in a 360° format allows not only a complete visualization of the image, but also ensures both interactivity and the generation of the feeling of touch, which is essential for the sale of sensory products.

Latest technology also enables the visualization of products not only in 3-D formats but also in real time, meaning that a product such as a watch that is displayed on the website may be viewed with the correct real time and if the watch has a metal strap the real light reflections on the metal strap will also be seen. When you cannot touch a product, you have to at least expect to feel that you can touch it or that you can visualize it exactly as it would be if you were holding it in your hands. This is the direction of interactive digital technology and will form a key component of client expectations in the near future.

3-D and zoom are indispensable in the visual e-merchandizing of sensory products as they not only provide a better view of the product, but also empower the website visitor to visualize products in their own individual mode. This demonstrates recognition of the client and reinforces their empowerment. When images are featured in static mode, they ought to be multiple alternative variations featuring exteriors, interiors, specific angles and a focus on special features. Close-up shots are also now a given and a luxury website that is yet to feature high-impact close shots has already been left behind.

Online interactivity influenced by movement may also be simulated through enabling the back and forth movement of static images that have been displayed in a manner that reflects harmony. For example the homepage of Karl Lagerfeld's website (see Figure 4.10) shows a line-up of young models dressed in the brand's creations. Upon clicking on any of the models, she advances towards the fore of the screen while the others retract. The general impression is that the models are lined up and waiting to be summoned to advance towards the website's visitor by a click of the mouse, but in reality each of the models' images is actually an individual image that has been embedded with the others on the page. This tactic enhances interactivity and provides a viewing option that has an even higher impact level than the standard slide-show view of products, which has become quite passé with the advancement of interactive and digital tools.

Figure 4.10 *Karl Lagerfeld uses embedded static images to generate the feeling of movement and enhance interactivity through a viewing option that is different from the standard slide-shows and the current widely-used horizontal navigation*

The sense of touch may also be simulated online through other interactive tools such as integrating the means of viewing catalogues or brochures by literally "flipping" them open with the click of the mouse, instead of the standard image view option. Accompanying this with a real "flip" sound has an even higher impact. A few luxury brands have effectively integrated online page flipping within their websites, notably the private jet company Ultimate Jets. In fashion and accessories, both Coach and Jimmy Choo have featured this tool in their catalogue browsing sections. Some others like Boucheron have also placed horizontal navigation of both images and text as a supplement to flips and a means of simulating movement.

Finally, the ultimate in enhancing the sense of touch through movement is by providing a highly personal and intimate experience through enabling the website visitor to "live" the virtual life on the website. This may be done through a customized personal avatar (see Figures 4.11 and 4.12). I'm sure you pretty much get the avatar concept but an avatar does more than aid in the visualization of products against the human form. It also enables an individual to craft their personal features on a human-like form in order to view products as they would appear exactly on them in real life. One such application that enables this has been developed by the Montréal-based company My Virtual Model™. This application, also known as MVP, has been developed as a 3-D visual merchandising tool particularly for fashion and accessories online retail and may be integrated within an already existing luxury brand's website. It comprises a virtual catalogue of human features such as height, weight, body shape, skin tone, hair and eye color, facial features and so on, which each individual chooses so as to recreate themselves in a virtual mode. This recreated self allows them to try on products such as clothes, bags, shoes and jewelry during a single online shopping trip or during subsequent visits. Since this avatar can be saved and returned to on the same website, it also provides an edge for online communications through virtual communities as it enables its users to explore other people's styles, make suggestions and recommendations, rate different looks and also publish their model on blogs and social networks. Of course, it is up to the luxury brand to enable this additional feature. There is more on My Virtual Model™ in Chapter 8.

Avatars may also be used in a simplified format that doesn't require the replica of each individual in a virtual format. In this case, the website may integrate avatars in several standard formats and each individual may choose the avatar that most corresponds to their form. American fashion accessories brand, Coach, was one of the first to include standard avatars on its website as far back as 2002, although these avatars have no human features apart

Figure 4.11 *American fashion accessories brand Coach was one of the first brands to feature an avatar on its website as a tool for product merchandizing. The avatar uses three standard sizes and two product view choices to enable shoppers to visualize products against the human form*

Figure 4.12 *My Virtual Model™, an e-merchandizing application that allows online shoppers to create a personal avatar with their exact human proportions, has been integrated into several websites including H&M, although luxury brands are yet to adopt it. This tool enables virtually trying on articles like clothes, shoes and jewelry and is particularly suitable for the e-retail of sensory goods such as luxury products*

from the human form in three sizes. Other e-retailers have also identified the need for the virtual trial of products online and one such player is Browns, which recently introduced a virtual changing room on its website although this doesn't feature avatars for the moment.

Flavor

How do you reproduce the sense of taste in the virtual world? How can brands like Jean-Paul Hévin or La Maison du Chocolat or Fauchon, whose products are basically based on taste, succeed online? Does this mean that they are restricted to using images, text and the occasional interactive flash and video to create a desire for their products online? What about brands like Dom Perignon, Rémy Martin and Château Mouton Rothschild whose champagnes, spirits and wines are renowned worldwide but their appreciation remains dependent on the arousal of the senses of taste, sight and smell. These brands not only require to be online, but also face the challenge of transferring their core brand promises through their online sensory codes. How could a client's taste buds be stimulated online without actually tasting the products? It's impossible to taste anything online, right? Yes, I agree that we cannot literally taste products online but do you think that our sense of taste can be stimulated virtually without actually making the product itself available physically? I believe so.

The stimulation of our taste buds and the arousing of the desire to acquire taste-based goods like champagne and chocolates could be successfully achieved online through the tactical use of web elements to focus on the sense of taste and its complementary sense. This approach means that the "reasonable" aspects of website development like navigation and functionality need to be relegated while those elements that enhance the senses need to be placed at the fore. To begin with, the descriptions of the products themselves must be strong, that means compelling, imaginative, concise and punchy. The accompanying images should also have a high impact and literally "diffuse" taste. For example, instead of featuring a static image of a hot meal set on the table of a luxury restaurant, the image may be made interactive by enabling the aroma to be emanated from the plate through virtual steam rising from the plate. This will surely have a higher impact than a one-page essay on how great the food tastes and how great the brand is. As already mentioned in this chapter, websites that focus on the mind rather than the eyes will have an edge in sensory brand communications and validation. A look at the websites of three renowned French gastronomy brands Dalloyau, Jean-Paul Hévin and La Maison du Chocolat will confirm what I mean by focusing on the eyes through text. Fauchon (Figure 4.13) on the other hand has applied visual and taste stimulus through images and e-merchandizing approaches on some of its website's pages.

Taste references may also be used to evoke the imagination of what the product may taste like. For example, not everyone may know what *foie gras d'oie* tastes like but they may be able to imagine this taste if they are told that it is rich, musky and delicate, and melts on the tongue like the smoothest butter and calls to mind the feeling of silk. An additional approach to evoking the sense of taste online is through testimonials of taste experiences posted on the website as well as organizing real-life taste events that are broadcast live or subsequently online.

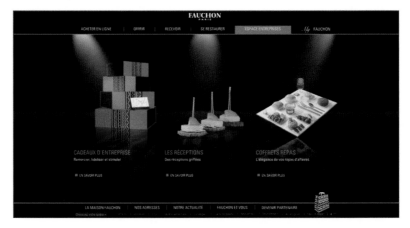

Figure 4.13 *French brand Fauchon uses visual and taste stimulus through images and e-merchandizing approaches to activate the taste buds on its website's pages*

Table 4.1 presents an overview of the online luxemospheric elements and their links to the human senses and Internet marketing strategies.

Table 4.1 The luxemosphere dimensions and relationship to the human senses

Human sense	Web element	Luxemosphere tactic
Sight	Visuals	− Strong welcome page introduction − High-impact home page − Brand-specific design concept − Harmonized color scheme − High-pixel and relevant images − Clear text font style − Legible text font size − Full-screen mode − Relevant avatars − Balanced graphics
Aural	Sound	− Brand identity-specific sound − Music variety − Multiple music options − Sound control tools − Section-specific background sound − Click-sound necessity − Voice narration choices − Balanced tone, pitch and tempo − Text listening options − Text translation possibilities
Smell	Scent	− Scent emission − Samples − Descriptions − References
Tactile	Movement	− Universal and selective zoom − Relevant slide shows − Full-screen videos − 3-D product view − 360° real-time product view − Interactive views − Alternative views − Interactive zoom − Flash animation − Flip catalogues − Horizontal navigation − Close-up shots − Avatar options − Changing rooms − Demos
Taste	Flavor	− Strong descriptions − Tasting events − Taste references − Testimonials − Taste diffusing images

the e-experience: creating more than a luxury website

If you've read up to this point then I may have succeeded in convincing you that online sensory communications and experience are essential to the success of a luxury brand's web presence and its brand reinforcement both online and offline. Both the mind and the subconscious play important roles in the relationship between a luxury brand and its public, therefore sensory e-experience cannot be over emphasized. Targeting the eyes online is like taking a shot of energy drink which wears out sooner or later, but focusing on the mind and the senses that drive it ensures that what people will remember long after the collections and visuals have changed is the experience they "lived" on the website.

Figure 4.14 gives you a visual idea of the luxemosphere concept.

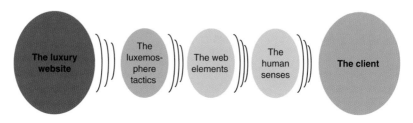

Figure 4.14   *The luxemosphere Internet strategy model*

Designing the "winning" luxury website

I'm pretty sure that many people reading these lines may concede that developing a website is fairly easy and doesn't necessarily require an extensive section in a book. After all, there are millions of websites existing in cyberspace and this wouldn't be so if website development were that complicated. This means that, generally, anyone with a fraction of a brain can read through *Web Design for Dummies* and manage to throw a few web pages together. But "developing" a website is not the same as "creating" a website. Neither is "building" a website the same as creating one. It is also not only about design and navigation; nor is it about only technology (flash or html?) and search-engine optimization. Nor only about developing an e-boutique and ensuring that sales can be made in as many currencies as possible. It is, rather, about giving life to a luxury brand in the virtual space through a balanced integration of all of the above-mentioned web features, and also ensuring that these bounce off solidly on everything that the brand represents. When you "create" a website, particularly a website that represents a luxury brand, there is so much more to think about than just putting up a few pages with nice photos and text in as many languages as possible.

Creating a luxury website is like embarking on a journey in much the same way that visiting a luxury website should be a journey of pleasurable discovery. The journey of luxury website creation (please notice that I haven't used the words "design" or "development") is multi-faceted. It comprises design and creativity, technical competence, business and marketing know-how, digital media expertise and a thorough understanding of the world of luxury and, particularly, the universe of the brand in question.

This means that in order to create the winning luxury website, the skills and expertise required could be summed up in five key areas:

1. Artistic and creative talent (for the design and aesthetics)
2. Technical skill in web and digital media (for the functionality and back-office)
3. Business and marketing know-how (for the content, communications and e-retail)
4. Brand dynamics and interpretation skills (for the virtual brand re-interpretation)
5. Luxury industry experience (for the luxury online positioning)

The reality is that it is almost a mission impossible for a luxury brand to identify a single individual with a balanced combination of these skills to qualify him/her as an expert in luxury website development. What this means is that a luxury brand is almost always required to create a team comprising members that exhibit an elevated level of skills in these areas. The reality, however, is that it is challenging to manage a team of business executives, artists, and computer geeks since they all speak different languages. The designers or "creatives" in the luxury sector are generally considered to exist in their own "floating bubble", while the technicians or "techies" are viewed as squares who just don't get it but have to be tolerated because their role is essential. The business executives and marketers as well as the brand "interpreters and inspirers", who are generally considered (or who consider themselves) as the "know-alls", usually have a hard time managing their marketing and e-business objectives in addition to the two aforementioned groups, not to talk of getting to grips with the sense of loss they often feel (even though many won't admit it) as a result of the newness of luxury online (see the Introduction to understand better). This is quite a dilemma, so what options does a luxury brand have to ensure that their website creation and maintenance process is seamless and that their online existence is optimized?

To begin with, the theory of *The Almighty Webmaster* should be thrown out of the window (no personal offence to webmasters). At several luxury companies, the person often in charge of creating and managing the website, as well as the Internet department or team, is the webmaster. In some other companies it is the graphics designer while at several other luxury brands, the Internet team is manned by (hold your breath) the store development manager who in most cases is still trying to figure out the difference between blogs and chat rooms. In this scenario, the king of technology, the webmaster, often focuses on the latest technology and the coolest software, applications, plug-ins and all kinds of Ps and MLs (PHP, ASP, HTML, DHTML, XML) and underplays the design and aesthetics and practically ignores (or forgets) the e-communications and the re-creation of the brand's codes online. Graphic designers, on the other hand, are often obsessed with creating "pretty" websites that have as much interactive flash animation, images, graphics, sound and videos as possible. Their accomplices are, of course, the people in advertising and PR who, together with their agencies, push for images, images and more images. Where the business executives are in charge, the focus shifts to the sales figures and revenues, therefore anything that would make people buy as much as possible from the website goes. And the brand interpreters? Since they have no clue as to what all this Internet business is all about but must show their enthusiasm anyway, they generally employ every trick in the book to demonstrate that everyone else doesn't understand the brand's DNA as much as they do and that they are all about to commit an "absolute disaster" online (even though they don't offer solutions for avoiding this disaster). And what happens when the executive with the most experience in the field of luxury (let's say 25 years) is put at the helm of the Internet department? Well, what happens? Your guess is as good as mine – nothing happens. And how do we expect something to happen when the guy's secretary hasn't yet managed to convince him that he doesn't need to have his emails printed out and left on his desk every morning? And that if he waits to dictate the responses, the person who sent the email may have probably forgotten about it. Pretty grim you would think, but it need not be so.

Before looking at the strategies and techniques required for the creation of luxury websites, it is necessary to suggest some key strategic issues that need to be addressed within luxury companies. I have put these issues in a framework that I would like to call the *Seven-Step Journey*, not because it is a wonderful theory that I've been hatching for half a decade but simply because it's easier to remember (and it also has nothing to do with "seven" being a mythical number). These steps would go a long way in ensuring that the website development project is executed from start to finish.

Step one: defining the strategic role

It may seem pretty obvious but every luxury brand must ask themselves the simple question, "Why do we need to have a website?" Is it because our competitors are all online? Or because we may lose some of our clients to these competitors? Or because we need to advertise and communicate? Or to provide such information as our location addresses and our brand story? Or for retail? Or just for the sake of being online? In the last fifteen years since the Internet became a permanent business channel, several brands were pushed to establish websites because of their competitors and others, to respond to clients' needs which were evolving even as these clients took up new technologies. But a luxury brand must believe in the importance of establishing a strong web presence through their own website before they are able to develop a winning website that emanates passion, experience and richness. If a brand hasn't yet recognized the importance of the Internet and doesn't believe in its power to inform, influence and reinforce, then the brand shouldn't go ahead with developing a website because it will be apparent through the website that the brand is online for the sake of it or for wrong reasons. If you make a quick tour of cyberspace and visit up to ten luxury brands' websites in a row, you will quickly be able to tell which websites were built with passion, knowledge and dedication to ensure a strategic online positioning. And by being online I don't mean registering the domain name and creating a one-page "coming soon" placeholder.

The definition of the strategic goal of being online leads luxury brands to take the basic and necessary steps towards their online presence. For example, only brands that are committed to using the multi-purpose functions of the Internet would think of registering variations of their domain name in several text combinations and characters. These are the brands that would buy such domain names as champagne.com and cognac.com in addition to their brands' domains. These are also the brands that would go as far as buying the .com, .eu, .fr, .it, .co.uk, .hk, .jp, .in, .ru, .cn, .au, .net, .br, .me, etc. combinations with their brand names. It is also these brands that will understand that domain names could also be registered in other text characters, and not only in Latin. Since 2008, it has been possible to register domain names in Chinese characters. If you're a luxury brand reading these lines, you know what to ask yourself. Also don't forget Greek, Russian, Bulgarian, Japanese, Arabic and other languages that have non-Latin written characters.

Step two: ensuring the right internal orientation

I'd like to come back to the point I made earlier about establishing a team of professionals with inter-disciplinary skills to ensure an expert approach to the development of the winning luxury website. This can only be successful if the orientation across all the departments within the internal set-up is attuned to the reception of innovation, which the Internet represents. Although the popular belief in the tech world is that luxury brands dislike the Internet and the employees of luxury companies are more inclined to resist the Internet culture than accept it (which I don't entirely agree with anyway), every company in every sector has needed at some point to re-orientate their internal team towards the requirements of new technologies. The luxury sector is no different. The Internet team cannot function in isolation from other departments and will often need to call on the creative directors, the product managers, the brand managers, human resources directors, the retail developers and the marketing intelligence directors. All of these parties do not need to be technology-savvy but they will have to be knowledgeable about the business opportunities that the Internet provides and believe in it enough to provide the required support to the Internet team. Whether it is through training sessions, workshops, seminars, simulations or whatever dissemination means is most effective, every luxury brand will need constantly to inform and form its internal orientation towards the realities of new technologies to ensure the smooth operations of its e-business arm.

Step three: developing a solid e-business plan

Before delving into this important area, I'd like to get the definition of e-business right. e-Business is not e-commerce; neither is it e-retail, for which it is often mistaken. Rather, it comprises the multi-faceted and integrated aspects of conducting any kind of activity online and through digital media including e-communications, e-marketing, e-branding, e-consumer analysis, e-commerce, e-communities as well as e-CRM, e-merchandizing, e-logistics, e-customization, the social media and so on.

In order to develop a solid e-business plan and model, it is imperative to ensure that every aspect of e-business is covered. Key issues include creating a firm e-communications approach; developing a marketing program that features product selection, display and management; understanding how the brand may be positioned on its website and in the entire cyberspace; re-creating the universe of the brand at every online touch-point; influencing the representation of the brand on the social web including blogs, vlogs, social networks, discussion forums, messaging platforms and other user-to-user communities; monitoring the evolution of luxury clients online in terms of behavior, attitudes and interests; developing selling strategies on the brand's website and on third-party websites, and managing the ensuing logistics and operations; strengthening relations with clients online and tailoring products and services according to individual preferences; and so much more. As you can see, e-business planning is quite extensive.

Step four: re-assessing the brand identity

Every individual who works with a luxury brand has a thorough understanding of what the brand represents in terms of identity, heritage, signature, codes and, in short, the entire universe and DNA. This is the first and foremost aspect that is made clear to all current and potential employees. Normally, a luxury brand doesn't need to conduct a separate exercise to educate the Internet team on the attributes of the brand but, in several cases, the Internet team will need to deal with "external people" like web agencies and digital media and communications companies and, in this case, the brand identity will need to be re-assessed (not changed, please). Assessing the brand identity means examining the core elements of the brand, which give it its life and promise to clients. This includes the dimensions of the brand's roots such as its name, symbol, logo, colors, language, history, heritage, manners; the brand identity dimensions including the personality traits and the image projection codes; the brand's positioning in its consumers' minds and in comparison to its competitors; the brand's promise or what makes it a source of value to clients; the level of awareness that the brand has attained and the actions that were taken to attain this awareness; the way the brand manages its relationship with its clients; and the sources of the brand's equity. All of these need to be addressed and thoroughly understood by each party involved in the website creation because the key source of value for luxury companies is, of course, their brand.

I've come across several cases of website creation projects where web agencies receive tens of pages of a luxury company's brand identity briefing (which nobody bothers to read by the way) as a way to inform them of what the brand represents. This is not enough. External parties that form part of the website creation teams have to be given the opportunity to experience the brand in order to assimilate its identity. Just as a luxury brand cannot function without its brand promise, the website creation project of a luxury brand will not be successful if all the parties involved in the creation process do not have the core DNA of the brand in their heartbeats. This may explain why several web agencies end up stamping their style (and not the brand's style) on every website they develop, leaving the brands to exist under the umbrella of their signatures. What a pity.

Sometimes it is the luxury brands themselves who sabotage their brand identities online, in some cases by getting carried away with highlighting special news such as artistic collaborations and special projects more than

(1)   (2)

(3)   (4)

Figure 4.15   *Louis Vuitton, which has frequently updated home pages (1), uses subtlety to communicate its homage collection with collaborator Stephen Sprouse (2) and a re-directed website to emphasize its relationship with the artist and the art world (3 and 4)*

their own brand identities online. For example, a luxury brand that launches an initiative in environmental protection does not need to plaster "green" on its home page unless it intends to change its brand personality from "chic and sophisticated" to "natural and wholesome" (as much as I recommend sustainable corporate practices). Of course, luxury brands should by all means feature interesting initiatives online but this should be done intelligently without over-shadowing the brand or, worse still, confusing the brand's public.

Step five: creating the "wow" website

I don't believe that there is a secret formula for the creation of luxury websites that would be suitable for every luxury brand in every product and services category. I also don't agree that there is a secret "10 ways of..." that is yet to be discovered and revealed by those that have more pairs of eyes than we mere mortals. What I know for sure is that the one-formula-fits-all approach doesn't apply to luxury website creation. The reason for this is simple – every luxury brand is unique and different in its identity, personality, image and core essence. Even though several brands currently have more or less similar product categories and ranges, their core brand attributes remain distinctly different and this difference is the source of originality and equity for each brand. This must not be taken for granted online because the impact on the Internet will be even more resounding than offline due to the global accessibility and availability of the Internet.

As you may notice, we went through four steps before arriving at the point of creating the website, which should tell us something: that luxury website creation is not as simple as following the guidelines in the "How to..." series. And we haven't even started the discussion. Luxury website creation comprises ensuring that all the elements of the back office (systems, softwares, applications and all the tech stuff) are integrated and balanced with the front office aspects such as the design, navigation and our most beloved luxemosphere. It also includes ensuring that all the fundamental elements of luxury and website design are represented and these include, although are not limited to, the design and aesthetics concept, the functionality, content, retail, community, customization and the support technology. These aspects are elaborated more in the next section.

By the way, if you've come across that someone who has a magic formula for creating a luxury website, I'll love to meet him or her (I could do with more eyes around my head).

Step six: testing and improving

Every beautiful thing takes time (and sometimes a lot of pain) to create. The luxury website is no exception. Just as skill, craftsmanship and precision is required in luxury product creation; and care, attention and excellence is required in luxury service experiences, so should be the website creation process. Some luxury brands develop their website creation plans with a time-frame of three months, which in many cases is not realistic. Sometimes three months is not even sufficient time to test the supporting back-office applications and systems needed before the website creation begins. Every element of the website, whether in the front office or the back office, must be tested, refined, modified and optimized before the website is launched. Every text must be read and re-read; every "I" must be dotted, "T" must be crossed and full-stops applied. Every language translation must be re-read and back-translated; every image checked and double-checked and every video and media file played and re-played. These checks cannot be over-emphasized.

The test period could be an internal pilot exercise but is not, however, the same as the soft-launching of the website.

Step seven: going live online (without soft-launching)

In 2008, Galeries Lafayette, the French luxury retail department store that has not only become a treasure land for shoppers but also a national monument, launched its e-commerce website. The highly anticipated event, which in some parts of France could be equated with awaiting the visit of a statesman, drew thousands to the online store for a tour and possibly to purchase some of the delectable goods that are displayed in the physical stores. The website launch turned out to be an anti-climax. Visitors were disappointed with the flash-heavy, long home page download, excessive sound interruptions, unnecessary background images, poor navigation and limited brand and product selection that the website had to offer. Many (including myself) experienced a "freezing" of the web browser when trying to log on to the website, as a result of the heaviness of the flash system. When Galeries Lafayette was questioned over this, their explanation was that it was "only a soft launch" to test the market. The public's reaction was "How could such a retail institution get it so wrong?" and I would add "after two decades of the Internet!" to that. I don't know about others but I haven't been back to the Galeries Lafayette "soft-launched" website since it froze my entire system some months ago and I lost several unsaved open files. I'll be going back when they decide to go for the "real launch". After all, I don't think anyone should buy the prototype of a luxury product if alternatives of the real thing exist elsewhere.

I don't think that I need to repeat that luxury brands who decide to create a mish-mash of a website in the bid to soft-launch it and gauge public reaction are on an expressway to fulfilling their death-wish, that is unless they wish to change their slogan to "What were we thinking?" The same applies to brands that decide to replace their home pages with a "beautiful" "Coming Soon" sign, during the maintenance or improvement of the website, as if the Internet is the same as an offline store where construction workers have to block off store entrances and streets to work on buildings. Brands like Versace and Escada have been victims of this in the past and more recently I've seen

Catherine Malandrino's "coming soon" sign-post although the "coming soon" conveniently didn't apply to the e-commerce part of the website.

Launching the luxury website should be done with ceremony, zest and the joy of bringing a potentially exceptional experience to both clients and potential clients. It should be a fanfare of pleasure and show dedication and passion. If your website creation is not yet at the level of being celebrated when it is launched, then by all means please avoid launching it.

The journey of luxury website creation should be that of discovery, curiosity, passion, interest, sensory appreciation and enjoyment. It is a journey that will ensure that all the touch-points of a brand are reproduced online and that the impact of the website on everyone who comes across it will be so high that they will always remember the experience and never sever their relationship with the brand.

Case Analysis 4.3
Web team analysis – Tony, the almighty webmaster

Tony wears glasses. Not the black rimmed fashionable designer type but the ones that have a frame the color of, well, somewhere between orange and shell fish. He is five feet eight inches tall but because he is also as thin as a magic wand and as light as a paper towel, everyone has the impression that he's actually taller. His long and thick hair also doesn't help matters. Also he walks with a slight swagger (which some people swear is a bounce) but no one is really sure if this is intentional or the result of a deformity, or worse, if it is as a result of the force of the air around him, which is arguably heavier than his body weight. He hardly speaks to anyone, always seems to be mumbling something under his breath along the corridor and seems not to be aware that other people exist. The only time he insists on a mandate is when he obliges everyone who wants to see him to confirm their appointment on his digital diary, which requires the creation of a profile and the acceptance of some terms and conditions to access.

Tony works in the Internet and digital media department of one of the major French luxury brands. He is in fact the webmaster, although this doesn't explain why people seem to be afraid of him or plainly prefer to avoid him. But everyone knows that you cannot avoid a webmaster for long in a luxury company for sooner or later you will need some "system input or output" that only he can resolve. Anyhow, Tony doesn't need to speak much. His authority does the speaking for him, for he reports directly to the CEO and no one can challenge him, not even the CEO himself because the CEO doesn't know what he knows.

So what does Tony know? And what does he do exactly on a day-to-day basis? Tony created the company's website and manages it. He is the king of technology that holds the key to how millions of people around the world see the brand online, and also offline. He can decide what he wants the public to think and he can actually make them think it. He intimidates those around him with his skills in technology and numerics and he doesn't hesitate to apply technical computing languages when he wishes to dismiss certain people, for example the marketing "self-gods" or the creative "fluffs". What drives Tony's adrenalin is the discovery of the latest and coolest technology and applications and their integration to his beloved website. Who cares about marketing and all its jargon on brand identity and brand equity? And what does a dressmaker or a bag designer know about technology? He is the one who knows and he counts and this is where his power comes from. If he didn't know what he knew, he's pretty sure that those desperate-looking people (at least when they come to his office) would never have spoken to him in a hundred years.

What Tony the almighty webmaster doesn't show, however, is that he doesn't have all the answers for a luxury website. He could have had the answers if he was working at Microsoft or Apple and he would have a ball as well, but in this world of luxury, he is sometimes lost in the flurry of the needs of the brand, the clients, the products, the design, the retail, the merchandizing and the absolute universe of the brand and its special DNA. But he is the boss right? So he cannot show his fear. And therefore he must focus all his energy on the latest technology, which is the source of his power. And there goes your luxury website.

Now to the main issue: creating the luxury website

Assuming that a luxury brand has successfully mastered what the seven-step journey requires and understands the intricacies of launching a website creation project, then the brand would be ready for the actual website creation.

Again, in order to make this process clear and easy to remember, I have once more called on the "number seven", this time not to provide a guide in the form of a journey but to act as the basis for an outline and structure for retention. This is not a hatch-plan and the fact that the framework arrived at number seven after careful analysis was quite a surprise (by now, you should be nodding and saying, "yeah whatever" so I'm not going to try to convince you further).

So let's get down to the business of the *Seven Cs of Luxury Website Creation* and if you have a problem with the number seven, you can make yours the Eight Cs and include "Creation" as your additional C, and I could give you a page in the next edition of this book for more elaborations.

The 7-Cs of luxury website creation

Earlier in this chapter, I devoted a sizable amount of space to the e-experience as an imperative aspect of a luxury brand's website. The same attention was also given to our newly coined concept of luxemosphere and its key role in enhancing the sensory appreciation of luxury products and services online. These two elements have been taken apart from the 7-Cs because they are the core aspects of luxury website creation that may not be compromised under any circumstances. Their place should be permanent, period.

The 7-Cs however may be altered as luxury brands could either adopt all of the Cs or apply them in phases according to the company's objectives and resources. For example, not every luxury brand may be ready to establish an e-boutique during the website launch and therefore in this case the 'C for Commerce' may not immediately apply. The same goes for the 'C for Customization' which requires the development of specific applications and supporting operational systems to materialize. However, it is recommended that, where possible, all of the Cs should be applied in the website creation process of a luxury brand.

The Cs are the following:

1. Concept
2. Competence
3. Content
4. Commerce
5. Customization
6. Community
7. Computing

They may be divided into two main groups. The first group comprises the first five Cs, which are directly linked to the front office; the second group consists of the last two Cs, which are powered through the back office. None of the Cs are, however, mutually exclusive and each of them needs both the existence and the optimization of the others to be able to function in an optimized manner.

The following section is devoted to the in-depth analysis of the Cs.

Concept

The website concept basically comprises the design and aesthetic elements. It is the main idea behind the design of the website and equates to the scheme that every aspect of the website will follow. While we cannot say that the concept is the most important C in luxury website creation, we can construe that the concept is the starting point. It is unrealistic to evaluate the dimensions of a website's navigation and content if the design concept is yet to be defined. In essence, what will you be navigating?

As anyone who has been involved in a design project or product launch knows, the first step is the idea generation, followed by the concept testing before moving on to developing mock-ups and section testing and finally validating the concept. This process is similar to the process of establishing the luxury website's concept. However, in this case, the design concept should follow the personality of the brand. There is no point designing a basic and classic website if a brand has an extravagant personality. When we visit Ferrari's website or John Galliano's, we don't expect a similar design concept as on the websites of BMW or Hermès.

The concept of a luxury website is often confused with meaning the same as its color or page layout, image distribution and navigational menu placements. These are all essential parts of the concept but they are not what drive the concept. It is rather the concept that drives these elements. When I say website concept, what I mean is the overall model, idea and notion behind the website. Is it based on a virtual dream land? A 3-D discovery world? A clipboard? A moving screen? A classic presentation? Horizontal navigation? It is important to understand not only the concept of the website, but also the link between the website, the brand identity and the potential online luxemosphere. Several luxury brands have adopted the classic website concept featuring the clean-cut but typical static and, in some cases, 2-D design concept with the basic idea of making a "presentation" rather than providing an experience. Some of the brands have added interactivity to this classic concept through images, videos and sound although the majority of luxury websites remain similar in concept. While classic website concepts are not a crime, it is time for luxury brands to rethink this approach and apply innovation in website design, as the classic website design concept is outdated and is now a given. With the advancement of digital technology applications, client expectations with regards to exceptional online experiences are on a constant rise and luxury websites are no exception.

A few luxury brands have however taken bold strides in creating website design concepts in a form that is more elevated than the classic presentation style that calls to mind Microsoft's PowerPoint. One such website is The Watch Avenue (www.thewatchavenue.com) (see Figure 4.16), initiated by the Fondation de l'Haute Horlogerie, the uniting body of luxury watch makers including Tag Heueur, Raymond Weil, Vacheron Constantin, Piaget, Audemars Piguet, Tissot, Longines, Hublot and so on. The website has been designed and developed as a real avenue with a line-up of luxury watch stores, complete with doors that swing open, window displays, trees and chirping birds. Its horizontal navigation enables the user to "stroll" down the avenue while taking in the environment or stopping at the news stand to pick up a magazine. There is also a human guide who will not hesitate to follow the user and provide directions and commentary. Upon entering any of the stores, the website visitor will be able to walk around the store and view product selections, watch the in-store television, converse with the sales ambassadors, enrol in the private club, obtain catalogues and interact with the brand in many more ways. All these are made possible through the 3-D application on which the website has been built. It provides a complete 360° experience and an elevated interaction with the brand. Another example is Cartier, which applies the brand's unique color codes in a horizontal movement format to give the impression of being in a rotating theatre of discoveries, through its website, Love.cartier.com, built to celebrate its Love collection. The website breaks from the traditional standard and square design concepts rampant in the luxury terrain.

Other luxury brands have taken the initiative to adopt design concepts that are out of the ordinary and in line with their brand personalities. One notable example is Viktor & Rolf, whose website's design concept is based on the brand's "maison", literally (Figure 4.17). The website is built as a house whose home page opens to the design duo descending the main stairway

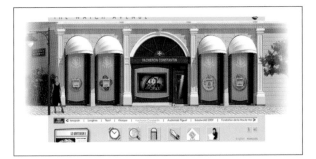

Figure 4.16 *The Watch Avenue has for the first time introduced a prestigious location concept to the virtual world and brought a complete 3-D experience complemented by human presence to the online shopping experience. In doing so, it has created a much-needed reference in the sphere of luxury online*

the e-experience: creating more than a luxury website

Figure 4.17 *Viktor & Rolf pioneers the use of bold virtual immersive 3-D website creation concepts in the luxury industry. The website, which is built as a real "maison," opens up with the designer duo greeting and welcoming each visitor to their world*

of the house's entrance and advancing towards the screen while welcoming the website visitor to their house and wishing them an enjoyable stay, all with the background of especially composed music that enhances the luxemosphere. A tour of the "house" reveals additional rooms, libraries, archives, design studios and even the room that acts as a "*parfumerie*" where the brand's fragrance is presented in a boudoir-like setting. Each door that opens is a clandestine discovery in an environment that is driven by experience through motion, strong visuals, sound and a unique luxemosphere. Although there is no e-commerce on this website, the originality of the design concept, exactitude of the virtual brand interpretation and richness of the luxemosphere all add up to the exceptional brand experience. Other brands that have attempted to create a concept based on a virtual 3-D house with several rooms are Rémy Martin, through its social network, GetInteresting.Com, although the experience provided on the website is less seamless; and Mauboussin, whose linear image display of multiple products on multiple pages integrated on a single screen calls to mind an attempt at reproducing Microsoft Vista's advert images. The constantly changing sounds and design ideas upon clicking on a new page don't help matters either. As mentioned earlier in the chapter, Christian Lacroix also took a bold step (in line with the brand's spirit) when it created a virtual fantasyland dedicated to its special collaboration for La Redoute. However, the downside is that the brand's main website itself was forgotten in this tide of innovation, leading to an inconsistency in the virtual brand image.

Although there is no magic formula to identify the right or wrong design concept for every luxury brand, when choosing a design concept, the following principles should be used as a guide:

1. Keep it simple but rich. There is no theory that stipulates that when it comes to creating luxury websites, the more complicated, the more luxurious. A look at LuxuryCulture.com (Figure 4.18) will underline that online superiority may be achieved through simplicity and sleekness. And when I discussed the Viktor & Rolf website earlier, did I mention how complicated it was? I don't think so.
2. Avoid having a black background color except if black is a part of your brand's signature colors. And no, black doesn't automatically mean luxury, online or offline.
3. Don't fall under the pressure of having a home page in the conventional sense of creating a separate page. A home page may not be necessary in all cases and, depending on your design concept, it could be skipped. Take a look at Love.Cartier.Com and you'll understand why the home page is not obliged to be a separate page.
4. Ensure that the website's concept is coherent on all pages and that, upon entering different sections and sub-sections, the visitor to the website does not feel that they are visiting a different website. Anyone who has visited Chanel.com lately will understand what I mean.

5. Create a powerful visual and sensory impact through the website concept. Luxury is all about the pleasurable and if your website doesn't lead to a pleasurable experience for the senses, then what is the point of calling your brand a luxury brand, at least online?

6. Understand that you may draw benchmarks for website concepts from outside the luxury industry. As I mentioned in the Introduction, luxury online is still in its infancy and has not come of age, therefore expecting to have a reference in every aspect of e-business in the luxury sector is unrealistic.

7. Understand that the website design concept needs to be regularly updated, particularly with the advancement of digital technology. Although luxury brands are expected to be timeless and coherent in brand and product presentation, this golden rule should be represented in the online brand presentation and not in applied technology and design concepts. For example, a classic luxury brand like Chanel doesn't need to retain the same home page for six years in a bid to maintain its classic brand attribute, does it?

Figure 4.18 *LuxuryCulture demonstrates that online superiority may be achieved through simplicity and sleekness*

Competence

The competence of a website is generally linked to its usability, which is powered by the navigation and the functionality of all the elements of the website. The website usability can be likened to the map of a city, intended to guide visitors. A good map always leads to the right destination but the best maps are those that ensure that the reader discovers the essence and soul of the city during their journey to the final destination. Having said that, a luxury website's competence lies in how user-friendly its navigation is, how easily visitors can find key information and, more importantly, how the navigation is used to propel the online experience. A key question is, "Does the website's functionality tools drive the user experience or is it the user who judges the brand based on their ability to manipulate the main sections and sub-sections of the website?"

Website competence has multiple dimensions. First, there is the navigation which allows the visitor to discover the website's contents. Second, there is the functionality which makes the website's tools efficient; and third, there is the overall usability which gives the website visitor the desire to extend their tour of the website and to discover the brand. All three aspects must work together in order to drive the desired user experience.

Navigation features such as menus and sub-menus indicate to the website visitor what direction they need to follow in order to find specific content and discover the brand. The placement of navigational menus and sub-menus is a key factor in influencing the online brand experience and the website's luxemosphere. While there is no right or wrong approach in the choice of navigational menu style, it is a known fact that most Internet users read from left to right and this affects their visual referencing for the layout of web pages. Therefore, a menu toolbar that is placed on the left side of the screen will have a different effect than if it were placed on the right side of the screen. The same principle applies to reading from top to bottom and from bottom to top. This explains why most websites place the sub-menus at the bottom of the page. Multiple menu bars on the same website should be non-repetitive and strategically placed. I've seen too many websites with the same navigational menu placed horizontally and vertically, in a bid to enhance clickability and visibility. This more often than not results in confusion and presents the brand as desperate.

An additional important factor linked to navigational menus is the choice of using a "drop-down" menu style or a "listing" menu style. The drop-down menu style regroups topics that are linked together under one title. The title is what is visible on the menu and the topics only appear when a mouse is moved over the theme. This approach is most suitable for the simple and sleek website design and has become more relevant even as Internet users become more savvy with technology.

In ensuring the smooth web navigation of a luxury website, interactive features that enable the feeling of movement on the website should be enhanced through easy access to these features. For example, on some websites, interactive flash animation is applied in the opening page of main sections while videos are grouped in a specific section. Other websites may prefer to integrate videos in multiple sections with a coherent structure, which is fine as long as the navigation is uncomplicated and universal effect leads to an enhanced luxemosphere.

Navigation could also be enhanced through the use of "breadcrumbs", which are texts placed in small sizes often towards the top of the screen.

These texts leave a trace of the pages already visited during the browsing experience. Breadcrumbs could be likened to footsteps and they are useful in retracing steps and in avoiding a sense of loss on a website. This is particularly important for luxury websites such as Chanel.com and Montblanc who have excessive sections, sub-sections, embedded mini-sites, micro-sites and multiple links.

Finally, there is the question of vertical and horizontal navigation. In the recent past, it has become *à la mode* for luxury brands to integrate horizontal navigation tools for both images and text views on their websites. While this demonstrates an evolution in luxury online, horizontal navigation should not be adopted because all the competitors have this tool, but because it is in line with the website design concept and other sensory and interactive elements. A luxury brand doesn't need to jump on the bandwagon of horizontal navigation just because it's in vogue.

Functionality has speed, security and softwares as its main elements. In order to ensure that a website is competent, it has to perform well. This means that its pages have to open swiftly and smoothly; that the downloads have to be fast; the videos have to stream in record time; and that the screen modes have to be easily altered and exited. In the case where there are opportunities to upload files, this also has to be fast. And the golden rule for videos is to enable control through play, pause, fast forward, stop, volume, full-screen and simple opting out. There is no point having a pretty website if it's not efficient. I'm sure you'll agree that the magic of the Ferrari is not only from the beauty of its design and color, but also for its performance. The same approach should be applied online. My observation is that, currently, luxury websites compromise the speed of their website features in their bid to integrate the interactive media applications such as Flash and Active X. In cases where this has been badly done, the web pages take forever to load and drive the clients away. Who wants to re-live the Boo.com experience ten years on.

An additional key element of a website's functionality is the security. Several luxury websites that have incorporated e-commerce have the additional challenge of ensuring that the transaction area is protected. While the issue of security is mostly linked to the transactions that take place in the e-boutique, security is also linked to the safeguarding of client information and the respect for their privacy. This means that the client information generated from transactions and subscriptions to newsletters and other programs must be kept in an exclusive database and may not be used or transferred to other parties. As has been emphasized throughout this book, luxury brands represent a promise to clients and this is based on an unspoken trust that the brand will keep its promise and even surpass the expectations of clients. Therefore, when luxury brands are tempted to share client information, even within the same group, in a bid to optimize relations, the result could be fatally negative.

Functionality is also enabled by software and applications that power the front office displays. In general, most websites are built in HTML formats where files can be stored in PHP modes. These applications are supported by most computers without additional software downloads but where a website is powered by Flash or ActiveX, which most people may have to download before accessing, then there could be the additional challenge of a wider adoption of the web features. While maintaining an innovative and avant-garde approach to the integration of advanced technological tools to their website, luxury brands should also ensure an understanding of the phase of technology adoptions by the target client.

Usability features on a website arouse a desire to discover the brand through an extended visit of the website. It is the general ease of use through elements that facilitate an enjoyable experience. These elements include language options, local content, screen modes such as full-screen, separate window pop-ups, print versions of images and text files, multiple product views, client call-back option, instant text chat option, background color manipulation, choice of background sound, image download option, video viewing options, cookie options and so on. The list of features that could enable a seamless online usability is endless but each element should be carefully thought out before being adopted. Some of these elements have posed particular challenges for luxury brands to integrate online, particularly the issue of language options and local content as well as the set-up of cookies.

As we all know, the luxury market is today more international than ever and the Internet has largely contributed to the global visibility of luxury brands. In line with this, it has become essential to provide website content in multiple languages, particularly for brands that have a global presence and those that aim to take advantage of the international traveling clientele. The emergence of new markets like Russia, China, Brazil and the Gulf States has further emphasized the need for multiple languages and local content on luxury websites. Despite this, several luxury brands still have the classic trio of English, French and Italian languages on their websites. This is often not out of a recognition of an international clientele but mainly because most of the brands are, well, French, Italian and either British or American, the latter group being the worst offenders. It is quite appalling to find that such international luxury hotel brands such as the Hyatt Hotels & Resorts and the Hilton as well as luxury fashion and accessories brands like Donna Karan and Dunhill are yet to realize that a single language on their websites is no longer sufficient. Assuming that everyone who makes an online hotel reservation or who desires to explore the world of an American or British luxury brand ought to understand English would be living in an illusion. In addition to language options, there is also the important issue of how the languages should be accessed. Should this be according to the geographical region, for example, based on the assumption that everyone in France would prefer to view the website in the French language and everyone in Australia would prefer English? In this case, if the website content is local, then the non-local language speakers would be excluded from what the brand has to offer that particular market. In the case where the language choice is according to language preference irrespective of location, then the brand would have no choice but to provide a universal content for all markets even if there are special programs designed for specific markets. And, of course, there is the additional challenge of providing language options according to the availability of e-commerce on the website and the markets of e-distribution. In this case, the brand that decides to sectionalize languages according to its e-retail markets will be forced to segregate the visitors who are not in the markets of e-distribution and deal with compensating them for exclusion. The majority of luxury brands are still far from this dilemma as the issue of language choices is yet to be given the attention it deserves. However, two brands that have taken strides in dealing with the language challenge, albeit through different approaches, are Louis Vuitton and Cartier (Figure 4.19). The former, which has integrated e-retail in eight countries, has opted for the "language equals location" approach, while the latter, which also has e-retail in multiple countries, has gone for the approach of "language equals choice". The difference between these two approaches is that Louis Vuitton is able to provide their website visitors with a clear and short path to making online purchases while experiencing the brand's universe on their way to the e-boutique. Cartier on the other hand enables their website visitor to create a large part of their own experience on the website while plunging them into the universe of the brand in which they could also discover the collections for subsequent purchases. Louis Vuitton is apparently seeking to optimize both experience and sales, while Cartier is seeking to optimize experience and relations, which could also lead to more sales. From which of these websites are today's clients most likely to purchase? And with which of these brands are they most likely to build a long-lasting relationship? I hear your answers.

An additional usability element that several luxury brands seem to be struggling with is how to use cookies to capture user information for both personalization and statistics without making this obvious and breaching client privacy. Although cookies are generally accepted by the average Internet user, due to their highly personal nature, this could also be a sensitive issue. Just to clarify, a cookie enables a web server to identify users of its website through their computers by capturing some information peculiar to each computer and storing this in a text file which is retrieved each time that computer is used to log on to the website. Several websites apply cookies without informing the website visitors, while others even go as far as imposing the enablement of cookies on computers before their websites may be accessed. Due to the fact that cookies collect information from all types of computers, including personal ones, several web users prefer to be informed about the cookie set-up of each website. I have come across some

(1)

(2)

(3)

Figure 4.19 *Louis Vuitton and Cartier approach language and location choices through different strategic tactics. While both use drop-down menus (2 & 3), the former enables local language and content generation through location and e-commerce (2) and the latter places an emphasis on language choice irrespective of location (3). Both websites demonstrate the importance of high-impact images and page layout for web page optimization, although Louis Vuitton's focus is perceived to be on "the buying experience" while Cartier is seen to be focused on the "online experience"*

heavy Internet users who simply refuse to accept website cookies and would boycott any website that imposes cookies on them. However, since cookies enable companies to understand their clients better through monitoring their website browsing habits, preferences and taste, it is an important tool for client recognition and, subsequently, the development of tailored products, services and experiences for clients. Since luxury companies are expected to play a leading role in client recognition and, at the same time, in the ethics of client privacy, their approach to the inclusion of cookies online is important. First, a luxury brand ought to inform the public of its use of cookies in capturing their personal information and this information should not be hidden in a sub-page of a sub-menu of the mini-site that has been integrated in the micro-site that no one is likely to find unless they spend five hours on the website. The information about cookies should be visible and clear without being technical, as Louis Vuitton has done on its welcome page. The retention by the website of the information about cookie-enabled preferences such as language choices and page preferences should also be the client's choice and not the luxury brands'. For example, Hôtel Le Bristol's website provides five language choices and, when a choice is made, the website visitor is asked whether they would like this choice to be retained or not. This means one more click but it's a click that will ensure numerous return visits.

The home page and the welcome page are also additional website competence elements that have been highly debated in luxury circles. The debates have centered on whether the two serve the same purposes; what these purposes are; and the necessity of having a welcome page that doesn't provide navigation but means one more click just for entertainment. To begin with the last issue and move backwards, a luxury brand ought to have a welcome page and unlike popular belief, a welcome page has a purpose and the purpose is not entertainment. I liken luxury website welcome pages to the door of a high-jewelry store. Have you ever visited Boucheron's store or Chopard's or Bvlgari's and found the door to the store wide open? That would be unlikely to happen, wouldn't it? You would normally arrive and have a doorman swiftly open the door for you and usher you into the store. The doorman would greet you in the local language and would immediately spot your language preference if different and switch to that. In many cases you would pass through an *entrée* where a sales ambassador would gracefully take your coat, umbrella or whatever you would like to get rid of while in the store in order to ensure that your experience is unspoiled. The ambassador would also greet you in your own language before ushering you into the store. So why should this be any different online? The welcome page is your entry door where you understand that you have arrived at the point of entry into the brand's online universe. The presentation and perhaps animation on the page serves as your welcome and when you choose your language and location, this welcome is further heightened. As you move on to the home page, you're passing the entrée and into the floor space from where you can access the different product displays. So you see that this has little to do with one more or one less click but everything to do with providing a unique brand experience.

Search-engine optimization and **web referencing** are additional areas of challenge for luxury brands. Popular consensus indicates that luxury brands need to optimize their searchability by paying for Google ads and placing their web links on blogs, social networks and entertainment websites.

I disagree with this suggestion. While I concede that a luxury brand should be found easily online, I believe that a luxury brand should invest in developing its social media referencing and offline brand awareness, as these will play a key role in driving traffic to its website. Brand communications online and offline are not mutually exclusive and go a long way in complementing one another. In your opinion, would someone looking for a black luxury handbag type in "black luxury handbag" in the Google search box or would they go to Gucci, Louis Vuitton or Hermès' websites? If you're wondering what lesser known brands should do in this case, then I would say use the social web to create an online buzz about your brand but invest in also creating a buzz offline simultaneously. Paying Google to list you first when people search for "luxury cars" or "luxury wines" will likely not get a brand very far in the long term. Luxury clients online will not always choose a Porsche or bottle of wine from *Chateau Mouton Rothschild* but they will also include you in their choice selection only if they know you and understand your brand message and believe in what you represent.

The competence is the backbone of a website and plays a key role in crafting the online experience through effortless navigation, functionality and usability. In formulating the most feasible approach to the competence features, it is important for a luxury brand to retain a focus on the evolution of digital media technologies and applications, as well as the adoption rate of these technologies by Internet users, particularly the target audience. Technology is constantly changing and the usability and functionality choices made for the website should reflect the core essence of the brand and add value to the each user's web experience. Wealthy clients expect exceptional experiences from every touch-point of the brand and this includes the website. Online touch-points are the different ways that a brand's universe may be experienced on the website, including videos, interviews, panoramic visits of premises and their neighborhoods, music, special collections, product demos, advertisements, care guides, special online events and so on. Enhanced experiences from touch-points are likely to strike a chord in the way the brand is related with.

To finalize, again here are a few tips for website competence optimization:

1. Understand the difference between a welcome page and a home page and optimize both for their symbolic and functional benefits.
2. Invest in a powerful welcome page and home page or whatever page people arrive at upon clicking on your domain name.
3. Never save the best pages for last. This is not the Grammy Awards ceremony.
4. Integrate control tools on all video and sound files. Please do so, for Pete's sake.
5. Avoid multiple sequential click-through pages. It leads nowhere, literally.

6. Don't believe that you're smart enough to get away with creating mini-sites, micro-sites and all kinds of digital files and interconnecting them to your website. It's tacky tacky tacky and so obvious.
7. Avoid cluttering pages with too much information. This *Marketing 101* presentation rule is also applicable for luxury websites.
8. Don't believe those people that tell you that if your website background color is not black, then you're not a luxury brand. *C'est faux*!
9. In all circumstances, avoid integrating heavy media files and graphics that require long downloads, especially on your home page. That is, unless this is your way of operating a one-man protest against luxury on the Internet.
10. Allow visitors to customize their choice of page views on the website. And no, it will not diminish their experience of the brand's universe.
11. Understand that language is a key issue that should not be ignored online. And when I say language I don't mean only grammar and expression, but also language options, access type, local content and special text characters.
12. Understand that domain names may now be registered in non-Latin text characters. And yes, you have to do something about it before some smart Chinese guy does.
13. Understand that 3-clicks to buy is not an academic theory but a real business tool for every luxury website.
14. Apply "breadcrumbs" as footprints on your website. If you're lost, then read from the beginning of this section.
15. Don't forget that all the benchmarks for each element of website competence as highlighted in this section are not necessarily drawn from the luxury sector. When reviewing web elements, don't forget the likes of Amazon, Apple and Nike who have precedented several web functionality and usability tools. Yes, they are not luxury brands but they got there first, sorry.

Case Analysis 4.4
Website competence analysis – anyone for cookies?

How would you feel if each time you logged onto your preferred website, you were instantly recognized and ushered in exactly as you wish, meaning in your preferred language choice, page settings, personalized content and perhaps even your preferred choice of products? Have you ever dreamed that a website could recognize you and modify the web pages for you? How about if that website happens to be that of a luxury brand? Well actually, part of this is now possible as luxury brands are presently able to collect information about website visitors through cookies. The downside, however, is that in most cases the website visitor is not informed of this and therefore not aware of it. Even worse, many of the luxury brands have not managed to create exceptional experiences with this data, at least from the client viewpoint.

But what are cookies?

The name *cookie* derives from UNIX objects called *magic cookies*. These are tokens that are attached to a user or program and change depending on the areas entered by the user or program. To move away from the tech jargon, cookies are simply text files that store information that is peculiar to each computer, which is used to identify web browsers. When an online user logs onto a website, a message is sent by the server that hosts that website to the web browser. The browser stores the message in a text file. This message is then sent back to the server and each time the browser requests a page from the server pertaining to that website, the text file is enabled. It is the text file that is linked to a specific computer which helps to identify the person that uses that computer to access the website. The contents of the text file could vary but all content is drawn from the computer and is unique to that computer. This could be private information or simply program codes contained on the computer. Cookies are, however, not used to run programs or launch viruses, but they contain information pertaining to a computer that is stored on the website's server. So it may be that an individual could have hundreds of pieces of data taken from their computer that are stored as cookies or text files on different websites.

The main purpose of cookies is to identify users and possibly prepare customized web pages and offers for them. When you click on a website using cookies, you may be asked to fill out a form providing such information as your name and interests. The majority of existing websites, however, collect and store information regarding your computer without this form and therefore without the user's knowledge. This information is packaged into a cookie and sent to the website's server which stores it for later use. The next time you go to the same website, the server can use this information to personalize your visit. So, for example, instead of seeing just a generic welcome page you might see a welcome page with your name on it. You may also be presented with tailor-made services like products and services collections and web page view preferences. The brand benefits from understanding clients better through monitoring their browsing habits, shopping preferences and page movement. Among luxury brands, however, the general practice remains that cookies are enabled without informing website users and the data collected from cookies serves the brand more than the client.

Should luxury brands inform clients of the use of cookies on their websites? Yes. Should they obtain permission from clients before capturing data from their computers? Yes. Should they play a leading role in client recognition and at the same time the ethics of client privacy? Yes. And should they tailor-make online experiences according to data captured by cookies? Of course.

Content

The content of a luxury website is integral to its richness, relevance and interest. It represents the brand's current status and draws from its past to ensure its future. It indicates to those visiting the website that the brand is not only the king of its world but that it is eternal. The content is considered by many to be the most important aspect of a website and this is not far from the truth for luxury brands. The content must feature authentic, compelling and relevant information that is more enriching than the standard PR-stunts that are pulled on numerous websites. In the assessment of website content, luxury websites ought to consider five key qualities to ensure the elevation of the status of the website: authentic, compelling, relevant, extensive and format.

A luxury website that desires to convince the public that it truly represents what it promises, must be authentic. The brand must present itself in its true and pure form and must demonstrate that its originality is derived from its unique heritage, story or whatever gives the brand its source of promise. This authenticity has to be communicated in a clear and transparent manner, which means no ambiguous expressions and no contextual statements. For example, if a brand is presenting the chronology of its history, there should be no gaps between the dates. If the brand passed through a period of inactivity, this should be presented in a way that demonstrates that despite this challenging period, the brand emerged stronger. The authenticity of a luxury website's content also derives from the local or standard nature of the information and general content provided on the website. For example, if the content is presented in a local language with information that is attuned to that market, it is often judged to be more authentic. In the case of standardized information and content, the brand has to present this in such a way that it has to feel right for each person in every market. The authenticity of a luxury website's content may also originate from the way the brand communicates on its initiatives towards sustainable corporate practices and social responsibility but again, these have to be genuine and not used as PR-stunts.

In addition, the message of the content on a luxury brand's website ought to be compelling. This comes from the clarity, conciseness and consistency of the language in its choice of words, style, tone, manner of expression. A luxury brand should speak the language of refinement, express knowledge through a unique culture and voice its beliefs through a compelling imagination. Whether it is in providing information on products, services, events, history or revealing the world of the brand, the message ought to evoke a dream and arouse a desire.

The content of a luxury website must be relevant. This means that it should be not only up-to-date, but also be in line with current expectations. For example, if I asked you if a luxury brand should have a video of Santa Claus on their website in July, your answer would probably be "Are you joking?" But several websites (not only luxury brands) have fallen into the habit of retaining content such as videos, interviews and text linked to events that have long passed. I won't mention names but I've visited a luxury website in May that still had a video that was created for a Valentine's Day collection. I've also seen winter menus of Michelin starred restaurants on their websites during the summer of the following year. Relevance also has to do with expert information, meaning that if you're a jewelry brand whose core material is diamonds, then you should have some information on your website about diamonds in general and how they are mined, cleaned, cut and turned into the beautiful pieces that end up in the stores. It also means that if you're a high gastronomic restaurant, you should provide information not only about your menu but also about the inspiration behind the menu, how you source your ingredients and your approach to cooking (not your recipe!). Relevance also has to do with ensuring that visitors to your website are able to find information about the types and range of products that are stocked in each store and the availability of the services that may be found at each location. If cheap hotels are able to provide information on their room availability, then why not luxury brands? There should also be an online booking system for store appointments, which is particularly important for luxury brands. De Beers is one of the few luxury brands that provide the opportunity for a store visit appointment to be made online.

The content of a luxury website should also be extensive. This means that there shouldn't be sparse information spread around two or three pages; the content must be rich. It should include the history of the brand or a chronology of its milestones, its philosophy, beliefs, vision, brand principles, production expertise, service approaches, products collections, service dimensions, corporate information, brochures and catalogues, store locations, access maps, Q & A, arts and social initiatives, advertising campaigns and so on. The goal should be that anyone who takes the time for an extended visit of the website should feel that they know the brand inside out.

In addition, the format of the content and information of the website makes the content richer. For example, long-winded text would lead nowhere if it were not presented in a legible format, no matter how compelling the expressions are. In other words, a luxury brand should provide content that can be watched, listened to, interacted with, downloaded, forwarded, recommended and discussed. It is not enough to quote what Karl Lagerfeld said last week; we should see Karl Lagerfeld actually saying it. And it is not sufficient to say that your hotel is located five minutes away from Central Park in New York; we should actually see an image of the hotel with Central Park in the surroundings and we should also be able to take a panoramic tour of the neighborhood. In this era of Google Maps and Google Earth, expectations have risen and words are simply no longer sufficient. The same principle applies to events, product care, product demos and so on.

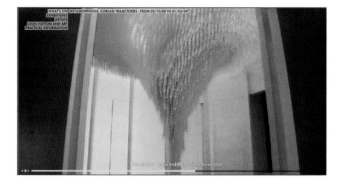

Figure 4.20   *Louis Vuitton enhances a rich experience by re-directing visitors to its Cultural Centre website on which the brand's art initiatives are highlighted*

Commerce

Online commerce or retail, which is directly connected with revenues and growth, is an increasingly relevant aspect of a luxury brand's website creation. As luxury markets expand to include an international clientele from both established and emerging luxury markets, it has become crucial to enable this wider client base to not only interact with the products and services, but also to be able to purchase them. Of course, the e-retail of luxury goods

(1)

(2)

(3)

Figure 4.21 *Browns, Matches and Net-A-Porter are three independent e-retailers of luxury products that are shaping the way luxury is sold online. While Browns demonstrates alternate views of the same product and complementary products suggestions (1 & 3), Matches has integrated specific zoom-in tools, strong product descriptions and a tracking device for recently viewed products (2, 4 & 5)*

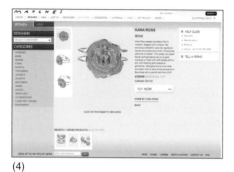

(4)

(5)

Figure 4.21 *Continued*

is not the same as the e-retail of mass market products. Luxury products are sold in extraordinary retail spaces and this shouldn't be any different online. The current practice among luxury brands, however, is to create e-boutiques that scream "buy now" all over the pages both through the text and through the general presentation.

In order to understand how to sell luxury online, it is important to identify the key factors that drive the shopping experience and sales in the e-boutique. This is the e-boutique format; the e-merchandizing style or the way products are displayed, viewed and interacted with; and the supporting e-CRM, in other words the facilities for instant client relations such as style advice and after-sales relations including returns, refunds and exchanges. The online service is also important.

In choosing the format of the e-boutique and the e-merchandizing of the products, the first key issue to recognize is that the products have to be elevated in order to enhance their value. In other words, the products should be treated like precious and delectable objects to be treasured and not like merchandise to be sold at all costs. This means that the product images, their display modes and the corresponding information should all be of the best quality and in sync with one another. In addition, the level of interactivity of the accompanying e-merchandizing tools such as zoom, 3-D views, alternative product views, product view history, color and style availability, collaborative filtering (i.e. complementary products and so on) should all be incorporated in a seamless manner.

Furthermore, e-merchandizing and e-CRM tools for instant access to style guidance, advice on product selections, care and use as well as alternative colors should all be made available. Also important in the incorporation of the e-boutique is the provision of after-sales support through a clear and simple format for refunds, returns, exchanges and store credits. Several luxury websites that have attained the glory of creating pretty websites are still found very much wanting in the area of client support, which is imperative for an elevated online experience. Surprisingly (or not), several luxury brands are yet to "get it" when it comes to e-commerce and several aspects of the e-retail of luxury goods are currently being led by independent retailers such as My Wardrobe, Browns, Matches and Net-A-Porter (Figure 4.21).

An extensive analysis of e-commerce is provided in Chapter 6, which is entirely dedicated to e-retail.

Customization

One of the most apparent factors to emerge in this age of the social web is the importance that online consumers attach to personalization and customization of everything online from web pages and images to products and services. The recognition and influence that social media such as blogs, social networks, messaging platforms and user-to-user communities have given to people means that they not only have a voice but now they also have clout and guts, and therefore have become highly demanding of personal recognition and attention. This has naturally led to the expectation of extraordinary personalized experiences with the brands that they have chosen both offline and online. They are product and services savvy, have also become masters of technology and call the shots regarding their online experiences. Meeting the needs of this client base is no easy feat and this may explain why the majority of luxury companies are still a far cry from applying the e-customization tools in web design, product selection and merchandizing and services formats.

Not surprisingly, independent e-retailers have leapt at the opportunity of customizing web pages, personalizing web contents and allowing clients to customize their own e-experience. Websites like Amazon sowed the seeds for this level of customization through recognizing returning clients and placing pre-selected products on the homepage according to their page view or shopping history. Although luxury brands and independent luxury e-retailers are yet to integrate this level of interaction within their websites, it is about time several questions linked to e-customization are asked. Is it worthwhile providing website visitors with the opportunity to customize the way they view the web pages through the text font size, background colors, sound and page layout? Is it necessary to use the previous web page views and shopping history of returning clients to influence the content or the order of the pages they view when they return to the website? Is it important for a luxury brand to integrate the opportunity for clients to create personal avatars in the e-boutique in order to enable them to try on products just as they would at home? I would answer a yes to all of these but again, all these elements have to be integrated in such a way that they enhance the luxemosphere and remain true to the brand's core essence. If utilized appropriately, e-customization tools could become a driver of sales and could lead to customer loyalty and brand affiliation.

Customization, however, has ethical dimensions that ought to be considered in order to ensure the right effect. This includes respecting client privacy and avoiding the misuse of personal information in a bid to target offers at website visitors. The client should be allowed to "permit" the website to apply the customization tools to them. These may be done through the options of enabling and disabling cookies, opting-in and opting-out of web pages' contents and e-newsletters and so on. Several websites oblige Internet users to enable cookies before visiting their website while others simply apply cookies without informing clients.

Several mass consumer goods retailers, such as Britain's Tesco, track online visits of their customers through their click habits and most frequent purchases. This information is used to customize their home pages to feature the products that they would most likely purchase the next time they visit the website. Others like French supermarket Carrefour have integrated customized pre-packaged shopping baskets with the items that clients frequently purchase and provide this readily during the next visit for a one-click-to-purchase effect. This should give some indication to luxury brands as to the dimensions of the collective experiences of online consumers, which they transfer across sectors.

In addition to the customization of web pages and contents, Internet and digital technologies also provide opportunities for products either to be entirely customized or to be dotted with touches of personalization. General consensus indicates that online product personalization, customization and co-creation is inapplicable to luxury because luxury brands are supposed to create a "dream", which means imagining what consumers desire before they even know it, and bringing this dream to life. I agree with the "dream" part but I disagree that luxury products may not be personalized or customized online. Why should a client who is willing to pay an additional amount of money to engrave their loved one's name on a diamond ring be prevented from doing so? And why should a personal touch such as one's initials not be carved into a gold-rimmed fountain pen? The reality is that these personalization and customization services already exist offline, but it seems that the thought of integrating them online somehow sends shivers down the spines of luxury Internet managers, even though it is actually more cost-effective to provide online and could potentially strengthen the relationship between the brand and its clients. A few luxury brands such as Louis Vuitton (Figure 4.22) have taken the bold step of providing product personalization online even if it remains restrictive in choice parameters. Others like

Hermès allow us to make a mini paper bag of its famous Kelly model, even if it is more of a game with no real purpose than a tool for client satisfaction. Notable initiatives have been taken by luxury cosmetics brand Maison Calavas (Figure 4.22), which allows clients to build their own make-up kits by selecting preferred colors and palettes of foundations, powders, blushers, eye shadows and lipsticks and assembling them into a complete make-up kit, which they may also purchase online and have home-delivered. Fashion brand Anya Hindmarch has also integrated an online personalization tool for its leather handbags, while this would be further enhanced with the personal virtual avatar model view as created by My Virtual Model.

As you may very well know, online customization of web content, products and services has not been pioneered by luxury brands but by such innovators as Dell and the Apple iPod, although luxury brands are expected to follow in these strides.

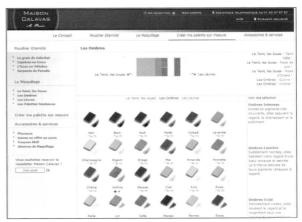

Figure 4.22 *Louis Vuitton allows online shoppers to personalize some products through an online service while Maison Calavas invites the online shopper to create their own make-up kits by selecting pre-existing color palettes*

Community

The emergence of the social web and online communities has given rise to the need for a change in how the "people" segment of Internet strategies are viewed and defined. Early online congregation points such as chat rooms and message boards, which used to be private affairs, have today given rise to the very public forums like blogs, social networks and virtual worlds, which have subsequently changed the rules of online marketing strategies. With 130 million people on Facebook and 150 million people on China's QZone, online consumers are crafting their own online experiences and making their own rules as they go, in environments that increasingly exclude corporate bodies and brands whether they are luxury or not. These platforms, which enable people to create and manage an online identity (whether real or not), communicate with and influence others, and participate in all kinds of online events are cropping up all over cyberspace at an alarming rate. With hundreds of thousands of existing blogs and social networks in any language you can think of and millions of users around the world, the power equation of the cyberspace has shifted from corporate bodies to the consumer market. The company or luxury brand is no longer in control of the way online messages are diffused, assessed and interpreted. They are now discussed and debated before they are either accepted or completely rejected. The social web brings people together and encourages them to talk through dialogues that are genuine and independent of any influence from corporations.

Since online communities have the capacity to change public opinion in a matter of minutes and, eventually, public behavior in short periods, it is about time their relevance for the luxury sector is assessed. The luxury sector remains lost as to how to approach the social web and the majority of brands concede that the luxury brands should not create online communities but should, rather, watch the social web and understand the modalities of its functioning. The problem with this standpoint is that it's been a couple of years since this watching exercise started and still nothing has been done by luxury brands in this regard, except, well, more watching and the occasional Tweeting. While I am one of those who do not go out advising luxury brands to create blogs and online communities, I believe that luxury brands should do more than "watch" the social web. Of course, observation and monitoring the contents of blogs is key to understanding the evolution of the mind-set of luxury clients but luxury brands may participate in the social web without exposing themselves to ridicule or losing their magic touch.

Essentially, there are two ways that a corporate body may participate in the current social web, the first being as an aggregator of consumers to the website. This approach draws people together on the brand's website not only to interact with the brand and purchase products, but also to discuss, share and exchange experiences linked to the brand. Before a company goes in this direction, they must first ensure that they enjoy a positive consumer-based brand equity and that they have a cult consumer following. Apple has pulled off a great online community on its website which congregates all the Apple addicts around the world (see Figure 4.23). It is their social network and the exchanges, contacts and level of connection and activity in the community are impressive. But then it's Apple, right? So before you hurry off in this direction, please ask yourself a simple question, "Am I Apple and can I pull it off?" On the other hand, even if you're not Apple and you think you can't pull it off, you may find your brand in a market such as the emerging ones of China, Brazil and India where the public may need to be educated on luxury in general, the brand, its products, how to use them and how to care for them. One of the reasons that the beauty online community Rose Beauty is so successful in China is that it not only contributed to raising a beauty consciousness among young Chinese women, but it also became a practical Beauty 101 class where everything is learned, shared and discussed, from how to apply lipstick and blusher to the steps to caring for all skin types.

The second approach that a luxury brand may adopt for online communities is by actually going out there and participating in the discussions, exchanges and forums, as individuals and real people and not as corporate bodies. The best way to inform and influence someone who posts a message on a social forum with the topic of "I hate Stella McCartney because her leather bags suck" is to inform them that Stella McCartney doesn't use leather to make her handbags and that she is also against animal testing and furs. If this information is coming from Jim the intern in the marketing department of Stella McCartney, more attention will be paid to what he has

Figure 4.23 *Apple has created a thriving online community, through the cult following of its brand that congregates and engages participants and observers*

to say because it is authentic and credible, and they know that Jim would not dare to lie to them on a public forum otherwise they would tear him down publicly and the impact on the brand would be worse. The rules of this world are transparency and independence of opinion and anyone who understands this is already headed in the right direction.

Again, further analysis of online communities is provided in Chapter 3, which is entirely dedicated to this topic.

Computing

Computing deals with the technology, programs, systems, applications, software and other tools that make up the back office of a website, which is required for effective functioning. Since e-business involves all electronically mediated activities including information exchange and transactions that support a range of business processes, it is essential that the appropriate technology powers these processes. Computing systems have the goal of enhancing the competitiveness of a luxury brand online through innovative technological support that may be linked to every aspect of the company's value chain and supply chain management. It doesn't necessarily involve only using technology to automate existing operations or processes, but also using technology to enhance and change these processes, where required. Optimizing e-business activities through computing, particularly for luxury companies, involves expertise in a breadth of different business areas including communications, public relations, marketing and sales, new product development, client relationship management, manufacturing, operations and supply chain management and inbound and outbound logistics. Computing also requires companies to tackle the need to manage the change process necessary for incorporating new processes and technology in multiple departments, as discussed at the beginning of this section.

Anyone that has ever been involved with programming and IT-based systems development already knows the difference between software and hardware but, since this is not a technical but a business book, it is necessary to go the way of basic definitions. The hardware comprises multiple physical components of a computer onto which the elements that perform the functions of the computer are loaded. These elements that perform the functions of the computer are collectively known as the software although they range from applications to programs, firmware, middleware, systems, testware and so on. The software has the role of ensuring the effective functioning of the website but before this can be done, the right choices have to be made regarding the necessary software that a website needs. For luxury websites, the focus, of course, should be on the applications, software and systems that would optimize the tools that have been integrated to ensure a high-impact web experience and brand image enhancement.

Luxury websites, of course, require the basic technology systems for web page appearance, speed, video streaming, downloads and other interactive media. In addition to these, luxury websites are also expected to integrate the systems that support capturing client online habits, managing their preferences and enabling customization, personalization and reward systems. In the case of an e-boutique, understanding clients becomes insufficient as these clients have to be monitored and their shopping habits will have to be integrated with their data and shopping habits in the offline stores. There is also the additional issue of managing an international clientele that shop online but also in different stores of the same brand around the world. Some of these clients may have multiple addresses, credit cards and even nationalities; therefore the software that ought to identify them online should also be able to transmit their data to a central point from which it will be distributed to the several retail points. This, of course, is easier said than done but these are the lines along which luxury brands should be thinking. More so, applications that support e-merchandizing such as product display and viewing modes, shopping assistance, product selection and trials as well as display preferences should also be enabled. In addition, payment systems, currency conversion, transaction tracking, delivery options, logistics and inventory control should all be powered by the best systems.

Computing is like the human bones that hold the body together. We do not see it but it has to be recognized and cared for, otherwise we will die and all that will be left is a skeleton, literally. This applies as much to humans as to luxury websites.

The journey of establishing an extraordinary online presence is quite long, as you may agree after reading this section. Luxury brands no longer face the sole question of having a website or even having the prettiest website around. This is now a given. The crucial issue is linked to the kind of experience that is provided on the website and how this affects the relationship with the client or general public. Creating a luxury website should have the goal of ensuring an immersive web environment and luxemosphere that would envelop each person who visits the website into the universe of the brand. It should seek to create intimacy through arousing human sensations that influence perceptions leading to a real love and respect for the brand. This is possible, of course, if the focus is on the mind rather than the eyes.

Chapter 5
Let's talk: communicating the luxury message online

> "The newest computer can merely mix ... the oldest problem in the relations between human beings, and in the end the communicator will be confronted with the old problem, of what to say and how to say it."
>
> —Edward R. Murrow

When the government of Venice produced the first handwritten newspaper *Notizie Scritte* in 1556, it was in response to the need to convey news on the economic, political and military affairs of the state in a quick and efficient manner. Long before this period, the Chinese were already using handwritten messages on silk to transmit information on the affairs of the state to government officials on a daily basis although this took time to produce, transmit and read, and lacked the desired quickness and efficiency of information dissemination. By 1582 China had began to publish newssheets for private broadcasts in and around Beijing. Gradually, the idea of the newspaper as a source of daily news for the public's digestion spread beyond China to other parts of Asia, even as it became widely adopted in Europe. The newspaper became popular when Johann Carolus published what has been recognized as the first modern era newspaper in 1605 in Strasbourg, then an independent imperial city in Germany and which is now in France. In no time, newspapers became adopted in Germany (1609), the Netherlands (1618), England (1620), France (1631) and Sweden (1645). The latter still publishes its first newspaper, *Oprechte Haerlemse Courant*, in an electronic format online. Stateside, the American population was not to get a taste of the newspaper until 1690 when Benjamin Harris published *Publick Occurrences Both Forreign and Domestick* and subsequently *The Boston News-Letter* in 1704 (Figure 5.1) which became the first continuously

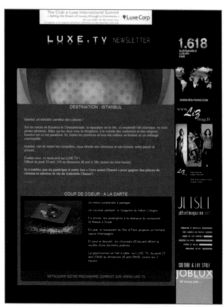

Figure 5.1 *The first continuously published American newspaper, The Boston News-Letter, which first appeared in print in 1704, was introduced to address the need to provide information and news in a quick and efficient manner. Four hundred and five years later, this need has yet to change, although the evolution of mankind has introduced a new channel of speed and efficiency of communications in the form of the Internet. Incidentally one of the current most efficient methods of online news transmission still bears the name "Newsletter" as exemplified by Luxe.TV and several other luxury media bodies and brands*

published newspaper in the US. Canada followed suit with the *Halifax Gazette* in 1751.

This was a time when international travel was at a very minimum and relations between countries and continents were sparse, yet the idea and need for the newspaper was imminent in all countries and societies and among all the people. Why? Because the human mind is constructed in such a way that it is constantly on the quest for knowledge, no matter how inconsequential this knowledge could be at times. The mind has to be fed with news and information in order to sustain it. It doesn't matter the means or the form, and in some cases the content is irrelevant, but news must be given as news is always sought.

This need also led to the publication of magazines – an offshoot of newspapers – which today exist in various areas, forms and shapes. Then the radio came along in 1895 as a fruit of the conviction and obsession of Guglielmo Marconi. The invention of the radio, complemented by the tele-graph and the telephone, revolutionized the world of media and changed the way news is accessed forever. The subsequent invention of electricity and the arrival of the cinema and television marked a point of no return not only in the way human beings communicated, but also in the way people lived and related to one another. People were no longer reading static text or listening to faceless voices but could visualize the sounds and information they received through viewing others in motion. They were visually stimulated beyond imagination and their creativity was stretched to unimaginable levels, leading to news and entertainments of different forms. After sixty years of television came another invention that would once again change the course of communications in unexpected ways – the computer and its first-born, the Internet.

Created in 1989 by Sir Timothy John Berners-Lee and Robert Cailliau as a form of collaborative sharing for scientific and military projects, the Internet has, since its founding, changed the face of the earth and shifted the behavior, attitudes and interests of entire generations in ways that are apparent but remain unclear in consensus. The patterns of behavior that have emerged from twenty years of interacting with the Internet are as far afield as the study of behavioral science itself. The unique difference, however, is that while the inventions of the past were focused on "channels", in other words the means of communications, today's communication is as much about channels as about the "exchanges" provided within the channels. The newspaper and magazine, which are the most impersonal of media channels, brought a one-way stand-off communication mode where the reader was "diffused" with news and information. The radio, another impersonal media channel, followed the same pattern of one-way information diffusion, although in recent years an element of interactivity has been injected through dial-in programs. Television also began with one-way information dissemination and together with the cinema has remained very impersonal over the last centuries. Today, the television is viewed by many as more of a channel of interruption than a channel of communications.

The arrival of the computer and the Internet brought a personal touch to media communications for the first time and set off the wave of innovation in interactivity across the other media channels. For the first time, people were able to control what they saw and were able to choose the information they wanted to access without it being imposed on them. They were able to make news and information come to them with the control of the mouse. They were also able to generate their own content through input and feedback. At last there was a channel that enabled them to be recognized. They suddenly counted and mattered. This level of interaction made the contents of the news more personal and made communications more relevant to them. The arrival of the mobile phone and its ability to stream data from the Internet as well as enable input and feedback finally broke down all the boundaries of impersonal communications, and took the control of media communications from the publishers and media companies to the individual. This third wave of this control movement is currently being felt through the social web and web 2.0, platforms existing online where everyone has the ability not only to control but to influence millions of people around the world through online content.

The world of media has changed and remains in continuous evolution. This is an undisputable reality and we can no longer go back to the days when newspapers, magazines and the TV were all that counted. The Internet has broken all the rules of communications and has destroyed all the unwritten codes of information dissemination. However, what has remained constant over the past centuries until today is man's need to communicate, to be informed, to exchange and to share. As long as human beings exist, there will always be a need to communicate but the form in which this communication will take place is what will continue to change and is to be continuously addressed.

Today's media communications is about appeal, interactivity, sharing, collaborating, creating, exchanging, influencing, decoding, transparency, value, content, richness, excitement, curating, instantaneousness, utility, relevance, participation, editing and design. The rules of the game have changed from push media to pull media. There is a change of attitude in media consumption and people no longer want pre-structured communications and irrelevant content. They are seeking to be instantly in tune with the media landscape because they are now the architects of their own news and information. With online tools like RSS feeds, newswire adoptions, newsletter subscriptions and instant messaging on platforms like Twitter, consumers are choosing what they want to see and hear, the frequency and increasingly the mode. This movement began with the Internet and has been made popular by the social web through blogs, social networks, user forums and chat rooms. It is spreading across the landscapes of TV, radio and magazines as attested by the popularity of the TV fast-forwarding service which allows adverts to be skipped and pre-recording services that enable people to record only the programs they're interested in to watch later. The TV is being referred to as an "old-fashioned idiot box" by an entire generation that has realized that they can very well live without television. On the print media front, the state is even more alarming. Printed newspapers are considered as "so yesterday" and the subscription rates of major international newspapers is dropping at an average of 7 percent annually. Apart from hotels, corporate bodies and associations, the newspaper circulation circuit is fast disappearing. Their publishers are resorting to TV adverts in a bid to re-awaken some nostalgia in the reading public. At the same time, newspapers have gone mainstream online, providing mostly free content and, in some cases, interactivity while depending on a business model of revenue generation through advertisements. Magazines, although still maintaining higher levels of circulation, are following the footsteps of newspapers in the online offering by providing free content in a bid to attract millions of readers and, subsequently, paid advertisements. On the radio front, the picture is not much better. This has become a communication medium that is accessed passively rather than actively, meaning when we are in the shower, in the kitchen, in the car, in the library or just to have some distant background sound.

This may sound like the end of the media sector but it need not be so. What is currently taking place in different societies on different levels is that consumers have simply changed and have moved on from an old behavioral pattern to a new mode of functioning that serves their self-interests and satisfies them better. The media world is therefore required to fine-tune its approaches to better suit the current environment, particularly in the context of luxury communications, which has a strong factor of emotional connection and a high level of expectations.

In the luxury domain, the mode of communications is quite peculiar and its struggle with the transition from the old system of talking "to" the public to the new way of talking "with" clients is apparent. Prior to the Internet, magazines and newspapers dominated luxury communications with television not so far behind. Luxury brands basically had one approach to media communications – disseminate information in a one-way form; and two choices of channels – print media and television. It was a question of the brands with the biggest budgets getting their ads on the most visible magazine pages and the best TV spots. The smaller brands with lesser budgets were left wallowing in the land of the unknown, swallowed by the giants while depending on word-of-mouth and the occasional luck of some editorial feature in a magazine that happened to have some free space. But the Internet has come along and changed everything, literally. The Internet is not TV and it doesn't function in the same way as print media either. It has brought with it a new set of rules that emphasize developing relationships directly with clients through one-to-one dialogue that doesn't depend on magazines and other one-way communications channels. It is about targeted relationship marketing, in other words talking to the right people in the right way with the relevant message that will capture and retain their attention. And their attention and interest is retained through dialogue and exchanges.

The web is a conversation and luxury clients are already involved in dialogues on different topics among themselves through blogs and the various user communities. They are also increasingly adopting these means as their source of indirect media communications. It's about time that luxury brands became a part of this world of exchanges. The Internet has provided a tremendous opportunity to reach wealthy clients in niche segments directly with targeted messages that cost a fraction of what big-budget advertising costs. Instead of buying a 30-second TV spot for a luxury fragrance advert that is run at prime time between the adverts of Head & Shoulders dandruff shampoo and cat food, why not address the hundreds of thousands of fragrance enthusiasts that are cyber-residents of online communities like the Blog Beauty Addict or the social networks, A Small World and Diamond Lounge? The web has shaped consumers' mind-sets in such a way that they view communications messages which they have not chosen as irrelevant "interruption", therefore they are likely to skip that fragrance advert to go to the rest-room or grab a coffee or something – and there goes your $100,000! Luxury communications used to be all about capturing attention. Unfortunately, those days are gone. The question that should be asked today is "How can we retain attention and make our brand remain relevant?" The answer is to develop and apply a feasible e-communications strategy that is relevant for today's client.

Communicating online is simply delivering useful content to the right audience at the right time through the relevant platforms in a manner that encourages exchanges, dialogue, sharing and inclusion. For an industry that derives a large chunk of its appeal and desirability from maintaining a certain distance from clients, it may seem that this is bad news. But the approach of inclusion in luxury online communications doesn't mean changing the appearance and message of the brand. It begins with identifying the right audience online and understanding the language they speak before talking to them in a way to which they will listen and respond. And when they respond, they are likely to bring along other parties because luxury clients no longer exist in isolation online but in interconnected communities with the clout to influence thousands of others at a time.

Giving way to the new communications style

For as long as the luxury business has existed, the relationship with the public through communications has been driven by creating a strong desire through projecting a fantasy world around luxury brands. This presentation, mostly using appealing images that could feature anything from models donning the delectable products to the products themselves presented in sumptuous environs, is aimed at telling the person looking at the images that their lives would have more meaning if they bought into this world. A peek into any luxury magazine could reveal a model in a provocative pose clutching her Dior handbag to her chest, a delicious looking couple dressed in Burberry trenches established in the English mews, a parade of young fashionistas on the streets of New York donning the most appealing clothes and accessories from Donna Karan, not to speak of the occasional image of a star like Beyoncé stepping out of private jets and limousines dressed in Jimmy Choo.

This is luxury brand image projection in its natural form and the choice of media ranges from magazines, newspapers and television, in that order. This mode of communications has been about advertising in a one-way "presentation" style with the underlying message of "Here we are – the great brand that you should be dreaming about. We don't know who you are and we couldn't care less because you will always lust after us anyway." These adverts are exclusively about appealing to the masses although targeted at the wealthy in the belief that they will let loose their pockets and head for the stores afterwards. It has also been about reinforcing the brand image and injecting more appeal and desire around the brand through advertizing campaigns that are based on creativity, albeit with a short lifespan.

luxury online

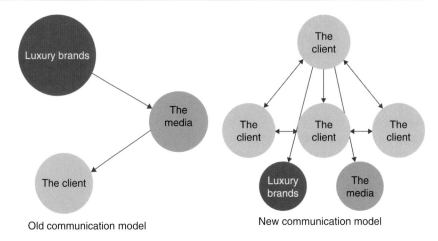

Old communication model

New communication model

Figure 5.2 *The model of communications and relations between luxury brands and clients has been radically changed with the arrival of the Internet. In the past, luxury brands had a supreme position in disseminating information to clients through the media, which also exercised immense control on the information flow from the brands to the clients. Today, this model is being challenged by the client, who has taken the reins of communications and relegated the brands and the media to the bottom of the communications mix while increasing the collective influence that consumers have on one another*

This communications style has, in fact, not been about communicating but has been more about "presenting" and "imposing" "luxury brands" images and messages to the public. This formula has always worked and the brands have been on a party roll with this easy communications style until now.

The landscape of luxury communications is changing and consumers are driving this change through the influence they are obtaining from the Internet (see Figure 5.2). For a start, luxury adverts are no longer viewed the same way as in the past. Seasonal adverts are no longer awaited with the anticipation of the past. The Internet has broken the boundaries by allowing the public access to view luxury adverts even before they appear in the magazines. Worse still, consumers now have the audacity to judge the relevance of the adverts and further accept or reject them following discussions and exchanges in online forums that involve thousands of people at a time. Most of this happens before the adverts appear on the paid pages of the magazines! When Louis Vuitton took on Madonna for its 2009 spring/summer advertisement campaign, the news was all over cyberspace even before the photo shoot took place in Los Angeles. Following the shootings, the images appeared online and blogs, social networks and user forums were all too pleased to pass it around, dissect it, discuss it and pronounce their judgment months before they showed up in *Vogue*, *Vanity Fair*, *In Style* and other print media. By the time the images appeared in the magazines, it was no longer news and consumers had moved on to other issues. The impact? Well your guess is as good as mine – *Vogue et al.* pocketed $millions in revenues from the advert, Madonna made a cool couple of millions if we're to believe the press and Louis Vuitton was left to be judged by opinionated bloggers and their comments and exchanges were accessible to the whole world. The impact of the print media has been challenged by the Internet and will never be the same. The control of the one-way media is finished, even in luxury. We are now in a new era and it's time for luxury brands to respond to this change.

Today's luxury client no longer waits for luxury adverts to come to them in the form of a glossy magazine spread or a bottom strip in a page-fold newspaper. They don't seek to be "interrupted" by endless fragrance advertisements while watching their favorite TV programs either. They are no longer enticed by one-way information dissemination, no matter how beautiful the model is and how delectable the products are. They don't want to be talked "to" but they seek to be talked "with". One side of the story simply doesn't work anymore. The new reality of luxury communications is that the social web has given rise to an emphasis on dialogue among consumers. A large chunk of this dialogue is centered on luxury brands and they are initiated and carried forward by those passionate about the brands and about luxury. Some of them passionately love certain brands while others passionately detest other brands for reasons that they do not hesitate to divulge. At the same time, they're pleased to display their affection and disaffection for luxury brands and products and, in the process, influence thousands of others – in some cases, millions. These conversations mostly have nothing to do with the glossy advertisements that luxury brands spend millions on but the participants have chosen dialogue on web platforms as their own mode of communication about luxury brands. This means that the stronger the dialogue, the stronger the brand – although it doesn't necessarily mean the more positively the brand is portrayed.

The way people access luxury has also changed and this is reflected in the way that consumers expect to view and interpret luxury messages through communications. Because people are now shopping online as well as offline and are increasingly being influenced by the social web in their brand and product choices, they have transferred a new attitude to the way they interpret communication messages from brands. This change of outlook is also reflected in the way they expect to receive luxury communications. They're no longer interested in receiving mass email newsletters that feature products that don't interest them while glorifying the brands; neither does it interest them to be inundated by pop-ups and banner advertisements all over the Internet. They also no longer seek the validation of luxury brands from the information on the brands' own websites but, instead, from their fellow consumers. Their new approach has to do with delivering them rich and relevant content in a format that reassures them that the brand is as much interested in their feedback as in their action through adopting the brand.

And in the meantime, what have luxury brands been doing online apart from repeating the usual mantra, "We're developing our online communications strategy which will soon be ready for us to share it with you"? The reality is that the majority of luxury brands have been somewhat lost as to the strategies to apply in executing effective online communications programs. Due to the Internet being significantly different from the structured and somewhat impositional style of offline media with rules and codes that are transferred from the media companies to the luxury brands and subsequently to the consumers, there still lacks a consensus in online luxury communications. The most widely adopted means remains banner and pop-up advertisements on media websites, as an extended arm of the print glossies. Several brands like Louis Vuitton, Yves Saint Laurent and Stella McCartney have recently boarded the Twitter plane, while others like Sonia Rykiel have taken the blogging path and several others have jumped on the Facebook bandwagon. The existing landscape is so because for a long time luxury brands have been led to believe that people access and relate to online media the same way that they relate to print media. They have been sold the online version of the cost per thousand (CPM) model through the number of clicks/unique visitors/page views per week/month/edition and all manner of other quantifying of the colossal fees charged for online advertisements. None of these, however, point to real information on user profiles, behaviors, attitudes and interests but indicate quantitative measurements that serve little purpose in evaluating the advert's effectiveness. This is hardly enough for justifying online luxury ads expenditure and measuring their returns. Online luxury communications is not about the same mass advertising approach that is applied offline. It is about targeted and direct communications powered by content that has a dual aspect of feedback, exchanges and collaborations between the consumers and the brands and among consumers themselves. It is time to throw the old style of relating with luxury clients out of the window. There is no point in continuing to resist the reality that the Internet has brought a form of direct access to luxury clients, which never existed before.

This is not to say that the mainstream media has lost its relevance or that it will die off eventually. The media will remain pertinent in luxury communications and will continue to play an important role in brand awareness generation and brand image reinforcement. Luxury brands will still get noticed in *Vogue* and *Elle* and new brands featured in *L'Officiel* and *In Style* will still get attention from the public, but this is no longer enough. The formula has extended from these vital aspects to include more efficient ways of reaching clients and potential segments in a direct manner online. And the irony is that the luxury brands that do a good job of telling their stories through the relevant online platforms and getting it heard by the right people and buzzed about online will also attract the attention of the mainstream media who will generate more news about it. When Christian Dior created a one-off advertisement teaser on the virtual world Second Life for its jewelry collection, it led to wide mainstream media coverage including a top spot on YouTube, although the advertisement was initially targeted at the Second Life community. In the same way, when Viktor & Rolf held on online-only fashion show in 2008, where everyone was invited, the ensuing buzz marketing surpassed the publicity many brands have generated in a lifetime.

Changing old habits is no easy feat, particularly in an area that has been governed by strict rules for professionals who know no other ways. But the rules have changed and therefore new habits have to be formed, period. How luxury brands can inculcate this two-way communications culture and infuse an element of intimacy in relating with clients without sacrificing the aura of the brand is where the challenge lies. And, of course, we shouldn't forget the all too important relationship with media companies. Here are a few points and tips which in my opinion will point the brands in the right direction:

1. The web is not an advertising medium and you do not need a media agency to buy online communications. The Internet is a multi-channel that serves more than advertisements. And media buyers are only there to confuse you.

2. Today's online communications is about building trust, educating clients in the right way, inculcating the luxury culture and fostering inclusion and exchanges. The days of one-way brand information imposition are gone forever. If you're still stuck in this way of thinking, please wake up for your own good.

3. The luxury client currently has the clout to accept or reject brand messages and influence thousands of people along the way. Communicating with the client online is no longer about attracting attention, but capturing and retaining interest through rich content presented in a format that encourages exchanges and interaction.

4. Communications is not the same as advertisements; neither is it the same as branding. Today's communications is a two-way exchange that is far from the one-way information dissemination that shows how desirable a brand is through an impersonal and cold glossy magazine page.

5. Advertisements should no longer be designed to appeal to the masses but to the relevant target audience.

6. Understand that you can measure the effectiveness of your online advertisements very well – something that is nearly impossible offline.

7. Understand that the same media buying approach that you have been using forever for mainstream media does not apply online. Forget about quantitative justifications online and focus on qualitative characteristics. The best websites to advertise on are not necessarily those that attract the highest web clicks, page hits or unique visitors. This is a trick. You have to know the user profiles, their attitudes, interests, behavior and expectations. You need to go beyond the surface and dig deep.

8. PR and marketing are no longer separate disciplines run by different people with a dissimilar set of agendas. The Internet has blurred the

lines between all communications activities and this requires a new approach.

9. Don't believe the people that tell you that the only way to generate awareness for your brand is through paid banner adverts on media websites. Unless you're Louis Vuitton or Cartier, you should go out there and tell your story, but make sure it is authentic and that you are doing so in a genuine and transparent manner. Even Louis Vuitton and Cartier are keeping clients is the loop through new media channels like Twitter.

10. Use your brand's website as the first point of communication with the public. Communication doesn't only mean adverts and newsletters but also comprises the sensory elements that are disseminated from your website's content and atmosphere.

11. Understand that multi-media has blurred the lines between print, television, videos and the Internet. Each communications channel crosses over to the other. The online and offline media worlds no longer exist in parallel but have arrived at converging points at several intervals. Can you name one TV station that doesn't have a news website? Or one magazine that hasn't yet created a blog?

12. Do not be tempted to start a blog or a community just because competitors are doing so or because your PR agency is telling you that it is the way to go. If you have to create a club or community, there should be a strategic purpose behind it and it should be executed on the right platform and without any errors, and not on Facebook only because it is easy.

13. Keep your eyes everywhere and your ears wide open. Subscribe to online magazines, monitor blogs, join social networks, activate news feeds, adopt instant messaging, subscribe to newletters, accept press releases and do whatever else that is needed to keep up with the web. For goodness sake do not fold your arms, say that the web is not suited to your brand – and then look down at your shoes when you hear me saying at a conference that luxury PR and communications people who don't subscribe to online luxury magazines are still stuck in the eighteenth century.

14. Finally, it is not more important for your advertisement agency to win awards than for you to win clients. Seriously, which side are you on and who are you working for?

The magazine madness

If you take a copy of any fashion or lifestyle magazine, say *Vogue*, *Elle* or *Vanity Fair* and flip through it, you'll get the impression that if we were to put numbers to it, 70 percent of the content would be advertisements and 20 percent would be editorial information on the products and services of the brands featured in the adverts and the other 10 percent on anything from horoscopes to features of the contributors and photo spreads of models wearing, wait a second, pieces from the brands whose adverts you have already seen. Even the letter from the editor, which is supposed to tell the reader what to expect from the magazine, is often hidden somewhere in the middle pages, suppressed by the mammoth presence of the adverts that surround it. The magazine world has sold its soul to advertisement revenues. The established luxury brands pay sums that run into hundreds of thousands of dollars for a one-page advert in a fashion magazine and emerging brands are left to sweat it to get some editorial coverage "because they are not advertisers", even if they have a great concept, fantastic products, excellent service and a strong message. This is how it had always been until the Internet came along and is on the verge of breaking all the rules ferociously guarded by media companies.

Even in the early days of the Internet, there was a flurry to reproduce the same model when mainstream print media companies introduced websites that reproduced the same news in their print versions. With online advertisement expenditure at a constant rise ($32 billion in 2007 and projected to reach $160 billion by 2012), media companies looked to retain a large chunk of this cake. This was the period when media companies, with ample support from PR firms and media buyers, sought to produce a web version of the CPM (cost per thousand) quantitative measurement that is supposed to justify an expenditure of $100,000 per page of advert. This basically followed the "counting" system that print media loves to dish out and on the web it translated to the numbers of daily, weekly and monthly visitors as well as the number of clicks per page, number of unique visitors per month, the number of newsletter subscribers and all kinds of numbers that could be waved in the faces of luxury executives to both tantalize and confuse them. But the social web (or web 2.0) came along and changed everything.

Online media now has its own mechanism and doesn't function in the way that print and television operates. The social web has provided a voice to the people and a platform for any brand (both big and small) to tell their story to an audience that increasingly listens, provides feedback and spreads the message. The Internet provides equal access and space to everyone who wants to be visible. The time has come for the exclusive media club that promoted the use of all sorts of jargon and obedience to strict rules, including excluding outsiders, to re-write its rules. The arrival of citizen journalists in the form of bloggers, and the opinionated consumer who doesn't hesitate to speak up in favor of or against luxury brands, has crushed the media barriers. Today, blogs like Style Bubble, Beauty Addict, Bagsnob.com and Purseblog.com have more community members and page views than the average mainstream magazine's website. The average fashion enthusiast now has the tools and competence to develop an interactive and highly aesthetic website with content that could compete with the *Vogues*, *Elles* and *Glamours* of the publishing world. The web has made everyone a publisher – that is, everyone who has a compelling story and understands how to tell it. The online media provides no exclusivity to any parties. It is with the same click of mouse that we can exit any media website that disappoints and it doesn't cost consumers anything. A new era has arrived in online communications that is challenging the "magazine madness" of luxury brands. It is no longer a question of banners, buttons, pop-ups, pop-downs, pre-roll, post-roll, leader-boards and skyscrapers. The tune of the music has changed and the current keywords are trust, content, engagement and accountability.

True, there is no reason why luxury brands should stop advertising on the websites of mainstream magazines but this should be done if the websites offer real value in terms of what online clients are seeking and not because they are called xmagazine.com. It is also not enough to say that an online magazine has a blog (hey, my 12-year-old nephew also has a blog) or that it has a community with several forums (which mostly lack real activity, to be honest). The reality, however, is that in most regions and languages it is not the online versions of the mainstream magazines that are pulling the weight of attracting and engaging the most readers within the online luxury client segment. Those that are providing real and valuable content and engagement have arisen from an array of independent pure-play online magazines led by the pioneering LuxuryCulture.com (Figure 5.3), which is so far the only online luxury magazine that can claim real "high gloss" status. Others are all responding to the needs of today's online luxury clients much more than mainstream media websites – for example, Prestigium.com, which has built a dedicated readership; LuxuryBriefing.com (Figure 5.3), which provides access exclusively to its subscribers; Luxe-Mag.com, which remains of the few online platforms focusing on informing and exchanging on luxury business issues; JC Report, which has grown from an independent editorial to an interactive online resource; as well as the recently launched Iconic Chic (Figure 5.3), which has also integrated an active blog. These should naturally be in the list of destinations for online luxury advertisements.

The magazine sector is still in its infancy online. Most of the mainstream magazines went online without a visible and feasible strategy and, as a result, started off by offering content for free with the anticipation of compensation in advert revenues. This approach by magazines and news publications was literally a death wish, except the moves made by the likes of the *Financial Times* and *WWD*, which were wise enough to restrict access through understanding that online clients will pay for valuable content and could ignore invaluable content even if it were free. The Internet has, however, evolved beyond information dissemination and the web is not about advertising. Placing an advert for Cartier's *Balon bleue* watch on magazine and newspaper websites can be considered as low in engagement if the audience is wrong. Also, in the past, luxury adverts used to be highly anticipated and speculated before they were released in the press. This was part of the buzz and excitement around the brand. Today they are previewed, screened, discussed and

let's talk: communicating the luxury message online

Figure 5.3 *Independent online luxury magazines like LuxuryCulture.com, LuxuryBriefing.com and IconicChic.com are setting the precedence in luxury online communications through features and tools that attract and engage readers focused on real and valuable content. Unlike Internet versions of the mainstream magazines, which still exhibit elements of corporate influence and agenda, the independent online magazines are considered as trustworthy and able to provide honest, objective and impartial news and content in a transparent manner*

approved or thrashed on the Internet months before they appear in the media. There are no surprises anymore.

There are however signs that the traditional media sector is beginning to understand the requirements of online communications, particularly for luxury products and services. Magazines like Style.com, Elle.com and GQ.com are now using interactive tools like videos, animations and congregation platforms like blogs, instant messaging on the likes of Twitter and communities to do better journalism. There are also signs that they are beginning to engage their audiences in their content by providing opportunities to comment, share, tag, forward and save articles. This move has been initiated by entrepreneurial journalists or those that may be considered as citizen journalists who are finding profitable niches online. Websites like the *New York Times* and the *International Herald Tribune* have launched video sections with short features and interviews as well as an online magazine, while the *Wall Street Journal* has created an online version of its *WSJ* lifestyle magazine and the *FT*'s *How to Spend It* now exists in a fully interactive online version that can also be downloaded. The competition is becoming rife and the crossover between magazines, newspapers and videos is becoming more common. Video interviews are no longer only for the likes of TV channels like The Luxury Channel and Luxe.TV but may now be found on any website that has an element of news including blogs and also e-retail websites.

At the same time, luxury brands are also starting to grasp the value of the conversations, interactivity, dialogue, sharing and trust that is built on media websites and their role in the choice of product placements. The main issue for the two parties remains, however, the best approach to milk the opportunity of the Internet and to optimize the brand's presence online while saving costs and generating higher revenues. And, of course, also enable the media companies to remain profitable.

Will print magazines disappear? Not likely, but their role will change as the Internet continues to provide direct access to news and information through several sources, including citizen journalists. Another factor that will affect print media is the evolution of the usage and assimilation of information in different luxury markets. In regions like the Middle East and South America where wealthy women spend entire days poring over *Vogue* and *Elle*, magazines will remain strong because these women need the magazine references to be informed for their shopping trips to London and Paris in the summer. However, does a NYC girl or a Parisian wait for *Vogue* to be released on the news stand before being informed of the latest trends? I don't think so. They may also skip *Vogue*'s website and go directly to their beloved blogs and social networks to dialogue with real people whose input and opinions they trust to be honest and independent of corporate influences.

One of the crucial issues in online communications remains that of trust. As online consumers evolve, they are learning to decipher and detect

Case Analysis 5.1
Creating a new culture for online communications through LuxuryCulture.com

In 2004, the landscape of luxury online communications was shoddy. Luxury brands were presented in the virtual world in a manner that brought their status as luxury into question. Brands' own websites generally followed two directions; either featuring a mix of excessive images presented in an over-zealous manner and flash animations clamouring to out-do one another; or the websites were presented in such a way that they could have passed for virtual extensions of factory outlets where damaged or left-over merchandise was dumped at the end of every season, with all manners of tricks to induce customers to "buy now". This gloomy online landscape, which lacked the rich experience that luxury brands work so hard to provide in the real world, ensured lacklustre relations between brands and clients online: until Yaffa Assouline decided to do something about it by creating LuxuryCulture.com (Figure 5.4). Everyone told her that it was impossible to reproduce the essence of luxury on the Internet and that the nature of the Internet meant that luxury would have to bend its rules in order to be online. Fortunately she didn't listen to them.

LuxuryCulture.com has opened a new chapter not only in the way luxury communicates online, but also in the way it presents itself in the virtual world. Yaffa Assouline challenged herself by going against all the so-called website design rules and in the process created a series of "firsts". LuxuryCulture.com was the first website to uphold and express the true essence of luxury and remains the only high-gloss luxury magazine online demonstrating true sophistication. It is the first virtual platform to demonstrate a striking balance between design, navigation, content and frequency. It is the first online magazine that promotes the universe of luxury worldwide while educating new luxury clients in emerging markets and reinforcing the luxury philosophy in established markets. It is the only destination that congregates both enthusiastic newcomers and connoisseurs of luxury in a pleasant online universe. LuxuryCulture.com is the embodiment of luxury in its true, pure and original form. Through its unique virtual atmosphere, it entices the mind, it speaks to the emotions, it pleases the senses.

Through its simple and sleek design, clear navigation, rich content and a unique atmosphere, the website brings news and views of the luxury lifestyle and art de vivre to the world through uncovering the worlds of fashion, art, accessories, architecture, design, concierge, hotels, spas, beauty, jewelry, timepieces, perfumery, private travel and every aspect of the beautiful life.

With over one million monthly visitors, over three million monthly page views and global readers from over 141 countries ranging from high net-worth individuals, international travelers, global citizens, city dwellers, country nomads, luxury professionals, new luxury clients and luxury connoisseurs, LuxuryCulture.com has become a reference for both individual and collective identities in the luxury world.

Presenting luxury as a culture and philosophy rather than as a product and commodity, the website has built a strong brand image based on elegance and refinement; an enriching and valuable content showing the luxury heritage with products and services with a strong and clear identity.

As a luxury brand that was created to demonstrate the culture of luxury using the virtual environment as its channel, LuxuryCulture.com today represents the pursuit of perfection as a religion and sharing it as a mission.

It remains the leading reference for the way luxury should present itself online. Luxury brands, take note.

Figure 5.4 *Before LuxuryCulture.com came along in 2004, online luxury communications were drab, uninteresting and presented in a bland manner. The general feeling at this time was that the Internet was unsuitable for luxury communications and that it was impossible to evoke luxury online. LuxuryCulture.com decided to challenge this by inventing horizontal navigation – which is now copied by everyone – and adopting simplicity while avoiding being trapped in building a magazine based on HTML for web referencing but, rather, introducing an all-flash website that has built its reputation on the exceptional experience that it provides*

websites that are transparent and those that have a hidden agenda. They now consider certain blogs as trustworthy as any traditional media, if not more. But both the luxury brands and media brands are learning as well.

Strategies and approaches for online communications

E-communication is the oxygen of luxury online presence: there is no question about it. Information about luxury brands, luxury products, services, retail, life-style and business circulate in cyberspace on millions of websites and through thousands of discussion threads. Every luxury brand ought to communicate online and demonstrate commitment to presenting the brand's image through a strong message, beginning from the brand's website. I still hear some luxury brands say that the Internet is not their "thing". They often say that a luxury brand needs to build its reputation in the real world and, if they do this suc-cessfully, the Internet "people" will speak about them. Well, the reality is that millions of other parties are doing the communicating for the brands that have refused to communicate online and in some cases the information distributed could be erroneous and negative to the detriment of the brand.

Luxury brands no longer control their online presence and the informa-tion that is passed about their affairs among cyber-residents. This is one of the realities of the current evolution of the Internet that we have to live with. The control of information flow between and among online consumers now lies in the hands of the consumers. With the abundant nature of information found online, people no longer wait for luxury news to come to them in the form of advertisements or unwanted pop-ups; they bring the news and information that they desire to themselves when they want it and increasingly in the format in which they want it. Through tools like RSS feed, newswire and simple permalinks and instant messaging services like Twitter, people are able to filter news and their sources while blocking those that they deem as interruption, including the luxury adverts and websites. So what is a luxury brand to do in this scenario?

Well for a start, there should be an integrated online communications strategy that complements and supports the offline communications plan, without replicating it. I have heard too many luxury brands repeat the mantra "We do not communicate with the public apart from through adverts". What a pity to rely on the often cold and distant "glossy" format of communications – which, by the way, is not real communications because it remains one-way. The new way to go is interactive communications and one of the most useful platforms for doing so is the Internet. But first, luxury brands must understand its potential, its scope, its mechanisms and its approaches. In order to arrive at this point, a real e-culture needs to be created and inculcated across the communications and press divisions of luxury companies.

Following this is the choice criteria for the destinations of the online communications. How does a luxury brand identify and select the most suitable website for its communications plan? Is every website that presents itself as "luxury" relevant for luxury advertisements? Are there websites where certain products are most suitable or should each brand advertise only the latest collection? What about editorial features of the products and services? What factors are the most important in choosing the suitable websites for communications? Is it the nature of the website? The fact that it is an independent magazine, an online version of a mainstream magazine, a blog, a social network? Or does it have to do with the design, aesthetics and visual appeal of the website? The monthly page views and traffic flow? The number of clicks per day? The number of unique visitors per week? Or the number of returning visitors per month? How does a luxury brand justify the online advert expenditure? And how can its effectiveness be measured? The questions linked to the choice criteria and techniques of luxury e-communications are endless.

My viewpoint is that to communicate effectively online, a luxury brand must first have an objective for communicating, then determine the message that it is trying to pass, understand its target audience online, identify the websites where they congregate or they visit, visualize the format of message that they will most likely respond to, evaluate the quality (not only the quantitative) of the website and its level of engagement and relevance for the target consumer group, and design a communications program that could be effectively executed to attain the objectives.

Figure 5.5 *Luxury online communication is required to be original, unique and coherent in style, content and message with offline message communications. Coherence, however, doesn't mean repetition but respecting the brand's heritage, identity and core DNA. Louis Vuitton, which has applied a 'shock therapy' approach to brand communications by alternating between visually stimulating seasonal adverts with models and celebrities and intellectually stimulating institutional adverts with international personalities, has maintained a level of coherence and has created a certain expectation and anticipation around the brand. The approaches to the execution of online communications campaigns are, however, significantly different from those of offline media campaigns and require a strategic online communications plan*

Figure 5.5   *(Continued)*

Then there is the format and content of the communication itself. Key decisions to be made in this regard are linked to the type of communications such as advertisements, exclusive events, private online shows, competitions and raffles and so on. The common practice in online luxury communications has been to simply "copy" what competitors are doing and reproduce the same format, changing only the logos and images. The Internet makes this level of sameness and the lack of creativity and originality more visible. Copying the advertisement concepts of other brands discredits a luxury brand, particularly online where transparency and openness rules and people are able to spot this in seconds. Worse still, they discuss it in blogs and mock the brands, which the whole world can also see.

Luxury advertisement concepts ought to be original, whether they are emphasizing products, styles, models, storylines, places, message or heritage, there has to be a form of uniqueness that is directly connected with the brand's essence and DNA. There should also be a strong element of coherence in image projection that stays true to the brand's identity. The advertisement visuals should be such that if one were to remove the logo on the image, it would still be apparent who the brand is. This is not to say that the brand should repeat the same advertisement concept or style every season and year after year. It simply means that whatever approaches a brand takes in advertisements have to respond to the set of expectations that the brand has created around itself among consumers. For example, Versace is known as a brand that courts Hollywood stars and this is reflected in the advertisements, communications and collections that have been coherent in projecting its "celebrity" undertones over the years. Louis Vuitton (Figure 5.5), on the other hand, has introduced a shock therapy in communications by alternating between seasonal advertisement concepts featuring a mix of models and celebrities, and intellectually stimulating advert concepts themed "core values" that reflect the brand's heritage in travel goods, with the goal of mixing excitement with stability. Patek Philippe, on the other hand, has been the message of heritage and family tradition to maintain coherence in its advertisements and build credibility and trust around the brand. Yves Saint Laurent and Bottega Veneta are other brands that have been coherent in using creative communications approaches both online and offline.

Communicating online is, however, not only a question of placing banner advertisements on media websites; neither is it about reproducing the advertisement images on the brand's website. It includes an integrated approach to creative and cross-communication that is both interactive and engaging. Whether it is through online advertisements, email newsletters, exclusive events and competitions, the real online consumer has to be reached, informed through rich content and be affiliated with through providing for two-way exchanges.

Communicating through the luxury brand's own website

Have you ever been to a luxury brand's website and, while navigating the pages, for a moment you thought you were on another brand's website because of visual triggers that reminded you of some other brand? Perhaps it was just a phrase, an image, a design, color, layout, products, offer or even a subconscious element that you can't quite pinpoint but which led to some form of memory recall of another brand. If you're familiar with browsing luxury websites or websites that are associated with the luxury industry like media and retail websites, you will likely have had this experience. If you haven't, you'll most likely do so in the near future, that is if things remain as they are. The general luxury landscape in cyberspace is one that is flavored with a high level of similarity that borders on sameness of website design and communications. This general lack of originality has led several brands to adopt a similar colour scheme that is quite different from their brands' signature colours (think black) and a communications concept that is incoherent with everything else that the brand stands for. The luxury website is a communications tool and an important point of departure for the brand's relations with clients. It should therefore embody all the elements that make the brand distinctive, different and original. There is no point having a black background on your website if your brand hasn't adopted black as a core signature colour reflected across its visual codes and triggers such as packaging and store concept. It also doesn't serve the brand any purpose to copy other brands' newsletter formats and send it to a database that includes clients who subscribe to several brands' newsletters, including the one that was copied.

Communicating through a luxury brand's website goes beyond the newsletter and "News and Events" section of the website. Luxury website communications follows two forms: tangible and intangible, or if you prefer, conscious and subconscious. The tangible or conscious communication includes using a combination of text, sound, movement and visual elements like images, colors, shapes, lines, layouts and videos to send a message to the online client. This message could range from brand image reinforcement, information about new products, stores, channels of distribution, collaborations and social responsibility and other initiatives that the brand is involved in. These should be presented in an interactive and engaging manner that allows the client to participate in the experience of receiving the messages. A simple provision to zoom on images or to download and print them injects a higher level of interactivity than static images. The website provides an opportunity to project a strong visual identity using the brand's well-defined visual codes. This has nothing to do with advertisements but should be designed and projected to complement the brand's advertisements. It should also be presented in such a way that if we were to remove the brand's name or logo, it would still be apparent which brand the visuals represent. Some luxury brands like Bottega Veneta and Van Cleef & Arpels have developed strong visual codes that combine several elements to project a strong message through their websites. The content should also include updated and relevant information designed to capture the attention of clients and engage them through enlivening the website. In February 2009, luxury lingerie brand Agent Provocateur created a spicy video featuring a couple and themed around its lingerie and Valentine's day, which was uploaded on its website. This video not only attracted substantial traffic to the brand's website but also made the rounds in the entire cyberspace and may now be found on websites like DailyMotion and YouTube. Viktor & Rolf also successfully executed a communications coup by hosting the first online-only runway show for its 2009 spring–summer collection, which was shown on its website in October 2008. This "open" show where everyone was invited not only generated unprecedented online and offline press but also contributed towards establishing Viktor & Rolf as a bold and innovative brand.

The content as a means of communication on a luxury website should be extensive and uniform. I often notice a lack of consistent information on the different language sections of the same website, which shouldn't be so. This, of course, is frustrating for luxury clients. This approach should also be applied to online magazines and clubs owned by luxury brands like Maserati since the attraction is not only based on rich and extensive content, but also on homogeneous content. The Maserati or Bentley owner in Moscow would also wish to know what the brand is telling his fellow owner in Miami.

The second aspect of website communication is the intangible or sub-conscious communication which enables message transmission through influencing the mind by triggering responses to the senses of sight, sound, touch, smell and taste. This form of sensory communication requires the use of a specific set of elements to influence the website's atmosphere and reproduce the desired feelings in people. These feelings are linked back to the brand image and validated by the tangible communication elements (this topic has been covered extensively in the previous chapter, in case you skipped it).

For online communications to be effective on a luxury brand's website, the tangible and intangible elements must be balanced. This means ensuring that the visual elements validate the sensory elements and that the sensory elements evoke the visual elements. Achieving this is quite challenging but brands like Bottega Veneta and Van Cleef & Arpels have been able to do so from their websites. These elements should, of course, be presented in a form that encourages inclusion and interactivity.

How can a luxury brand foster collaboration through its own website? Does it mean allowing consumers to discuss the brand freely and have an input in its design and offerings. Should luxury websites allow user-generated content to be uploaded on the website? Should luxury brands foster this closeness or will it break the intriguing distance that ever enchants the client to the brand? The keyword is creating an environment that projects inclusion and collaboration which ensures that the client feels that they are recognized and that they count while allowing the brands to have control over the web-site content. Prada managed to achieve this through its "Trembled Blossoms" animation competition where a competition was held for the soundtrack. Everyone was invited to join and the brand selected the best soundtrack, which was announced and subsequently used by the brand. Boucheron also communicated a collaborative spirit though its "Precious Moments" initia-tive online, where people were invited to inscribe a recap of their precious moments on a wall on the brand's website. These initiatives ensure that a brand builds its reputation and credibility; enhances the "desire" factor and creates a more intimate bond with clients.

Case Analysis 5.2
Using the online runway as a communications tool

Every season the runway shows of major luxury fashion brands congregate industry insiders, celebrities and the fashion press around the world for a series of exclusive events. These seasons define trends, drive purchases, reinforce identities and ensure the execution of the retail strategies for the subsequent periods. It is also a time when new talents are identified, contacts reinforced and business networking optimized. For these reasons, the notion of an Internet-only fashion show was unthinkable until Victor & Rolf brought this into question by presenting its 2009 spring–summer collection exclusively online (Figure 5.6).

Viktor & Rolf opted for an innovative short movie filmed in a setting that represents the brand's virtual salon accessible on their website. The show presented only one mannequin, Shalom Harlow, who modeled the entire collection on a podium resembling a real-life runway. The show was presented against the background of supporting music and special effects that enabled the multiple appearances of the model on the podium through multiple footages, which resulted in a high visual impact. In addition, emphasis was made on the angles from which the models were viewed, which may not have been possible in a real-life show. At the end of the show, the model appears once again in multiple footages while making a bow as the designers look on from above.

This fashion show was initially accessible to an invited online audience who were also able to view the backstage fittings, hair styling and make-up, before access was given to the public. Realizing this virtual runway show took fifty technicians working in filming and production, in addition to the artists and creative assistants involved in the styling.

The show generated substantial buzz and editorial credits for its originality and visual effects and, as you may imagine, enabled the brand to attain a level of worldwide communications that could not have been possible before the arrival of the Internet.

Figure 5.6 *Online communications through a luxury brand's website requires creative and cross-marketing measures that feature a high element of interactivity and participation. Viktor & Rolf exhibited an innovative and creative flair in communications by hosting the first Internet-only runway show on its website in 2008. This original and interactivity communications not only excites and entertains, but also enables buzz marketing both online and offline.*

Communicating through online media websites

If you take a quick tour of the websites of mainstream luxury and fashion media, you will likely notice how similar their looks and features are. The majority have the same sections: trends, style, people, beauty, love, celebrities, culture, events, videos, blogs, forums and communities and, in some cases, look books and style books, in addition to the usual sections: news, contact, advertising and home page sections. Upon clicking on any of the sections, you will likely come upon pages with minimal text and tons of images presented in flash and static structured forms that often appear in frames including feature tools for zoom, slide-shows and control for the videos. A look at the newspaper websites will show that they mostly have the same design concept, navigational menu structures and text and image layouts. Even the logos of most are placed at the same spot, and the banner and pop-up adverts appear in the same way. On the independent online magazine cover, the first thing you may notice is that they all have black as the main color theme leading to a uniform array of black backgrounds. Luxury websites, for their own part, are doing their best to demonstrate the current craze for horizontal navigation by adopting it on nearly every page, even on websites that have a concept that isn't necessarily enhanced by this feature. Just as luxury brands went through the fever of black color themes and backgrounds a few years ago, today everybody seems to be on the bandwagon of horizontal navigation.

Why this level of sameness, you may wonder? One factor that could explain this is that there is still no real consensus in luxury online communications and all the parties involved in communicating online have been trying to carve a niche for themselves in the quest to understand the dimensions and mechanics of online communications.

The online media world is vast. To begin with, there are the mainstream media websites that have nearly all developed Internet versions where we currently find luxury adverts in the form of banners, pop-ups and videos. Then there are the independent online media websites like the e-zines Luxury Culture, Luxury Design and Luxe-Mag and the TV platforms Luxury Channel and Luxe.TV, which mostly have rich editorial content but in which luxury adverts are seldom featured. And then there are the social media websites like YouTube, Facebook and Style Bubble which are powered by citizen journalists and cyber-residents and feature luxury content in different forms ranging from adverts placed by both the brands and consumers to videos uploaded by the brands and those created by consumers themselves to content generated by the public through discussions and debates.

The power behind these different forms of media is shared by the four principal parties in the online communications world – the luxury brands, the mainstream media, the independent media and the clients. None of these is more powerful online than the others. The Internet provides them with uniform space and access to send their message. In the early days of the Internet starting from the late nineties, the luxury brands wielded the power in online communications, first through their websites and subsequently through their ability to negotiate online media coverage with the mainstream press. Then online communications went through a period of power-shift from the brands to the mainstream media from the early noughties, when the latter created a formula for selling advert space through measurement techniques like website traffic, page clicks, advert clicks, unique visitors, subscribers and so on and managed to sell this to luxury brands who, for their part, were most grateful to have the all important numbers for justifying online advertisement expenditure and demonstrating potential returns on this investment. The scenario changed once again with the arrival of independent Internet-only magazines like LuxuryCulture.com, Prestigium.com, Luxe-Mag.com, Billionaire500.com and FashionMag.com. These magazines brought a turning point to online communications through presenting websites that feature more than text and images but are created to represent everything that luxury stands for – creativity, originality, purity, elegance, richness and splendor without being overtly extravagant. These e-zines have succeeded in using the right doses of all the luxury website creation ingredients – design, content, usability, atmosphere and content – to create what has been described as "the first online glossy" in the case of LuxuryCulture.com and "the ultimate luxury resource" in the case of Prestigium.com. They also brought an awakening to mainstream media websites on the requirements of representing luxury online as attested by their popularity and success. Since then, the looks of media websites have been undergoing a constant face-lift and the landscape of online communications a continuous evolution.

Today, with the advent of the social web, the picture is again different. The arrival of citizen journalists who are behind millions of blogs, social networks, user forums and all manners of user-to-user communities, the face of luxury online communications has changed. In contrast to the former system, where information about luxury brands was diffused directly by the brands through their own websites and those of the media, the social web generates its own brand information through its users and moderators. It is a medium that is more receptive of messages originating from independent parties than those from corporate or intermediary parties. This movement has influenced online consumers to assert their power and has led to a scenario where the public now decides which of these parties are the most credible.

In addition, the lines that separate all the forms of media websites from shopping websites is also blurring. Today, e-retailers like MyWardrobe.com have integrated magazines and video series within the e-boutique to entertain shoppers while they buy and to foster higher expenditure. On the other hand, e-zines like LuxuryDesign.com and LuxuryCulture.com have also incorporated retail elements on their websites featuring products sold on e-retail websites to which the readers are redirected upon clicking on the desired product, while Luxe-Mag.com has facilitated participation and community through its discussion platform. On the mainstream media front, video series and TV series are now common on the online versions of mainstream magazines and newspapers like the *New York Times* and *Architectural Digest,* the while the websites of TV stations like, BBC and CNN now feature blogs, podcasts and communities. Each of these is now sharing the same space online and trying to grab the attention of the same public.

The consequence is that today there is much confusion regarding the best approach to take in representing luxury online and, until now, the criteria for choosing media websites for luxury communications remains unclear. The current scenario has also led luxury brands to view pure-play independent online magazines as irrelevant for communications programs. There is also the question of justifying the advertisement expenditure on magazines that are believed not to wield the same level of power and influence on luxury consumers as mainstream magazines such as the likes of *Vogue*, *InStyle* and *GQ*. The reality, however, is that mainstream magazines are no more influential on luxury clients online than independent online magazines or social media websites for that matter. Online consumers seek interactivity and engagement and any website that is able to provide this in high doses will count in their destinations. They are also more website loyal than brand loyal and will therefore stick to the media websites that "deliver" irrespective of the category they belong to.

So what is a luxury brand to do in this scenario? How can all these news and information media be assessed and filtered in order to identify those most suitable for each luxury brand?

The answer lies in crafting an integrated online communications strategy featuring multi-media channel programs and effective measurements for the returns of advertisements (see Figure 5.7). This is what the Internet now represents. It is not enough for luxury brands to upload the videos of the latest advert campaign on YouTube or DailyMotion; neither is it sufficient to create excitement through exclusive online fashion shows on e-retail websites. While these schemes contribute to the reinforcement of the brand's online communications, they ought to form part of a feasible strategy that will guide the brand's online presence and ensure continuous progressive returns (see Figure 5.8). The strategy should feature an assessment of the multi-media platforms, the features on each media website irrespective of the form, the profiles of users, the reach and traffic flow of the regular readers (not unique visitors, please), the level of engagement and participation of the websites and how much the website respects the luxury codes and represents the spirit of luxury.

The social web communications dilemma

I often hear people say that luxury brands should create blogs and integrate online communities to their websites. Several of them also say that luxury brands ought to have official clubs and forums on social networks like Facebook and MySpace. Other parties have said that luxury brands have no business on the social web. They claim that the social web is for the masses

let's talk: communicating the luxury message online

Figure 5.7 *The online media world currently features websites that are applying multi-media elements in an integrated form and subsequently blurring the lines that separate mainstream media websites, pure-play e-zines and social media websites. It is now common to find video series on mainstream websites; editorial articles on TV websites like Luxe.TV and The Luxury Channel; discussion platforms on e-zines like Luxe-Mag.com; TV series on e-zines like Billionaire500.com*

and associating luxury with it would render it banal. I have always agreed that brands shouldn't have blogs particularly integrated on their websites but I have also always disagreed that luxury brands should ignore the social web. They simply cannot afford to do so. Luxury brands should not only observe and monitor the social web but, should also participate in the social web in an intelligent way that befits the brands (this has been addressed in Chapter 4, if you skipped it). This participation also includes communicating through the various social media.

As has been illustrated throughout this book, the social web and the social media have brought about a new and different way of relating with consumers. The period where luxury brands handed "down" information to clients is fast

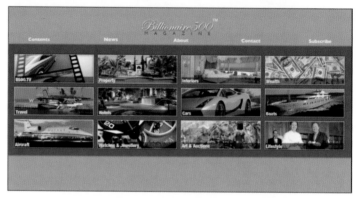

Figure 5.7 *(Continued)*

receding into the past. Luxury clients no longer want to be "talked to"; they want to be 'conversed with', even as they maintain control of the conversation. Whether luxury brands make themselves available for these conversations or not, the clients are conversing among themselves and influencing thousands of fellow consumers through these conversations. They are active, passionate and independent, and their autonomous viewpoints have led to trust and reliability. They are not only providing glowing recommendations of brands that they love, but are also ferociously condemning brands that they are disappointed with. The latter could have substantial consequences on the perception and long-term value of a luxury brand.

The social web's key features are recognition, inclusion, dialogue and collaboration and its keywords are community, trust and sharing, through conversations, opinions and content which all go a long way in influencing consumers and shaping their perceptions. Dialogue and exchanges between consumers and luxury brands on the social web doesn't mean that the brands should open up the online communications channel in a public forum and allow people to play with their image in an uncontrolled manner. It also doesn't mean that luxury brands should invite the public to give their viewpoints on

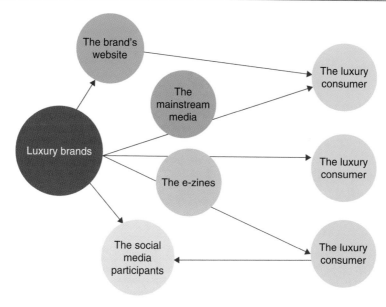

Figure 5.8 *The current online communications model requires luxury brands to reach the client through several channels and intermediaries. This presents a real opportunity for developing intimate relations with clients but is also beset with challenges*

how the products or services or advertising campaigns should be designed. Communicating through the social web should be on the level of the overall brand experience. It should be about enabling the cyber-residents on the social web to feel an intimate link with the brand. The key is to reproduce the same feeling in them as the social web. They have to feel that they are recognized, that they are respected, that their opinion is important and that they count for the brand. For example, organizing a competition where people can submit ideas generated for a specific project for a luxury brand could be a first step. Also, providing access to brand discovery events through the social media could be another means as well as using the social web for product previews and teaser campaigns. This is the first step to inclusion and participation and will generate buzz around the brand. People on the social web are there to talk and they will talk irrespective of whether a luxury brand is communicating with them or not. It is better for the brand to give them something good to talk about.

Luxury brands can also use the social web to inform and educate the public on key issues that affect the brands and the industry in general, as well as the steps that the brands are taking to address these. For example, several brands like Ermenegildo Zegna and Louis Vuitton (Figure 5.9) have been at the forefront of promoting sustainable practices and environmental protection causes in the luxury sector and the social web could be a means to reinforce these initiatives through raising the level of awareness among the

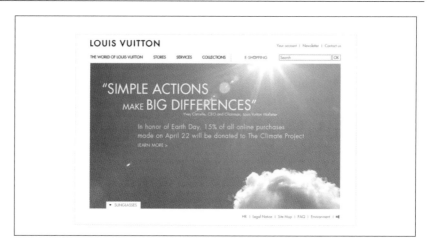

Figure 5.9 *The online social media present an opportunity for brands like Louis Vuitton and Ermenegildo Zegna, which are active in environmental causes, sustainable practices and the fight against counterfeiting, to communicate their initiatives while educating the public and enhancing social consciousness on these issues*

public. Brands like Burberry, Dior and Gucci, which are active in the combat against counterfeiting, could also use the social web as a platform for educating the public on the dangers of this trade and its adverse effects on the wider society. Educating the social community is also as important as informing the bloggers and moderators of social websites for a stronger joint message. Instead of reproducing advert videos and slogans on YouTube, why not create a thematic high-impact video with a strong message on an issue such as counterfeiting or fair trade? Or even broadcast this message in the "Luxury Leaders" section of The Luxury Channel's website?

The social web is also an effective means of tracking consumer perceptions of luxury brands and their mind-set evolution. Monitoring conversations and exchanges among people on the social web, as well as generating discussions on subjects that form key customer concerns and general thoughts about key issues of the luxury business such as the future of luxury and the meaning of luxury, could also be rewarding to brands.

In addition, communicating on the social web can be through viral marketing or word-of-mouse. Viral word-of-mouse is the key to spreading brand awareness but since this has no control by the brand, the brands have to address the "spreaders" through clear and appealing messages. Viral marketing, above all else, should be content-based and not based only on the transfer of images, flash animations and videos. The recipient should be able to go further by a click or a link. Viral marketing doesn't have to reach millions of people for it to be effective as long as it reaches the right people who will likely take the action desired by the brand, that is become customers and also invite other "likelies" to be customers. In fact, viral marketing in luxury works best in small and controlled online environments and communities such as A Small World where you know who the message is reaching.

To approach the social media strategically, luxury brands must be vigilant and monitor conversations about themselves as well as their competitors. It is the responsibility of the brand to correct misinformed impressions, to influence perceptions positively without manipulation and control, and to ensure that the overall brand essence is projected. On the social media, the voice of the people is heard loudly and clearly and if luxury brands play their cards right, their voices could become joint forces.

Doing it well and avoiding the don'ts

Luxury online communications shouldn't be the long-winded and complex process that it currently is today; neither should it follow a strict and structured format in strategy definition and execution. Communicating online is not about structural guidelines; neither does it follow cyclical patterns. It is, rather, a question of identifying the online media platforms that are the most suitable for every brand and its audience while monitoring the evolution of the Internet and the invention of new media platforms. As luxury brands adjust to the vast offerings and requirements of online media, the following tips, I believe, will be useful in developing and executing effective media programs:

Don'ts

1. Don't lose the dialogue with consumers. The web today is a conversation and consumers no longer want to be talked to but to be conversed with.
2. Don't believe the people that tell you that the luxury brand's website is not a communications channel.
3. Don't underestimate the power of indirect communications that are sent through the multiple mixed messages on a brand's website or those of its associated websites. In other words, don't be like the luxury brands that have cheapened their image over time through desperate messages – "Sales", "Up to 70% off", "Last Chance on Free Delivery", "Buy Now or Never" and all kinds of unappealing subject lines that totally throw luxury consumers off.
4. Don't think that you need an online media buyer to help you understand how to communicate online. It's a farce!
5. Don't underestimate the power and influence of independent e-zines and the social media. They have the clout to congregate millions of people at a time and these people are more website loyal than brand loyal.
6. Don't forget that luxury e-communications are comprised in the Internet, which is also accessible through mobile phones. In other words, make provision for mobile communications in your digital marketing plan.

7. Don't forget the keywords of online communications in the current context – transparency, interactivity, engagement, inclusion, collaboration, trust and respect.

Do's

1. Do make creativity and originality your watchwords. It no longer pays to have a website that looks like the twin sites of competitors.
2. Do have an online communications plan with an integrated feasible strategy.
3. Do follow the evolution of the Internet and technology and stay ahead of the game in order to refine the online communications program accordingly. If you can't keep up, ensure that you keep the people in the know close to you.
4. Do understand the positive influence of the newsletter. This all too powerful communications means, which has been in use since the days of *The Boston News-Letter* from 1704, still retains its clout. Even the first Swedish newspaper first published in 1645 still exists today as an online newsletter. That should tell us something.
5. Do provide extensive information and a coherent message in all markets. Don't be deterred by the specificities of certain markets like the cyber-policing in China. Several countries like South Korea and Japan have a high density of cyber-residents who are able to detect information marginalization.
6. Do integrate online communications with offline messages. These two channels are not mutually exclusive but should function as complementary channels. The great thing about instant messaging social websites like Twitter is that you can integrate what you're doing offline in your messages.
7. Do understand that the effective online communications should feature richness in content, engagement through interactivity and intimacy in collaboration.
8. Do have a plan for evaluating the effectiveness of online media communications.
9. Do monitor consumer-generated media (CGM) regarding your brand and understand that this includes not only unsolicited adverts on YouTube, but also positive feedback or negative complaints. If you don't know how, you can adopt applications like the Digilant that enable this tracking in multiple tracking in multiple languages in real time!
10. Do have a plan for a high frequency of online media communications.
11. Do apply creative and cross-marketing initiatives in communications, including features on editorial retailing websites. And please also do keep in mind that this list is not a magic success formula, because you need to keep up with the evolution of technology.

Chapter 6
The art of selling the dream online

> "Selling Luxury is a dream and there should be no nightmare issues lurking behind that dream."
>
> —quoted from *Luxury Considered*

At a recent dinner, I had the privilege of being in the company of several luxury professionals, including the creative director of a major luxury brand, the CEO of a PR firm, a fashion journalist and the owner of a Parisian atelier that creates exceptional luxury accessories for major international luxury brands. Among the interesting conversations of the evening was talk about a newly launched luxury leathergoods and accessories brand and its approaches to communications and public relations. When someone asked about the brand's store location in Paris and around the world, I replied that the brand had a global online store on its website, from where its collections are retailed and shipped worldwide, in addition to plans of a store-in-store opening at Galeries Lafayette and other department stores in Europe. My highly respected table companion then said pointedly, "Yes I know that they have the Internet and all that stuff but I meant to know where the *real* store is located." I was quite lost as to what to answer to this comment because he had obviously not understood me. The implication of this statement is that the e-boutique of the brand in question was not considered as a "real" retail location. This unfortunately remains the stance of several luxury brands despite the likes of Louis Vuitton, Tiffany's and Gucci which continue to generate substantial revenue online.

Until 2004, several luxury brands had not given any thought to retailing online. The mantra of most of the French luxury brands at this time was that the e-retail (I prefer this term to e-commerce, which sounds too mass-market) of luxury goods was marketing *à l'américaine,* which basically means an orientation towards selling at all costs, even if it means price discounting and bombarding clients with offers ranging from free shipping, 24-hour deliveries and all manners of promotions that would lead the client to "buy now". The general perception was that this approach was for mass-market products that didn't require an enhanced shopping experience or an elevated brand image to retail. Most luxury brands were also conscious of the fact that the Internet was still perceived at this time to be a channel distribution for price-discounted products and a destination for people looking for "deals" and "steals", some of which included counterfeit or fake luxury products.

It took the likes of Louis Vuitton, which first introduced e-retail in the US through e-Luxury.com in 2002 and subsequently in France and other European destinations from 2005, and Gucci, which first started retailing its products online in the US in the same year to change this. These brands were considered by other luxury brands as profit-driven "sell-outs" that were in the process of damaging their brand values by placing their products in a mass-market channel. Other US high-end brands like Coach and Tiffany's which had developed e-retail were also considered as brands that would never be able to claim true luxury status. It was during this time that two of the most reputable French luxury brands bluntly confirmed to me that they would never put their products to be sold online. Their stance has, however, changed since, fortunately for them, although they're both apparently playing the catch-up game and performing poorly online.

In the meantime wealthy consumers were buying everything online, from flight tickets to entertainment, electronics, furniture and home equipment. They were also using the Internet for a vast range of services including banking, trading, investments, academic learning and even e-health programs. Even as this wealthy group transferred their e-retail expectations from the collective experiences that they had garnered from purchasing other types of products online, several luxury brands turned their eyes away from e-retail. The media also accentuated this aversion to e-retail. It was not until 2006 and 2007 that major magazines like *Vogue*, *Elle* and *Glamour* considered making the inclusion of the website addresses of their featured brands a requirement for the editorials and adverts – the telephone number of the store was more important, although one can easily obtain the telephone number and address from the website!

However, the landscape has changed and, with the evolution of technology, the luxury sector and those that are affiliated with it have come to realize that the Internet is an essential complementary channel to offline retailing. Also, the advancement of security and payment systems has contributed to dispelling the fears related to protecting personal information and exposure to fake goods. The advent of the social web and exclusive online communities that congregate the wealthy have also contributed to overcoming the idea that the retail of authentic luxury goods can only take place when clients are able to "touch and feel" the products in their hands.

It is no longer news that the wealthy are all online and make up a substantial segment of the cyber-resident population. From New York to San Francisco, Mexico, Sydney, Tokyo, Beijing, Hong Kong, Mumbai, London, Paris, Milan and Berlin, the world's wealthy are hooked online. Recent statistics from Forrester Research indicate that in 2008 the British expenditure online for selected retail items including clothing was 40.5 billion euros, in Germany the figure was 27.5 billion euros and is expected to reach 27.9 billion euros in France in a few years. Already in France, clothing ranks first on the list of the most frequently purchased item online ahead of travel and cultural items such as books and DVDs. In the US over $2 billion was generated from online purchases of sensory goods like clothing, jewelry and accessories by mid-2008. As we know, the luxury segment is well represented in this area. In Europe, 150 million people make online purchases on a regular basis and these clients are generally more satisfied with their online purchases than the experiences they have in retail stores. Mainstream e-retailers like France's Carrefour and the US's Wal Mart have developed seamless online shopping experiences through applications that enable the storage of shopping baskets with pre-selected and pre-packaged products that enable clients to make purchases with only two clicks. Others like Office Depot have streamlined online shopping through a multi-segment search tool that enables products to be found quickly and dropped into shopping baskets instantly. These experiences are being transferred as expectations from these mainstream websites to luxury e-shopping by the same clients. The clients also expect to have an exceptional shopping experience on luxury websites in an enhanced online environment as a result of the high factor of emotions and sensory responses in the relationship between luxury brands and luxury clients.

Although the issue of selling luxury products online has been visited and revisited several times in the last decade, the question of the suitability of luxury products and services for e-retail continues to be raised. This stance is no longer relevant. Luxury is currently sold online and there is no reason why integrated e-retail shouldn't be a complementary channel or even the sole channel for a luxury brand's distribution. It is surprising that this issue, which was discussed, debated, reviewed and concluded several years ago, is still being evoked today. With the significant advancement of digital technology, interactive media, client management applications and sales and logistics support systems in the last decade, there is no longer any justification as to why luxury shouldn't be sold online. The Internet has evolved through four main phases (see Chapter 1), each of them providing an opportunity for assessment, understanding and development of an integrated e-business strategy that includes e-retail and other dimensions. Those that have been left behind in this wave of progression, of course, will continue to resort to the same ten-year-old excuses that luxury is incompatible with the Internet and that luxury brands devalue their brand equity by being online. If well crafted and executed, a luxury brand's e-business strategy has the potential to make the Internet the platform that could propel the brand to a status of global brand awareness, brand image reinforcement and client acquisition and retention – all for the fraction of the cost offline.

Of course it is challenging to sell luxury online and this is not in doubt. This challenge is also enormous and requires expertise in understanding the key strategic issues linked to both the front office (e-boutique development, e-merchandizing, e-branding, product selection, sales services etc.) and the back office (e-logistics, transport and deliveries, after-sales services, security and privacy, sales support systems, content management applications, interactive media software and systems and so on). In addition, several intricacies of the retail of luxury goods also need to be evaluated, as the luxury shopping experience is different from the usual shopping experience.

Due to the sensory nature of luxury products, their purchase entails high aesthetic appreciation using all the human senses. This often requires physical store presence, which is absent in the online environment. The Internet also lacks the exclusive and prestigious locations where the luxury stores are situated. As soon as luxury products are placed in an e-boutique, they become available for and accessible to all. In addition, there is also the issue of the "virtual" interpretation of a luxury brand's identity as well as the reproduction of a luxurious atmosphere that befits the brand online; and, of course, dealing with the bridge of "mass" and "status" online. These concerns are justified and thankfully can be overcome with the aid of digital tools and a strategic mind-set attuned to accepting and embracing the inverted approach of dealing with luxury online.

Luxury e-retail is not about having a beautiful and colorful website or an e-boutique that shows the latest flash technology. Neither is it about copying the websites of competitors and changing the background colors and logo. It is also not about price discounting or plastering the websites with "buy now pay later", "free shipping now", "two for the price of one now", "clearance sale now" and all manner of "now" that scream "I am desperate to make a sale" and reduce the website to the status of an Ali Baba store while sending jitters down the spines of luxury clients (apart from those coming for a one-off experience).

It is about a completely integrated process that includes strategy formulation, planning, execution, monitoring and improvement. It is about taking advantage of tools that provide an opportunity for optimizing retail in an elevated form and relating with clients in a more intimate way. It is about creating a shopping environment that appeals to all the senses and results in a "wow" experience which will get clients hooked on the website and returning for more. It is about exceeding sales expectations and substantially reducing operational costs. It is about understanding that e-retail has changed the way luxury is viewed, accessed and interacted with and that this phenomenon is permanent. Just as there is no going back to the days before the Internet, there is no more going back to the days before luxury became available to be bought online. Luxury e-retail is about being in tune with the twenty-first century business environment. It is simply about being as smart as wealthy clients who have all taken up the Internet in unexpected ways.

The 360° e-retail experience

Luxury is no longer viewed the way it used to be in the past since the Internet came along. Luxury websites can now be accessed by anyone who desires and at any time. Information about luxury products is diffused online as soon as they hit the stores and in some cases even before they arrive at the stores. The images and videos of the runway shows of luxury fashion brands often show up on blogs and e-communities before media websites or the official websites of the brands. Luxury hotels are no longer able to keep the styling and decorations of their master suites secret as the images are now divulged rampantly on travel and hospitality blogs and communities. Luxury brand information, corporate practices and manufacturing methods can now easily be found online as well as special projects and collaborations with artists and designers. It is also now common to find multiple "making of" videos of luxury advertisements and the like on websites such as YouTube and DailyMotion. This is a reality that we must accept and deal with. It is, however, not the end of the world and it doesn't mean that luxury is now available to everyone and that luxury has been "democratized", as several parties are prone to claiming. Although you may be able to access all the information you want about Boucheron online, you still need to have 23,000 euros in your pocket to be able to purchase the Caméléon ring.

The accessibility of luxury information online is actually a positive rather than a negative factor. It provides the brand with a unique opportunity to set its website and e-boutique apart from the countless websites that provide information on the brand like blogs, social networks, third party e-retail websites and other user-to-user communities. Let's say that you're looking for information about the Cartier Love collection and you type this keyword in Google, you're most likely to have a list of thousands of website references that feature information, images, discussions and exchanges on the Love collection. If you decide to skip Cartier's official website but opt to read independent commentary and reviews from blogs and user forums, you are likely to discover people's opinions, judgments, validations, recommendations, ratings and perhaps also rejection of the collection. If you decide, however, to visit the official website of Cartier afterwards and find yourself immersed in a highly pleasing online environment with a luxurious atmosphere that promises to lead to a magical shopping experience, you are likely immediately to draw the difference between Cartier's website and the others. But if your experience on Cartier's website is the same as the one you had on the blogs and social networks, then we could say that Cartier has a problem with optimizing its website experience (which, by the way, is not the case as I write).

The easy access of luxury websites coupled with the progression of online experiences towards "shared" rather than "individual" experiences has led to a different way of interacting with the Internet and with luxury. Online consumers no longer rely on information from corporate websites; neither do they

Figure 6.1   *Cartier is one of the few luxury brands that has clearly distinguished the web experience of its Love Collection website from that of the numerous websites where the collection is featured. While blogs such as Luxist provide a forum for presenting, discussing and sharing information on the collection, the web experience presented in the community spirit of blogs is expected to be enhanced and validated by the brand's official website*

accept the information diffused by media websites without question. Their interaction with luxury brands online is now on a 360° basis in which they obtain, review, discuss and share information on brands before making a purchase decision. This information flow is no longer vertical (from the brand to the client) but is now lateral (from clients to fellow clients) and increasingly excludes the brands. Luxury clients are not only seeking interaction with those who share their tastes and passions, but also input and feedback about brands. Their point of reference is shifting from the information provided by the luxury brands to the perceptions that their fellow consumers have of the brands. Several among them no longer even bother to validate the commentary of their fellow clients regarding brands as there is currently a strong factor of trust among consumers online. They have understood that they have the power of expression through blogs, a strong position through their ability to congregate and independence in their choices and channel of receiving messages. As a result, luxury clients have become more demanding and currently seek a complete 360° shopping experience with either brands or luxury e-retailers. This mode of communication and functioning in turn contributes to how they view luxury brands both individually and collectively. It means that online shoppers expect to find the same level of engagement that they have on the social websites from luxury websites. They expect to be engaged through interactive features as well as be given the possibility to engage others through conversations, feedback and exchanges that come in the form of conversing, sharing, recommending, companion shopping, creating, customizing, trying and collaborating and so on.

As I write, the majority of existing luxury e-stores remains in a basic almost pre-formatted style that seems to have a single motto of "sameness". While clients' expectations have evolved from one-dimensional to a more complete e-shopping experience, most luxury e-stores have remained static. This is true for both products and services. Since the majority of luxury brands do not currently offer this enhanced e-shopping experience, clients are seeking and obtaining it from independent e-retailers who are continuously integrating features to take advantage of this gap. One such e-retailer, MyWardrobe.com, has applied the features that cater to this demanding consumer base seeking support from fellow buyers and style experts while shopping online. The website offers not only products and shopping services, but has also incorporated features such as a blog, a TV channel, videos, discussion boards and exclusive private sales events for a 360° interaction. The website goes a step further by featuring designer interviews on its integrated online television "My TV" and posting topics linked to its merchandise and website sections on its integrated blog. Shoppers may comment on the blog postings or TV features and may also click within the blog to "shop the look" directly from the e-boutique section of the website. All of these features enhance the feeling of "belonging" and "community" and assure the shopper that they are part of a group whose opinions count.

The 360° web experience can be summed up in six different steps and any luxury e-retailer that ignores these steps risks losing out on attracting the attention of the online shopper, who is already prone to being distracted by the hyperactivity of cyberspace. These steps promote interactivity, engagement, dialogue, collaboration, sensory appeal and sharing. It is no longer a question of accessing a website, finding an appealing product and clicking to purchase it. It is now about online companion shopping and sharing a collective shopping experience. It is about applying tools to "watch", "comment", "share", "send", "tag" and "suggest" before finally arriving at "purchase". The days of relying on endless videos, flash animations and slide-shows of images to entice clients to purchase items online are over. Online consumers' expectations have shifted gear and when they arrive on a luxury website, they expect to feel that they are in the right environment and that the website enables them to amass influence. This evolution, which follows the steps listed below, and is illustrated in Figure 6.2, will be continuous and the brands that capitalize on utilizing its tools to attract clients online will be able to develop intimate relations in the short term.

- Step one: website access
- Step two: watch
- Step three: blog and post
- Step four: browse
- Step five: select and purchase
- Step six: share

Step one : website

Step two : watch

Step three : blog and post

Figure 6.2 *MyWardrobe.com is one of the independent luxury e-retailers that have understood that luxury clients have evolved from the one-dimensional experience to wanting a more complete e-shopping experience. They currently seek the level of engagement that enables interacting, conversing, sharing, recommending, companion shopping, creating, customizing, trying and collaborating while shopping. Through its integrated TV channel, blog, interactive shopping features such as advice and tips, My Wardrobe provides a 360° shopping experience that is both memorable and empowering to the client. Luxury brands are currently far from providing this level of integrated offering online*

Step four : browse

Step five : select and

Step six : share

Figure 6.2 *Continued*

Crafting the integrated e-retail strategy

Luxury e-business executives are constantly under pressure from senior management to perform miraculous sales figures online. In the slow economy, which has touched luxury brands in nearly all categories, the Internet is viewed by many as one of the last options to reach sales targets. Its relative cost-effectiveness, coupled with a wider reach and extensive data-capturing capabilities, has suddenly made e-retail appealing to luxury brands. Some of the luxury brands that used their e-boutiques as dumping grounds for products that were under-performing in the stores are suddenly expanding their range online. Those that sniffed at e-retail a few years ago are currently trying to optimize sales returns online. The tables have been turned and with this frenzy has come a certain disorientation. Most of the confusion stems from the fact that the majority of the brands that are suddenly trying to sell online are doing so without an integrated e-business strategy that would guide the online practices to assure desired sales levels. The direction taken by these brands is one of creating an online store without first establishing a solid e-presence backed up by a strategy. The result is often disappointment with the low activity in the e-store and the consequence is under-performance.

To be able to sell luxury online successfully, brands need first to craft an e-business strategy and plan that will develop all aspects of their web presence before integrating e-retail in this mix. Luxury e-business strategy doesn't have to begin with e-retail. In reality, defining a brand's web presence through e-retail could have adverse results. It can lead to avoidable mistakes and making the brand unappealing due to a lack of prior online presence and experience. The ideal approach of e-retail would be to follow a systematic process of launching an appealing website with rich and interactive content and incorporating the e-boutique within this environment. Online luxury shopping should be an enriching and pleasurable experience in which clients are engaged with every aspect of the website and not only the e-boutique. Engaging clients means ensuring that the website features the appropriate elements in its interface with the front office and that these are supported by the required systems in the back office. The web elements that are suitable for one luxury website are not necessarily those that are the best for another. Just as each luxury brand is distinctive in its DNA, the websites and e-boutiques should represent this distinction by featuring elements that are fitting for each brand.

In addition to front and back office systems decisions, the integrated luxury e-retail strategy follows tactical choices in product selection, pricing approach, countries of distribution, service approaches and channel integration. These aspects are further analyzed in the following steps.

Step one: the location choice

Following the decision to sell online, the first assessment a luxury brand ought to make is that of the markets that the e-retail activity will serve. This choice could range from countries, regions and states, and will subsequently affect linked issues like pricing, currency, warehousing, transport, after-sales and several types of legal issues. Although the Internet is global in reach and the ideal choice would be worldwide distribution, it is not always feasible due to regulations, logistics and complex processes. The choices that a luxury brand makes in terms of distribution should, however, reflect a commitment to expanding the geographical reach in time. Whether a brand begins with single-country or multi-country shipping, there should be a long-term plan to incorporate global shipping through the e-boutique. The Internet is the most cost-effective means of luxury retail and this advantage shouldn't be undermined. Independent e-retailers of luxury products and services have understood this value and are capitalizing on it.

Step two: product selection

The question of identifying the right products within a brand's range to retail online is often raised. In the early period of e-retail, the few brands that were bold enough to venture into e-retail like Armani took the prudent approach of placing a few items within their collections online as a means of market and channel testing. Others like Hermès used their e-boutiques as a retail outlet for the products that under-performed in the stores, tagging them as "gift selections". As these items began to record high sales and the demand levels increased, the brands understood that the Internet had greater potential. The popular viewpoint that the complete range of a brand's product shouldn't be placed online began to be dispelled, although it is yet to be entirely addressed.

The choice of products to sell online should follow the strategic objective of e-retail for the brand. Is the e-store's purpose to generate revenues or to act as a window to the brand and its collections? For example, it is apparent that the e-boutiques of Louis Vuitton and Gucci are for sales revenue generation purposes, which justifies their wide product range at different price points. In the case of Boucheron and Cartier, whose overall price points are significantly higher, the e-store's purpose could be more to diffuse the brand's signature and tantalize the public.

Product selection should also follow the peculiarities linked to shipping and security for each product category. The best-sellers of the brand should also be considered.

Step three: pricing approach

One of the major misconceptions of the Internet in its early years was that it was a channel for price-discounted goods. This assumption has since been clarified but not every luxury brand has got around the idea that the Internet doesn't mean low prices and discounts. Luxury brands are not obliged to take the price-reduction route online and there is no justifiable reason to do so. Brands like Louis Vuitton, which never has price reductions, are applying the same principle online. Luxury brands need to have a coherent pricing approach online and offline to accord with client expectations. Although the ideal pricing approach for a luxury brand online is to avoid rampant discounting in the e-store, when prices are reduced, this should be done in an intelligent and transparent manner that doesn't literally kill the dream that the brand offers.

Step four: e-boutique development

Creating an appealing e-boutique is now a given. Luxury clients no longer expect a basic and "square" online store with, literally, a line-up of beautiful products. Their expectations currently run higher and they are seeking e-boutiques that offer a world of discovery and immersion into a brand's universe. The e-boutique has to engage them in an elevated way and they have to be stimulated by the virtual surroundings. Attaining this effect requires the integration of specific web elements and e-tools in the front-office interface and the back-office support. They are to be completely included within the entity of the website and not only within the e-boutique, in order to complete a total experience. If you take a quick tour of the existing luxury websites with e-boutiques, you are likely to notice a high factor of sameness either in structure or presentation format. This level of similarity can no longer be accepted by clients who expect luxury brands to be distinct in their e-shopping environments.

The tactics for e-boutique development have been further analyzed in the following sections:

Step five: e-tools incorporation

The pleasure derived from visiting an e-boutique is often as a result of the successful application of the web tools that enhance the user experience. These range from product visualization elements such as zoom, 3-D, spin and flip; to e-merchandizing tools like personal avatars and virtual models; e-customization tools like product engravings and co-creation software; as well as client management tools like companion shopping applications and virtual shopping assistants. These elements ensure that the web experience is rich and that clients receive the level of engagement they currently seek.

Step six: service optimization

The Internet provides one of the best opportunities to serve luxury clients in a personal and intimate way. With the access and affordability of data capturing applications that enable the identification of clients and the presentation of their shopping histories, habits and preferences, luxury brands no longer have an excuse for ignoring personalized relations with online clients. Technology has also made it possible for clients to be assisted in the online shopping exercise by providing styling tips, advice on collections and care guides. When luxury brand customers shop online, they expect a level of service that goes beyond one page of FAQs or an automated babbling avatar called Miss Q. They seek to be able to chat instantly with virtual shopping assistants who understand their needs and are able to provide style solutions. They also expect to be able to have an interactive shopping experience in which they will be able to invite others to view collections with them, contribute commentary, make recommendations and perhaps purchase together.

The service expectations also include the provision of several options to instantly connect with a (real) sales representative by phone, email, chat, call-back or voice messaging systems. Enabling extra features for information, entertainment and exchanges will also go a long way to increasing purchase probability. In addition, extended services that include product customization and personalization, web page and web content personalization as well as formatted service preferences will contribute to a memorable shopping experience.

Step seven: back-office support

It is clear that a website is not able to function effectively without a sound support system powered by the appropriate software and applications. Luxury e-stores, which are particularly expected to be content-rich and image-heavy with advanced interactive applications, are particularly required to have the rock-solid back-office systems. Also, the fact that the luxury business doesn't make any provision for errors and that luxury clients are also unforgiving of errors means that luxury e-stores must function seamlessly at all times. The e-boutique is also not expected to close for maintenance at any time since shoppers in different time zones are attracted to the online store around the clock. Fortunately, advanced technology has been able to provide systems that enable the upgrading of a website while still keeping it running.

In addition, applications that power usability and e-merchandizing features like multiple product views, select and zoom, spin and flip, speed of page downloads and navigation should also be in optimal form at all times. Uncompromising back-office support systems also include applications for the protection of personal information such as credit card details as well as addresses, nationalities, dates of birth and so on.

Step eight: client management

Fulfilling and exceeding the expectations of luxury clients online should be the goal of every luxury e-retail website. This can only be achieved if the focus is on ensuring an enhanced shopping experience rather than on selling as much as possible. A positive shopping experience, of course, leads to a higher purchase probability.

Effective client management is far from simple data collection for mass email blasts or the registration of client preferences for endless propositions to "preview" collections. It includes mining the data to extract information that will enable targeted marketing communications and meaningful offers that would likely lead to higher expenditure by the client. Bombarding clients with standard emails containing irrelevant information every two days will serve a brand little purpose, even if the brand has 10 million email addresses in their database.

Step nine: modeling the e-retail

The choice of a model for e-retail is crucial for sales optimization and brand positioning. The ideal e-retail model for a luxury brand is apparently the integration of an e-boutique that features the appropriate product range to meet the objectives of the e-retail. But several questions need to be answered before an e-retail model may be defined: Should the brand display the entire collection in the e-store or only selected products? What criteria should be used in the selection? Should the brand display the prices of all products or not? Should the prices only be discovered at the end of the product discovery journey just before check out? Should the e-store be closed and made available to only a select few by invitation? Should the website be accessed only by logging in with a password? Should the e-store only act as a shopping window without enabling instant shopping but making this available only through contacting the brand by email? Should the products be shipped worldwide or to specific countries?

Several parties have challenged the sale of luxury products online and contend that if a luxury brand is to retail online, the e-store should be closed to the public and made available only to a selected VIP clientele to access by special login and password. Others have claimed that the most suitable model for luxury e-retail is to display the products and their prices to tantalize the public but make purchasing them possible only through the phone or by email. My viewpoint is that these models are not applicable in the current luxury marketplace. There is no strategic reason and justification as to why a luxury brand's e-store or entire website should be closed to the public and made available to only a "happy few". Does the brand ever close its store to the public in the real world? Also, why should a luxury brand restrict shoppers who wish to buy online by not giving them the option of clicking and purchasing? By now, I suppose you'll agree that these viewpoints represent conversations held ten years ago when luxury e-retail was still in the experimental phase. Today, clients have moved on and so should luxury brands.

Step ten: channel integration

The backbone of the luxury business is retail, irrespective of the channel in which it is conducted. Today, the Internet provides an additional complementary and cost-effective means of selling luxury products. This has made it possible to reach a wider market and to increase sales revenues. It has also brought with it several challenges and an increasing phenomenon which luxury brands have to deal with. The key challenge is linked to the integration of every aspect of the two main retail channels (offline and online) across product selections and merchandizing; in-store service and after-sales; client traffic, data collection and management; as well as sales performance, targets and forecasts.

The progressively important phenomenon that a dual retail channel has brought about is that of reconciling client data of an increasingly international clientele. It is now common for a luxury brand to have a client (let's call him John Smith), who shops from the brand's stores at different locations, say London, Milan, New York, Singapore, Paris, Tokyo and Hong Kong as well as online. John may also have triple nationality (which is common these days) and possess two different passports which he may use alternately to identify himself in the stores. He may also own four different credit cards which he could switch during his purchases in the stores and online. John could also own apartments in New York, London and Hong Kong, meaning that he has three addresses which he could also use during his shopping depending on where he is. John spends an average of $1 million annually on luxury items, which means that he's an important client that should be retained at all costs. During a recent visit to Paris, John decides to do some shopping in the same brand's store. At the payment counter he is asked his name and, upon keying it in, the sales representative realizes that there are over two thousand John Smiths in the database. John is asked for his passport number and he gives his British passport number, which he last used to shop in Hong Kong the year before. Upon keying in this number, John's record is retrieved and indicates that he lives in London and spent $75,000 in the last year in the brand's London and Hong Kong stores. He makes his purchase and leaves. What the brand's database failed to capture is that John makes purchases from the brand's e-store on an average of once every two months and that he has spent nearly $1 million on the brand's products shopping online and from the different stores around the world, mainly with his American and Brazilian passports and several credit cards. Since the information against John's records doesn't reflect his high expenditure, the brand fails to include him in the VIP database and therefore do not treat him as one. John remains a gold mine that is yet to be tapped by the brand and could potentially walk away one day without the brand realizing it.

The opportunity of luxury e-retail can only be optimized if the systems that man the store retail are integrated with that of e-retail and interconnected with all the brand's stores around the world. To further tap into the wealth of data amassed through these channels, the brand must foster a spirit of solidarity among the sales ambassadors responsible for the different stores and for Internet sales. It is not uncommon to find sales representatives of different stores and sales channels competing with one another for the same clients and sales turnover. While the spirit of competition encourages store results, this should not be to the detriment of the brand's overall performance.

Channel integration also extends beyond store services to include aspects of the after-sales services such as returns, exchanges, refunds and repairs. For example, a product purchased online should easily be returned exchanged offline. Also clients should be able to reserve items in a store from the

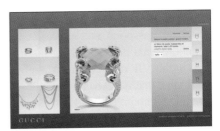

Figure 6.3 *Successful e-retail modeling follows addressing key issues linked to website access, product selection, price display, purchase methods and shopping enablement. Louis Vuitton, which has a wide selection of its product range available for e-retail, has opted to display the prices of its haute joaillerie range without enabling the e-retail of this product category due to the high price point, which exceeds €25,000. Boucheron, on the other hand, displays and retails its entire range online including pieces that cost above €25,000; while Chaumet, which doesn't have an e-store, has refrained from both e-retail and price display. Gucci, on the other hand, whose jewelry range is retailed at a slightly lower price-point than the other brands, enables the e-shopping of this category and other product ranges. e-Retail models ought to reflect a luxury brand's online positioning as well as integrate the online channel with the offline retail*

e-boutique and also book store appointments through the website. These services may sound quite obvious for a luxury brand but, apart from De Beers, which provides a store appointment booking service from its website, not many luxury brands offer a two-way client service package from the Internet.

Creating the luxury e-boutique

In February 2009, Valentino held a champagne cocktail reception at its *rue de Faubourg Saint Honoré* store in Paris, inviting not only loyal clients but any self-professed Valentino fan in the general public. Bally followed in the same social gathering spirit a few weeks later, this time expanding the reception to include a brunch and drinks that lasted well into the evening at its *Boulevard des Capucines* store. Meanwhile across the pond in London, Selfridges was offering clients psychic help in the shape of "professional intuitive" style advice, while Browns introduced a free shoe-repair service at its newly launched shoe boutique on Brooke Street, and Liberty offered craft classes. In Milan, luxury stores were enthusiastically whispering the offer of out-of-hours shopping services, chauffeur-driven cars, house calls by personal shoppers, style advice and all manner of concierge services. Prada decided to take the frenzy further by inviting fashion industry personalities including Carine Roitfeld and Alex White to dress its store windows in Paris, New York, London and Milan. All of these initiatives point towards one thing – service and excitement. This is not to say that luxury retailers previously lacked service offerings, but the current slow economy has re-ignited the kind of creativity that targets the pocket through surprises, excitement, entertainment and involvement. All these aim to provide an elevated service that spells higher value for the client, which goes beyond pretty products. Luxury retail has suddenly become about offering clients the emotional connection that they seek with the brands and lifting their spirits in an environment that is wrought with recognition, respect and service. The latter is currently challenging "location, location, location" as the most important mantra in luxury retail. Luxury retail has also become less about giving more of the same thing and more about an enhanced shopping experience and service. It has become less about placing the store "above" the client and more about including the client "in" the store. Luxury retail has, in short, become about optimizing sales and reinforcing brand positioning through service, service and more service.

The surprising reality is that the level of attention currently being paid to service is lacking in doses online. Even as e-retail is becoming commonplace in the luxury arena, brands continue to give little attention to offering online shoppers the kind of tantalizing services that abound in retail stores. Although the Internet renders a luxury brand more visible and exposed to both clients and admirers, the general state of luxury e-stores remains unimpressive in comparison with the brands' offline presence. As highlighted at the beginning of this chapter, the impression one gets after a quick tour of luxury e-stores is that there remains a relatively low commitment level to retailing luxury products in enhanced online environments. Luxury brands generally strive to establish a befitting presence through the physical stores but the same brands then go online to present their products in tacky websites and e-stores that haven't been given much strategic thought because the e-store design was decided by a web architect or systems developer.

Creating a luxury e-store is challenging. It requires strategic thinking and an outside-the-box approach that should exclude comparisons with competitors' websites but include creating value for shoppers. It should be about taking the client on a journey of immersion and discovery that will eventually lead them to offer their credit card information without regret. This process comprises intricately examining the main elements of the front-office display and the back-office support systems, and fully integrating them in a virtual store that will evoke excitement and strike an emotional chord with the client.

The front office

In 1998, when the general feeling in the luxury industry was that luxury products were unsuitable to be retailed online, the creators of the fashion e-retail website Net-a-porter.com defied this by launching what has since become a pacesetter in luxury e-retail and one of the main online destinations for luxury e-shoppers. Other bold independent e-retailers like BrownsFashion.com, MyWardrobe.com, Vivre.com, CoutureLab.com, 20Ltd.com (Figure 6.4) and Matchesfashion.com have since been established and in nearly all cases have been running successful online businesses. Mainstream luxury retailers including established department stores and independent boutiques have since nearly all set up e-retail activities. Their arrival before several luxury brands on the terrain has meant that they are setting the precedents in luxury e-retail practices and have relegated the brands to the background. They have also evolved alongside luxury clients in their adoption and familiarity with Internet and multi-media technologies, while leaving the luxury brands tootling behind. This explains the reason that the concepts and offerings on luxury e-stores remain a far cry from those of independent boutiques. The brands have concentrated on acquiring the best technology and support systems (thanks to big budgets) albeit creating "sickeningly" similar e-stores. The independent e-retailers, on the other hand, have generally invested in building e-stores that strive to use digital tools to maximize interactivity in shopping environments that are rich in content. Although many of these online stores still lack that optimal 360° total immersion experience that the client is seeking, they are well on their way to achieving this through an integrated approach to front- and back-office elements.

The major front-office interface features required for creating an optimal e-store begin with the design and presentation of the website. The first decision to be made in this regard is the format in which the website is to be presented. Should it be in interactive flash mode, which supports image presentation, or in HTML, which is optimal for text-based referencing on search engines? The tendency has been for luxury e-stores to be flash-based while most of the independent e-stores and department stores have opted for HTML-based websites. The overall design concept and product presentation formats have to be considered in making this decision. In the early days of e-retail, most of the pioneers began by creating online stores in which products were presented in a "square" format within frames. Several e-stores of department stores like Saks Fifth Avenue and Neiman Marcus are still at the "square" stage. The subsequent e-retailers jumped on the bandwagon and the trend of e-boutiques that resembled boxes in a puzzle game began. A few years down the line a few online stores were changed and their new versions featured a black background. Suddenly nearly all luxury online stores caught the "black" bug and the landscape changed to black. Currently, the bug has moved from black to horizontal navigation with the proliferation of e-boutiques with horizontal navigation modes since Luxury Culture introduced this in 2004 and Gucci popularized it from 2005 (Figure 6.4). The appearance and presentation of luxury e-boutiques, however, do not have to be uniform and clients are likely to be put off by the sameness of luxury websites. The same applies to luxury services websites like hotels and resorts as well as other categories ranging from automobiles to private jets. Just as it is crucial to overcome store windows that look the same on major luxury shopping streets around the world, it is also essential to avoid sameness in the design concept of online stores.

Usability and navigation are both essential aspects of the front-office interface. Usability has to do with the ease with which the shopper can move around the e-store, browse the products available, make selections and purchase. It is basically what features have been incorporated in the e-store to make the browsing process more interesting while increasing the chances that the shopper will view the full range and make a purchase. It includes the classification of products according to type, seasons, collections, colors, styles, occasions, trends, events, complements and so on. Some e-retailers like Net-A-Porter have included categories that are powered by interactivity such as videos featuring seasonal trends directly from the runway shows, with commentary, as well as themes presented in a magazine format with flip-through pages on which the shopper may click and buy. Others like BrownsFashion.com have incorporated categories for "stylist's suggestions", "insider's favorites", "hottest new entries" and "labels for less". Matches.com approaches product classification through an editorial format with themes that range from "frills" to "patterns" and "geometry", while Coach has created a clipboard of pre-selected products as its homepage image. Vivre uses a style diary of its founder named "Eva's World" to enhance interactivity and intimacy through providing style tips and product recommendations. Features of the website's products in mainstream fashion magazines are used for product classification

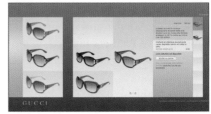

Figure 6.4 *Luxury websites and e-stores have a tendency to sameness in concept and appearance. The level of copy-cat activities in website design is so high that every new feature risks becoming adopted rampantly until the next wave of change arrives. This makes distinction and uniqueness a near impossibility in the looks of luxury e-stores. Two of the pacesetters in adopting the horizontal navigation appearance, LuxuryCulture.com (which invented it) and Gucci.com (which popularized it) have however strived to maintain their originality although the concept has been widely copied. Another luxury website that has succeeded in differentiating itself is the independent e-retailer 20Ltd, whose website has been developed to reflect its unique concept of retailing twenty pieces of twenty exceptional luxury products at any given time*

and to enhance find-ability (see Figure 6.5). These all point to the objective of increasing the probability that the shopper will view the entire collection on the website and ensuring that they have as many options for selection as possible. In the case of luxury services provided through the website, it is also necessary to provide clients with multiple options for appealing packages presented in an interactive and enjoyable format. For example, a luxury resort could provide vacationers with options for selecting the location according to their reason for traveling or according to the occasion they are celebrating. Other options could include the features in the hotel, seasonal packages, local events and so on. The more the choices given, the longer the

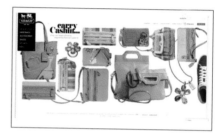

Figure 6.5 *Matches.com, Brownsfashion.com and Vivre.com have all approached product classification in creative ways that go beyond the standard categories of type, season and gender. Matches employs an editorial format through themes and trends; Browns adds a new dimension through an online Style Advisor, Insider Favorites among others; Vivre uses style notes and press features; while Coach uses a clipboard of pre-selected products as its homepage screen. The more options shoppers have for product viewing and interactivity, the higher their purchase probability. Directly-owned luxury e-boutiques as well as luxury hotels & resorts could borrow a leaf of creativity from these pacesetters*

shopper will be likely to spend on the website and the higher the chance that a sale will be made. Luxury shopping doesn't necessarily have to be a matter of "1-click to purchase". After all, selling luxury is about selling a dream, which is a journey of discovery, and not about selling DVDs or books.

The front office also features e-merchandizing elements, in other words, the manner of display of the products and the ways that the client may view them.

Figure 6.6 *The majority of existing e-stores has incorporated interactive features like zoom and alternative view options for product visualization. Most of these enable selecting and zooming in on specific parts of the image and, although these features are visually stimulating, consumers are currently asking for a more personal type of interactivity through the web and physical channels. Oscar de la Renta goes a step further by providing full-screen zoom of static images for a higher online visual impact and an offline personal shopping service to complement the online offering leading to an entirely personalized shopping experience*

It is now common to find zoom, 360° and spin applications as well as alternative views and matching styles, integrated in online stores. Also commonplace are tools that trace the pages viewed, tools that suggest complementary products and those that filter preferences in order to pull up items that could correspond to the shopper's tastes. Online shoppers also expect to find product information including details, size charts, materials, care guide and tools to forward, share and add commentary and wish lists or ask a style expert some questions. These features are all a given and are no longer elements that could captivate the online shopper. What luxury clients expect from e-boutiques in terms of merchandizing are tools that will enable them to interact with the products in a collaborative environment that thrives on inclusion, fun, immersion and overall enhanced value. One such tool is the use of a virtual model in the form of an avatar to try on products or test them against a human form or image. This is particularly relevant as the sensory nature of luxury goods means that there is a strong factor for the need to interact with the products on a more personal level (Figure 6.6).

Avatars were first introduced into the fashion accessories arena by Coach in the early noughties. This tool was integrated in the e-store to enable shoppers to visualize the appearance of handbags against a human form. The avatars appeared in two standard sizes (short and tall) and could display the bags in two formats (hand-held and shoulder-hung). Although this introduced a new level of interactivity in e-merchandizing, Coach's virtual model remained restrictive as its two-dimensional and static nature prevented the shopper from personalizing the product views. Since then, the technology that powers virtual models has evolved and three-dimensional avatars have been invented. One such application is My Virtual Model (MVP) created by the Montréal-based company of the same name (Figure 6.7). MVP enables the creation of a 3-D human avatar in a personalized format through integrating the body features that match closely with the shopper's appearance and enabling products to be tried on this model. For example, let's say a shopper visits Dior.com and finds that the brand has incorporated this application in its e-boutique, the shopper can proceed to re-create himself or herself in the store by selecting the exact height, weight, facial features, skin color, hairstyle, body shape and other multiple dimensions. This model can then be used to try on products like bags, shoes, jewelry, clothing, eyewear, watches and so on. MVP also enables the shopper to store their personal avatars for future retrieval and to transfer them to friends for comments. This tool not only increases purchase probability, but also goes a long way to ensure client satisfaction and retention as well as compensate for the lack of human presence in the e-store. The company has also created My Virtual Showroom, which uses the same principle and application of MVP to power the re-creation of physical spaces from store interiors to offices, homes and showrooms.

Another e-merchandizing application that corresponds to the level of interactive online shopping that clients currently seek is the Online Makeover kit created by Taaz, which enables hairstyling and make-up artistry on real human photos. The application allows shoppers to upload their photos online and subsequently test out different looks on their faces by selecting hairstyles, colors, length and thickness. Taaz also produces hundreds of make-up options for lips, eyes, cheeks, brows and face. It even allows the users to plump their lips, whiten their teeth and change the color of their eyes with contact lenses! This total re-looking enablement is a sure booster of the online shopping experience (Figure 6.7).

The days when zoom, flash, flip, spin and 360° product views moved online shoppers to take out their credit cards are over. Luxury e-shopping currently requires more involvement and collaboration powered by the e-store but controlled by the shopper. The challenge for luxury brands and e-retailers lies in not only grasping the attention of the shopper and aiding them in finding and viewing the products, but also in engaging them through a collaborative shopping environment that thrives on creativity and sharing. The future will be about companion shopping, individual styling, interactive media manipulation and access to web profiles on extended peripheral devices including mobile phones. Consumers will also expect to be able to view products in 3-D real time, which is quite different from the 360° product spin that currently exists in static image formats.

The front office interface elements that are essential for sales optimization include all the features that are connected to serving the client. When people are shopping online, they are aware that there is no human being present on the website but they would still like to feel that there is someone behind the screen somewhere available for them. This is where e-CRM tools come in. Serving online shoppers shouldn't be about data collection, FAQ sheets, talking avatar assistants and automated product suggestions. It should be about providing tools for instant access to sales representatives, personal shoppers, technicians

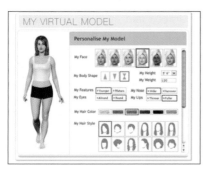

Figure 6.7   *Online shoppers are no longer wowed by basic features like zoom, flash or 3-D product views. Their expectations for interactive online shopping include the enablement of personal virtual models to enhance product visualization against a realistic human form; as well as interactive kits for product testing and trials. Two of such applications that could easily be integrated in the e-store of luxury websites is My Virtual Model and My Virtual Showroom, which allows shoppers to virtually re-create themselves online and their environments; and Taaz, a re-looking kit that enables shoppers to try on different facial looks prior to shopping*

or whomever the online shopper would most likely seek to get in touch with. Luxury online stores ought to have tools for instant live chat, call-back sms, email, express dial in addition to automated shopping assistance that should feature dimensions of the most frequently demanded services. The same applies to after-sales service offerings which should be clearly stated and easily available.

Shopping for luxury products online should also feature a high element of product and services customization and personalization. Online shoppers have become demanding due to the influence they have garnered on the social web and also from being spoilt for choice. The wide accessibility of luxury brands and products has led them to seek products that offer a personal touch whether it is bespoke or standardized. Also, with the ease of the integration of applications for customizing products and services, clients expect to see provisions for product personalization from luxury websites. A few luxury brands like Louis Vuitton (see Figure 6.8), Guerlain and Anya Hindmarch allow online shoppers to personalize a limited range of products online, mainly through a few letters indicating their initials, inscribed or painted on the leather goods. Others like Maison Calavas allow online shoppers to create and package their make-up kits from a range of colors, while Fendi has recently introduced the opportunity to personalize its baguette bag through a paint-brush kit that comes with the bag of coated canvas. Although Fendi provides no means of trying out design samples of the bag online, this bag is retailed on websites like e-Luxury.com. Product personalization goes beyond allowing clients to put a few letters on a product; it presents a real opportunity to foster creativity and inclusion and to strengthen the cord of intimacy between the client and the brand.

Online customization and personalization is tricky and challenging because it stretches beyond products and must now include services in web experiences. Technology currently allows websites to track clients' online shopping

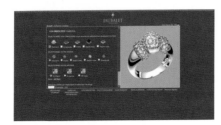

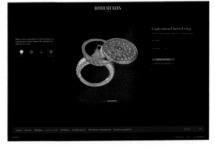

Figure 6.8 *Web-enabled customization and personalization of luxury products, services and web experiences rank high among the expectations of clients from e-boutiques. It allows for more client inclusion and satisfaction while fostering intimacy and creativity. Although several luxury brands provide bespoke and personalization services offline, there has been a low commitment towards integrating this in the online offerings and extending it as a complement to the offline channel. Brands like Louis Vuitton provide online personalization for a limited range of leather goods, while Guerlain has an online personalization service for its perfume bottles and has also extended the personalization of its Rouge G lipstick from its Parisian stores to its website through a competition. Along with Boucheron, the French high-jewelry brand Jaubalet is one of the few luxury brands to incorporate an integrated product customization process through its website*

and browsing habits, and this information could be crucial in customizing their visit to the e-store through page view order, product presentation format and even background color and design possibilities. Online customization should also be integrated with offline customization offerings to enhance the feeling of a complete inclusion in clients. Multi-channel customization and personalization means providing similar options through the two channels as well as performing dual communications to enhance the value of the offering. For example, when Guerlain launched its Rouge G lipstick in April 2009, the brand provided clients the opportunity to personalize their lipstick cases with their names or initials over a two-week period. This offer was only available from the brand's Parisian stores. To compensate for this while at the same time creating a buzz, Guerlain launched an online competition with a more extended time period on its website where anyone could play to win a lipstick with their personalized message of ten characters. Each participant was encouraged to invite others and the more people invited, the higher the chance of winning a personalized lipstick. Although this initiative encourages buzz marketing and enhances the awareness of the product, it would serve the brand higher returns and client retention if it became an integrated offering. On the other hand when Fendi launched the initiative for the customization of its baguette bag, to celebrate the bag's 10th anniversary, one would have expected this information to be disseminated from the Fendi website or stores but, at the time of writing, this wasn't the case although the news was all over cyberspace. Consumers were talking about it but there wasn't enough interactivity and excitement to encourage purchase. The luxury car industry is also known to run competitions and rallies initiated online but these initiatives require a high level of interactivity to generate the desired involvement and buzz among the target audience.

Interactivity plays a key role in defining the dimensions of the luxury e-boutique. The type and level of interactivity that clients are seeking has, however, changed. They are no longer seeking interactive elements for the sake of interaction; they are on the lookout for e-shopping features that will add value to their shopping experience. Incorporating flash-powered interactive kits that thrive on movement and downloads, but serve no real purpose, is viewed as a waste of time by today's intelligent online client. A visit to Hermes.com leads to a section with an interactive kit that includes all manner of flash-based games (even if nobody understands the rules) and products in motion (even if nobody can figure out why they swing, open and close and what is coming next) as well as various paper pattern designs of the Kelly bag (for people to print, cut and create miniatures, in case you're wondering) and numerous other features that I leave you to discover by yourselves. Although these are all in interactive modes, their place and value for the online client is very much questionable. In addition, media elements that improve interaction such as videos, sound and animations are now prolific and no longer excite shoppers. The new order of online shopping interactivity calls for rich and valuable content that provides an elevated form of interaction with the products. It means presenting the offering in a creative and stimulating format that could include magazine editorials, content generation, video narration, companion, avatars and social shopping as well as blogs and user communities. It is, however, essential to identify the features most appropriate for each brand and e-store.

Case Analysis 6.1
Changing the rules of online shopping with My Virtual Model™

In 1997, Louise Guay and Jean-François St-Arnaud had a vision. They knew that the Internet was on the verge of re-writing the rules of retail forever and that both retailers and consumers would go through a significant re-orientation process as a result. They also understood that not everybody would be ready for this change and that only a few would be able to identify the right course in order to take advantage of the opportunities of the new direction . They weren't sure that they had all the answers either but one thing they were certain of was that people would not accept being restricted by the Internet on any level and that, within a short time, they would expect to receive the same (if not higher) level of service and offerings that they receive when shopping in the real world. They set out to do something about it through creating a breakthrough technology that enables the re-creation of personalized human forms online in the form of avatars baptized My Virtual Model™ (MVM).

The first release of My Virtual Model™ in 1997 brought a major step forward in online customer service. Since then, MVP has created a standard for virtual identity through interactive and companion shopping powered by 3-D and personalized touches. As the world leader in virtual identity and the innovator of personalized shopping, MVM has also set a precedent in incorporating online social media elements within the retail environment.

How does it work and what is all the hype?

MVM basically allows e-shoppers to re-create themselves in the form of a personal avatar or virtual model which they can use to try on products including apparel, jewelry, handbags, shoes, eyewear and watches. The creation of the virtual model follows a process of choosing features that closely resemble the shopper through a multiple selection of suggestions for face, hair, form, height, weight and skin-tone. The personalized virtual model is then used to try on preselected products which the shopper may visualize. The goal of the product trials is, of course, to create the feeling that the shopper is looking at themselves in the mirror instead of on a computer screen. An additional possibility for creating a personalized virtual model is to upload an existing head-shot photo of the shopper and integrate it with the dimensions of the body selected from the given options, leading to a realistic human 3-D avatar. The virtual model can be saved, retrieved, forwarded and shared. It may also be used to track weight loss and as a tester of pre-selected products from multiple brands.

The company behind MVM also introduced My Virtual Model™ Imail in 2002, an innovative marketing tool that offers a unique, fun and simple interactive MVM Dressing Room integrated in an e-mail. The company has also launched MVM Showroom, which allows online shoppers to visualize hard or soft goods in customizable sets based on the 3-D technology that made My Virtual Model™ possible. The application can be used as a simulator for interior store and home decoration and helps to overcome the anxiety of how a room would appear if remodeled. The company's latest product 'BrandME I am the brand' lets users display several brands in their virtual wardrobe and post them on their personal online page where visitors can comment on them. This has led to the creation of a thriving online community that congregates both shoppers and those seeking an outlet for their creative juices.

The applications, which are fast and easy to use, may be incorporated within any e-store and are already in use by Sears, H&M, Adidas, Speedo, Levi Strauss & Co and so on. Its benefits go beyond converting shoppers to buyers by lessening the fear factor, but also improves profitability by increasing revenues while cutting costs. It's been determined that online shoppers using My Virtual Model™ solutions spend more, buy more and return far fewer items, resulting directly in reduced shipping and handling costs for the retailers. It is also an essential tool for content management and digitized services.

As online shoppers become familiar with this technology and use it as a yardstick for their expectations from luxury e-stores, this level of innovation in personalized shopping will become the norm. The brands that will be left behind by the wave of change in virtual identity will spend more to catch up.

The back office

The back-office support system of an e-boutique refers to all manner of software, applications, systems and codes that ensure that the website is running efficiently. They form the backbone of the website and, without their optimization, it would practically be impossible for all the front-office features to run. The back-office elements cover a wide-ranging scope from stock tracking and inventory management, transaction and payment processing, dispatch, logistics, returns, refunds, cancellations, information processing, data management, content management, privacy and security of transactions, and security of deliveries.

Supporting all the aspects that make up the complex nodes of the back-office systems requires expertise and investment in the right technology. It also calls for a flexible approach to change and improvement as constant updating will be with the evolution of technology. Online shoppers do not expect to be inconvenienced by systems breakdowns or website closures as a result of maintenance and are, of course, not expected to become victims of this. Luxury brands should also avoid outsourcing crucial back-office segments that could touch on client management and may potentially result in leaving the brand's image at the mercy of the sub-contracted company. And, of course, it is essential to avoid being associated with sub-contractors that understand neither a brand's positioning nor its clientele.

Creating an exciting and interactive luxury e-boutique that demonstrates recognition and inclusion is the order of today's online luxury shopping (see Figure 6.9). Service is the keyword irrespective of what a brand is selling and online luxury product retail should not be separated from selling luxury service.

Case Analysis 6.2
The La Redoute horror story and its lesson for luxury e-retail

If you've ever had a real-life nightmare, the type that made you feel like you were in a dream or that you were living right out of a horror movie, you will likely understand what Caroline experienced in her quest to shop online with French retailer La Redoute, which although not a luxury retailer has had a long-standing collaboration with Christian Lacroix and is owned by PPR, the same group that owns the Gucci Group with brands like Gucci, Yves Saint Laurent, Boucheron, Bottega Veneta, Stella McCartney, Sergio Rossi and several others. La Redoute demonstrates how companies that lack a solid e-retail strategy that is in tune with client expectations can create nightmares in client relations, retail service and customer experience. A important lesson in outsourcing can also be learnt here.

Caroline was drawn to Internet shopping for two practical reasons. First, as a 40-year-old senior marketing executive of a global telecommunications company she had enormous responsibilities managing both global operations and a global team. She also had a young family with three children, a husband, two dogs and a home to cater to. So as you guessed, she is one of those millions of city dwellers whose biggest problem is the lack of time. To top off the complex mix, she also suffered from chronic backache, a result of twenty years of being hunched over in front of computers and people. This, plus the lack of time, meant that she couldn't afford the luxury of getting the two-hour weekly massage recommended by both her doctor and friends. So she opted for a quick-fix solution by deciding to buy an electronic massage sofa which would enable her get a massage while helping her kids with their homework. Again, the problem of time meant that she was left with the single option of finding the suitable massage chair and purchasing it online. This however didn't bother her as she was already a prolific e-shopper and could navigate the Internet world with ease. If only she had had any idea that she was in for a horror story.

It took a few minutes and a quick search online with keywords in Google for Caroline to find a variety of massage chair choices and e-retailers. After a quick overview of each, she opted for La Redoute which offered a variety of massage chairs on its website at a competitive price of €811.75. Upon making the purchase, she was informed that she would receive her order within fourteen days and that she would be contacted one day prior to the delivery date to fix a precise time. While she felt a great sense of relief upon making the purchase, she was a little taken aback by the long delivery time-frame of two weeks but anyhow, at last she could obtain the treatment she needed for her back.

True to the words of La Redoute, she received a call one day prior to the proposed delivery date but it was not to fix the time of delivery; it was to inform her that the delivery would be made two days later and that the timing would be confirmed the next day. She accepted the information without protest. However, on the new date, there was no delivery to her great surprise. She also didn't receive any phone call or email from La Redoute informing her of the reason why her sofa hadn't been delivered as confirmed. The next day she called the company in anger, expecting to receive a valid reason for this level of unprofessionalism and, after being passed around on an automated recorded message for nearly twenty minutes, she was finally able to speak to a sales representative, who informed her curtly that La Redoute didn't deal directly with matters connected with logistics and deliveries and that she would have to call the company to which La Redoute had outsourced logistics and find out what happened to her sofa, and promptly cut off the line. Appalled by this information, which she believed she must have mis-heard, Caroline called La Redoute back and, after a further twenty minutes, she spoke to another sales representative, who seemed delighted to give her the same information which underlined that, in other words, it was up to the client to sort out the problems that arose as a result of the company's negligence. She was given the phone number of a company called Sogep and asked to call them and sort out her issues. By this time Caroline was in a rage but she went ahead and called Sogep, where someone confirmed that her delivery was scheduled but had to be cancelled because of logistics issues – and nobody bothered to inform her!

She was told that in order to book another delivery date she had to contact the company that was in charge of deliveries for Sogep and book directly with them. She was promptly given the phone number of a company called SED and was informed that she should quote a reference number to identify herself when she called them. When she asked who SED was and what business they had with her sofa, she was informed that it was the transport company to which Sogep, the logistics company, outsourced its deliveries. They were the only people that could sort out issues with delivery timings. Caroline couldn't believe her ears. Was she, a supposedly valuable client, actually being passed around like a worthless intruder for a product that she bought which the useless retailer hadn't bothered to deliver? She just couldn't accept this treatment and so she called La Redoute back and, after much argument and insistence on speaking with a supervisor or director, someone came on the phone, introduced herself as the Client Manager and informed her that they could do nothing for her and she had to follow the instructions of the logistics company and dropped the phone. By the way, this lady had no idea who SED was! Feeling helpless, Caroline called SED and after several minutes explaining who she was a new delivery date was booked for five days later. On the said day, there was a repeat episode and no delivery was made; she received no phone call, neither was there an email informing her of the reason for the no-show. She tried to contain her fury as she called the delivery company the next day where someone informed her that the driver actually departed to make the delivery but had to turn back because he couldn't find a parking space. What a useless excuse! When she enquired why nobody bothered to call her to inform her, the person on the other end couldn't think of a further excuse. She apologized and promised Caroline that the delivery would be made the next day before noon. Caroline decided to give them a final chance. The next day, as you rightly guessed, there was no delivery, no call and no email. Caroline called La Redoute, Sogep and SED yet again. At La Redoute she was told that she was rude, at Sogep she was informed that the company no longer had any business with her delivery and at SED the person on the other end of the line dropped the phone when she expressed her feeling of their incompetence and unprofessionalism. Finally, upon the second phone call to SED where she threatened to call her lawyer, she was given a new delivery date for the next day. Your guess is as good as mine – there was no delivery.

Caroline had reached her limit. She called La Redoute and asked for an immediate refund. She was told her request could not be processed until the sofa had been returned by the logistics company Sogep, who by the way needed to obtain the sofa back from the transport company SED. The estimated time-frame for this was six weeks, that is if Caroline followed up immediately by cancelling her delivery file with SED and subsequently Sogep. After this, then the refund request could be made and would be dealt with within three months. This meant that she would probably not get her refund for another five months! And she had already spent nearly one month running after her sofa to be delivered. By this time she was sure that she was in a nightmare! How could a company in the twenty-first century function in this way and demonstrate an apparent lack of recognition and respect for clients? It was beyond her comprehension. She was on the verge of suing the company because of their inability to respect their obligations but she figured that she didn't really have the time to pursue a lawsuit. She shopped online in the first place because she didn't have time. But she had to resolve this matter once and for all. She decided to take a day off from the horror story and the next day, armed with a voice recorder, she called the three companies involved in this mess and recorded the phone conversations which she planned to use in her lawsuit.

At SED, upon obtaining the representative's name and informing her that the telephone conversation was being recorded, the rep promptly dropped the phone. Caroline called back and asked the rep if she actually dropped the phone on her, a customer, in the middle of the conversation and the rep shamelessly lied, saying that the line was cut off. Caroline insisted on speaking to the director of the agency who came to the phone and rudely informed her that her case was too complicated for them because their drivers reported arriving for the delivery with no one present. He so much as called Caroline a liar and neurotic who took pleasure in harassing people, before dropping the phone on her. She was speechless. It took her a few minutes to get herself together before her call to Sogep, the second company involved in this soap opera of incompetence. She was immediately asked to stop calling them as they had no business with her anymore. Caroline thought this must be a joke and realized that she was wasting her time so she called La Redoute.

At La Redoute, she refused to drop the phone until she was put in touch with the Director of Client Services, whose name she promptly noted after informing her that she was recording their conversation. She recounted her nightmare story, told her what she thought about them and their incompetence, negligence and dysfunctional structure and further informed her that if she didn't receive her refund within 48 hours, she would sue La Redoute and would implicate her in the lawsuit. The "director" promptly retrieved her file and duly informed Caroline that it indicated that the delivery for the sofa was made twice and there was no one at Caroline's residence to receive the sofa. Again Caroline couldn't believe her ears – this story was becoming more incredulous. She had concluded that they were unprofessional but she hadn't thought that they would resort to lying. She realized that she has underestimated them. Caroline confirmed that this was a blatant lie and "Madam Director" indicated that she would investigate the matter and ensure that Caroline received her refund within two weeks – which according to her was an enormous step as she had to fit the request in their "quick response" program. Caroline's decision was made – if she didn't receive her full refund by the specified time, she would take them to court. In the meantime, she still had to find a solution to her aching back, which was getting worse.

Two weeks later – and exactly seven weeks after making her online purchase – she obtained her refund in the form of a cheque (she had paid by credit card) accompanied by a toneless unapologetic letter signed by a so-called "Director of Client Relations". She threw the letter in the trash and decided to put this horrible experience behind her but, first, she warned everyone around her from family to friends and colleagues to avoid La Redoute like a plague. But La Redoute wouldn't have it. The following week she received a package with numerous reduction coupons to shop from the store. The following week another pack arrived and the week after it was a letter informing her that she had a "gift" reserved for her which would be immediately dispatched upon her next purchase. A few days later she began to receive emails from La Redoute nearly every day, with offers for discounts, free shipping and all manners of desperado sales moves to get her to shop with them. Were these guys nuts? What kind of company was this? Didn't they realize that she would never spend her money in their store and that she would ensure that no one she knew did so? She was still wondering these when three weeks after obtaining her refund, she received a phone call from Sogep to find out her availability for the delivery of her sofa. Oh dear!

This is not a fictitious story but a true story of events that took place between 2008 and 2009

Luxury clients want to be recognized, they want to be remembered, and they want to be shown that they count and there is no better way to provide this than through elevated service. With the significant advances made in content and data management, online shopping services can now easily include personalization on all levels, product suggestions and even recognizing clients' birthdays as well as those of their family members for whom they may also shop.

In addition, recognizing the e-boutique as an extension and complement of offline retailing will reward a luxury brand more than positioning the two channels as competing stores. Consumers who congregate online are also increasingly meeting offline and are creating communities around luxury lifestyle dimensions. Online websites that cater to the wealthy are also establishing offline clubs where customers can meet like-minded people. This has a consequence in their collective experiences which they transfer to shopping for luxury goods online. On the other hand, e-retailers such as Fashionista.com are challenging the formula of restricting e-retailers to the online channel. The

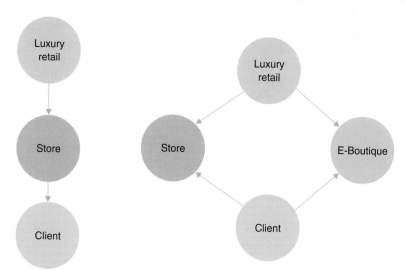

Figure 6.9 *The structure of luxury retail has changed with the arrival of the Internet. Clients currently purchase both online and offline and expect to receive a uniform brand experience and elevated customer service on the two channels. Luxury brands are currently required to integrate the two distribution channels to complement one another across the board*

website is one of the few retailers that moved from a pure-play e-retailer to a real physical store located at 22, rue Saint Sauveur in Paris.

Although every luxury brand worth its salt should own an online boutique, those that currently have no e-retail activities have, however, not committed any crime. It is not imperative to create an online store at the same time as launching a website but it becomes a death sentence if there are no plans to do so in the medium term. The goal, of course, should remain making shopping fun for the client through content and interaction both online and offline.

The discount dilemma

Every fashion season ends with whispered messages passed among luxury industry insiders. These messages make their rounds quietly but surely from journalists, buyers, clients, associates, friends to those considered as the "people" that luxury needs to keep its juices flowing. They are not whispers that recall the magnificence of the collections or the new talents to be courted and revered; neither do they contain juicy details of the latest drug or sex-related scandal in the luxury community. These whispers are the form in which information on the private sale events of luxury brands are passed around. The dates, time, location, collections and access are divulged and this information is kept among the "happy few". From Place Vendôme to Avenue Montaigne, Pont Neuf and Champs Elysées, the locations could be far apart but the purpose remains the same – to dispose of the unsold stock at discounted prices in a private and hush-hush environment. The invitations to these private sales have become as sought-after as those of fashion shows and their appeal as high as the front-row seats at fashion shows. When brands like Hermès, Dior or Chanel hold their private sale events, the lines at the entry point are formed hours before the indicated start time and stretch for miles although each attendee is supposed to have a personal invitation and guaranteed entry. The case is no different in the luxury automobile industry where the practice of price-cutting is a continuous practice that doesn't follow seasonal patterns. Luxury brands have managed to turn the disdained practice of price discounting into an art form and have guarded the confidentiality surrounding the private sale events from the public, that is until now.

The current slow economy and subsequent decrease in shopping expenditure that it brought about has led luxury brands to rethink the question of price discounting. In the frenzy of confusion that followed the credit crunch of 2008, several brands were pushed to adopt flexible pricing policies. Since then, price reductions have started to show up in the stores, albeit in discreet corners, while additional offers are being tactfully proposed to clients who have the potential to spend large amounts of money. In September 2008, a new chapter was opened on the price-discounting scene. Christian Dior decided to hold a public seasonal sale for several weeks (actually, for as long as the stock lasted), in which anyone with some cash in their pocket was invited. There were no formal and private invitations and there was no discreet store corner display. All the merchandise were displayed in the same open space and given the same level of high visibility. The difference, however, is that the products were not in the Dior store. The brand had hired a section of a renowned Parisian museum and converted it into a temporary store for the end of season sale. The opening hours were the same as the store's and the attention and service were no different. The location, however, remained discreet and there were no window or public displays that indicated that there was a sale going on with price cuts at up to 50 percent off the original prices. Despite the fact that this was a discreet pop-up sale store it was widely discussed in the Parisian fashion circles and within days the entire collection was sold out. The effect that this strategic approach to price discounting had on the client was that of special privilege irrespective of the fact that it was open access, and that of confidentiality despite this store being common knowledge. In addition, the coherence with the Dior shopping experience as well as the location choice added a touch of originality and appeal to the sale event. Consequently, even the wealthiest of clients weren't ashamed to be seen rummaging through the collections and the brand suffered little damage to its image and positioning. You may be wondering if Christian Dior reproduced the same feat online and the answer is no. Why? Simply because the online channel is an open platform where the whole world has access to both information on price slashes and the opportunity to purchase.

The issue of price discounting has been a recurring debate in the luxury sector for a long time. Apart from brands like Louis Vuitton and Annick Goutal that have a clear and strict "no discount" policy, several brands like Gucci, Hermès, Chanel, Armani, Dior, Fendi as well as jewelers like Cartier, Boucheron and Bvlagri have all been seeking ways to overcome the discount dilemma. Most have adopted in-store discount of selected products displayed in a discreet format while others have an "open" discount policy which is offered to clients on a one-to-one basis. Although price-cutting doesn't necessarily enhance a luxury brand's image or add to its equity, this is not a practice that brands involve themselves in out of choice; they do so due to necessity. Let's face it, the inventory has to be cleared at some point and old unsold stock has to give way to new collections because not every brand has the clout of Louis Vuitton which has practically zero unsold seasonal stock. The brands that have approached price-discounting with an intelligent strategy have been able to pull off price discounting unscathed but the Internet has made tackling this dilemma more challenging.

The accessibility and availability of the Internet is both a blessing and a curse for luxury brands. It provides the advantage of being a propeller of brand awareness, communications and positioning but at the same time is a promoter of over-exposure and image dilution. The latter is particularly linked to price discounting and has led to the question of whether luxury brands should discount online or not, and if they do, how this should be approached. With price comparison websites like BuzzFeed, NextTag and Shopittome, access to prices is now available with one click and price transparency has never been as vital as at present.

For a start, when "sales" are held in the physical stores they are often placed in discreet corners such as at the back of the stores or upstairs to avoid reducing the desire for the newer collections and screaming "desperate". There is no reason why the same discreet approach shouldn't be applied online. In fact, the Internet requires a higher degree of discretion due to its wide accessibility. It is quite appalling to visit a luxury brand or retailer's website and find a wide sign screaming "Sale" from the home page. Some brands like Valentino have, however, understood that when online price discounting is approached with discretion, it is actually more appealing to shoppers and more enhancing to the brand image. Although the brand displays a sign indicating its sale event on its home page, it is presented in a way that blends with the rest of the website and not in neon-green or blood-red to grasp as much attention as possible. Oscar de la Renta has even gone a step further by creating an entire section on its website called "The Outlet", a corner where the brand quietly retails its previous season's stock at reduced prices. The presentation and display of this section is no different from the rest of the website and shouldn't be (see Figure 6.10).

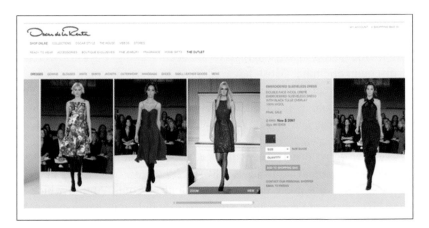

Figure 6.10 *Price discounting may not always be avoidable for luxury brands and e-retailers but when it is done online it should be approached in an intelligent and tactical way to avoid damaging the brand's appeal. Oscar de La Renta which practices online price discounting has discreetly integrated the "sale" pages to blend with the rest of the website while e-retailers like Net-A-Porter have approached discounting with fanfare*

Tips for online price-discounting

In an ideal world luxury brands shouldn't reduce product prices, particularly online. But because we don't live in a perfect world, the following tips could be useful in dealing with the issue of price discounting:

1. If price discounting is not in your brand's policy, do not be forced to reduce prices due to pressure from the economy. Luxury clients are still spending on luxury goods, albeit in a different way, while demanding all-round value from the product and the brand. If your brand concentrates on providing this value, you may not need to reduce your prices.
2. Approach price discounting online the way you do offline. That is, if your discounted products are discreetly displayed in a corner of your physical store, do so online by creating a corner for the items with reduced prices (not on the home page please).
3. Anticipate how the online public may react to your brand's price reduction. Every product or service type has its specificities and peculiarities and the way clients may react to the price cut of a fragrance is not the same way they may react to the price cut of jewelry.
4. Apply a coherent pricing strategy in both your direct e-retail and that of independent e-retailers who sell your products. There is no point having a "no discount" policy if your products may be found at reduced prices all over the Internet.
5. Don't believe the people who tell you that you cannot avoid price discounting unless you're Louis Vuitton. If you have the right systems and policies in place and have invested in your brand, you could be able to avoid discounting online. In this case, please do so by all means.

The sample sale syndrome

In 2001, when Jacques-Antoine Granjon had the vision of launching VentePrivée.com, the first private sample sale website, he had no idea that he was on the verge of introducing a new chapter in the second wave of Internet revolution, not to speak of opening a can of worms in the process. Introducing a new way of e-retail characterized by a restricted environment both in access and sale period, price discounts of up to 70 percent, limited access to members only as well as an invitation-only format for membership, VentePrivée redefined online shopping, particularly for sensory products of brands with a high brand equity. Although VentePrivée is not dedicated exclusively to luxury products, it has created a special space for the sale of luxury products on its website called VP lounge where brands like Dunhill, Sergio Rossi, Bottega Veneta and Christophle have made appearances. In the process, VentePrivée has built a dedicated community of online shoppers who snap up products within minutes of their going live, including thousands within the high-income bracket.

Since the arrival of VentePrivée, several independent ventures have been launched under the same principle, many of them specializing in the luxury segment, duly baptized "sample sale" websites. The US-based Gilt Groupe leads the way, having been created in 2007 and since generating a membership exceeding one million members who are frequent buyers. Collections ranging from clothing to leather goods from a line-up of brands including Valentino, Oscar de la Renta, Ralph Lauren, Sergio Rossi and Giorgio Armani have all been retailed on the website at prices marked down as much as 70 percent off the original prices. Its format of access by membership only and its sale period restriction to 36 hours has ensured that elements of exclusivity and discretion have been maintained. Others like Ideeli.com, Koodos.com and PrivateOutlet.com have incorporated elements of this formula to appeal to an extended clientele. Outnet.com, the recently launched website from Net-a-porter.com that is uniquely for the sale of its products at reduced prices, has also introduced 72-hour "pop-up" sale events, incorporating the formula created by VentePrivée and popularized by the likes of Gilt. On its launch date on 16 April 2009, several of its pieces were sold out in the first ten minutes. On the home decor front, websites like MyFab.com is also moving to change the rules of the online retail of luxury furnishings and home fashion. The website, which works directly with the manufacturers, introduces weekly sales based on themes, styles and brands. Price reductions are often between 50 percent to 70 percent and sale periods are also restricted (see Figure 6.11).

What is the consequence of the abundance of sample sale websites for luxury brands and what impact would it have on the way consumers perceive the brands? Does it affect the factors of "desire" and "dream" that luxury brands work so hard to create and nurture like a treasure? When clients are able to buy a Baume & Mercier watch at 70 percent discount, will they ever buy another watch from the brand at full price? If a Gucci bag's retail price moves down from €2,000 to €450 will consumers still crave to have the handbag at all costs? Will the appeal that Gucci holds for them diminish? Will they perceive the brand as highly as they do other luxury brands?

Sample sale websites are taking the Internet back to its initial positioning as a channel of retail for price-discounted goods or for deals and steals. If you remember the early days of e-retail in the mid-nineties, online shopping was viewed as risky not only because of security issues, but also due to its perception as a retail channel for a mix of low quality-low priced and fake products. What has changed in this mix since is the low-quality and fake dimension because, with time, consumers have become savvy enough to detect fake and low quality products and e-retailers have also built their reputations and credibility. The issue of pricing, however, remains the only point that is yet to find a common consensus among luxury brands and it is becoming more complex with the spread of sample sale websites. What will happen to luxury brands in this environment? How will luxury retail and e-retail sustain itself with the sample sale competition from independent retailers? What about the price transparency that is supposed to rule online? Does it make sense for a luxury brand to have an online store with full-priced items while providing stock to sample sale websites to be retailed at discounts? Or should luxury brands follow this direction by launching their own discount-based websites just as they do offline through private sale events? Wouldn't this make more sense instead of having sale reductions on the same website as the full-priced items? Would this not be the same as launching a lower-priced range just like Armani has done with the "Exchange" or Valentino with the "Red"? The questions abound and answers must be established before luxury e-retail can move on to its next phase.

Luxury brands have no choice but to acknowledge and accept sample sale websites and find a way to work with them to achieve the common goal of higher market performance and brand enhancement. Finding a position of compromise in this scenario is a real challenge as several brands are yet to define an integrated e-retail strategy. Even as this segment remains in its infancy, the following factors should however be considered by both luxury brands and sample sale e-retailers for a mutually beneficial relationship:

1. Online sample sales have an impact on consumer psychology, no matter the format in which the sample sale website is presented. Although controlled access and restricted sale periods help to maintain a level of exclusivity around the sale, the reality is that everyone knows that it is possible to obtain certain brands' products at a significantly reduced price. Before jumping on discount websites, a luxury brand should first evaluate the potential impact on client perceptions and make a value assessment to ascertain if the long-term impact on the brand could be traded off for the short-term benefits of sales returns.
2. Sample sale websites fuel the desire that a value-driven client segment has for luxury brands and products and introduces them to luxury brands and the world of luxury consumption. The websites also serve a segment of old luxury clients and enables them to be flexible with their brand choices.
3. The sample websites that will bring the most tangible and intangible value to luxury brands are those that understand how to be a brand themselves. Luxury brands offer symbolic benefits to clients that are derived from the universe created around the brand. Only an e-retailer who understands and respects this will be able to apply the luxury codes to their service to luxury clients. This doesn't only mean presentation and merchandising but also includes packaging and communications.
4. Offering a fantastic online shopping experience on a discount website infuses some magic and ensures that shoppers return. Although the low prices may initially attract them, it is the customer service that will top off the experience. This means a great product assortment, visually stimulating display, high-impact and appealing images, rich information, instant assistance and overall entertaining and fun content. These features are even more

required in a discount environment to ensure the client that there is no value reduction in terms of the brand promise even if the prices are lower.

5. Luxury brands should understand the collective value that discount e-retailers provide to each brand by understanding the range of brands displayed on the website. The effect on a brand's perception if the products are retailed on the same website as mass brands with a much lower positioning will be different from a brand that is retailed on a site with fellow luxury brands. When a client visits a discount website and finds information on sale events for Sergio Rossi, Dunhill, Morgan and Fossil on the same page, their evaluation of the luxury brands in this group could be clouded.

Figure 6.11 *Several independent discount websites that resell luxury products have emerged since VentePrivée.com introduced this concept in 2001. Today, websites like Gilt.com, MyFab.com, PrivateOutlet.com, Koodos.com and The Outlet offer luxury products from a wide variety of brands at prices as low as 80 percent off the original prices. Luxury brands have no choice but to acknowledge these retailers and find a balance in collaborating with them and sustaining the brands' aura*

The temporary ownership movement

The age-old concept of borrowing and renting, which saw a modern twist in the wealthy segment through the introduction of fractional and collective ownership of property like housing and private jets, has been taken yet to another level by the Internet. Since 2004, when US-based Avelle.com (formerly Bagborrowsteal.com) and Frombagstoriches.com were introduced to provide loaning services of luxury handbags and jewelry, the temporary ownership movement has been quietly making its entry into other markets and altering the way clients relate to luxury brands and products. Today France has Sacdeluxe. fr, Japan has Newell and even Australia has caught the bug with MilaandEddie. com, all with full-serve lending services of luxury handbags, jewelry and accessories which are apparently thriving. These websites are highlighting the secondary market value of luxury items and changing consumer attitudes towards ownership. In the context of shortening product cycles where luxury brands seem to launch cruise and capsule collections every two weeks, the temporary ownership attitude of clients seems to have found a justification. The consequence is a shift in the value-systems of clients and a change in the parameters through which they evaluate luxury brands. And the impact on luxury brands could be either of two ways – the fueling of the desire actually to own the products and the reluctance to purchase luxury products, likely from different client segments.

The luxury product loaning business, which mainly began with low-ticket items like the entry-point $400 handbag, have elevated their offering to include higher-priced items, limited edition products and couture pieces. It is now common to find the current season's handbags available for rent just days after their release. Also, there are no restrictions to the brands available. From Louis Vuitton, Dior, Chanel, Hermès, Prada, Armani, Valentino, Bottega Veneta, Mui Mui, Dolce & Gabbana, Gucci and Cartier, the brand and style assortment in the handbag section of these websites is as rich as any luxury department store floor. They apply a formula of getting the product mix right, ensuring that they are duly covered by insurance and presenting them in a desirable format. The websites also feature interactive content like a blog and in some cases a user community, creating a spirit of inclusion and sharing. Their subscription-based approach as well as member-only offers including private sale of seasonal handbags have also contributed to their growing popularity.

Luxury brands, on the other hand, initially showed reticence in accepting this off-shoot of luxury e-retail and were suspicious of the websites passing off fakes as authentic products. Also, the lack of direct control over the distribution of the products, the inability to ascertain the quality and state of the "used" products, the level of service provided, the packaging and presentation of the products, as well as the effect of bypassing the shopping environment and experience provide areas of concern for luxury brands. Since luxury brands cannot pretend that product-lending services do not exist or that the temporary ownership movement is not in full swing, they must find a way to overcome its challenges and ensure that the impact on their brands is more positive than negative. This may sound like a mission impossible but in my opinion, understanding the following factors and features of product-lending websites could help along the way:

1. Websites that provide luxury product-lending services are capital-intensive and take a high stock risk. This means that if the owners were not confident of the market opportunity they would not have launched the businesses. Their market analysis identified the changing attitudes of consumers and the potential appeal for alternating between brands without creating a permanent bond through specific products. This reality is vital for brands to assess the model for production and retail cycles as well as client management models.

2. Temporary ownership websites are susceptible to product category shifts and trends. People tend to borrow more of the products that are in fashion

Figure 6.12 *Rental websites like Sacdeluxe.com and MilaandEddie.com have opened a new chapter in the way luxury products are accessed from the Internet by creating full-service rental businesses that allow clients to borrow luxury products from handbags to jewelry, watches, sunglasses and accessories. Their arrival has contributed to the shift in the way consumers relate to luxury brands and products as well as the introduction of a new segment of consumers to the luxury universe. This movement also has an indirect impact on the trade of fake luxury products by providing an alternative option to people that may have been tempted to purchase fake luxury items*

and less of those that are classic. These services could be a way for clients who do not necessarily buy pieces from every collection to interact with brands on a more regular basis with lower risks.

3. Rental companies could easily fuel the desire to own the products that are borrowed. Since borrowing means testing through usage, it could also be the beginning of a long relationship between a client and a brand. Both Sacdeluxe.com (Figure 6.12) and Avelle.com have revealed that the majority of their clients are educated well-placed professionals who also have the means of purchasing the products that they borrow at full price and this could be a real opportunity for luxury brands.

4. Temporary ownership websites are able to reproduce some of the codes through which luxury functions, such as exclusivity through waiting-lists for certain products; elevated brand image through packaging and presentation; restricted access through membership-only services; and high-impact experience through client services. These all add up to reassure the client that they are still within the luxury universe.

5. Rental companies contribute indirectly to combating counterfeiting of luxury products. Consumers who may have considered purchasing fake luxury products could be enticed into to borrowing the authentic products due to the low price factor and this could be their point of conversion from fake product clients to the consumers of authentic luxury products. It could also be an educational process and eye-opener for them to appreciate the difference between a well-crafted product and a knock-off version.

6. Rental websites could become information resources for luxury clients who have no intention to rent but are seeking the latest collections, styles and trends of as many brands as possible on a single website.

Sellers and counterfeiters

The Internet is currently in its second wave of boom, following the dot-com crash and this time its evolution has been moving slowly but surely in multiple directions. While, on the one hand, the control of e-retailing luxury goods has been placed in the hands of brands and retailers, on the other, it has also provided an opportunity for consumers themselves to carve a market not only for buying but also for selling. eBay has been at the forefront of client-to-client commerce through a controlled auction format, but specialized websites that focus on specific categories such as luxury and fashion are also emerging. One such website is Portero.com (Figure 6.13), which is a portal that allows individuals to resell their used luxury items to other people through an auction-bidding system.

The auction website was founded in 2004 to offer the public access to the luxury lifestyle through pre-owned products in excellent condition. It strives to be a marketplace for people controlled by people. Products are retailed across a broad range of luxury categories including accessories – handbags,

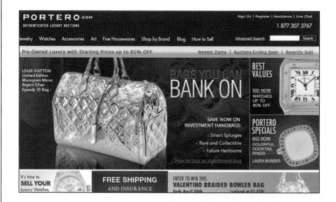

Figure 6.13 *Portero.com, which introduced the concept of reselling authentic used luxury products online through auction-bidding, has brought about an additional arm to the availability of luxury goods through the Internet. Although there are no set prices and the highest bidder gets the product, the website strives to build its credibility through the authenticity of the products and the excellence of its client services. Like rental websites, this movement could have an indirect positive impact on the trade of fake luxury products by providing an alternative option to people that may have been tempted to purchase fake luxury items online*

luggage, shoes, jewelry, sunglasses, scarves, wallets, pens, watches, fine home ware and art. Brands whose products have been bid for on the website is a roll call of all the major international luxury brands including Louis Vuitton, Goyard, Gucci, Balenciaga, Lalique, Armani, Georg Jensen, Tag

Heueur, Salvador Dali, Yves Saint Laurent, Hermès, Chanel, Oscar de la Renta, Zenith and Cartier to name a few. There are no fixed retail prices and auctions could go on as long as there are bidders until the final auction date. The last highest bidder gets the item and sometimes they might be lucky to snap up an item at a low price. In most cases, the prices are lower than the original value at full price but in some cases the auction prices have exceeded the original prices. The auction company's model is based on a mix of extended brand and product selection and expert product information, authenticity of all goods and dedicated customer experience to ensure a luxury experience. They are also known to have partnered with selected brands like Lalique and Robert Lee on different levels. The objective is to bring authentic luxury items of enduring value to a public that appreciates their worth. This formula has apparently led to the success of this company. As with rental websites, auction websites such as Portero could indirectly contribute to combating counterfeiting and educating the public on its effects.

While websites like Portero who strive to establish credibility by empha-sizing the authenticity of the products featured on its website, the Internet abounds with thousands of websites that are defying international intellectual property laws by blatantly retailing counterfeit luxury products to an interna-tional market. Websites like Highreplica.com (which claims to be operating out of China even though they could very well be based in a San Francisco backyard), Basicreplica.com (which failed to state their location but admit-ted that all goods were manufactured in China) and Replicashandbag.com (which has no corporate information) are now commonplace online and pose a continuous challenge for both luxury brands and luxury clients. The key issue with cracking down on their operations is in tracking their locations, gathering enough evidence to prove their operations and working with the legal authorities concerned to bring them to justice. As you may well imag-ine, this is almost like a mission impossible as these websites exist in a vir-tual space and operate from various countries with different outlooks and jurisdiction towards intellectual property issues. Luxury brands are, however,

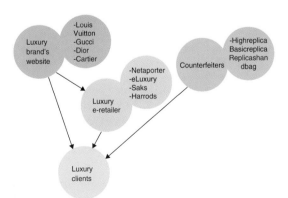

Figure 6.14 *Access to luxury products online was previously through three principal sources; 1) the luxury brand's own website; 2) the luxury e-retailer's website; 3) the counterfeiter's website. Today, this formula has changed drastically and luxury products may now be purchased through various means and forms online*

luxury online

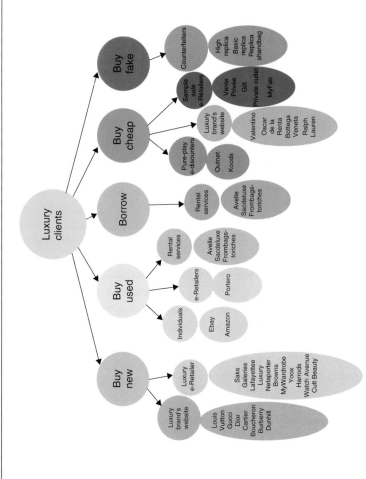

Figure 6.15 *The complex structure of the current luxury e-retail structure. The control has moved from the luxury brand, who previously decided which retailers to work with, to the consumer who now has ten different choice options for obtaining luxury products online. Luxury brands have lost a large degree of control in this scenario and must address the issue of product availability and client evolution with the several parties currently involved in online luxury retail*

required to strive to find creative and complementary means of combating online counterfeiting through educating the public on how to detect fake products and the dangers of partaking in its trade.

Since the mid-nineties, when e-retail established itself as a permanent channel of goods distribution and luxury retail joined the movement, the way luxury is presented and sold online has undergone significant positive changes. From the days of Boo.com, when the bubble came crashing, to the days of Net-a-porter.com and eLuxury.com, when the rules were redefined; to the arrival of Vuitton.com and Gucci.com who paved the way for other brands; to the reverse modeling of Portero.com and Avelle.com; and finally to the arrival of VentePrivée.com and Gilt.com, luxury e-retail has been through several phases and will continue to evolve. The approach of luxury e-retail has shifted from the direct control of the brands and retailers to that of shared influence and access with independent parties and consumers themselves. This calls for a new, flexible and outside-the-box rethinking of the online distribution model as indicated in the illustrated models in Figures 6.14 and 6.15. It calls for including new features and opportunities that could enhance a luxury brand's appeal to its audience while protecting the brand image and enhancing the brand equity.

Chapter 7

e-people are real people

"The 'now' culture of the Internet (mobiles and laptops) convinced us that if we do not have everything on our finger tips, we will immediately transform into one of these impatient, red-faced people cursing each lost millisecond."

—quoted from *Luxe to 2011*

I am often surprised when I hear of the efforts made by luxury brands to separate online clients from offline clients. The initiatives that reflect this practice range from creating separate client management programs and systems, segmenting client offers according to shopping channel and grouping VIP clients not in terms of overall expenditure but from the amount spent on purchases made on each sales channel. Worse yet is when the retail employees in the physical stores compete with the managers of the online stores for clients and sales revenue levels. This reality has led to hoarding client information, resistance towards creating synergies in client management programs and all manner of dysfunctional habits that contribute to the detriment of the brands rather than their advancement.

The reality is that there is no line that separates online luxury clients with offline consumers. In most cases, it is the same people who shop online who are also buying in the physical stores. In fact, the first adopters of Internet shopping in the early days of luxury e-retail were those clients who already had established relationships with luxury brands. Their familiarity with the brands was a natural reassurance for shopping in the virtual environment and they were using the Internet as an extended form of their overall relationship with the brands. Progressively, other groups joined the online shopping crowd and the Internet also became a channel of brand discovery for people to be introduced to luxury brands with which they further interacted through shopping offline. Although online people may exhibit different characteristics due to the specificities of the Internet, their collective behavior towards luxury brands is influenced by their transferred experiences from the real world. It is the same client shopping on the two channels and they are looking for a uniform and coherent brand experience, which means that there should be strong synergies between these channels and everything about client management on either channel should complement rather than compete with the other.

e-People are real people and they are even exhibiting more "realness" in the current global economic slowdown where the Internet is playing multiple roles from offering an avenue for discreet shopping of high-ticket items; to acting as the vehicle for a voyage in the search for discounts, steals and deals; to being the window through which the world of luxury is discovered and desired. These multi-roles have led to significant rises in the number of wealthy shopping for luxury online from 9.5 million in 2008 to the expected +27 percent annual growth between now and 2011. Of the approximately 6.6 billion Internet users, this figure represents a mere 0.6 percent but, in terms of revenue generation, is easily a substantial proportion of total online expenditure of discretionary goods in which luxury forms a significant proportion. It is also interesting to note the wide age range of luxury online shoppers with no age group dominating, although the youth segment (15–34 years) account for slightly over half (55 percent) of online luxury shoppers while those from 35 years upwards make 45 percent of all luxury purchases online. With the constant progress being made in technology applications and the support of governments and such bodies as the European Union – which has been at the forefront of initiating reforms to encourage the growth of online shopping – the Internet is poised to remain a major playground for the wealthy.

Understanding the wealthy online goes beyond evaluating their income levels and expenditure. As much as it is important to view their statistics and progression, it is also crucial to understand their attitudes, interests, expectations, behavior and evolution – in short, what drives them to the Internet and what moves them when they arrive online.

A look at the current luxury client

Anyone who believes that today's luxury client is the same as the one of the last decade is in for a surprise. The luxury client has changed and their perceptions and outlook to luxury have also evolved. This is not only due to the Internet, although the arrival of digital technology and interactive media, coupled with the instant communications and transparency that it enables, has definitely played a key role.

What has happened to the luxury client in the last ten years is remarkable and significant in many ways, as it has been a decade of profound change on multiple levels and in many facets. First, the global economic boom of the nineties continued almost uninterrupted well into the early noughties albeit slightly affected by several set-backs – the Gulf War, the Asian crisis, September 11, SARS – in different degrees around the world. This coupled with the explosion of Internet and digital technologies and their vast business opportunities set the perfect backdrop for unprecedented wealth creation which also stretched to the creative and entertainment industries as well as sports and manufacturing. The support of the capitalist market structure in most developed economies and the access it provided to instant cash, credit and capital led to the change of status for a substantial segment of different populations. As this trend spread around the world through the globalization machine, different attitudes towards money emerged and materialism, consumerism and instant gratification became the order of the day. With the opening up of the access to wealth came increased international travel and convergence of cultures, which subsequently led to the global consumption culture that is very much present today. All these set off a course of international expansion of the luxury market as never seen before. Luxury brands like Louis Vuitton, which multiplied their global store numbers from two in 1977 to 130 in 1989, took a massive turn to internationalization and as I write the brand has 430 stores around the world. Other brands like Giorgio Armani, Gucci and Cartier have not been far behind with store openings worldwide. Even American brands that have been known to stick to the home territory due to market size and economic gains began to take bold steps beyond their shores, with Tiffany's moving from ten stores mostly in the US to 184 stores around the world in just ten years.

The international market opportunities also meant that luxury brands were gaining access to new territories with consumers characterized by different cultural and aesthetic codes as well as perceptions and definitions of luxury. The vastness of these markets, including parts of the US, the extended EU, China, Brazil and Russia, and the potential they held for future revenues prompted certain brands to introduce multiple junior lines within the product ranges, setting off a trend of accessible and affordable products through sub-brands created within the parent brand. Mini-versions of major luxury houses including Valentino Red, Armani Exchange, Just Cavalli, D&G and Versace's Versus were born, giving rise to what has been called by many "masstige" or accessible luxury consumption. This movement also led to the success of high-end brands like Coach and Proenza Schouler and the introduction of several others like Massimo Dutti, Juicy Couture and Rock & Republic, whose models have followed the "accessible luxury" route or what some may call "high-end luxury". The luxury client that emerged in this scenario became one that viewed luxury with not only desire, but also as an extension of themselves and their lifestyles.

As all these were taking place the barriers of entry into the luxury market were being broken down, new brands began to emerge in several segments to compete with the established brands. The Internet became the vehicle behind this with its vast opportunities for visibility, communications and retail. The boom of the latter has played a key role in the current reality of the changing mind-set of the wealthy towards luxury. The freedom of access to information about luxury brands which the Internet provides has led to the closing up of the distance that previously existed between luxury brands and the public. Anyone can access luxury websites and can become a part of the brand's online universe (including those without the means to acquire the products) and this has challenged the way luxury presents itself and the way clients perceive luxury.

The next wave of evolution came with the materialization of the emerging luxury markets – China, Russia, India, Brazil, the Gulf States and, increasingly, Mexico – that are currently considered as those that will carry the luxury industry forward in terms of growth. These markets, peppered with their dynamic economies, new wealth expansion, emergence of wealthy segments and an insatiable thirst for everything luxurious, have brought a revolution in consumer perceptions towards luxury. For example, on the top of the "to do" list of the average wealthy Chinese tourist visiting Paris is a trip to the Louis Vuitton store on the Avenue des Champs Elysées, even if it often requires queuing outside the store entrance for hours before being let in. Russia, where the number of luxury stores has grown to over 400 in just five years, has been ranked among the highest revenue generating markets for brands like Burberry both on home soil and through Russians traveling or resident abroad. Emerging luxury consumers are predicted to outnumber the core luxury clients of today within ten years. These new luxury clients, whose ideas of luxury and attitudes to its consumption are geared more towards the projection of a new social status and an "ideal self" and less towards the portrayal of a luxury culture – although this varies in degrees in each market – are on the verge of changing the way luxury is perceived. In addition, the next eleven countries identified as those that will cause the next wave of boom in the global economy following the predicted twenty-five years of domination of the BRIC countries (Brazil, Russia, India and China) are showing signs of consumer groups gearing up for luxury consumption. Their arrival will bring yet additional dimensions to the socio-cultural influences with regard to the perception of luxury.

On the other hand, there is a rise in the social consciousness among luxury clients in established markets regarding such issues as environmental protection, ethical practices, corporate responsibility, fair trade and sustainable practices of luxury companies. The outlook of this client base has been as a consequence of the perception of "over-availability" of luxury offerings across different markets and the accessibility of luxury brought about by the Internet. As a result, the definition of luxury for many has been within the scope of intangible factors rather than tangible products. This social consciousness has further been heightened by the crash of the financial systems of 2008 and the resulting global economic recession. In seeking solace and recompense in an uncertain climate and what appears to be an unknown future for many, the movement towards luxury sustainability has found its forte and has led to one too many propagators among luxury clients.

The social web phenomenon and the revolution it has brought about through giving a voice to the people and making any and everyone a potential brand evangelist, judge, opinion-leader, influencer, advocator or destroyer has also led to a change in the luxury client. Today, the luxury client is not only savvy and demanding, but is also bold, assertive and powerful enough to steer thousands of others in favor of or against a luxury brand through the unprecedented tools of the social media. Blogs, social networks, discussion platforms and all manner of user-to-user communities have produced a global flock of citizen journalists whose opinions are causing constant change in the way luxury is viewed and perceived by entire generations. This wave has also led to behavior change in the way consumers relate to luxury both in the real world and in the virtual world. They have become product and services savvy and have also become masters of technology who call the shots in their online experiences and transfer these into expectations in their offline interactions with luxury brands.

What these changes and the current climate have produced is a set of contradictions and paradoxes linked to who the current luxury client has become today and what their real profile looks like. On the one hand, luxury clients have shown traits of ongoing enthusiasm for luxury offerings while, on the other hand, signs of "luxury fatigue" are apparent. Some parties are even saying that luxury is dead and that the word "luxury" shouldn't be pronounced anymore. I personally think that this claim is quite ridiculous. And even luxury clients don't believe that luxury is dead.

Luxury is not dead. My opinion is that luxury is just no longer understood. This has arisen from too many people who don't have the culture of luxury currently having access to luxury, therefore rendering it banal. If you've heard the story of the young wealthy Chinese businessman who guzzles down his McDonald's cheeseburger with a bottle of Dom Perignon champagne in a glass cup just because he can afford to buy it, you'll see what I mean. Do we say, in this case, that champagne is dead? Of course not. What we need to do is to educate the young man and open his eyes to the understanding that champagne is not consumed with cheeseburger and that it should be poured in a tilted flute, which is held by its stem before being drunk.

If a portrait were to be painted of today's luxury consumer, it would feature the following characteristics:

1. *Smart and savvy*. Luxury clients no longer buy into the type of luxury portrayed by non-genuine brands that claim the luxury status for quick returns. Today's client can smell brands that don't live up to the luxury qualities from miles away.
2. *Informed and knowledgeable*. With instant access to digital information, the luxury client of today has the ins and outs of luxury brands at his or her fingertips. The surprise element has been suppressed and the client is

now more difficult to please and tantalize. Luxury brands have to work hard to attract and retain the informed client's attention.

3. *International.* Today's luxury client is increasingly a globe-trotter and it is not uncommon for them to shop at major luxury cities, where they increasingly own homes or extended businesses. This means that they expect recognition and coherent brand experiences at every shopping location and channel both offline and online.

4. *Empowered and influential.* The Internet and the arrival of the social web have given power to luxury clients in ways unimagined. Today, by evoking a simple conversation or debate on a blog or social network, luxury clients are able to influence the opinions and perceptions of millions of people towards luxury brands, both positively and negatively. Luxury brands have to understand this world and how to represent their brands in it.

5. *Demanding, impatient and insatiable.* The multiple offerings that luxury clients are inundated with from different channels of sales and communications have led them to be spoilt for choice. As a result, they have become demanding and difficult to please and expect instant gratification. Brands now have to woo, court and dance to their tunes.

6. *Socially and culturally aware.* The world has changed tremendously and become more global in the last two decades and luxury clients have evolved with it. The consequence is a convergence of cultures and social habits and exposure to the differences that make all societies unique. This has led wealthy people to seek niche brands and products that truly represent the fine tradition and craft of each culture.

7. *Individualistic yet communal.* This is one of the paradoxes of today's luxury client who shares collective experiences with thousands of others on the social web while experiencing individual interactions with luxury brands. Their overall feeling towards luxury brands is a result of their shared linkage between these two channels.

8. *Saturated with luxury offerings and information.* Today's luxury client is over-loaded with information and has become a specialist detective in filtering out the details of brand promises that they deem unworthy of their time. The luxury fatigue that is currently rampant means that they are searching for real substance from luxury brands.

9. *Flexible attitude.* The luxury client of today has undergone an attitude overhaul. They no longer crave association with only one brand or an entire collection from one brand; they are prone to defining their own styles by mixing and matching. They are also open to disposing of luxury products through sales and second-ownership sales as well as acquiring used luxury products, borrowing some and even collectively owning some like yachts, cars and jets.

10. *Convenience-driven.* Again, the Internet has provided a most convenient and less intimidating channel of interaction with luxury brands and this has sparked an attitude towards convenience as a key factor in accessing luxury

products and services. For a large proportion of luxury clients, their choice of shopping channel is dependent on convenience but they still expect the overall brand experience to be enriching, irrespective of channel.

11. *Seeking bespoke and made-to-measure.* The wave of increased access to luxury products and services by an expanded client base as well as the maturity level of luxury consumption in some markets has led to increased demand for made-to-measure and customized products and service experiences.

12. *More website loyal, less brand loyal.* Luxury clients exhibit varying degrees of differences in their behavior online versus offline. In the physical world, their choice criteria for brand preference range from the brand's reputation, products, services and overall experiences. Online, however, their preference for a luxury brand depends on the offerings and experience the brand offers on its website. In other words, if a luxury website doesn't deliver the client moves on. After all, it only takes one click and half a second.

13. *Seeks to connect, share and dialogue online.* Today's web experience is about conversing, exchanging, sharing and collaborating and the luxury client is not left out of this revolution. They seek to share their passion for luxury brands with other cyber-residents and increasingly trust the independent opinions of their fellow consumers in these forums.

14. *Expects to be in charge.* The voice that the social web has given to the luxury consumer has led to their belief in their control of the relationship with luxury brands. They expect to be in charge of defining their needs and how they want to be served by luxury brands.

15. *Socially responsible.* Today's luxury client cares about the world in which they live. There is a strong movement towards social responsibility, ethics, environmental protection, fair trade and other initiatives geared towards the well-being of society. The brands that are involved in genuinely supporting these initiatives will likely feature at the top-end of the choice list of clients. And the clients are smart enough to sniff out the brands that intend to use sustainability for PR stunts!

Cracking today's luxury client

Well, we've seen that today's luxury client seems to be a tough cookie to crack. What opportunities do luxury brands have for grabbing and holding the attention of this client base? What do they really want and expect from luxury brands? How can they be served and related with in order to ensure their affiliation with brands? What about their exposure to thousands of luxury brands at a time on the Internet? How is this changing their expectations and outlook? And what will be the impact of the global economic recession on their attitudes towards luxury? The answers to these questions lie in the behavior of luxury clients, both online and offline.

The luxury client is seeking a deep and intimate relationship with luxury brands that emphasizes recognition, respect, dialogue and collaboration.

Today's client is fed up with being ignored. They don't want to be a part of the faceless names on the database lists used for mass email blasts, neither are they seeking to complete luxury brands' statistics for website traffic. They have a face and a voice and they want brands to recognize them at every touch-point. The days of anonymous marketing are over and the client of today is attuned to rejecting brands that don't give them the recognition they seek. The luxury consumer's current state of mind is such that they are likely to lose quickly patience with brands that don't deliver exceptional products, services and experiences. Luxury brands will have to prove themselves to this clientele even as they continue to be spoilt for choice and as the competition becomes more widespread.

The same set of expectations applies to the e-experience garnered from the brands' websites. Today's client is seeking a "wow" web experience from brands that is in line with what the brand offers in the physical world. They desire to discover a coherent brand universe online and offline. For them, the channel of access to a luxury brand shouldn't take away the brand experience and the virtual world of the brand should be as stimulating and immersive as the real world. A luxury brand's website should strike an emotional chord with the client and build a bond of intimacy. This is what will drive them to discuss the brand in the social web and "evangelize" the brand's positive attributes online and offline. Achieving this goes beyond creating a pretty website with easy navigation and usability and ensuring security of transactions; it also requires interactivity in high doses and excellent client management features with real human contact. Collaborative features including customization, personalization, dialogue and community are also important ingredients in this mix. As repeated throughout this book, the mass availability and wide adoption of the Internet has given rise to a new online social order where consumers are piloting exchanges about brands through dialogue, debates and mass collaboration. And thousands are actively participating in these conversations. A look at the hundreds of user groups formed around luxury brands on online communities like MySpace and Facebook will confirm this.

The keywords required to cracking today's luxury client, both online and offline, are: *inform, entertain, influence, empower, impact, content, participate, observe, listen, understand, update, evolve, engage, real, trust, connect, advice, influence, opinion, customize, personalize, co-create, tantalize, court and wow.*

The brands that integrate the right mix of the online and offline elements that reproduce these qualities are already on their way to the client's heart.

The international luxury client

The typical luxury jewelry client found on the client lists of brands such as Bvlgari, Cartier, Boucheron, Chopard and Van Cleef & Arpels are international jet-setters that feature two distinct groups: celebrities and socialites;

and the ordinary man or woman who could be anything from business mogul to a sportsman or simply a young executive who has adopted an international lifestyle. These clients' shopping habits for luxury products such as jewelry or fashion and accessories is such that they are frequent buyers and spend substantial sums, often upwards of $10,000, during each buying activity. This figure can stretch to $millions.

The core characteristic of this clientele is not only their wealth status but also their unique positioning in the international scene. The majority of them are multiple home owners with several addresses in different cities and countries. They also increasingly have dual and triple nationalities with different passports that they use according to their locations and destinations. Not surprisingly, they also easily have several credit cards linked to banks and financial institutions around the world, which they alternate as they shop. As we may imagine, this clientele is likely to shop for luxury products in different cities, using different credit cards and passports as ID.

Let's say that there is a Cartier devotee among them who has an apartment in Paris, another in Miami and yet another in Dubai, meaning three addresses; and shops at Cartier in all these locations as well as other Cartier stores around the world (Figure 7.1). If he also happens to have dual French and American nationalities and switches between the two passports when shopping, in addition to also switching between his Amex, Visa and Mastercards, he is likely to fall within the bracket of clients with multiple profiles in the luxury store databases depending on the type of systems being used. Cartier's store in New York may have him listed as an American client resident locally and may have a recording of his shopping history in the US. Cartier Paris could have a parallel profile of him with a recording of his shopping history in France, this time as a French client resident locally in Paris. Other Cartier stores around the world could have parallel profiles with details that are dependent on the address, passport and credit card that he uses when shopping. Let's say that this client spends an average of $1 million on Cartier products annually in about ten of the brand's stores around the world. If we break down his expenditure in each store, we may find that he could be spending as little as $5,000 in one store and as much as $300,000 in another store. As a consequence, in one store he could be classified as a VIP client while in another store he may not make the VIP list. It could also happen that he may not be on the VIP list of any of the stores at all, depending on the spread of his expenditure. But, in reality, he is a real VIP client that should be treasured and pleased at all costs. The point is that the brand doesn't know this and has therefore overlooked him and could potentially lose him to competitors.

This scenario is common in the current luxury market. In fact, several luxury brands have admitted that they lose an estimated 15 percent to 25 percent of their VIP clients as a result of the lack of integrated key information about international clients. And 15 percent of clients that spend $millions on a brand is not a joke!

To make the matter worse for luxury brands, this international clientele has its own specific attitudes, demands and expectations. In addition to their expectation of being recognized, respected and accorded VIP treatment across every store and online, these clients also expect luxury brands to remember their tastes, habits and preferences and to use this information to tailor offerings to them for a refined shopping and brand experience. This poses a real challenge to luxury brands that can only be overcome with the integration of the appropriate client management and rewards systems.

Figure 7.1 *The global increase of high net-worth individuals has led to the rise of a segment of luxury clients with international profiles who shop in luxury boutiques around the world. These clients, who increasingly have multiple nationalities and passports, several homes and addresses, and numerous bank accounts and credit cards have proved a challenging demographic for luxury brands to cater to as a result of the difficulties in capturing their personal data and tracking their multiple profiles. At the same time, they increasingly expect brands that have extensive store networks around the world, like Cartier, to recognize them, understand them and provide them with tailor-made offerings in products, services and shopping experience both online and offline*

Rewarding the online luxury client

Once upon a time, when luxury was solely a combination of the art of crafting beautiful products and selling them in intimate environs, the best clients that frequently purchased these products were known to the designers, store owners and shopkeepers. They formed personal relationships that stretched beyond the store walls. In addition to knowing their names, tastes and preferences, the designers and store owners also knew their families, friends, lifestyles, homes, pets and even their birthdays. Maintaining a strong relationship with this clientele was so important that the owners of the luxury *maisons* often invited them to their homes for meals and festivities. The clients, on their own part, reciprocated by being loyal to the *maison* and committed to the designers.

Today, this has changed. As a consequence of the expansion of the luxury market that now includes international territories and a near-global market, the majority of today's luxury brands have clients running into hundreds of thousands, and in some cases millions, of people around the world. You will agree that it is impossible to know all their names by heart and to invite all of them to dinner. But this evolution of the luxury market has brought with it something that didn't exist in the past – technology – which if exploited appropriately could enable luxury brands to reproduce the intimacy of relations with clients in days gone by.

To begin with, the technology that supports client data management both on the Internet and offline should be top-notch and capable of capturing data, integrating it across channels and locations, streamlining it in a way that clients may easily be found and pulling its main elements together for personalized offerings and experiences. The beauty of technology is that it provides infinite opportunities to capture client data, monitor their shopping habits and tailor specific offerings to them. If effectively applied, technological support can be a real stepping stone for brands in their quest for a substantial mind-share of luxury clients. How can this be achieved? Here are a few tips and points:

- Client management programs don't begin and end with responding to customer queries and ensuring that shoppers receive adequate advice. It includes an integrated approach to guarantee that the experience that clients have with the brand is enriching, uniform and coherent across every touch-point, whether by telephone or email and through the website or physical location.

- Managing clients online is not only a question of sending email newsletters as frequently as possible – no matter how interesting it is and the number of links it has; neither is it about monitoring website and shopping traffic. It also has to do with ensuring that clients visiting the website do not feel the lack of human presence. This may be achieved by incorporating elements that lead to immediate access to client managers through instant dialogue tools such as "click to call" and "client call back". These tools should be made available for clients in different world regions.

- Integrating online and offline client management systems is a must. As highlighted throughout this book online shoppers also experience luxury brands in the physical world on many levels and they seek coherence in these experiences. This can only be provided if the client is recognized, remembered and served in the way he deserves across every touch-point with the brand.

- Luxury brands have always refused to adopt Fidelity Cards, Affinity Cards and other forms of reward programs, maintaining that this removes the dream factor from luxury purchases and "massifies" luxury consumption. While this argument is sound, it is time for luxury brands to explore ways that technology could support client regrouping through using cards for client recognition across different channels and touch-points.

- In following the same pattern of aversion to reward cards, luxury brands have also frowned on branded individual credit cards provided to clients for shopping, as well as payment plans such as the installment payment programs widely practiced by luxury boutiques in places like Brazil and Bulgaria. The domain of branded credit cards has been ventured into by the likes of Giorgio Armani, Roberto Cavalli and Alexander McQueen mainly on a design level. Branded payment cards could also provide an avenue for overcoming the client identification crisis that luxury brands experience with an increasingly international clientele.
- Rewarding luxury clients could also take the form of special access to events online and offline as well as access to exclusive web pages and content. Several luxury car brands like Porsche and Ferrari are currently applying this, particularly online, and on the beauty front Parfums Christian Dior is leading this through its VeryDior club.
- Online luxury clients could also be rewarded through mining the database to propose personalized offerings to clients according to their page views and interests. This is likely to yield higher results than mass email marketing and will also go a long way to making the client feel recognized and respected. This could also be transferred to the offline offerings.
- Online luxury clients who regularly shop or visit the brand's website could also be rewarded by being invited to be among the select few to collaborate with luxury brands on different levels, whether it is through ideas generation, co-creation, special visits or brand's events. These steps will surely strengthen the bond existing between the brand and clients.

From e-people to what people?

Digital technology has dramatically changed the mind-set of an entire generation and has reshaped several economies and societies in less than two decades. There is no doubt about this. It has also resulted in several consumer cultures and sub-cultures, most of them linked to luxury directly and indirectly. Because of instant messaging through smart phones, the Internet, social web platforms – blogs, online communities and virtual worlds – and portals like YouTube, MySpace, Flickr, Skype and Digg, tens of millions of people all over the world are instantly aware of what is going on everywhere in the world at the same time. These digital elite with high doses of disposable income amassed from an entrepreneurial culture are defining a new set of rules for luxury experiences while challenging the ways luxury brands relate to them. Their current expectation is that luxury should come to them rather than they go to luxury and also that luxury products should be available to them when they want it and how they want it – in other words, attuning the offerings to everyone's needs for instant gratification. All these expectations are in addition to the demand to be recognized and courted irrespective of whether they are clients or not, as long as they have visited the luxury brand's website once.

To make matters more interesting, the global financial crisis and its spin-off credit crunch is leading to even further changes in the psychology of luxury clients and further shifts in value systems, mind-sets and social consciousness on multiple levels. This coupled with globalization and the presence of luxury brands on the world economic stage has ensured that there is no escape for luxury brands in the cultural revolution that was ignited by the Internet and has been propelled by globalization and now the recession. The mentality of luxury clients is changing worldwide and it is apparent that this is on a profound level. These changes are also evolving in multiple directions although it is not yet clear which of these directions will dominate the new culture that will emerge following the strong winds blowing over the economic crisis. One thing for sure, however, is that what is currently taking place on the luxury consumer front has never been experienced before in the luxury domain.

The current global recession marks the first time that the luxury sector has been touched by a worldwide crisis as an industry. Unlike the previous hits that luxury has taken in the past for short periods, including the Gulf War, September 11 and SARS, the current crisis is significantly different. First, it is not event-driven and doesn't touch only on tourist spending, but also on domestic purchases of luxury. Second, it is impacting the luxury business as a consolidated "industry", which was not the case in the past. Let's not forget that before LVMH, Richemont and the Gucci Group came along, the luxury sector was a group of design and trade-driven activities dominated by small and successful family businesses. Today, the scene has changed and luxury has become an important economic force with a concrete structure, operational mechanisms and consensus in management systems. Third, the recession is coming at a time of an important power-shift on two levels, first between luxury brands and consumers and, second, between the economic force of occidental versus oriental countries in terms of luxury consumption. The "traditional" luxury countries – France, Italy, Spain and the UK – together with the US and Japan have for a long time wielded the force of influence in luxury purchases and, as a result, exported the idea of western luxury to the oriental countries – China, the Gulf States, Brazil, Russia and India. Today, these latter countries, together with the likes of Mexico, hold great promise for the future survival of the global luxury business. This, of course, will bring with it several cultural consequences.

Where is the consumer in this mix and in what way will they be affected by the current climate? Although it is quite challenging to understand clearly the direction of the next wave of evolution of the luxury client, it is clear that luxury consumers are at a crossroads between the virtual melting pot, the shifts in luxury consumption and the economic crisis. Here are ten indications and pointers for brands as we all make efforts towards making sense of it all:

1. Consumers will re-interpret luxury according to their idea of what provides them with value. This re-definition of value will follow a new order of evaluating the brands that are able to deliver what they promise not only in terms of well-crafted and exceptional products with the best quality, but also an overall positive experience garnered from the way the brand presents itself, respects its clients, contributes to its society and acts responsibly. Consumers will not stop spending on luxury but they will only buy what corresponds to this new order of interpretation and represents true value to them. The recent record-breaking auction sales of Yves Saint Laurent and Pierre Bergé's private art and interiors collections which fetched €374.4 million ($477 million), significantly higher than the forecast €200 million to €300 million, right in the middle of the financial crisis, attests to this. Investment is the keyword here.

2. Luxury clients will adopt online shopping to a greater degree than in the past. Those that already buy online will use the Internet channel recurrently while those that have resisted using the Internet to purchase luxury products and services will most likely adopt the channel. This will arise as a result of two opposing factors. First, there is the current movement away from street shopping which has suddenly become "unfashionable" in a climate where job losses are a daily occurrence. Shopping in discretion has become the order of the day and there is no better place to do so than online. Second, there is the factor of discount shopping that has become more accentuated due to the rise of markdown and sample sale websites as well as the awareness of cutting back on expenditure in the face of an uncertain future for many. In addition, the phenomenon of the social web and its unique nature of assembling hundreds of thousands of people to connect, dialogue and influence one another will gear a new population towards online shopping.

3. Consumers will purchase luxury differently from the way they accessed luxury in the past. This will happen through alternating between different channels of distribution including physical stores, the Internet and mobile shopping. The same client will increasingly experience luxury through both channels and will seek uniform brand experiences online and offline. Consumers that are experienced with luxury purchases who know their tastes and the brands that are able to satisfy their style demands will be savvy and confident enough to spend $thousands on the Internet without blinking, just as they do offline. Also, as mobile technology evolves, they will progressively adopt this channel for access to luxury.

4. The ample changes in the luxury segment and the rise of a multitude of brands that claim to be "luxury" without necessarily having luxury offerings, will lead consumers to be fatigued with luxury, so to speak. This will give rise to several trends, chief of which will be a higher demand for made-to-measure or bespoke products. Personal and discreet luxury will become the order of the day and "bling" and "it" items will be discarded, even in emerging markets. Consumers will also increasingly demand the opportunity to personalize standard products and their expectation for this will also be transferred to the Internet channel.

5. The youth generation empowered by a digital culture and the social web will re-define the way that luxury brands relate with clients. The independent, transparent, open, communal and collaborative nature of the social web will lead to a new global youth culture that thrives on assertion and expressiveness. The chunk of this generation belonging to the youth segment will transfer their virtual experiences to their real-life expectations from luxury brands and will influence older segments in this movement. They will become more in control in the relationship with luxury brands.

6. The luxury client will continue in the evolution towards social consciousness and the recognition of virtue and value in ethics, environmental protection and daily sustainable practices as true luxury. They will increasingly judge and adopt luxury brands on the basis of their transparency in issues such as fair trade, environmental protection, charitable contributions and overall corporate social responsibility. The responsible luxury client will emerge as an entire segment and such trivial issues as courting and worshipping celebrities will be "out" while individual value will become "in". Although this movement will be powered by the established luxury markets and will evolve in varying degrees in different markets, the emerging markets will catch up in no time, thanks to information access and exposure garnered from the Internet.

7. The new luxury client will also place "service" and "experience" at the top of their requirements for luxury to fulfill its promise to them. Service experiences could easily become king over the products as a source of long-term relationship with the brand. Luxury clients have always invested in their relationships with brands and they have been taken more or less for granted, until now. They now require brands to take them seriously and to go out of their way to offer great experiences that will keep them happy. The brands that fail to meet this criterion will be crossed off the list. A case in point is the recently opened Georg Jensen New York flagship store on Madison Avenue, offering a store concept of the Danish lifestyle in the context of a home with Danish furnishings and other elements including fireplaces, leather sofas, food items, chinaware and sound systems by Bang & Olufsen. Despite coming along in the middle of the recession, the store has become an important destination

for luxury shoppers seeking enhanced service and exceptional experiences linked to a lifestyle.

8. In an uncertain economic climate full of contrasts and paradoxes and pressured by an urgent need to have instant access to everything, a segment of luxury clients will seek the opposite – patience, peace and quality time in a fast-paced world. They will expect to find this in the solace of luxury stores and environments and in the reward of the products and services obtained.

9. The luxury client from emerging markets will begin to show signs of departing from the tag of "nouveau riche" consumers who have little luxury culture. The hard lessons learnt from the global recession in countries like Russia, China and United Arab Emirates and the new attitudes to money that will emerge following the financial crisis will introduce a new way of perceiving luxury. For this clientele, in no time it will be less about logos and more about the total value of the collective elements of luxury. Again, this will be accelerated by increased exposure to the Internet and instant digital communications.

10. Finally, the luxury customer will show creativity in adopting and mixing and matching luxury. As with every period of scarcity and limitations, creativity in luxury will emerge in high doses and this will be championed by the consumers. They will also expect brands to get over the current "sameness" of luxury and up the creative notch.

As the luxury client evolves and new consumer cultures emerge, luxury will need to remain true to itself by retaining an uncompromising stance to the qualities that have given it its credibility. Luxury brands will also face the challenge of educating an entire generation on the meaning of true luxury and inculcating the culture and philosophy of luxury in their consciousness. This will be no easy task in the face of a younger generation whose present and future is built on digital technology and the freedom and independence that it provides. Luxury brands will, however, need to adopt the appropriate approach in order to fulfill the changing expectations of luxury clients, while remaining true to their core values.

Chapter 8

Beyond the Internet: mobile technology and innovation for luxury

"Utility is when you have one telephone, luxury is when you have two, opulence is when you have three – and paradise is when you have none."

—Doug Larson

If someone were to mention to you that a luxury brand is a living thing that needs to be fed and nurtured like humans, animals and plants, your first reaction would probably be that the person is crazy. If the person went ahead and insisted that luxury brands go through the same stages of growth as human beings, from infancy to childhood, teenage, adulthood and old age and that each life-stage requires luxury to be and act in a certain way, you will likely conclude that he has lost his mind or that he has suddenly woken up on the wrong side of the age of philosophy.

The truth is that a luxury brand can be considered as embodying the same characteristics as a living thing because it touches on emotions, arouses strong feelings and moves people to feel and act in ways that may often seem illogical or surprising to them and others. Just as music and cinema have the potential to move emotions in people, true luxury represents more than objects and surroundings but is an embodiment of feelings, emotions and sentiments that live within people and, in certain cases, manifests with every pulse and breath.

If we were to put luxury in the context of life-stages, we could say that luxury is currently mature and is going through the stage of adulthood because luxury has been a part of humankind since time immemorial. However, if we were to take luxury as a consolidated industry and an economic force on the global market scene, the life-stage we would designate it would be different. In this case, luxury would be best described as being in its late teenage years.

This is because the luxury sector did not previously exist as an "industry" with a structured consensus in management and an integrated approach to business operations. Until the three largest luxury groups – LVMH, Richemont and Gucci Group – were created in the late nineties and early noughties, the luxury domain was interspersed by a group of families involved in the art of creating, producing and retailing the finest quality products ranging through leathergoods, fashion, jewelry and fragrance. The luxury sphere, however, remained a domain of "activities" rather than an economic "sector".

Today, this has changed – although this change is fairly recent. LVMH, which came along and transformed the way luxury functions, was created in 1987, Richemont came along in 1988 and the Gucci Group was consolidated shortly afterwards, although its parent company, PPR, had been in existence since 1963. For the next decade, these three groups and the brands they own – Louis Vuitton, Christian Dior, Fendi, Dom Perignon, Moët & Chandon, Tag Heueur etc. for LVMH; Cartier, Van Cleef & Arpels, Piaget, Chloé, Dunhill, Mont Blanc etc. for Richemont; Gucci, Yves Saint Laurent, Bottega Veneta, Sergio Rossi, Boucheron, Stella McCartney, etc. for the Gucci Group – would define the creative and business practices of the luxury sector on a global market level. Their arrival brought about a change in the way luxury functions where, instead of relying solely on artistic direction, the management aspect became the force that drives both the creative and business outputs of luxury.

During the several years these companies have been in existence, a modern luxury industry has been born. Where there was traditional bureaucracy, there is now streamlined business mechanics. Where there was resistance to change, modern innovation has been adopted. Intelligent branding and marketing techniques have replaced a cold, aloof and distant relationship with clients. An international approach has been adopted in the place of regional supremacy while talent, creativity, craftsmanship, perfection and skill remain obsessively nurtured. Social factors and environmental issues continue to be immensely respected and the industry continuously strives towards positively influencing social and economic evolution. An example can be drawn from LVMH's acquisition of a minority stake in ethical fashion brand Edun. This combination of key success factors is responsible for the continuous growth and evolution of the luxury sector. Needless to say, the birth of the modern luxury industry and the emergence of a consensus in its management systems and business approaches have accelerated the evolution of the industry and, at the same time, revealed several challenges that must be addressed in its development.

The main challenging factor of growth in the luxury industry is technology. In addition to dealing with the paradoxes of the Internet, digital media and technology, the luxury sector must face up to other facets of technological advancement. Luxury must find an equilibrium in adopting technology in creation, production, retail, management and general operations. Just as technology is an important aspect of the lives of late teens and early adults, it has also become imperative for luxury to ascertain its place in the current digital-driven world. The beat of the global economy is based on this digital pulse. Technology and innovation are currently required across every aspect of the luxury business, starting from material sourcing, production techniques, retail development, store merchandizing, client management, logistics and transport, strategy development, operational models and so on. It translates itself through mobile technology and the opportunities for m-commerce; it supports the applications required for data capturing and management; it challenges the approaches to sensory marketing through neuro-marketing techniques; it provides a different outlook to store merchandizing through distant-assortment methods; it reshapes the looks and functions of products through high-tech materials; and it introduces a new look to product customization through body scanning methods. There is no escaping the fact that technology will play a key role in defining the growth of luxury in its next life-stage, and the earlier luxury brands address the issues linked to technology the better.

The mobile luxury debate

The mobile phone is the most personal of all the communications media existing today. If I ask you to tell me precisely where your car keys or house or office keys are at this moment, you may not be able to do so, but if I ask you to tell me precisely where your mobile phone is or to show it to me, you would likely produce it immediately. Let's admit it, we all have intimate relationships with our mobile phones and, to a large extent, it controls us in different ways. I've seen too many men and women become frantic in public places in a bid to find their ringing phones in their handbags, briefcases and pockets. The mobile has turned the coolest and chicest of women into disheveled neurotics in the frenzied panic attacks following its loss. It has become more than a companion but a treasured solace for those lonely ones that find themselves with no one to speak to at cocktail parties or at public events. It has also become a tool for people to exhibit their importance, particularly in public places – airports, train stations, banks, fashion shows – and in most cases, their self-worth and their pocket-size – think the Boucheron and Vertu co-branded phone. Lyrics have been sung about the mobile phenomenon and its rendering of everyone from business executives to fashionistas, celebrities and politicians to slavery status – think Silvio Berlusconi at the 2009 NATO meeting or Angelina Jolie at press interviews – and its sheer power over the youth generation who view having a mobile as a necessity equated to eating food and drinking water.

The arrival of the Blackberry and iPhone and other smartphones have even made matters worse. Our peace of mind has been stolen forever. Frantically (or should I say neurotically) checking one's Blackberry every five minutes is now a pastime for many and it would not be surprising if this is soon listed in official forms under the "hobby" section. The result is that the arrival of the mobile has changed the way we communicate, think, live, act and relate to one another. And even those that have refused to acquire mobile phones are also affected because the wider society is feeling the impact of this revolution.

The mobile revolution is not a question of a youth culture but is taking place across all generations, geographical regions, age groups, cultures, religions and societies irrespective of economic state. Today, approximately 2.5 billion mobile phone subscribers exist in the world. Globally, there are twice as many active users of SMS as there are active users of emails. In 2007 alone, more than 2 trillion text messages were sent worldwide and this number was estimated to reach 2.5 trillion messages in 2008. People read SMS typically within an average of 15 minutes after receipt and they respond typically within 60 minutes, no matter how busy they are. To add to the mind-staggering figures, around 280 million people use 3G (third generation phones) worldwide, and by 2010 this number is expected to reach 800 million. At the moment, there are 100 million people around the world who use their mobile phones to connect to the Internet constantly. This is, however, not surprising because as far back as 2005 more than thirty countries in the world had reached 100 percent mobile penetration and the rest of the world is not far behind. Even in the most remote parts of developing Africa, Asia and South America, you are more likely to find people with mobile phones than road signs.

Mobile technology is a global phenomenon that knows no boundaries and it has led to a real market opportunity for companies in several sectors to take advantage of its prospects. Not surprisingly, the luxury sector has jumped on the bandwagon, first through mobile devices launched in collaboration with mobile phone manufacturers, and subsequently through mobile marketing campaigns that feature promotions, events and new product information. In 2006, Dolce & Gabbana collaborated with Motorola to create the Razr Gold amidst great publicity and fanfare, and shortly afterwards the Giorgio Armani and Samsung co-branded phone was launched with the same enthusiastic flair the brand is known for. Prada didn't waste time and soon associated with LG to produce a co-branded phone while Hugo Boss opted for a single brand mobile phone. Christian Dior and Tag Heueur also went the way of building their single-brand phone, complete with customized systems and content. On a higher level of positioning, Boucheron collaborated with high-end phone company, Vertu, to create a bejeweled limited-edition phone that came in only 8 pieces and was retailed for $310,000 per piece (see Figure 8.1). All these initiatives have demonstrated boldness in venturing into new territories but have generally failed to create sustainable appeal of the luxury brands. This is because the focus of these initiatives has been on product extension through the mobile "device", which remains a disposable item. On the contrary, the core features that wealthy clients appreciate in mobile phones are the design, the functions and the content. They expect the latter to be rich and personalized as the brand experience ought to be more elevated when it comes to relating mobile technology to luxury.

As luxury brands have become more accustomed to mobile technology, a few brands have shown a shift in developing branded applications integrated as content within mobile phones. An example of one of the first luxury brands to follow this direction is the Hotel Plaza-Athenée in Paris which offers its guests a mobile phone with a GPS system application containing the addresses and maps to Paris' most exclusive boutiques, restaurants and tourist attractions. The application also enables instant connection with the concierge service of the hotel through click-to-call and provides the opportunity for the guests to download the application on their own mobile phones. This real and rich content that both informs, entertains and reassures has been an essential tool in creating intimacy between the hotel and its clients as well as leading to a higher number of returning visitors.

In July 2008, Chanel also launched an application for iPhone users to view its Fall–Winter 2008–2009 Haute Couture Show. iPhone users could watch a video of the fashion show and, through the touch-screen functions, they could window-shop future collections and zoom in on details of garments or accessories. The application allowed click-to-call to make an order and offered other features such as store location, images and access to the news feed of the brand. Users were also able to use the brand's logo as a screen-saver on their phone as a way to reinforce brand presence. The application was targeted at young, female, smart and sophisticated Chanel affiliates and its aim was to evoke a sense of belonging to an exclusive community recognized by the brand. However, limiting the application to iPhone owners was no guarantee to exclusivity.

Also, although the application could not be perceived as intrusive by customers – they are the ones to decide whether or not to download it – its anonymous, impersonal and mass nature diminished its effect on clients. Today's luxury client base seeks more than mass entertainment; it has also become accustomed to being recognized, respected, communicated with on a one-to-one basis. They also seek avenues to relate with luxury brands through dialogue and exchanges. These are the aspects that the Chanel application failed to fulfill.

Chloé shortly followed in the same direction by creating an iPhone integrated application through which users were able to view the latest fashion shows and contact a boutique via a touch-to-call function (see Figure 8.1). Again, there was no additional value in this application because all the functions that the phone offered could easily be accessed on the Internet and, frankly, clients will always prefer to watch a video of a fashion show on a large computer screen than on a mobile phone screen, unless they have no choice.

Figure 8.1   *The arrival of mobile technology has led luxury brands to explore the several options for being omnipresent in the lives and consciousness of clients. The debate for the integration of mobile technology with luxury has been in two distinct areas: mobile devices versus mobile applications. While brands like Chloé and Chanel have opted for content-based applications, others like Boucheron and Prada have taken the route of mobile devices. Both strategies are aimed at attracting the client to the brand, although the latter is more exposed to the risk of the disposable nature of mobile phones as a result of technology and style evolution*

On the mobile marketing front, Dolce & Gabbana also ran a campaign in partnership with Nokia in June 2008. The campaign promoted the brand's teen-focused fashion catalogue, while increasing awareness during the Men's Fashion Show in Milan. The icons on the phone led consumers to a D&G mobile Internet site where they could download a branded game and wallpaper to their handset and view a catalogue. The strategy was to reach young consumers on their mobile handset through a fun campaign that would encourage them to spend time with the brand, as well as forward-generate a buzz. Armani Exchange also conducted its first SMS-based marketing program in 2008 through a text-to-win promotion. It encouraged people to text the keyword "AX" to a short code for a chance to win a $1,000 shopping spree. These mobile marketing initiatives remain interesting but have become basic requirements for a clientele seeking more engagement with luxury brands.

Ralph Lauren has led the evolution of luxury m-commerce by launching a mobile commerce service to allow clients to buy products from their handsets through a dedicated mobile site that is powered by Quick Response (QR) codes in advertisements. QR is an application that enables customers to shop via their camera phones by sending a photo of a two-dimensional image shown in print advertisements or store windows. The QR code will then take the client directly to the m-commerce portal to shop for the specified item. To elevate the offering, the service provides entertainment through access to the brand's magazine, a style guide, exclusive videos and special sports news. Clients are also provided the option of signing up for Ralph Lauren mobile alerts for a wide range of information including store openings, events and collaborations. The portal is free and open to anyone with a supporting mobile system. At the time of writing, another luxury brand, Hermès, has indicated interest in pursuing m-commerce in its technology integration.

These examples, which indicate the interest and flexibility of luxury brands in mobile technology, also reveal that, so far, luxury brands have approached mobile marketing and retail initiatives as an independent platform rather than an extension of an integrated multi-channel effort. Mobile technology works best in the context of a complementary medium that supports the overall marketing and retailing activities of a brand. It is a platform that has the potential to complete the client's overall experience of a brand's universe and ought to be made a part of an integrated marketing strategy. One of the few brands that has demonstrated progression in this direction is the auto brand BMW, which launched a mobile campaign to promote its first X6 Sports Activity Coupé in the US, as part of a multi-channel strategy to enhance client relations. It created a dedicated mobile WAP site and enabled access through texting a keyword to a number. The site provided information including the car's specifications and dealer information, as well as interactivity through slideshows. Jaguar also executed a similar campaign in the US for its XF model, which included among other choices, the opportunity to order a brochure or book a test drive of the car. Its success rate has been high, particularly in the area of downloads as well as locating dealers to arrange test drives.

It's now common knowledge that interactive mobile initiatives increase the level of engagement between luxury brands and clients. As one of the most responsive media of communication, it is ideal for relationship marketing because it is personal, individual, and omnipresent, has high penetration and is a two-way means of communication. Mobile technology has the power to keep brand names consistently and effectively in the minds of clients. It enables the development of personalized communications and allows brands to capture accurate customer intelligence based on behavior. Its impact can also be measured in real time. Its low-cost and easy and quick set-up format also means that it provides a real source of cost-effectiveness and value. All of these benefits point to the reality that mobile technology should form a core aspect of a luxury brand's multi-channel communications and retail strategy. In addition, m-commerce, which is growing rapidly, is expected to surpass wired e-commerce within 10 years. The real question at the moment is how luxury brands may take advantage of mobile technology and adapt it to the requirements of luxury.

The mobile debate in luxury circles so far has been whether to focus on mobile phone devices, in other words the hardware, or whether luxury brands should concentrate efforts on the contents, in other words the application software. I guess the question should be rephrased as "Should we design and create a phone and plaster our logo on it?" Or "Should we design the contents of a phone, and include exclusive interactive information and branded content?"

While the former will provide short-term status returns (for the clients that depend on brands to reassure them and others of their wealth status), in the long-term it has the risk of damaging the brand's positioning. After all, the nature of mobile phones is such that people do not have a life-long relationship with them but dispose of them as technology and styles evolve. I bet you that many who acquired the Dolce & Gabbana phone or the Giorgio Armani phone in the last two to three years have probably disposed of them and moved on to the new Blackberrys and iPhones. When people throw a product with an Armani logo on it in the dustbin, it definitely does something to their perception of the brand. The latter question, however, has the potential of acting as a bridge in building intimate relations with clients through recognition, respect and collaboration. Providing interactive and enriching content that informs, serves, entertains and inspires in a format that is simple and can be shared, will serve a luxury brand better than launching telephone model after model.

It is, however, essential to understand the type of relationship and interactivity that consumers have with their mobile phones. It is also imperative to monitor the evolution of mobile technology and the advantages and limitations of existing applications and formats. For example, mobile marketing campaigns which basically follow an SMS format are powered by 2G mobile phones and only allow brands to contact existing and potential customers via 160 character SMS or by direct voice calls. The current collection of 3G mobile phones offers the opportunity to engage customers through rich content and greater interactivity. With the increasing numbers of 3G users, the possibility to reach customers directly anywhere at anytime, as well as the sheer size of the global mobile population, is enormous. Luxury brands have the potential to use mobile technology not only as a communications channel, but also as a sales and client engagement channel. And mobile technology is in constant evolution, therefore latecomers will have a lot of catching up to do.

If the question "How can luxury brands approach content-based mobile applications?" is still nagging in your head, then read on.

For starters, when designing mobile marketing or mobile retailing initiatives, luxury brands have to ensure that clients will experience its value on all levels and are able to relate it to the universal brand experience across other channels. This basically means giving them a coherent experience and ensuring that their contact with the brand is enriching and enjoyable. That means also ensuring that:

- the initiative is not and will not be viewed as intrusive.
- it is designed in such a way that the user is reassured of the privacy of their personal information and their control over its use.
- the client's authorization is obtained before bombarding them with marketing content, in other words that they "opt-in" to use the service.
- the relevant content is provided to the right people, in other words tailoring the message to be appealing to the recipients.
- access to the mobile service retains an element of exclusivity and control whether in terms of timing, location or client group.
- the application enables customization and personalization on some level whether through product suggestions or matching client preferences or enabling them to customize the appearance of their pages within the application.
- the application allows them to share the content with others or to transfer it to other devices like computers or protected web pages.
- the application enables a two-way conversation with the brand by allowing users to provide feedback.
- the application is a part of an integrated marketing program that is linked to other channels which users may also access.
- the mobile initiative is practical and easy to use. Nobody has time for complicated applications anymore.
- the application is interactive, engaging and visually stimulating. If it's boring, people will just simply move on.
- the application is consistent with the brand image and positioning.
- the factor of third-party dependence for integration and execution is considered and that this does not affect the client.

Now to the question of how?

Whereas mobile technology may not have a high impact of areas like design and production, it can greatly influence customer experience, therefore implementing mobile marketing initiatives using methods that will enhance client experience should be applied. Instead of the standard SMS, MMS, Bluetooth transfers and so on, luxury brands should opt for the more interactive use of Short Codes, GPS, 2G- and 3G-based mobile applications, as described below.

Shortcodes: Also known as CSC (common short codes) are short telephone numbers usually consisting of five digits that are used to send SMS and MMS messages from mobile phones. They are currently used for wireless services like television voting, polling, ordering ringtones, making donations, queries and search engines. Shortcodes are easier to remember, although they are billed at a higher rate than SMS or MMS messages.

Bluetooth: Bluetooth is a wireless technology that enables equipped phone devices to receive data and voice at a short range of an average of ten metres. The connections can be from a single point to another point or from a single point to multiple points.

GPS: The GPS (Global Positioning System) is a system of satellites that orbit the earth. The system enables people with ground receivers to pinpoint their geographic location.

2G and 3G: The technology of the former enables digital voice encoding. This mobile technology has steadily evolved over the last few years with increased bandwidth, packet routing, and the introduction of multimedia. 3G, on the other hand, provides enhanced multimedia including voice, data, video, and remote control as well as broadband and high speed of upwards of 2 Mbps.

Mobile applications: Mobile applications are programs that are designed to perform a specific function directly for the user. They are designed to feature the content that the brands desire to provide and can be downloaded by users. They could include videos, images, music, text and other features. Mobile applications are becoming more widely adopted due to the greater processing abilities and storage capacities of the latest generations of phones from brands like Motorola, Apple, Samsung, BlackBerry and HTC.

Mobile recognition software: This type of software is able to recognize images by comparing its resemblance to a previously populated image database on a server. Images can be sent from the mobile device to the server via MMS or email. The software can be used to send information back to a user when there is a match between a photo taken and an image in the database. Technologies and mobile devices can be combined to create a number of customer services and marketing applications. For example, people could be invited to interact with a program or editorial content provided on another medium, like TV voting, quizzes, radio contests, ringtone or logo requests and editorial feedback. The main fields of applications include media and entertainment, brand awareness, customer acquisition, customer retention and loyalty programs.

Location-based services: Using technologies such as Bluetooth or GPS, location-based services (LBS) are services that exploit knowledge about where a user is physically located and relevant information may be sent to their mobiles based on this knowledge. For example, if a client of Prada who has "opted-in" for this service is within 1 kilometre of a Prada store, he could receive a message reminding him of his proximity to the store and informing him of the new collections within the store. For years, location-based services have been seen as offering a great potential for brands. Although there has been a lot of hype around this, applications have been fairly limited until now. Bluetooth has enabled the development of marketing applications such as the possibility of sending messages to anyone with a Bluetooth mobile device walking within a short range of a store. But Bluetooth can have a damaging impact on the perception of mobile marketing by consumers who feel that receiving messages whenever they are within range of a transmitter is unwanted, annoying and intrusive. This is why they should be given the option to "opt-in" for the service.

Click-to-call (also called CTC, click-to-dial or click-to-talk): This service uses an icon, button or highlighted phone number placed on a mobile device, application or website. Upon clicking on it, the user either triggers a call from a company representative for direct interaction or the phone number begins the calling process directly. Similar to auto-dialling, the user only has to click once on the shortcut rather than having to dial all the digits of a phone number. One significant benefit of click-to-call providers is that it allows companies to monitor when online visitors change from the website to a phone sales channel. It also provides a seamless multi-channel brand interaction for clients.

One-click purchase (also called express purchase or one-click buying): This refers to the technique of allowing customers to make online purchases with a single click, with the payment information needed to complete the purchase already entered by the user previously. More particularly, it allows the online shopper to purchase an item without using the shopping cart software. Instead of manually inputting billing and shipping information for a purchase, the user applies the one-click service with pre-defined address and credit card information for a seamless shopping experience.

M-commerce (or m-retail):   This is simply the process of buying and selling products and services through a mobile device. It enables users to access the Internet and a mobile website without plugging into a device. M-commerce is expected to experience high growth as mobile content delivery becomes faster and more secure. Industries expected to benefit the most from m-commerce include apparel and services. M-commerce provides an opportunity for luxury brands to extend this channel as a complement to e-retail and physical store retail. The consumers who are likely to use this service are those who already have an established relationship with luxury brands and are seeking a higher level of engagement and deeper interactions.

Mobile loyalty programs: This refers to loyalty programs that use a mobile device rather than a card as the repository of the advantages provided to program members. As in all loyalty programs, benefits to members can include rewards, special access to events, product previews and customized offers. Its main opportunity lies in its ability to extend the brand relationship with customers and provide a value-driven interaction.

Mobile ticketing: This service is linked to the sale of tickets for events. Instead of sending a printed ticket or asking the customer to print it at home, the ticket supplier sends an electronic ticket (or m-ticket) via SMS to a mobile device in the form of a mobile barcode. This barcode can be quickly read and validated directly from the mobile device display screen with a dedicated reading device. This method is becoming increasingly popular since it allows ticket buyers to avoid long lines and enables ticket sellers to eliminate printing and distribution costs, and also provides a better service to clients. It is increasingly used for concerts, sporting events, cinemas, theme parks, trains and other public transportation.

M-coupons: This technology functions with the same principle as mobile ticketing. In this case, a barcode is sent via SMS or downloaded from a website and can be read in-store via a special device, thereby providing the customer with a discount or a special offer without the need to use paper.

The small size of mobile devices offers both an advantage and a disadvantage for luxury brands. On the one hand, people always have their mobile phones on them and can therefore be contacted directly and instantaneously. On the other hand, the small size of the screens, the low memory capacity and keypad can limit how much information consumers are willing to read, how long they will store the message and whether they will be willing to respond. One way of overcoming this is by adding value to the consumer, which is critical to the success of any mobile marketing initiative. Relevance is also essential in order to add value. This means that consumers expect the content to be highly relevant to them as individuals. The very personal nature of the mobile phone compared with other media demands an approach to individual relevance and personalization.

Luxury brands will therefore have to do more than the current practice of sending information based on user preferences or targeting particular times of the year like birthdays, Christmas or Mother's Day. Relevance means more than just getting the right substance or content to the mobile user. It also includes format and style, medium and timing of the message. This must be carefully managed because the mobile can be more intrusive than other means of communications due to its ubiquity and personal identity. Also, the personal identity of the mobile device is a difficult aspect to manage. Luxury brands need to understand the degree of personalization needed to maintain relevance. At the same time, they also need to be careful not to appear too personal since some people may not appreciate the idea of the brand appearing to be too friendly (for example, beginning a message with "Hey Mickey" instead of "Dear Michael").

Mobile technology now enables luxury companies to connect with customers before, during and after the shopping experience. It provides opportunities for brand awareness, need generation, influence on the purchasing decision, customer experience and service improvement, as well as brand affiliation, which leads to frequent purchases. It can also enable brands to create customer databases that allow the direct measurement of campaign effectiveness as well as more effective future campaigns thanks to the storage of data on customer preferences. Mobile has the power to inscribe luxury brands permanently in the consciousness of consumers across all demographics. As the most personal and one of the most powerful media in our expanding wireless world, mobile technology presents an undeniable express connection between luxury brands and clients. However, before jumping on the mobile bandwagon luxury brands must ensure that the implications of using mobile technology as well as the suitability of this medium for customers within their specific target groups is well understood. Otherwise, the risk on the long-term brand equity would be higher than the cost of adopting mobile technology and this may not be worth it after all.

As we look to the future, it is clear that mobile technology will play a role that is even more significant than the possibilities described here. Evidence already indicates that there are existing technologies that enable mobile phones to pick up and read dynamic data on objects carrying micro chips that don't require any contact to be activated. These micro chips, which are already increasingly replacing bar codes in consumer goods, will enable interaction with different kinds of products without touching them or even being in close proximity to them. For example, with a few clicks on a mobile phone we would be able to check the origin, composition and use of different kinds of products within a store. This technology will also increasingly lead the way for the interconnectivity with objects of daily life such as electronics and home ware. Imagine being able to use your mobile to activate your alarm clock, start your coffee machine, check the weather forecast on a digital screen and update yourself on the traffic condition. In this world, the mobile will become even more personal and will drive an unprecedented level of expectations from luxury clients. This is the future and luxury brands should be prepared.

Technology and innovation for luxury

The unique and long-standing relationship between luxury and avant-gardism means that luxury brands are expected by the public to be leaders in innovation in all its facets. The consumer population – comprising both those that purchase luxury and those that don't – look up to the luxury sector to pave the way for others in bringing products and services inspired and supported by technology to the market. This doesn't mean that luxury designers should become the next Steve Jobs or that brands should turn into the next Apple, but it does mean that luxury brands are expected to respond to a changing world in which the way products are made and marketed has been transformed by the arrival of digital technology. For a sector that inspires many, it means embracing technological functions and applying them across every aspect of design and creation as well as in business and retail operations. This includes material sourcing and functions; product and process design; operations and logistics; retail, merchandizing and client management; as well as other multiple aspects of the value chain including communications, public relations, marketing, brand management and business strategy. Successfully pulling off the integration of technology support to these business dimensions means adopting a forward-thinking orientation as well as a proactive approach towards applying new technologies as they evolve.

Until now, the question of using digital technology to support a luxury brand's activities has been raised mainly in the areas of website design, digital media production, e-retail and client management. In some cases, applied technology has been adopted for client data management and in supporting POS systems. On rare occasions, designers have used digital aids to stimulate product design and visualization but, apart from these areas, the use of technology in both the creative and business aspects of luxury have been limited. Technology, however, has much to offer luxury beyond these areas, evident from recent innovations in areas ranging from design to new product development, store merchandizing and sourcing materials for a wide range of products including clothing and accessories. Some of these innovations, which have been identified as having the potential to exert a high level of influence on the way the luxury business functions, are presented and assessed in the following sections.

Creating products through body scanning

If you are one of those people who are between sizes and have difficulty in finding clothes that fit to a "tee", or have ever wondered if a day would come when everyone would be able to have their clothes fitted before being made – without paying the price of bespoke – well, it looks like your days of wondering are over. The way clothing is designed and created is on its way to being revolutionalized thanks to a new technology that is powered by an application that scans the body form.

Body scanning is a new technology that is helping to shift the focus of clothing design and production from mass-design and mass-production to customized pieces with individualized sizing and design features. This functions by scanning the body and feeding the appropriate dimensions into a system, which then allocates these dimensions to the clothing's design features to ensure an outcome of a perfectly fitted piece of clothing. The application is suitable for every type of apparel for men, women and children. If you own a pet, it could also be useful. Its arrival has been as a result of advanced research in the identification of the possibility of using digital technology for mass customization while allowing the client to be a part of the design and production process. Through adopting technology that enables quick and efficient production, body scanning has brought about made-to-measure clothes at quick turnaround times en masse. This has made competitive prices possible, meaning that consumers seeking perfectly fitted clothing are able to obtain them at prices that don't mean breaking the bank.

Customized clothing production is, however, not an invention of the twenty-first century. A trip down memory lane will reveal that until the early part of last century, the majority of clothing was made one piece at a time, often by a single tailor or dressmaker. With time, for women who were mostly homemakers, learning dressmaking and sewing at home became the norm. However, from the 1900s, the developments of the industrial revolution, which also introduced mass production techniques, changed the way clothing was made. The invention of mass pattern-making machines and industrial sewing machines led to the introduction of ready-to-wear, which launched the modern age of apparel production. Homemade clothes went out of vogue and it became more economical to buy ready-to-wear mass-produced clothing than to have it made-to-measure. After nearly one hundred years of ready-to-wear produced en masse, this system seems to be coming to the end of its cycle and the evolution of both technology and society is taking us back to the course of having made-to-measure clothing, albeit differently.

Currently, consumers worldwide, particularly those that fall within the luxury bracket, are seeking differentiation in many forms through what they wear – clothing, accessories, handbags, shoes, jewelry and so on. Their desires include access to clothes that fit perfectly and are distinctive and different from those of others. To satisfy this need would mean that the clothing provided by brands has to fit each client not only in terms of size, but also in terms of body shape. That means that each person would need to be measured before the clothes are made. As you and I know, this is quite impossible for brands that have hundreds of thousands of clients. The current structure of clothing manufacturing means that it is not economically feasible for a luxury brand to provide made-to-measure clothing or accessories en masse, neither is reverting to the old system of dressmaking for each client applicable today. However, the advancement of digital technology has led apparel manufacturers worldwide to experiment with economical strategies that individualize clothing for each customer by offering a variety of design and fit options. This has led to the arrival of the "just for you" clothing which uses body scanning methods to produce fitted clothing en masse. One of the pioneers of this evolution is the company Bodymetrics.

The London-based company first launched its body-scanning concept at London's department store Selfridges and subsequently at Harrods. The high-tech approach to body measurement and scanning was presented through an installed pod within the store which people could walk into to scan whole or parts of their body in a 3-D format. The technology came about as an off-shoot of research conducted by the University College London on the "national sizing" of the British population. Today, the technology aims to enable people to have access to the most body-flattering clothes for their exact size, shape and style, including dresses, suits, skirts, blouses and even jeans. The Bodymetrics pod has currently been adopted by several brands at Harrods including Vivienne Westwood and Nick Holland.

Although the technology is still in its infancy and requires support from well-trained technicians and sales representatives, over time it is expected to become widely adopted as the market gets accustomed to it. At the same time, there have been some mixed feelings among luxury brands on its adoption. Some contend that it will finally address the dullness of the uniformity brought by ready-to-wear. It is also believed that it will overcome the lack of accuracy that often occurs from measuring by hand, which may not allow all of the body's contours to be perfectly taken in. Other parties believe that introducing technologically supported applications into bespoke in the form of "speed tailoring" is a contradiction and a discredit to the authenticity of the hand-made craftsmanship of the original made-to-measure format.

While this argument is yet to be clarified, another version of custom-made clothing selection en masse has been introduced to the Internet through a virtual try-on concept. Although this is more aligned to trying on clothing virtually rather than creating and making clothing, it follows the same

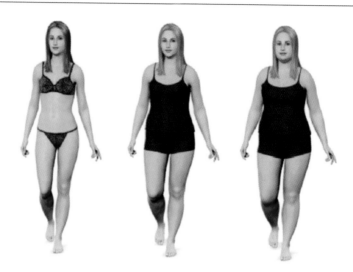

Figure 8.2 *Technology that enables customization of products for made-to-measure sizing such as the body-scanning method invented by Bodymetrics, as well as those that support style selection such as the Personal Avatar introduced by My Virtual Model, have brought an evolution in made-to-measure luxury product creation en-masse*

principle of made-to-measure. This application, called My Virtual Model (see Figure 8.2), works by allowing customers to take their own measurements or to select pre-determined sets of measurements that are closest to theirs. Parameters that allow the input of information about the general body shape can also be entered including the dimensions of the waist, hips, shoulders, torso and so on. Facial and hair features may also be selected such as style, colour, shape and so on. Following these, the online application then generates an image of the customer's body shape and displays it on the screen for confirmation or modification. After confirmation, the customer selects clothing styles from the website and tries them on the virtual image or model and, if it fits well, the item is purchased. Companies, brands and retailers mainly in North America such as Lands' End, Levi Strauss, Lane Bryant, and the Wedding Channel have adopted this application. It not only allows the customer to visualize the appearance of the clothing on their bodies – just as they would if they were looking in the mirror – but it also enables people to be more in tune with their bodies and understand the type of clothing that suits them best.

The real opportunity for body scanners and virtual models lies in using their applications to enhance client satisfaction and relations both online and offline. As consumers become more demanding of personalized products and services, such technology-based enhancers will be required more in luxury product development, retail, e-retail and client management.

Extending the product through innovation

In 2008, Louis Vuitton created the first luxury digital product called the Soundwalk. The product which exists in an entirely digital format for MP3 usage is based on an imaginative voyage of three Chinese cities through voice narrations and sounds evoking the locations. Its aim was to stretch the imagination of the listener by taking them through a journey of the senses in the form of sound. The Soundwalk, whose inspiration came from the brand's core heritage as a luxury luggage company, features a narrative of Shanghai, Hong Kong and Beijing through the voices of three celebrated Chinese actresses, Shu Qi, Gong Li and Joan Chen. The narratives transport the users to the streets of the cities by reproducing their sounds and evoking their atmosphere while firing the imagination through the soothing voices and the ideal choice of words of the narrators. The sound guide is also flavored with pieces of information about the three women's lives, dreams and expectations that mesh into an interesting storyline. They also project intimate insights into what it means to be a part of the Chinese culture. Through these cosmopolitan cities, the narrator shares Louis Vuitton's philosophy of travel as a form of discovery and enrichment, and brings both an intellectual and entertaining dimension to the brand's qualities. Although the Soundwalk follows a one-way communication approach, it allows the Louis Vuitton client to make the experience personal by downloading the product in an MP3 format that may then be replayed at will. This not only entertains, but also extends the time spent with the brand and subsequently enhances the relationship with the brand.

Through a step away from tangible products, the brand used the Soundwalk to mark a turning point in the relationship between luxury and technology in product extension. It also reintroduced the question that had so far only been whispered in luxury circles – where will the line be drawn between luxury and technology? Skeptics used the opportunity to pronounce a death sentence for brands that had made technology their forte. These parties share the viewpoint that luxury is only about the respect for tradition, heritage and skill that is passed on from generation to generation, and nothing more. Despite this outcry it wasn't long before another luxury brand, Hermès, picked up the baton by developing the "Contre-Temps", a digital diary or assistant with multiple functions, based on the technology behind the electronic paper, also known as e-paper.

The Hermès digital diary is designed as a pocket (or handbag) device and could pass for anything from a hand-held digital assistant to a simple hard-drive. It opens up through two opposing sliding doors and is based on the e-paper technology and futuristic flexible OLED touch-screen. The diary also contains a tactile interface, an electronic organizer, photo-sharing, email, GPS, a transport waiter, RSS readers, Internet connection through wifi and several other functions. It has been described as the ideal digital jewel for the modern woman who can easily slip it into her Birkin or Kelly bag, unlike a laptop, which takes too much space no matter how small the dimensions. Designed by Alexandre Fourn, this digital product perfectly combines technology with the elegance of the e-paper and external design. E-paper, by the way, is a display technology designed to portray the appearance of ordinary ink on paper. Unlike a conventional flat panel display, which uses a backlight to illuminate its pixels, electronic paper reflects light like ordinary paper and is capable of holding text and images indefinitely without drawing electricity. E-paper is not the same as digital paper, which is a pad to create handwritten digital documents with a digital pen.

The launch of the Contre-Temps will mark the first time that a tangible digital product will be created by a luxury brand – that is, if we stop counting the number of co-branded mobile phones created by luxury brands and mobile companies in the recent past. This could herald a new age for luxury product extension based on technology.

What client needs or expectations do products like the Vivienne Tam-HP or the Louis Vuitton's Soundwalk fulfill? Are these product types suitable for luxury brands? These products have emerged as a result of the progression of the luxury market and as a response to the changing needs and expectations of luxury clients. Before the arrival of the Internet and its supporting digital media technologies including mobile, luxury consumer needs were simply based on the scope of traditional luxury products like clothing, handbags, shoes, jewelry and watches; and services like hospitality, gastronomy and transport. Today, the story is different because consumer mind-sets have evolved following two decades of interacting with digital technology. Expectations have moved beyond the placid acceptance of the output of luxury creative machinations solely within the traditional product range. A digital-based hole has been created that needs to be filled and luxury brands who are proactive enough to view this as an opportunity can fill this gap through tangible digital-based products (for instance, the Vivienne Tam-HP) or intangible digital-based products (such as the Louis Vuitton Soundwalk) (see Figure 8.3). Luxury consumers also expect luxury services companies to go the digital way through providing unique devices that complement the services or launching new services entirely based on digital technology or media. It is time for luxury brands to challenge themselves in ways that will ensure their place in the world of a generation of consumers whose references are drawn from their interactions with the Internet, digital media and mobile technology. This generation of global millennials know no other way of thinking and the impact of their collective experiences transferred from the technology world will continue to be felt on a worldwide level. Luxury brands will need to think in a different way and adopt digital technology not only as a business support, but also as an extension of products and services.

Brands that provide paper versions of books – such as Louis Vuitton's City Guides – will have to assess the need for an e-book version or a branded

Figure 8.3 *The introduction of the first digital product, the Louis Vuitton Soundwalk, as well as the development of the Vivienne Tam-HP ultra-portable laptop clutch, are likely to herald a new era in the range of luxury products and services, from the traditional to the modern, driven by technology. While the former is an intangible product based on sound and voice narration existing in an MP3 format, the latter is a personal computer created to be as mobile as the modern user. These two products share the common characteristic of being transported as personal companions and are a response to the evolution of the mind-sets of current luxury clients, which has resulted from 20 years of interacting with the Internet and digital media*

EZ Reader; those that publish print magazines will need to re-think the relevance of paper versus e-paper; and those brands that provide concierge services will need to re-evaluate the accessibility of these services and perhaps introduce devices with e-applications for 360° interaction round the clock. And why not client recognition cards with multiple personalized functions provided to the brand's VIP clients? Or a digital-based service that enables VIP clients to communicate instantly with their dedicated sales representative? Or even watches equipped with noise and CO_2 sensors to monitor air pollution? Or a branded pedometer to encourage walking, discovery and well-being? The possibilities are endless and luxury brands will have to find ways to adopt new technologies extensively across products and services categories. Introducing iPod cases and iPhone cases in the product range is no longer enough. In an age where devices like the EZ Reader, a featherweight digital book, that is able to display up to 8,000 pages of text without recharging will become the order of the day, luxury brands will be expected to do better than MP3 player cases as a claim to technology.

Even as forward-thinking brands pave the way for the creation of a unique place for digital technology in luxury offerings, there remains a wide resistance to this movement. Despite the skepticism surrounding luxury and technology, brands like Louis Vuitton there are which has boldly ventured into the technology terrain and hasn't lost its place as the most profitable luxury brand in the world – even in the face of the current global economic slowdown.

Re-defining product functionality through materials

If you've been following the luxury landscape over the last decade, you will probably have noticed an increasing level of similarity – and, in some cases, blatant sameness – in product design across fashion, accessories, jewelry watches and even beauty and fragrance. Apart from seasonal colors and trends, which are supposed to direct creative output, there has been a general leaning towards uniformity in product design rather than differentiation through distinct signature styles. Some seasons have featured clothing, handbags and shoes that are so similar in style that it is nearly impossible to distinguish the brands and to understand which brand was copying the other. In other cases, the packaging and labeling of products like cosmetics, skincare and fragrance have been so similar that they could easily pass off one for the other. In fashion, particularly ready-to-wear, the case is even more apparent. Styles, colors, shapes and even materials are copied. The runways of fashion shows look like a reproduction of one show and the sameness of the models doesn't help matters. Although this apparent lack of creativity cannot be excused in an industry that is supposed to be driven by creative and aesthetic distinction, it may be deduced that it has arisen as a result of the limit which creativity has reached, particularly in fashion. As we know, fashion operates in cycles and this, together with trends, societal moods, cultural factors and other inspirations, could determine the design direction that designers take for, say, clothing. In some cases, designers could interpret these factors in the same way, which could lead to the production of similar-looking clothing that may be interpreted as "copied". In terms of design itself, we could even say that there isn't much that could be invented anymore and that experimentation is now limited in scope. But in cases like clothing and handbag design, there is much that can still be done with materials like fabrics and hardware. These could become the new source of creativity that the industry needs, particularly in the current context of "sameness" that some have described as the "creative crunch of luxury".

For years, sports apparel companies have been investigating the application of technology as a support for sporting performance through the fabric used in making sportswear. Companies such as Nike and Adidas have taken large strides in this direction, leading to breakthroughs in breatheable fabrics. Examples are the Nike Dri-Fit and the Adidas ClimaCool, which both deliver extra functions like high-tech moisture, body heat conversion and the generation of coolness to heated zones. These features have, however, been perceived more as functional than symbolic and, as a result, have been restricted to the "functional" sectors like sports.

When it comes to luxury, the advent of using applied technology in finetuning materials for products was considered as unnecessary and unappealing until the initiatives between luxury fashion designers and sports companies, notably through the collaboration between Stella McCartney and Adidas. The collaboration, which led to the infusion of style with function, also incorporated high-performance fabrics that keep wearers both dry and cool. It opened a new chapter on the application of technology to fabrics used for luxury apparel. Since then, several luxury brands have been experimenting with techno-support in fabrics and one brand that is pioneering the use of applied technology in sourcing, refining and adopting specific materials to product design and production is Versace. The brand has consistently introduced materials supported by high-tech layering and surface texture like cotton and silk for different effects on the body including cooling, conserving heat and UV protection. Decorative effects like high-tech embroidery have also been worked into the brand's collections. Other brands that have also consistently shown a leaning towards investing in high-tech fabrics are Lanvin and Balenciaga. While the former has used high-tech fabrics in its shoe design to enhance functionality and comfort when walking and running, the latter has applied breathable fabric that is often found in extreme sportswear to luxury prêt-a-porter. In addition, lingerie brands like Wacoal have used technology to innovate the functionality of underwear through the inventions from its research laboratory. Notable are the "Good Up Girdle" which is an underwear that lifts, moulds and shapes the buttocks; the "Body Shaper" which eliminates body rolls; and the "Hip Walker" which slims the silhouette and tones the buttock muscles as the wearer walks. These products are most effective with continuous use and have been proved to be efficient by hundreds of thousands of users around the world.

Apparel companies around the world are also developing innovative methods of combining different types of materials to produce fabrics that are both luxurious and functional which may be used for luxury ready-to-wear and even haute couture. One such company, AK Apparel, has invented a patented fabric technology that provides performance on-demand for a wide range of materials (Figure 8.4). The technology is based on layering single-type or multi-type fabrics with a shell and a base that perform different functions. The features include UV protection at up to a rating of 25; anti-microbial action, which traps bacteria and releases it during a normal wash cycle; temperature management, which keeps the body cool during hot days and heats it up during the cold ones; moisture transfer, which transports moisture away

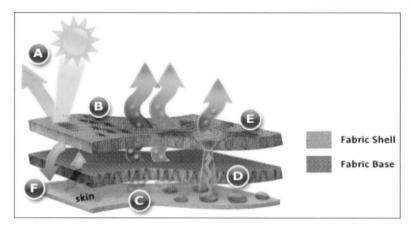

Figure 8.4 *Apparel companies like AK Apparel, which has invented fabric technology for a wide range of materials through technology based on layering fabrics with shells and bases that perform different functions including UV protection, anti-microbial, temperature management moisture transfer, moisture wicking and ventilation, are proving that technology could support the aesthetic beauty and appeal of luxury apparel*

from the body to the outer layer of the fabric where it can quickly evaporate; moisture wicking, which uses surface moisture and sweat wick to accelerate evaporation, keeping the body dry while aiding in the regulation of its temperature; and ventilation, which infuses fresh air, free from bacteria into the body through vapours created by body moisture exit. This may sound too fantastic to be true or may be perceived as unsuitable to luxury products but the technology that has led to these innovations may also be applied across various fabric types.

Technologically supported materials enhance the functionality of luxury apparel, which in turn complements their aesthetics, and increases their appeal. The materials may also be used as a source of enticement for a new segment of consumers that are either driven by sports activities, well-being or by technological innovation. Moreover, applied technology in fabrics can easily be integrated in organic materials through mixing and layering different types of fabrics that could create an appealing output. In addition to enabling clients overcome the stereotype that organic materials are drab and unappealing, this move could also lead luxury brands to endear themselves to a new generation of socially-conscious luxury clients.

Store merchandizing through innovation and interactive screening

The grand opening of Giorgio Armani's multi-million dollar Manhattan store in February 2009 – right in the middle of the global recession – drew the kind

Figure 8.5 *The interior of the futuristic Giorgio Armani store on New York's Fifth Avenue, which was created to feature the best in contemporary design and architecture, marks a departure from the consistency that has represented the luxury retail landscape in the last decade. Such bold retail moves that focus on aesthetics and atmosphere currently require being complemented by technological innovation that boosts in-store shopping, interactivity and merchandizing*

of attention that could be likened to major box office premiers. Apart from the line-up of celebrities including Victoria Beckham and Leonardo DiCapro, also present was an official delegation of New York City Council including the Mayor, Michael Bloomberg, the Chancellor of the New York City Board of Education Joel Klein and Caroline Kennedy who spearheads the city's Public Schools Fund. They all assisted in cutting the store opening ribbon. Needless to say, this was as much a fashion event as a political and social one.

The megastore, which was conceived as a single, fluid space providing uninterrupted inter-communication through shapes that are impossible to categorize geometrically, is an architectural accomplishment and measures 43,000 square feet. It displays the brand's main Giorgio Armani collection as well as those of the sub-brands Armani Exchange and Emporio Armani over four levels and also houses a futuristic restaurant and a chocolate shop. Such architectural extravagance can only be found in the luxury business, irrespective of the state of the economy (see Figure 8.5). Other brands like Louis Vuitton, Cartier and Gucci have also been known for spectacular store architecture and opening extravaganza. When Louis Vuitton opened its Hong Kong flagship in 2008, it was an all-night show-stopper featuring entertainment that ranged from ballerina performances to a concert by Kanye West and, when it opened its store in Bucharest, the Romanian Prime Minister found time in his busy schedule to attend the ceremony. Gucci's New York Fifth Avenue opening was an extravaganza of a party hosted by Madonna and a line-up of celebrities.

The show, however, often continues beyond the store openings. Luxury stores around the world are regarded as retail and entertainment cathedrals and architectural masterpieces. As exemplified by the Prada store in Omotesando, Tokyo; the Louis Vuitton store on the Champs Elysées in Paris; the Cartier store on Paris' Rue de la Paix; and the Dunhill House on London's Davies street, the interiors of luxury stores can be described as marvelous spaces that embody the best in architectural design. The sumptuous atmosphere created within the unique store environments and complemented by delectable products often assures a rich experience for anyone who walks into the stores. This inimitable space has the potential of immersing people in the brand's universe and endearing clients to the brand if completed by an offer of the best in shopping service.

Undoubtedly, luxury brands spend millions in store architecture and interior design in a bid to create exceptional experiences for shoppers and visitors. Most of the efforts are concentrated in the store designs, and a high degree of attention is given to the materials used in the production of the decorative pieces. These often lead to the creation of aesthetically pleasing environments, which are visually satisfying and in some cases can stimulate sensory responses. However, luxury retail is evolving and the luxury client is seeking more from the store environment to complete their rich experience. Store beauty, ambience and service are no longer enough for them, as their expectations have increased over the last decade. Clients now want retail experiences that go beyond the collective enjoyment of the store environment. They are seeking features that speak to them individually. They want interactivity in an intimate way. They are looking for brand exchanges, which are directed to them and no one else. It is no longer enough for them to have over-zealous sales representatives trailing their every move or intruding in their thought assessments. They want the kind of shopping interaction that they can control at will. They want a combination of attention, interactivity, entertainment and, of course, a wide product selection to complete their shopping experience. One of the best and most effective means of meeting these expectations is through technology.

In the recent past, technological breakthroughs that support store merchandizing and retail experience have made it possible for shoppers to interact with products and store features in ways previously unimagined. For example, it is now possible for people to call the attention of sales representatives or "sales concierges" by touching a button on a touch-screen display as is used at the Levi's store in Berlin. The store also features interactive terminals and a wall of screens in the form of shelves which provide multi-functions ranging from an interactive display of the brand's history to the portrayal of the brand's signature 501 jeans. Apple, another store that is known to use applied technology to enhance its store experience, has also featured sections within its store that use the support of touch-screen simulations to evoke unique experiences. Notable of these are the "Genius Bar", "One to One Program" and the "Pro Lab" featured in its Boston store. Nike has also integrated applications for product customization in its stores around the world through the NikeiD concept where shoppers can choose the colors, sizes and features of several parts of their Nike shoes as well as inscribe their names or expressions on it.

On the luxury front, the use of technology within retail stores remains limited to the widely adopted flat screen televisions that feature a mix of the brand's products, runway shows and history among others. This is, however, no longer enough and the time has come for luxury brands to be challenged in the way that store experience and merchandizing is presented. We can herald brands like Armani which used its newly opened New York flagship store – designed as a futuristic space of seamless movements – to mark a departure from the line-up of luxury stores that strive for consistency. These brands have, in the process, fallen into the trap of "sameness", which explains Armani's efforts to break the mold of identical, monolithic and repetitive retail spaces that luxury has bowed to in the last decade. According to the brand, sameness now belongs to the past and cannot match the experience offered by a totally original store through the aesthetic excitement of fine, contemporary architecture. However, even Armani's contemporary architecture is no longer enough for today's digital-minded luxury consumer. This beautiful architectural masterpiece must now be complemented by digital techniques that will further add to the immersion that clients feel in the store environment.

There are endless possibilities of how luxury brands could use digital technology to enhance the shopping experience and ensure a stronger affiliation with the brand, even in an increasingly crowded marketplace. Ten suggestions on how these may be approached are as follows:

1. Dressing room interactivity in the form of enabling the use of touchscreen mirrors installed in fitting rooms. These could enable the viewing of the product being tried on, in all the variety of colors, shapes and sizes that it exists in, without the shopper having to find them on the shop floor or calling the attention of a sale representative. The interactive view can simply be achieved by inputting the product code followed by a simple OK on a screen. This will not only add excitement to the shopping experience but will also lead to a quicker product selection. It will also help to curb the current practice where shoppers avoid the fitting rooms and, instead, take clothes home to try on. Interactive dressing rooms will drive shoppers to try on clothes and subsequently reduce the rate of product returns as a result.

2. Responsive mirrors that enable shoppers to see pictures of themselves in all the items they try on. This means that instead of narrowing the choice to the shopper's memory recall of the way the clothes fitted, they can actually place images of themselves on the responsive or interactive mirrors to visualize the clothes and their fitting collectively. This will likely increase purchase probability and will go a long way in ensuring

an enhanced shopping experience. Prada is already experimenting with this technology in some of its US stores.

3. Body scanning as an aid for product trials. Again, this could be a support for the dressing room dilemma where the shopper will not need to physically try on the pieces selected but will be able to view them against her body replica on a screen. The shopper could scan their body, which would be transformed into a 3-D virtual model and used to try on products like apparel, bags, shoes, jewelry and so on in various colors and sizes without tasking themselves physically. This feature could also enable shoppers to drag and drop pieces from the collection to their replica 3-D virtual body on the screen to visualize how they would look wearing the clothes. Needless to say, this could be a tool for indulging in personal styling and product interactivity. It could also enable the shopper to view a wider range of the collections within the store that their physical eye may have missed. It would also be an excellent tool for suggesting matching and complementary products in a visual format that the client may not have thought of. The screen could also be of varying sizes including a life-size where the 3-D virtual model could appear in the real body dimensions, replicating the life-size mirror.

4. Personal avatars of virtual models that may be created by clients and stored in programs installed in store cabin displays with an account login and password to be retrieved each time the shopper returns to that store or any of the brand's stores around the world. The avatars could be used to try on products and could also act as a complement to the physical product trials. In this case, the product code could be entered and the screen could display the variety of colours and sizes in which the product exists and all of these could be tried on the avatar and viewed on the screen.

5. Social and collective shopping, whereby a shopper is able to share the images and details of their selected pieces through a touch-screen that gives shoppers the option of inviting others to be a part of the shopping experience. In this case, instead of the standard practice of taking pictures of items with mobile phones and sending them to friends through MMS, the shopper will simply need to click on a web link to log on to a website where friends could be invited to view him or her shopping directly and may post their comments. This feature will not only increase purchase probability but will also make the shopping experience fun and inclusive by allowing people to communicate as though they were shopping together. Some luxury retailers like Japan's Mitsukoshi and the US's Bloomingdale's are already trying out facets of social shopping in their stores.

6. Sales ambassador alert through installed call buttons located at specific points in different sections of the store. This would enable shoppers to press a button and call the attention of a sales representative if needed. This is particularly essential for large stores and will help to prevent situations where clients are standing around the store waiting to be served

or, worse still, leave the store due to the lack of availability of sales staff. The call buttons are particularly essential for fitting rooms. It has been proved by researchers that when shoppers have a high level of interactivity and a pleasant experience in fitting rooms, it increases their likelihood of buying the item three or four times more than if they didn't try the item on or had a bland experience during the fitting.

7. Product availability and identification selection through a touch-screen that will enable clients to check the availability of a specific product in a store. This will particularly serve as a complement to Internet shopping as shoppers may obtain product codes from the brand's website and prefer to try them on in the store before purchasing. In large luxury stores that have multiple floors, finding such products and seeking help from sales ambassadors may become a dilemma that this option could help to overcome. It should, however, be featured in a format that doesn't replicate "self-service" in order to avoid the risk of robbing the shopper of the brand experience and the enjoyment of the luxury shopping.

8. 3-D animation display screens that provide the same effects as 3-D movies. This is a new form of technology that powers the visualization of images on a specially formatted screen in the kind of 3-D form that stimulates the feeling that the images are coming away from the screen and advancing towards the viewer. This fantastic invention, which is being pioneered by French company Artistic Images, is not only useful for high-impact interactivity but, also as a form of extended and complementary visual experience from that which may be found on a luxury brand's website. For example, if a luxury brand has integrated 3-D product view in real-time on its website, it would make sense for the 3-D display screens to be placed in the physical stores for a coherent continuous experience. This is particularly important as luxury consumers currently transfer their collective experiences from the web to the physical world and vice versa.

9. Store window interactivity through providing mannequins in 3-D spinning display modes or screens that stimulate real life 360° views rather than the present static format. Another possibility is interactive screens in store windows that change the colors and styles of the models displayed instead of the single model displayed on static mannequins. This is not only visually stimulating, but also adds an element of brand entertainment to both shoppers and passers-by.

10. Finally, luxury brands could enhance the current format of cramped dressing rooms by adding lighting that is closer to daylight and increasing the size of the rooms to allow for more movement and also to enable the shopper's companions to join them. And why not provide sofas in the fitting rooms? Let's not forget that fitting rooms have become important touch-points for brands and they deserve as much attention as the main shop floors.

Featuring digital technology in the shopping environment will become inevitable for luxury brands in the near future as clients transfer their collective experiences from Internet and mobile technologies to their expectations from physical store environments and offerings. Recent research by TNS indicates that 73 percent of shoppers worldwide anticipate using technologically driven tools such as touch-screens in dressing rooms in the next five years. This calls for urgent action from luxury brands. The brands that will lead the way in this direction will undoubtedly establish a strong positioning among increasingly digital-minded clients in the long term.

It is apparent that the landscape of luxury has changed as a result of the arrival of digital technologies on the Internet, through mobile phones and as a result of technologically driven innovation. The vast scope of these applications and systems provides real opportunities to support different aspects of luxury business operations. Their applications within several aspects of the luxury value chain will, however, need to be approached strategically and applied through a defined process to complement and enhance the spirit and heritage of each luxury brand.

Chapter 9
A look at the best and worst practices of luxury online

> "Taking one's time is not a luxury of the past. In today's world, everything is expected to be instant. And yet time is needed to meet the requirements and standards of high quality… to fashion products …. to finish them according to the rules of the craft, to add the meticulous finishing touches. To find time to advise clients on choices… so that they are assured of a harmonious and refined product… This is luxury. And so we will continue to work in this manner. For a long time to come."
>
> —Gilles Nouaihac

There is a famous saying that goes, "in the country of the blind, the one-eyed man is the king". This reminds me of the state of luxury e-business in the early part of this decade when I became active in luxury Internet marketing and e-business. During this period when the landscape of luxury online could best be described as nightmarish, the resounding phrase of the luxury brands that were bold enough to have ventured online was: "Our website is now better than that of 'X' brand, so I think our e-business has been achieved." The general feeling was that technology and luxury began and ended with having a pretty website which would enable a brand to say that they were on the Internet. Therefore, for most of the luxury brands that I was dealing with, it was a question of competition in terms of which website would have the most advanced digital features and functions. Several years down the line, the landscape of cyberspace has changed dramatically and the relevance of the luxury brand's website has been challenged by the proliferation of social websites which congregate luxury consumers of all ages, locations and professions. The competition is shifting from luxury brands against brands to luxury brands against social media websites. However, the spirit of competition that existed among the brands ten years ago still underlies certain decisions that are made with regard to luxury online.

Although visible progress has been made by luxury brands online, the fact remains that the companies that have shown the most proactivity in adopting best practices in e-business are not found within the luxury industry. It is a common and acknowledged fact that luxury brands draw their references for several aspects of e-business – communications, branding, retail, merchandizing, social interactions etc. – from companies outside of luxury such as Apple, Dell, Nike, Levi's, Nespresso and several others in multiple sectors. These companies, which may share one or two attributes with luxury, do not necessarily have the culture, spirit and mechanics of the luxury business and therefore it has been a real challenge for luxury brands to interpret the e-business best practices drawn from them to the strategic and operational requirements of each luxury brand. This has posed an ongoing problem in the luxury online landscape and explains why it has been nearly impossible to find a website owned by a luxury brand that serves as a benchmark for single or multiple aspects of luxury e-business. This also explains why you will find that my analysis of best practices features more independent websites than luxury brand owned websites. In terms of worst practices, I have refrained from making an extensive analysis due to the fact that there are just too many worst practices and I would have to write an entire book to go round all of them. Hopefully this picture should change soon. I would, however, like to add that this analysis is made on an independent and external basis and solely represents my thoughts, viewpoints and opinions, which have been developed from nearly a decade of ongoing practice in luxury e-business. You are, of course, welcome to disagree with me, and in this case I hope the disparity of opinions would lead to better luxury e-business practices.

The Watch Avenue challenges the virtual location notion

It is generally believed that the most important feature of physical retail is location. In the case of luxury retail, the qualities of the location include

Figure 9.1   *The Watch Avenue (thewatchavenue.com)*

a strong factor of exclusivity, prestige and affluence. In the Internet virtual world, the notion of location has been rendered irrelevant by the mass availability and accessibility of uniform website content irrespective of the user's location. The Internet as a whole became a universal destination and the websites existing in its sphere jointly became collective nodes of this destination. The universal nature of the Internet means that there is no location-based exclusivity, no prestige drawn from surroundings and no affluence depicted by the size of the website or the status of the visitors. Every website has equal opportunities for existence and visibility, and issues like company size or the number of loyal clients are irrelevant for the existence of a website. This has meant that the only opportunities for luxury brands to distinguish themselves online was through creating powerful websites with rich content and a unique atmosphere that would immerse the user in the brand's universe.

These characteristics of the Internet, which have been well, established and accepted in the twenty years of its existence, are being challenged by the arrival of a newly created website, The Watch Avenue (thewatchavenue.com) (Figure 9.1).

Piloted by the *Fondation de la Haute Horlogerie* (The Foundation for High Watchmaking) and developed as a collective effort of the member brands – Rolex, Tag Heueur, Vachern Constantin, Longines, Hublot, Tissot, Audemars Piguet, Chanel, Piaget and several others – the website was created to break every rule of luxury website creation. It discarded the approach of static pages in 2-D that provide limited interactivity but, rather, went for a complete 3-D format that provides a full immersive experience. It opted for genuine humans with real body movements over lifeless avatars and introduced a mix of natural sounds instead of playing melodies. It chose to display real store images in 3-D instead of static photos and used embedded televisions to display videos and images instead of pop-up windows. The website is created as a real virtual avenue complete with everything you will find in a physical luxury shopping street, including a line-up of stores with sumptuous window displays, a news stand, bill boards, street signs, public seats, a small park and even trees and flying birds not not to forget the habitual city sounds like cars honking, trains and birds chirping. The set up of the website emphasizes an exclusive location and invites a stroll down the two principal streets, First Avenue and Second Avenue. The presence of a companion in the form of a young lady who welcomes the user to the website and follows them as they move through the street also provides a touch of human presence and complements the natural environs.

Although it features information and no retail at this stage, the website is an embodiment of interactivity and luxury brand immersion and has set a precedent for the future direction of luxury websites.

Concept

The concept of The Watch Avenue is based on providing a complete and immersive 360° virtual experience (Figure 9.2). The website is built to provide an optimal web experience that will ensure the erasure of the barriers of the lack of human presence in the virtual world. The idea is to provide a prestigious virtual location that congregates prestigious brands in a single web destination with unique interactive features that replicate the elements of luxury. Its core value emanates from its focus on a 3-D experience that emulates the experiences in the real world. Its emphasis is on replicating physical store elements combined with real human attributes to ensure that the person visiting the website is so immersed in the online universe that he or she forgets that they are having a person-to-screen experience.

Figure 9.2 *The Watch Avenue: concept*

Design and aesthetics

Unlike the multitude of luxury websites that abound in cyberspace, the website's design and aesthetics refrain from the over-zealous application of multiple interactive elements like flash, slide-shows and videos but, rather, focuses on strong design concepts based on a 3-D format (Figure 9.3). The exterior of the avenue opens up with an image of a square from where the website visitor is redirected to First Avenue and Second Avenue with a line-up of stores. The design is such that each store's exterior and interior maintains the unique visual identity of the brand. For example, the interior of the Hublot store is based on the brand's signature black color and this complements the strong and masculine style, layout and interior fittings and decorations. The Vacheron Constantin store on the other hand features a design concept based on the brand's contemporary style which is complemented by the oak wood color undertones of the interior fittings and decorations. The exterior design of the avenue is, however, consistent in its visual replication of an exclusive and prestigious location.

Figure 9.3   *The Watch Avenue: design and aesthetics*

Atmosphere

One of the strongest features of The Watch Avenue is its unique atmosphere that evokes the feeling of being in a special place (Figure 9.4). As soon as the visitor arrives on the website, he immediately feels that he is in a prestigious atmosphere. This is achieved by the emotive mood that is generated from the intimate and rich ambience that is only found at exclusive locations. Gliding through the website's main avenues is reminiscent of a stroll down the beautiful tree-lined Avenue Montaigne in Paris amid the most luxurious of stores and hotels. Upon entering any of the stores like Piaget, Audemars Piguet or the Fondation de la Haute Horlogerie, the website visitor is further taken through a journey of sensory pleasures induced from a unique atmosphere of each website. At the Foundation's interior, we immediately feel the intellectual and profound ambience and the power of the organization's heritage and group of brand members. Vacheron Constanin is charged with the energy of innovation combined with heritage, while it is impossible to miss the elegance that embodies Piaget from its store interior.

Figure 9.4   *The Watch Avenue: atmosphere*

Usability

The focus of The Watch Avenue on creating an immersive virtual environment has not sacrificed its functionality (Figure 9.5). Despite being in a complete 3-D format with a 360° view, the website is easy to use and is a pleasure to navigate. Upon entering the website, the visitor is greeted by a young lady who welcomes them to the avenue and invites them to take a stroll. She also indicates her presence throughout the visit and invites the visitor to click on her should they need help. The navigational menu doesn't follow the standard vertical or horizontal line-up but is, rather, represented in flashing dots on different parts of the web pages. For example, a dot in the interior of a store may lead the visitor to another section of the store, say upstairs, or may lead to the television where videos may be watched. With the dots, it is easy to move around the stores and in and out of several sections of the avenue. To facilitate the usability, the website also features real sales representatives who may mostly be found at the interior entrance of several stores like Raymond Weil and Audemars Piguet as well as the Watch Foundation. Their presence is not only reassuring, but also provides an alternative functionality as they can be clicked on for help.

In addition, there are several menus for extensive information on the products displayed in the stores, news about the brands, the archives of the Foundation and other content. These are presented in a variety of ways from pop-up pages to embedded pages depending on the nature and extent of information.

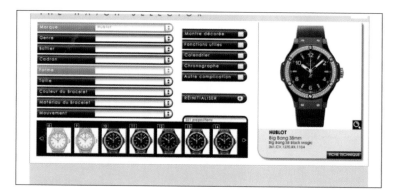

Figure 9.5 *The Watch Avenue: usability*

Content

This website wins top grades for rich content presented in an interactive and stimulating format (Figure 9.6). The discovery of the content is like a journey through a treasure island. Its features, including product collections, brand histories, the watch-making art and craft, archives, press information, narratives, and visually arresting product images, are all presented in a way that

Figure 9.6 *The Watch Avenue: content*

is balanced and stable. Although the amount of information on this website is vast, it is sectionalized according to brand and presented in such a way that the website visitor is stimulated to discover more content. The content is highly interactive and is displayed in a variety of formats, including videos and animations. When a brand arrives at this point in its web offerings, we can say that the website has attained a level of high stickiness and has reached a high probability of affiliation among the public.

The Watch Avenue has set an important precedent in the way luxury presents itself online and has introduced the new approach to addressing the question of online location. Watch out for off-shoot concepts in the years ahead.

Luxury Culture paves the way for the online luxury experience

Before Luxury Culture (LuxuryCulture.com) (Figure 9.7), the independent online magazine created by media veteran Yaffa Assouline, came along the

Figure 9.7 *Luxury Culture (luxuryculture.com)*

landscape of luxury online was what can best be described as "bland bland bland". Luxury websites all looked similar and Internet Managers of respective brands pre-occupied themselves with focusing on outdoing one another with as many images, videos, animations and pop-ups as possible. The question of representing luxury in its true and pure form in the virtual world was often raised but the general feeling was that this was impossible due to the nature of the Internet as a mass and classless platform. This led to the consensus that luxury would have to bend its rules to stay online. But would luxury brands have remained true to the status of prestige if luxury products were presented online like yogurt or toothpaste? The reality is that, at this time, there was no luxury website that simulated the core values and elements of luxury and there was no media website that had the combined qualities that could befit a luxury advertisement or communications – and there aren't many still. This led to luxury being rendered banal online and the consequence was that the Internet would eventually rob the luxury population of the culture and philosophy of luxury. This concern led to the vision behind the creation of Luxury Culture and also behind the choice of its name.

From the outset, Luxury Culture set out to challenge the way luxury presents itself in the virtual environment and, in the process, became one of the few references of luxury online. In its bid to create an environment that embodies the true characteristics of luxury, Luxury Culture questioned the form and manner in which Internet functionalities are integrated and challenged the display of text, images and information online. In the process, it invented horizontal navigation, developed a concept that is based on a two-way interaction – even without a community – and demonstrated how simplicity could be used to attain sleek sophistication.

Concept

The concept of Luxury Culture (Figure 9.8) is based on presenting luxury in its true and pure form through an online space that is simple yet rich in content and experience. The website aims to inform, entertain and form both luxury connoisseurs and amateurs in the culture of luxury. It demonstrates true luxury as a philosophy emphasizing the vastness of the luxury culture through the art of the appreciation of the fine things in life. The concept of Luxury Culture is such that the website strives to indulge every one of its visitors with the trappings of luxury and embrace the lovers of the *art de vivre* in an online world that they are likely to adopt as their own.

Design and aesthetics

This website is an embodiment of the use of minimalism to attain the sleek, smooth and sophisticated elegance that is found at the core of luxury (Figure 9.9). With its uncluttered pages, harmonized color scheme, visually

Figure 9.8 *Luxury Culture: concept*

arresting images, balanced use of icons and text, unique text display format, style, font and size, the website strikes a real equilibrium in the mix of low on features and high on style. Its uncluttered pages as well as its intelligent approach to advertisement all ensure that it offers a seamless experience. You will not find pop-ups, banners or flash ads on this website. Advertisements are embedded in a section aptly named "Brand Gallery" and other forms of communications include ads appearing in the interval between one page closure and another's opening in a non-obstructive way. Luxury Culture also achieves aesthetic harmony through maintaining a consistent black background in all sections and using a white background within the image and text box set in the dark background to highlight and emphasize on the page's content.

The website is also the only luxury website that welcomes each visitor with a quote on the definition of luxury and thanks you politely after your

Figure 9.9 *Luxury Culture: design and aesthetics*

visit. Luxury Culture demonstrates that it is possible to have "high gloss" online and epitomizes what in French is simply *la classe*.

Atmosphere

Needless to say, Luxury Culture emanates a unique and rich online atmosphere that is stimulated by the strong impact of its images, the display of its content and the use of features like sound and movement (Figure 9.10). Although millions of websites have these features, on this website they have been presented in a pure and unobstructed manner that offers each interactive element in just the right dose and blends the entire pages to create a harmonious impact on the senses. Upon entering this website, one quickly senses what can be best described as a cool breath of rich fresh air in the online universe. The mood that is evoked in the website's ambience is strong yet relaxing and this is derived from a unique blending of the signature color black with the varying colors of the products and services featured. The vast scope of luxury offerings that the website covers – fashion, art, architecture, interiors, transport, timepieces, jewelry, beauty and so on – also gives it a character of knowledge stimulation. On this website we almost feel as if our eyes, ears and all human senses are being opened to enjoy a pleasurable experience.

Figure 9.10 *Luxury Culture: atmosphere*

Usability

This is one of the easiest websites you will find online in any category or sector in terms of usability, functionality and navigation (Figure 9.11). As an innovative website that challenged the way information is presented online, the website was at the forefront of creating horizontal navigation instead of placing text and images on par in the standard scroll-down form. In addition, from its home page it also presents its main pages and sub-pages through a

Figure 9.11 *Luxury Culture: usability*

sleek line-up of sections which open up to other sections. The main navigational menu on the subsequent pages is in the form of a drop-down that is neither hidden nor obstructive. The categorization of the sections that suggest articles has also been approached in a clear and coherent manner. The interactive tools for "send", "forward", "print", "back" and so on have been represented with icons rather than unnecessary text. This website understands and recognizes that, after twenty years of interacting with the Internet, the online user has become intelligent and has moved on from elementary website interaction. Moving around Luxury Culture is a real pleasure and indulgence.

Content

The content of Luxury Culture is rich, engaging and informative (Figure 9.12). As an online luxury magazine, it strives to provide entertainment and the most

Figure 9.12 *Luxury Culture: content*

up-to-date information that will enable its readers to be in the know regarding luxury irrespective of their location. Luxury Culture, however, doesn't focus on providing information on trends. It leaves that to others and focuses on the type of content that is rich enough to be relevant for always. Its approach to luxury is as a timeless concept and this is visible in its approach to its content. The text of each article, interview and feature reflects a unique choice of words and manner of expression that is complemented by the accompanying wealth information presented with relevant images, videos and ample links to other websites for supplementary information.

The instantaneous nature of digital communications means that people can obtain trends-related news in a matter of milliseconds but what sets Luxury Culture apart is the timelessness and significance of its content, which is sure to remain enriching even for years to come.

Luxury Culture's arrival on the landscape of online communications and its success in breaking stereotype codes linked to online communications has led to a "wake-up" call for not only the media sector but also the luxury industry as a whole. It demonstrates on every level that the Internet can be matched with "high-gloss" and that luxury should be featured only in online environments that are befitting of luxury.

Viktor & Rolf changes the look of luxury online

To launch its spring–summer 2009 collection, Viktor & Rolf did something that everyone in the luxury fashion world would have sniffed at as being impossible, had they been told in advance. The brand decided to exploit the power of the Internet to maximize its communications and minimize its costs. It opted out of the usual Parisian runway show that sucks millions of dollars out of the pockets of designers and, rather, went for an online-only fashion show featuring only one model – Shalom Harlow – who strutted down a virtual runway in the brand's entire collection with multiple versions of herself appearing simultaneously (Figure 9.13). The digitally enhanced video of the show was uploaded on the brand's website and everyone was invited to watch. The result was what can be described as "mind-boggling". Within hours of its upload online, the news of the first "Internet-only" fashion show spread all over cyberspace like wildfire. Within a few days it had made its rounds on millions of blogs in the blogosphere and had become the hot topic *du jour* on social networks and several user communities. It wasn't long before the mainstream press picked it up, both online and offline, and the website became one of the most visited and most linked websites within one month. Fashion buyers flocked to the online show and those members of the general public that wanted to get a taste of the inside scene of the fashion world made the website their online destination. Needless to say, the brand got enough press and buzz to last it

Figure 9.13   *Viktor & Rolf (viktorandrolf.com)*

a lifetime and, in the process, set a standard in luxury online. The applause it has received for this move has simply been as a result of utilizing the immense potential of the Internet and demonstrating an understanding of the state of mind of luxury consumers who have also been substantially influenced by the digital revolution.

Viktor & Rolf brought the same unconventional approach to the recently re-launched website. The brand decided to take the bold step of doing things differently online by going against every luxury website design conventional wisdom – in other words, refraining from copying competitors' websites. The result is the creation of a website that envelopes visitors in a completely unified universe of Viktor & Rolf. The website is a journey of not only visual inspiration, but also one of sensory stimulation and an exceptional online experience.

Concept

The Viktor & Rolf website is created on the concept of a real "*maison*", into which every guest who decides to come by is welcome (Figure 9.14). This concept means that the website is developed entirely in 3-D format to emphasize the impact of the kind of immersive environment that can only be found in real houses. The website emphasizes that the highest form of satisfaction that can be obtained from a luxury brand is a pleasurable experience and this underlies the integration of each of its elements. The result is that of creating a unique feeling of being in a special space, a home where we are not alone but accompanied by the people that make the home alive – Viktor & Rolf.

Figure 9.14 *Viktor & Rolf: concept*

Design and aesthetics

Viktor & Rolf's website uses a unique combination of a digitally enhanced architectural design concept with human elements and movements to create a seamless aesthetic (Figure 9.15). Its design concept, which is based on a 3-D format, enables the simulation of an online experience that goes beyond text, images and videos. Its design is not based on multiple web pages – in fact, there are no pages – but on a unified experience of a journey through a house full of treasures. The color undertone is icy light grey, which adequately conveys the strength of color, shapes and visual elements of the product images featured

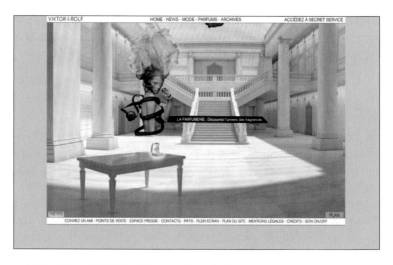

Figure 9.15 *Viktor & Rolf: design and aesthetics*

throughout the website. The design concept is one of classical architecture enhanced by modern shapes and interactivity. The clarity and luminosity of the different rooms and sections of the "house" makes the design concept stand out.

Atmosphere

The atmosphere of this website is charged with both energy and depth (Figure 9.16). One cannot help but feel the profundity of the world the designers have built around their brand. This feeling of creative wealth and respect is sensed through a 360° total experience of every section of the "house". It generates the kind of vibes that can be felt in the physical work rooms and studio of the designers. It uses interactivity, sound, melody, voice and strong visuals to evoke an ambience that embodies the core character-istics of the brand. The possibility of creating a unique online atmosphere has often been challenged by Internet opposers who contend that a luxurious experience cannot be created online. I invite those that adhere to this view-point to take a tour of the Viktor & Rolf online universe.

Figure 9.16 *Viktor & Rolf: atmosphere*

Usability

In spite of the use of advanced digital technology in its development, this web-site has struck a unique cord by enabling simple navigation, efficient function-ality and overall easy usability (Figure 9.17). Even an Internet novice will find the ease of use of the website pleasurable. Its navigation has combined the use of hidden tabs – which come to life with the movement of the mouse – with the standard horizontal menu and sub-menu presented discreetly on top and beneath the screen. This layout ensures that there is no interruption in the experience of journeying through the website. This experience is also enriched

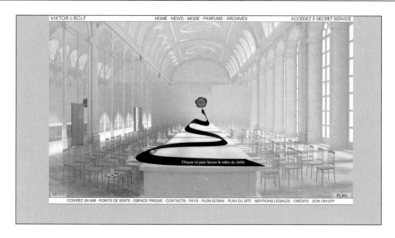

Figure 9.17 *Viktor & Rolf: usability*

by the simulated movement that is made upon clicking on one of the links that appear in different sections. For example, if the user desires to go to the "perfume room", he is transported into this room through simulated movement that takes him from his standpoint towards the door, which opens as he approaches and takes him into the room. What more could a website visitor ask than to be carried around in a beautiful house?

Content

Figure 9.18 *Viktor & Rolf: content*

The content of this website is what I would describe as sufficient (Figure 9.18). It doesn't go overboard, neither is it minimal. It provides just the right amount of text, images, videos, sound, animations and movement to ensure that the visitor's rich experience is coherent in every section of the "house". In addition, the presence of the designers on the website – who make an appearance in the company of their pets – elevates the content and reaffirms to the visitor that they are not alone in the "house".

The information on the brand, its history and heritage, designers, style, collections, products, press articles and other content are aptly displayed in different sections of the "house" which the user discovers as they make their tour. This ensures that the visitor is stimulated enough to prolong their stay on the website and, in the process, their enjoyment of the company of the designers.

This website, which has broken the conventional style that luxury websites have been following for over a decade, will surely be a benchmark for years to come.

Learning from the worst practices

It is not a very easy exercise to evaluate the worst practices of luxury online. First, there are just too many culprits and I would need an entire book to point out what is wrong with luxury online through website illustrations. Second, these worst practices are not entirely a death sentence that the brands and websites have imposed on themselves, as there are several internal factors that have led to the sometimes nightmarish nature of luxury websites – although this is not an excuse. Third, every luxury brand is unique in its identity, personality and essence, and one man's error may not necessarily be another's therefore highlighting these could lead some brands who do not fall within this bracket to relax their efforts.

In spite of all these, however, it is quite disheartening to find the websites of established brands in a state of incoherence in online experience and poor performance. For example, a visit to Chanel will reveal a website that is divided into three main sections – fashion and accessories, fragrance and beauty, and fine jewelry and watches. Upon further exploring the website, one can't help but be dismayed by the level of disparity in presentation and the incoherence in the brand experience that the three sections provide. While the fashion and accessories section focuses on providing as many images and videos as possible, most of which appear in high resolution, the beauty and fragrance section goes to the opposite extreme by featuring text and product images that are of such a poor quality that it hurts the eye. This is a horror for beauty aficionados, who need to read the labels and content information of skincare and cosmetics before purchasing and, moreover, for those that wish to print, as there is no opportunity to do so. A move to the fine jewelry and watches section and, again, we feel that we are on a different website. The style, concept, layout, sounds and experience is completely removed from the other two sections. The impression is that this website is a series of independent micro-sites that have been haphazardly embedded together.

A look at the Dior website and we also get the impression that we're moving through the universes of different brands according to the section of the website in which we find ourselves – and there are also too many sections and categories, which makes it easy to get lost. Hermès, on the other hand, seems to have chosen to change its brand image online, as there is no section of the brand's website that corresponds with the core identity and values of the brand to which clients can relate. If this is not the brand's intention, then it is all the more confusing and clients just don't "get" the website. Galeries Lafayette is not far from the ugly picture, with its flash-heavy pages that take forever to load, unclear navigation and static merchandizing. Several luxury brand and luxury retailer websites as well as media sites fall within the worst practice exemplifiers in several forms, including blatantly copying one another's styles and concepts – think Mauboussin and Paule Ka. But as I have mentioned earlier, this is not a self-imposed death sentence but indicates that luxury websites need to wake up to the fact that more is needed online and that luxury clients are no longer buying into this sub-standard online offering.

As I have emphasized throughout this book, luxury consumers have evolved after twenty years of interacting with the Internet. It no longer makes sense to offer them the same recipe that was used a decade ago. Just like you do not give a twenty-year-old baby food, luxury clients should not be given sub-standard web experiences. They will simply move on to other websites that have something better to offer. It's as simple as that.

To end on a positive note, it is important to recognize that in the last decade there has been a progression in the level of consciousness of the impact of the Internet on the luxury business and how this has changed both luxury clients and the way luxury conducts its affairs. Several brands and companies have taken bold steps – and prudent risk – in demonstrating that luxury and the virtual world can co-exist in a mutually beneficial manner. These pace-setters, who have been mentioned throughout this book, are the brands that will carve a core niche and client following for themselves if they continue in the direction that they have been going. Although mistakes will still be made and errors will still be committed – this is for sure – the key success factor for establishing a successful online presence would be for luxury brands to embrace digital technologies completely and maintain a forward-looking approach towards innovating and evolving with technology. There is no more going back to the days "before" the Internet, therefore luxury brands have the responsibility of being online in the way that befits luxury. As Gilles Nouaihac says, "luxury should not sacrifice its core values in a bid to meet the demands of the 'right now' culture but should use the richness of its world to envelope a clientele that is hungry for elevated experiences". There is no better way to demonstrate this than online.

Epilog
Q & A with Uché

1. Why did you write this book? Did it come about as an accident?

I have nurtured the idea of writing this book for about five years. It came out of several gaps that I discovered through my work as a business consultant for luxury brands. Irrespective of the country or product category, I noticed that luxury brands were struggling with the same issues and challenges. Some of the most resounding of these were linked to how to create a luxurious experience in the virtual world and how to reproduce the DNA codes of a luxury brand online. Many brands were also struggling to understand which products to sell online and how to do so without sacrificing their innate qualities and identities. I knew that I would write this book one day as I carried it around in my head for five years, so it wasn't an accident.

2. Why write the book at this precise moment, in 2009?

There are two main reasons. The first is that the arrival of the social web, or what some people prefer to call Web 2.0 or Web 3.0, has led to an explosive transformation of the mind-set of luxury clients, both online and offline. Attitudes, interests and general behavior have changed dramatically in the last few years. This has led to a real revolution that is challenging the way luxury presents itself and also what clients expect from luxury brands. This movement has also been reinforced by the global economic recession and its impact will further be felt in the next few years. I felt that these issues required urgent attention. The second reason is that the World Wide Web is celebrating its twentieth anniversary this year and there couldn't be a better time to make a contribution to this wonderful invention that has transformed the entire world and humankind.

3. Which luxury brands have the best websites?

I am often asked this question and my response is usually the same. There is none. This is not because luxury brands are not smart enough to have the best websites but simply because there is no pre-set magic formula for creating "the best" website. Representing luxury online involves several intricate strategies and approaches that have to be individually developed and executed in line with each brand's identity and core essence. Also, the degree of application of web elements like design, functionality, atmosphere, rich content, systems and applications varies between brands. The goal should be to create a coherent and unique experience across the entire board.

I find it often surprising to see how much time and energy luxury brands spend comparing one another's websites in a bid to become "better" than competitors. These brands often focus on the design and visual appeal rather than the total experience and complete brand immersion. Creating a luxury website should not only appeal to the eyes but also to the mind because long after the colors and design are forgotten, the virtual experience will always be remembered.

4. What do luxury consumers look for on a luxury website?

Consumers have been interacting actively with the Internet for the past twenty years and this exposure has led to constantly changing expectations. At the beginning of the World Wide Web, they were driven by curiosity to discover the virtual world and therefore they were easily attracted and pleased by beautifully developed websites. Today, this is no longer enough. The constant evolution of the Internet has led luxury consumers to believe that they are the center of the online universe. This means that they expect to be recognized and interacted with on a personalized level, whether it is through products, services or other offerings. Today's luxury consumer is seeking to be engaged by brands online and they will accept nothing less.

5. What should luxury brands do about blogs, social networks and virtual worlds?

Albert Einstein once said that *"Not everything that counts can be counted and not everything that can be counted counts".* think this should be the watchword of luxury brands as they get carried away by the excitement of the social web and by the competition of accumulating fans and followers on platforms like Twitter and Facebook.

I've heard many people say that luxury brands should create blogs, social networks and private islands on virtual immersive worlds like Second Life. I don't entirely subscribe to this idea because of the very nature of the social web and luxury itself. The social web acts as a congregation point for people to connect and express themselves through dialogue and exchanges. It thrives on independence of thought and draws its credibility from its objective nature. It is a medium created by the people for the people. Placing a luxury brand in this mix and expecting to have the same results is quite tricky, except the luxury brand is prepared to be entirely open, transparent and accepting of both positive and negative content. Most luxury brands are not ready for this. It is true that the active users of social networks are seeking brand engagement and intimate relations but I believe that luxury brands can fulfil their expectations without directly creating blogs or jumping on the bandwagon of social networks like Facebook, Myspace, Twitter and so on.

Integrating the social web in luxury is similar to learning a new language at an advanced age. It's a real challenge for luxury brands, especially as most brands have been used to communicating mainly through images and little text for a long time. Today the social web obliges communicating mainly using words and luxury brands have to learn to evoke desires and dreams through text. How do you make people dream using 140 characters on Twitter? Here lies the main challenge.

The answer is in understanding the phenomenon of the social web and how it is transforming people's mind-sets and the attitudes of an entire generation. This will lead luxury brands to understand the right approach and platform to adopt. The majority of luxury brands are yet to grasp the world of social networks.

I've seen several official communities created by luxury brands on websites like Facebook and My Space and most of them are poorly executed and they generally do not respect the codes of social networks like having a real two-way conversation with the people on the networks. Social websites provide people with an individual voice and a face, and it is quite difficult for corporate bodies to reproduce this. However I strongly recommend that luxury brands should closely monitor social websites as the information gathered on these networks are essential for tracking the evolution of consumer mind-sets and devising communications approaches. With the evolution of technology and the possible expansion of social networks in new dimensions, there will be several more possibilities. But the most important factor is to have a strategy.

6. How can a luxury brand select the right products to sell online? Should they sell everything online?

This is also another question I am asked all the time! I think that luxury e-retail should be approached very carefully, as there are several issues linked to it. First, the purpose of e-retail should be established and some questions should be answered: Is it purely for revenue generation? Is it a means of brand communications and image reinforcement? Is it an avenue to increase desire through inaccessibility? Is it a way to capture client data and reinforce relationships? Is it a means of channel integration? The answers to these should enable a luxury brand to decide whether to place the entire product collection for online retail and if not, which specific products to sell online. Second, there should be a core integrated strategy behind e-retail operations, otherwise it could fall apart.

7. You introduced the concept of the luxemosphere as a core aspect of luxury online. Can you explain the idea behind this?

Luxemosphere is coined from two words "luxe" and "atmosphere". Its meaning is obviously the creation of a luxurious atmosphere in a specific environment, both online and offline. It has been presented in the book as an essential aspect of ensuring a powerful online experience through sensory communications, which is very important in luxury. Luxemosphere uses different tactics to achieve a specific ambience that could evoke sensations in people. As we know, luxury is all about pleasure that results from a high degree of sensory appreciation, and positive sensory vibes go a long way in assuring a high-impact experience. In the online context where there is no direct human-to-human physical contact, this factor is even more important.

8. Is it true that luxury brands that don't have websites will stop existing?

Of course not. This is not likely to happen. However, what will happen for sure is that the luxury brands that avoid having their own websites will lose control of how their brands are represented online and, subsequently, how the brand is perceived in the real world. It is already happening with the arrival of the social web, where brands no longer control what consumers say or show about them online. The user is now in charge and has taken the reins of control in cyberspace. The most important means for luxury brands to address this phenomenon is to emphasize their brand heritage and value through having a high-impact website.

9. How should luxury brands approach other innovation-based areas like mobile and merchandising technologies?

The integration of technology and innovation in luxury doesn't end with the Internet. Technology may also be applied in product design and extension, material sourcing, store merchandising and mobile technology. Did you know that technology that enables body scanning for made-to-measure clothing now exists? Or that it is possible to try on clothes in fitting rooms through a recreated virtual model without ever putting the clothes on? Or that interactive mirrors in dressing rooms can enable distant and collective shopping? Or that the mobile phone can be used to capture sensory data on different products? Or that materials for clothing can now filter bacteria while conserving body heat or generating coolness? The possibilities for the integration of technology in the luxury field are endless.

10. What advice do you have for young and emerging luxury brands regarding the Internet?

I think young brands are extremely fortunate to be operating in the digital era. Every aspect of launching and growing a luxury brand has been made easier by technology. It is now possible to attain global brand awareness status in a relatively short time frame as a result of the Internet and instant communications. Product development, retailing, communications, sourcing, production and international expansion are all opportunities for young brands in the short term. My advice to emerging brands is to take full advantage of the digital media and new technologies, and never to think that they are too small or too young to act big!

11. Did you face any challenges while writing the book?

Endless challenges! First, I had to deal with web content that was constantly changing. Sometimes I used some websites to illustrate some points only to find upon completing that section that the website's contents had changed or that the entire website had been completely re-designed. This meant that I wrote some sections and chapters several times and I constantly added content until the very last minute of editing. Also, it was quite a challenge to convince some brands to release statistics linked to their website traffic, online sales turnover and other sensitive information. Eventually many of them did. Despite these, in general the challenges led me to strive to give the best to the book and I hope it has paid off.

12. What was the best part of writing this book?

I totally enjoyed every moment of writing *Luxury Online*. I guess it also comes from having an ongoing consulting practice in luxury e-business. Another enjoyable aspect of this book was hosting Club e-Luxe, the executive club for luxury e-business professionals. The involvement with Club e-Luxe meant that I was immersed fully in luxury e-business on a daily basis and it was easier to understand the challenges as well as identify the right approaches and technologies to overcome these. I also received enormous support from luxury brands too numerous to mention. People were generous with their time, insights, viewpoints and feedback. Since I wrote parts of this book during several business and personal travels, it was a real benefit to know that no matter where I was, I only needed to send an email or make a call to brands and they often responded instantly. I don't think I would have been able to write this book without this level of support.

I also received great support from my team at Luxe Corp, whose patience and flexibility in working around my pressure cycles and endless deadlines went a long way in making completing this book possible.

13. Did your previous book *Luxury Fashion Branding* influence the contents of this book?

Definitely. As soon as *Luxury Fashion Branding* was published in 2007, I knew that I was ready to write this book. I had so much to say in the e-business section of the previous book but couldn't due to limited space. Also, most of the questions I was asked during the book's presentation were related to the Internet and technology, and it was apparent that the issues in these areas had to be addressed. In addition, publishing *Luxury Fashion Branding* in full color also made me realize that this book had to be in produced in full color as well.

14. Any downside to writing this book?

Yes! As a result of the thousands of luxury websites I had to visit in my research and the many fantastic new brands and products that I discovered in the process I am now broke from shopping online!

15. Can you tell us which is your favorite luxury brand?

Sure. I'll tell you when I'm ready to be out of a job!

* Interview conducted by Sara White Wilson

Bibliography

Books and Journals

Aaker, D. A. (1996) *Building Strong Brands*, New York: The Free Press.

Aaker, D. A. (2003) "The Power of the Branded Differentiator", *MIT Sloan Management Review*, 45(1), 83–87.

Aaker J. L. and Maheswaran D. (1997) "The Effect of Cultural Orientation on Persuasion", *Journal of Consumer Research*, 24 (3), 315–28.

Aaker J. L. and Sengupta J. (2000) "Additivity versus Attention: The Role of Culture in the Resolution of Information Incongruity", *Journal of Consumer Psychology*, 9 (2), 67–82.

Ailawadi, K. L., Lehmann, D. R. and Neslin, S. A. (2003) "Revenue Premium as an Outcome Measure of Brand Equity", *Journal of Marketing*, 67(October), 1–17.

Alleres, D. (1990, 2003) "Luxe – Strategies Marketing", *Economica*, 1.

Atwal, G. and Willimans, A. (2009) "Luxury Brand Marketing", *Journal of Brand Management,* 16(5–6), March–May.

Berry, C. (1994) *The Idea of Luxury*, Cambridge University Press, UK.

Bialobos, C. (1991) "Luxe: le palmarès européer des marques", *L'expansion*, 412, September, 122–5.

Bourdieu, P. (1984) *Distinction: A Social Judgment of Taste*, Nice, R. (trans), Harvard University Press, Cambridge, MA.

Burt, S. and Sparks, L. (2002) "E-commerce and the Retail Process: A Review", *Journal of Retailing and Consumer Services.*

Cailleux, H., Mignot, C. and Kapferer, J. N. (2009) "Is CRM for Luxury Brands?", *Journal of Brand Management*, 16(5–6), March–May.

Chaffey, D. *et al.* (2000) *Internet Marketing*, Pearson Education Limited, Essex.

Chaffey, Dave (2007) *E-Business and e-Commerce Management*, 3rd edn, Pearson Education, Essex.

Chaston, I. (2001) *E-Marketing Strategy*, McGraw-Hill Education, London.

Chevalier, M. and Mazzalovo, G. (2008) *Luxury Brand Management: A World of Privilege*, Wiley.

Club e-Luxe Quarterly (2008) Issue 0010, Second Quarter.

Club e-Luxe Quarterly (2008) Issue 0011, Third Quarter.

Club e-Luxe Quarterly (2009) Issue 0012, First Quarter.

Club e-Luxe Quarterly (2009) Issue 0013, Second Quarter.

Cocanougher, A. B. and Bruce G. D. (1971) "Socially Distant Reference Groups and Consumer Aspirations", *Journal of Marketing Research*, 8(August), 379–81.

bibliography

Copeland, T. M. (1923) "Relation of Consumers' Buying Habits to Marketing Methods", *Harvard Business Review*, 1, April, 282–9.

Cornell, A. (2002) "Cult of Luxury: The New Opiate of the Masses", *Australian Financial Review*, 27 April, 47.

Coyler, E. (2007) "Luxury Brands Confront Web 2.0", Brandchannel.com

De Jonghe, An (2008) *Social Networks Around The World: How is Web 2.0 Changing Your Daily Life*, BookSurge Publishing.

Dennis, C., Fenech, T. and Merrilees, B. (2004) *E-Retailing*, Routledge, UK.

Dior, C. (1957) *Dior by Dior: The Autobiography of Christian Dior*, Weidenfeld & Nicolson, UK.

Dubois, B. and Paternault, C. (1995) "Observations: Understanding the World of International Luxury Brands: The Dream Formula", *Journal of Advertising Research,* (July/August).

Dubois, B., Laurent, G. and Czellar, S. (2001) "Consumer Rapport to Luxury: Analyzing Complex and Ambivalent Attitudes", Consumer Research Working Paper no. 736, HEC, Jouy-en-Josas, France.

Gillin, Paul (2009) *The New Influencers: A Marketer's Guide to the New Social Media, 2009*, Linden Publishing.

Gunter, B. and Furnham, A. (1992) *Consumer Profiles: An Introduction to Psychographics*, London: Routledge.

Gürhan-Canlõ, Z. and Maheswaran, D. (2000) "Culture Variations in Country of Origin Effects", *Journal of Marketing Research*, 37(3), 309–17.

Harris, L. and Dennis, C. (2002) *Marketing the E-Business*, Routledge, UK.

High Net Worth Report (2009), January/February. www.ledburyresearch.com

Holbrook, M. B. and Howard, J. A. (1977) *Frequently Purchased non Durable Goods and Services*, National Science Foundation.

Holt, D. B. (1995) "How Consumers Consume: A Typology of Consumption Practices", *Journal of Consumer Research*, 22, June, 1–16.

Holt, D. B. (2002) "Why Do Brands Cause Trouble? A Dialectic Theory of Consumer Culture and Branding", *Journal of Consumer Research*, 29(1), 70–90.

Holton, R. H. (1958) "The Distinction between Convenience Goods, Shopping Goods and Speciality Goods", *Journal of Marketing*, 3, July, 53–6.

Jupiter Research, available by subscription at www.forrester.com

Kapferer, J. (2004) *The New Strategic Brand Management*, Kogan Page, London.

Kapferer, J. N. and Bastien, V. (2008) *The Luxury Strategy: Break the Rules of Marketing to Build Luxury Brands*, Kogan Page, London.

Keller, K. (2003) *Building, Measuring and Managing Brand Equity*, New Jersey, Pearson Education.

Keller, K. (2009) "Managing the Growth Tradeoff: Challenges and Opportunities in Luxury Branding", *Journal of Brand Management*, 16(5–6), March–May.

Krishnamurthy, S. (2003) *E-Commerce Management*, Thomson Learning.

Le Journal du Net, www.lejournaldunet.com

Le Reste, E. (2008) "Enhancing Retail Customer Experience and Brand Value Through Mobile Technology", June, presented at Club e-Luxe Summit, 2009.

Lindstrom, M. (2008) "Buyology: Truth and Lies About Why We Buy", *Broadway Business*.

Lipovetsky G. and Roux, E. (2003) "Le Luxe Eternel", *Editions Gallimard*, Paris.

Luxury Briefing (2006) Atlantic Publishing, London, March.

Luxury Briefing (2008) Atlantic Publishing, London, April, July, October, December.

Luxury Briefing (2009) Atlantic Publishing, London, February, April.

O'Shea, Michael (2005) *The Brain – A Very Short Introduction*, Oxford University Press.

Okonkwo, U. (2004) "Redefining the Luxury Concept", BrandChannel.com

Okonkwo, U. (2005) "Can the Luxury Brand Atmosphere be Transferred to the Internet?", Brandchannel.com

Okonkwo, U. (2007*) Luxury Fashion Branding*, Palgrave Macmillan, London.

Okonkwo, U. (2008) "The Birth of the Modern Luxury Industry", Luxe-Mag.com

Okonkwo, U. (2009) "Sustaining the Luxury Brand on the Internet", *Journal of Brand Management,* 16(5–6), March–May.

Okonkwo, U. (2009) "The Luxury Brand Strategy Challenge", *Journal of Brand Management,* 16(5–6), March–May.

Phau, I. and Prendergast, G. (2000) "Consuming Luxury Brands: The Relevance of the 'Rarity Principle' ", *Journal of Brand Management*, 8(2), 122–38.

Porter, Joshua (2008) *Designing for the Social Web*, New Riders Press.

Roux, E. (1991) "Comment se positionnent les marques de luxe", *Revue Française du Marketing*, 132/133(2–3), 111–18.

Roux, E. (2002) "Le luxe: Au dela des chiffres, quelles logiques d'analyse?", *Revue Française du Marketing*, 187(2), 45–7.

Roux, E. and Floch, J. M. (1996) "Gérer l'ingérable: La contradiction interne de toute maison de luxe", *Décisions Marketing*, 9, September–December, 15–23.

Savigny Partners Newsletter, (2008) December. www.savignypartners.com

Scoble, Robert, and Shel, Israel (2008) *Naked Conversations: How Blogs are Changing the Way Businesses Talk with Customers*, John Wiley & Sons.

Scott, David (2008) *The New Rules of Marketing and PR: How to Use News Releases, Blogs, Podcasting, Viral Marketing and Online Media to Reach Buyers Directly*, John Wiley & Sons.

Silverstein, M. and Fiske, N. (2003) "Luxury for the Masses", *Harvard Business Review,* 81(4), 48–57.

Silverstein, M., Fiske, N. and Butman, J. (2004) *Trading Up: Why Consumers want New Luxury Goods and How Companies Create Them*, Portfolio Books, New York.

Tancer, Bill (2008) *Click: What Millions of People are Doing Online*, Hyperion.

Todaro, Miguel (2009) *Internet Marketing Methods Revealed: The Complete Guide to Becoming an Internet Marketing Expert*, Atlantic Publishing Company.

Truong, Y., McColl, R. and Kitchen, P. (2009) "New Luxury Brand Positioning and the Emergence of Masstige Brands", *Journal of Brand Management,* 16(5–6), March–May.

Tungate, M. (2005) *Fashion Brands: Branding Style from Armani to Zara*, Kohan Page, London.

Universal McCann (2008) www.universalmccann.com

Veblen, T. B. (1899) *The Theory of the Leisure Class*, Houghton Mifflin, Boston, MA.

Villacampa, E. (1995) "Luxe et magasins populaires", *L.S.A*, 1238, 50–2.

Weber, L. (2007) *Marketing to the Social Web*, John Wiley & Sons, USA.

bibliography

Weber, L. (2008) *Marketing to the Social Web: How Digital Customer Communities Build Your Business*, John Wiley & Sons.

Xiao Lu, Pierre (2008) *Elite China: Luxury Consumer Behaviour in China*, John Wiley & Sons.

Articles

"A State of Fantasy" (2007) *NewsWeek*, 30 July.

"Alternative Universe" (2007) *NewsWeek*, 30 July.

Amed, Imran (2008) "How to Recall Second Base Online", *Financial Times,* February.

"An Online Playground for the Rich and Fabulous" (2007) *International Herald Tribune*, 12 September.

"Ask Us" (2007) *In Style*, October.

Atwal Glyn, Khan Shaziya (2009) "Western Fashion Brands Miss Mark with Indian Trendsetters", *Admap*, January.

"Bagsie a Front Row Seat" (2008) *Grazia*, October.

Benhamou, Bernard (2009) "L'internet des objets", *Esprit*, March–April.

"Beyond Blogs" (2008) *BusinessWeek*, 2 June.

"Brrr, Designers Are Reflecting Climate Change" (2007) *International Herald Tribune*, 9 February.

"Bucking the Downward Trend" (2008) *WWD*, 2 October.

BusinessWeek (2005) "What's the Worth of Blog Search?", 11 July.

BusinessWeek (2007) "The Future of Tech – Global Youth", 2 July.

BusinessWeek (2007) "Luxury's Rising Son", 6 August.

BusinessWeek (2008) "Stalking the Next Big Thing"; "Let's Grab Google's Gazillions"; "Beyond blogs", 2 June.

Catherine Colin, (2008) "Le Design à Portée de Souris", *Les Echos Série Limitée*, 67, October.

"Children of the Web" (2007) *BusinessWeek*, 2 July.

Commerce et Image: "Le Grand Ecart", *CB News*, 964.

Dargan, Brian and Hunt, Mathew (2007) "CGM: The Power of the Margins", *Admap,* April.

"Dressing Rooms of the Future" (2008) *Forbes,* 22 July.

"European Firms Seek Minority Partners" (2008) *WWD*, 31 December.

"Facebook Reportedly Near Accord Over Origin" (2008) *New York Times*, 8 April.

"Fashion Stocks Still in Demand" (2007) *International Herald Tribune*, 12 September.

"For the Latest in Virtual Fashion, Just Add 3-D"(2007) *International Herald Tribune*, 26 September.

"Getting Luxury Goods Online" (2008) *TIME*, 23 June.

"How Companies Are Marketing Online: A McKinsey Global Survey" (2007) *McKinsey Quarterly*, July.

"Inside the Bespoke Revolution" (2009) *AgendaInc*, May.

"L'Hommage du Vice à la Vertu" (2008) *Le Nouvel Economiste,* 4–10 December.

"L'Industrie de Luxe Se Prépare à un Sensible Ralentissement" (2008) *Les Echos*, 24 June.

Le Journal du Net (2009) 4 April. www.lejournaldunet.fr

"Le Luxe Déploie ses Petites Séductions" (2008) *Le Monde*, 27 November.

"Le Mexique est Le Quatrième Consommateur Mondiale de Luxe" (2008) *Le Monde*, 19 February.

"Le Phénomène de la contrefaçon se sophistique" (2008) *Le Monde*, 13 December.

"Le Secteur du Luxe Pourrait Entrer en Récession en 2009" (2008) *Le Monde*, 14 November.

Lee, Barry (2007) "Web 2.0. Attracts Brands Looking for Customer Interaction", *Admap*, April.

"Les Blogs Dictent Leurs Modes" (2009) *Le Figaro*, 26 February.

"Les Marques Relancent le Soap Opera sur le Web" (2009) *Le Figaro*, 22 February.

"Les Ventes et la rentabilité des marques de Luxe Reculeront en 2009 et 2010" (2008) *Le Monde*, 13 December.

"Let's Grab Google's Gazillions" (2008) *BusinessWeek*, 2 June.

"Luxe er Stars, Une Stratégie à Tout Prix" (2008) *Prestigium.Com*, December.

"Luxury Brands and Marketing in Virtual Worlds" (2007) KZERO Research.

"Luxury Isn't Dead, But the Word Might Be" (2008) *The Wealth Report*, 17 January.

"Luxury Lifts Off in Cyberspace" (2007) *International Herald Tribune*, 9 October.

"Luxury Online Virals" (2009) *AgendaInc*, May.

"Luxury's Breaking Point" (2009) *CNBC European Business*, April.

"Luxury's Rising Son" (2007) *BusinessWeek*, 6 August.

"Modern Notions on Home Sewing" (2007) *International Herald Tribune*, 4 October.

"Moving Toward a New Internet" (2009) *Le Monde/The New York Times*, 7 March.

"My Life Without TV" (2008) *TIME*, May.

"My Online Panel" (2008) *Admap*, March.

Newsweek (2007) "US's Broadband Penetration is lower than even Estonia's", 2 July.

Newsweek (2007) "The Good Life", 30 July.

Peterson, Chris (2007) "CGA: The Creative Destruction of Agencies", *Admap*, April.

"Prada appelé à aider de ses foiurnisseurs" (2009) *FashionMag*, March.

"Putting a New Spin on a World of Natural Fibres" (2008) *International Herald Tribune*, 12 August.

"Rich Shoppers Prefer Their Luxury Online" (2008) *The Wealth Report*, 27 October.

"Richemont to Hire Wikstrom to Revive Chloé" (2009) *Bloomberg*, March.

"Roam un-free" (2007) *NewsWeek*, 30 July.

"Second Life, Une Seconde Economie" (2007) *Le Monde*, 23 July.

Sheldon, Nigel, "Consumers' Changing Relationship with New Technologies" (2007) *Admap*, April.

"Six Ways to Make Web 2.0. Work" (2009) *McKinsey Quarterly*, February.

"Social Networking for the Rich" (2008) *The Wealth Report*, 7 August.

"Stalking The Next Big Thing" (2008) *BusinessWeek*, 2 June.

"Stealth Wealth" (2007) *Newsweek*, 9 July.

Stelter Brian, (2009) "CC.com is Hoping to Win Surfer's Love", *International Herald Tribune*, 19 January.

"Sur Mesure" (2009) *Aeroports de Paris*, March.

"Survey Charts the Rise of Online Luxury Shoppers" (2009) *Linkshare*, March.

"The Internet From Space" (2009) *Bulletin*, March.

bibliography

"The Rise of Luxury Social Networks" (2009) *AgendaInc*, May,

The Wealth Report, (2008) 104(3), 15 March, The Luxury Institute.

"Troping Alexandra, Small World that May be Getting too Big" (2008) *The Guardian*, 1 September.

"Two Faces of People Search" (2008) *Financial Times*, 25 April.

"Visibilité à l'international pouir les marques de luxe, Google ne suffit plus!" (2009) *IC Agency*, 16 March.

White, Roderick (2007) "Web 2.0.: Consumers Take Charge", *Admap*, April.

"Yen Worries Luxury Companies Even More Than Weak Dollar" (2007) *International Herald Tribune*, 6 February.

Glossary of luxury online terms

The digital world is full of complicated terms, acronyms and all manners of jargon that are not easy to understand and nearly impossible to remember. When you're a creative person, a designer or a business executive, it is even more tasking to differentiate between ASP, HTML, PHP, DHTML, and the like. This glossary clarifies some of these terms and also acts as a reference for some of the words related to luxury in the context of technology and digital media.

Note: This is not a dictionary. The following definitions have been written from my understanding of tech jargon as it exists today. Of course you're welcome to disagree…

2-D Web Platforms (two-dimensional online platforms). These are basically websites that enable the viewing of its contents, including text and images from a static or 180-degree angle. Most websites and online platforms existing today are in 2-D.

2G Mobile Network (second-generation mobile phones). These are phones that are based mainly on digital voice technology and limited text capabilities. Most mobile phones introduced in the early days of GSM technology are 2G phones.

3-D Web Platforms (three-dimensional websites). These are online platforms that enable web interaction in a 360-degree format, such as the virtual immersive world platforms Second Life and Kaneva. 3-D elements may also be integrated in ordinary websites for product viewing and merchandizing. The future of the web is likely to be based on 3-D features.

3-G Mobile Network (third-generation mobile phones). These are mobile phones that feature enhanced multi-media functions in addition to voice, data, video, and animation. In most cases they offer an integrated web portal and fast internet access.

Active X. ActiveX controls are small program building blocks created by Microsoft to distribute applications that work over the Internet through web browsers. Examples include customized applications for gathering data, viewing certain kinds of files, and displaying animation. They run on the computer rather than on the server. To cut the jargon, Active X controls simply enable an enhanced viewing and interaction of web pages with rich content, period. And no, you don"t need to see this program when online, and neither do you need to give it a second thought.

Ad Server. A software that manages online adverts by programming the appearance of the adverts on pre-selected web pages. It also provides the statistics linked to the advert campaign. Basically it means that when you see a banner ad on a media website, it is not by accident.

Add On. An extension of software that ensures additional functionalities on a website.

ADSL (Asymetric Digital Subscriber Line). This is an internet access provider that permits high speed connections and facilitates the easy viewing of rich web content like animations, videos and images. Majority of web users today connect to the internet via ADSL (except those left behind in 1995).

Adware. A software that can be installed by a website author that enables the automatic appearance of adverts on the website's pages, based on prompted keywords that have been pre-purchased by the advertiser. Most blogs have adware that enables adverts depending on the words used in the blog's text and they are compensated based on page views and clicks on the adverts. Many view this as a cool way of making money.

Affiliation. A system of inter-linking websites through other websites with the goal of web traffic generation and transactions. This approach uses the placement of web links on "partner websites" to ensure visibility and increase the probability of visits. The generation of traffic is often compensated through a commission on visits, sales, contacts or other exchanges.

AOL (America Online). One of the early internet companies to provide people (yes, mainly Americans at first) with access to the Internet and such features as email, chat rooms, search engines and news content... that is, until the likes of MSN, Yahoo and Google came along and life became a bit tougher.

Application. A term generally used to refer to a software or system with specific functionalities and features. Applications may be web-based, mobile phone-based (think iPhone apps) or computer-based.

Artificial Intelligence. The use of technology to demonstrate and reproduce features and functions that would normally be performed by human beings and powered by the human brain. For example, robots demonstrate artificial intelligence as well as several other electronic devices and systems that make your life easier (and lazier). Did I hear someone mention Google?

Applied Technology. This term is generally used to refer to the integration of technology in the real and virtual worlds through both application support systems and technology devices. For example, using an interactive store window display that senses human presence could be refered to as applied technology.

ASP (Application Service Provider). A system that powers functions like online adverts or email marketing programs and provides statistics on their results.

Augmented Reality. The use of virtual features and elements in the real world and the integration of physical features in the virtual world (yes, it is possible!). This means basically bringing the virtual world to the physical world and vice versa. Holograms are a good example and the Six Senses by Pranav Mistry is also another example. If you're still in doubt, go to Google and type in "Tokyo Hotel hologram concert" and blow your mind away.

Auto-responder. A software that sends an automatic email to people either as a prospection or as a response to a click or a sent email. Did this really need explaining?

Avatar. The reproduction of a virtual human form either in 2-D or 3-D. Avatars are generally used for online product displays and merchandising.

Background Spoofing. The practice of filling background web pages with keywords to enable search engines like Google and Yahoo! artificially to increase the referencing of the websites.

Backoffice. The entire support system that ensures the functioning of a website.

Banner Advert. Online advertisements that generally appear on the top horizontal bar or the side vertical strip of websites with a re-direction to the advertiser's website upon clicking. They often feature images and animations and are increasingly interactive.

Black List. This is a list of web servers identified as the originators of "spam" emails. It is also sometimes refered to "spam detector" and enables the automatic deleting of emails from these servers. Nearly every web and email managing application features this service. If you don't have it you're doomed to a life of cursing your mailbox, your computer and the invisible spammers.

Blog. In simple terms, a blog is a web journal that can be written by anyone. In more sophisticated terms, a blog is a website that offers a record of a person (or a company's) thoughts, viewpoints and reactions on a specific subject or interest area. Blogs have recently emerged as the sensation of the social web phenomenon and have become highly influential to consumers.

Bluetooth. A wireless technology that enables devices like mobile phones or computers to receive data and voice at a short range of an average of ten meters, from point to point.

Boo.com. A fashion e-retail website that was one of the major victims of the dot.com crash of the late nineties. The website (eighteen months in existence) is often used as a reference for the worst online practices. As the saying goes, "Don't do a Boo please…"

Broker. People or companies that sell or trade in email databases and advise web companies on online client segmentation and email marketing targeting. If you've ever wondered how your email address got in the hands of a certain desperate e-retailer or media website, now you know.

Buzz Marketing. An online marketing technique that consists of literally making a lot of "noise" around a new website, product, service or offer. Buzz marketing doesn't use a single means for its diffussion but integrates all online media forms particularly the social media, for its communications. It thrives on creating a real online sensation that will entice readers enough to spread the news.

CGA (Consumer Generated Advert). These are advertisements of existing products and services created by individuals independently of the companies. They are often created by people that are passionate about the brands. Thousands of CGAs exist on websites like Youtube.

CGC (Consumer Generated Content). This is content about a product, service, concept or company generated by people independent of the companies. CGC could be in the form of text, images or animations. The social web thrives on CGC.

CGP (Consumer Generated Product). This is when consumers go as far creating products or concepts for a company mainly due to what they may percive as missing in the brand's offerings. These are often not counterfeit products but products created out of love and affiliation to a brand, or so they say.

Click. The action of clicking with the mouse on a web link, web page or advertisements. The number of clicks are often used to measure the popularity of the web content.

Clicktag. This is a code integrated in websites that contain Flash-based content. Clicktags enable these clicks to be registered and used further in web and advert traffic monitoring.

CLV. (Customer Lifetime Value). This simply means the value of a loyal customer to a brand over their lifetime. In other words how much money a brand can milk from individuals before they die, assuming that they remain loyal to the brand. CLV has a specific formula of calculation which I won't go into here (find it from a Google search) but all I can say is that whenever this term is mentioned in the board room there is excitement.

Channel Integration.   The integration of the features, functions and systems of a company's online practices with its offline practices for operational optimization.

Chat Room.   An online computer network where participants exchange messages and conduct conversations in real time. In addition to providing collaborations and connections, chat rooms have been popular for online dating...

CNET.   A website that specializes in technology product reviews, news and price comparisons, free software downloads, daily videos, and podcasts. Simply put, it's a destination for every tech junkie and also those looking for freebies.

Cookie.   This is information that a website puts on the hard disk of a computer to remember something about the computer and its user for future use. The information stored on the cookie is left on the client's server and is typically a record of the user's preferences and browsing habits when using a particular website. It is possible to disable the cookie function for specific websites. And no, I don't know how come this is the synonym of the biscuit, sorry.

Conversion.   A term generally used when a first-time website visitor is transformed from a simple visitor to one that conducts transactions on the site, in the form of purchases or subscriptions.

Conversion Rate.   The rate of converting website visitors from well visitors to shoppers.

Cost of Acquisition.   A term used to describe the average amount of money required to be invested in acquiring a potential client from an online advertisement.

CPA (Cost Per Action). This is the amount of money paid to "partner" or "affiliate" websites that provide links to other websites, based on the actions taken by visitors to the affiliate website. These actions could be in the form of clicks, downloads, subscriptions, transactions, or simply visits. Several luxury brands use the CPA model to remunerate bloggers and social media websites. Shhhh...

CPC (Cost Per Click). This is the remuneration of "partner" or "affiliate" websites that provide links to other websites, based on the number of clicks originating from the partner website.

CPL (Cost Per Lead). This is the remuneration of "partner" or "affiliate" websites that provide links to other websites, based on the number of contacts originating from the partner website.

CPM (Cost per Thousand (Mille). This is the cost attributed to an advertisement based on every thousand printed copies of the publication in which the advertisement appears.

Crawler.   This is a software (sometimes referred to as a robot, a spider or a bot) that search engine websites use to search the web in order to identify the most used keywords in different categories for web page classification and archiving.

CRM (Customer Relationship Management). Marketing programs and techniques that have the objective of ensuring that clients stay loyal. While in the past the focus was on "managing" clients, currently the objective is to "engage clients".

Cross Selling.   A means of direct marketing where an online shopper is given the suggestion and possibility of purchasing products or services that are complementary to their original choice. In other words, a kind of enticement (or tick?) to buy more and more. This is sometimes also called "Collaborative Filtering" and is powered by an application software.

CTC (Click to Call). This is an icon, button or highlighted phone number placed on a mobile phone, application or website which enables users to trigger a call from a company upon clicking on it. It is often used in customer care or service support contexts.

Cyber-residents.   This is used to refer to the millions of people around the world who live parallel lives online as offline. If you're reading this book, you're probably one of them (sorry, us).

Cyber-policing.   A term used to refer to the control of Internet and web content access by those more powerful than others (think China and North Korea).

Cyberspace.   The entire World Wide Web is also known as the cyberspace.

Cyberworld.   *See* cyberspace.

Cyworld.   A South Korea-based online social network that congregates its users to connect, share, dialogue and interact. It is one of the most active social networks in the world and also launched an English-language version based in the USA which closed recently.

Digital Media.   This refers to all the media platforms and tools that exist in the digital and internet contexts.

DHTML.   (Dymanic HTML). This is a name for a set of technologies used to create web pages that update themselves as the user interacts with the website. The updated elements could be the fonts, positions, layout and graphics which are rendered more interactive depending on several factors like the size of the user's screen.

Dot Com Era.   A term generally used to refer to the second evolutionary phase of the web from the mid nineties to the early noughties. This period was particularly marked by the rampant launch of e-retail websites and businesses many of which went bankrupt by the early 2000s. *Also see* Boo.com.

Double Opt-in. This is a term used to confirm a web user's authorization for either a subscription (such as a newsletter) or the adoption of a service. It allows a double verification of the intention to subscribe. *Also see* Permission Marketing.

E-boutique. This refers to an online store. The more elegant term "e-boutique" is favoured by luxury brands over "e-store" or "e-shop", both of which denote the sale of commodities rather than objects of desire.

E-branding. The representation of a brand and all its characteristics and dimensions online. This is explained in depth in *Luxury Fashion Branding*.

E-business. An integrated approach to every aspect of the internet business, comprising of marketing, branding, retail, client management, website design, digital media, social media and several others.

E-commerce. The sale of products and services online. When refering to the sale of luxury products online, please use the term "e-retail", thank you.

E-communications. Every aspect of communications online starting from a company's website to paid advertisements, social media, buzz marketing, cross marketing, and so on.

E-community. A term used to refer generally to online communities in general.

E-CRM. Online marketing programs and techniques that have the objective of ensuring client loyalty both online and offline. This is mainly linked to e-retail after sales services and client affiliation programs. *Also see* CRM.

E-culture. The current internet culture that is changing the characters, behavior, attitudes and complete comportments of entire generations.

E-learning. Online learning programs that often consist of distance or collective learning methods and experiences. And no, it is not for dummies looking to avoid supervised exams.

E-experience. Online experience derived from af company's website and its total offerings in the virtual world.

E-logistics. The logistics systems that support the e-retail activities of a website.

E-marketing. An integrated approach to every aspect of strategic online marketing comprising of the product, the pricing, the communications, the positioning, the clients and the processes.

E-merchandizing.   The use of technological tools in the display and presentation of products and services in the online boutique.

E-paper.   A display technology designed to reproduce the appearance of ordinary ink on paper. It is based on a technology that enables the reflection of light like ordinary paper and is capable of holding text and images indefinitely without drawing electricity.

E-people.   A term used to refer to online users or consumers. *Also see* Cyber-residents.

E-retail.   *See* e-commerce.

E-shopping.   Simply put, this means shopping online.

E-store.   *See* e-boutique.

E-zine.   This refers to online magazines that don't exist offline in parallel.

Email.   Who doesn't know the meaning of email? Seriously, I don't think it is necessary to define email but there may be someone out there looking for a simple way of explaining its meaning to their grandmother, so here goes: "Email or electronic mail is the a system for sending and receiving messages electronically over a computer network". Good luck with explaining the meaning of a computer network.

Email Alert.   Information originating from a website destined towards the mailbox of usually thousands of people on a database. The purpose is often to solicit, inform, sell or simply bother people's peace of mind.

Everquest.   An online based 3-D fantasy-themed multiplayer game. It is based on role playing in real time and is one of the several online massive multiplayer games that could become addictive, so watch out.

EZ Reader.   A small and lightweight digital device that enables the storage and reading of hundreds of thousands of book pages. The pages use a paper-like e-ink technology designed to enhance legibility even in bright light environments.

Facebook.   An online social network that connects people with friends and others linked to them through work and play. It is generally used to keep up with friends or connect with new ones, although many now view it as a modern disease due to its high adoption rate and addictive nature. This social network has recently been adopted by several luxury brands many of whom are focused more on outnumbering their competitors' fan base than really understanding the nature and value of the network and consider if it is right for their brand.

Feed.   This is a system that converges or aggregates web contents from different sources according to pre-identified the interest areas. Several online magazines and media websites use this system to build their own web content according to the interest areas of their readers.

Firewall. A system integrated on a computer or a server for protection against intrusion from unsolicited advertisements, emails, information or web content. It may be put in place by web-hosting companies, individuals or enterprises. In simple terms firewalls are what you need for a peaceful online existence.

Flash. A macromedia format provided by Adobe that enables the reading and visualization of text, images and animations on websites.

Flickr. An online photo management and sharing website that enables the exchange of images and social interactions around them.

FriendFeed. A website that allows people to build customized content with friends on other collaborative sites according to what they have shared, including news articles, photos, videos and comments. It basically customizes web content according to people's interest areas. And of course it's free.

Geek. A person who is considered to be inordinately dedicated and addicted to technology in all of its forms. The general perception of a geek is a boring intellectual whose world revolves around somewhere between computer codes and wires in an office hidden in the dark and lonely end of the hallway of a large corporation. In many cases he (or she) is also imagined to wear dark-rimmed glasses and to posses the strange power of being fully alert irrespective of sleeping an average of two hours per night and downing an average of twenty cups of coffee per day. And no, I am not a geek.

Google. Let's try this: type in "google" in Google and see what comes up. That's your definition.

Google Bombing. The (unethical) practice of using the keywords that describe other websites' activities to increase the visibility and referencing of the unethical company's website. In other words the purchase of either the keywords linked to specific companies or the integration of their web page linked in the background of other websites to increase their visibility on Google searches. This practice equals stealing and no amount of tech jargon can justify it so watch out offenders as Google bombing is now under surveillance by authorities.

GPS (Global Positioning System). A system of satellites that orbit the earth and enables people with ground receivers to pinpoint their geographical location.

GSM (Global System for Mobile communications). A digital mobile phone technology that is the predominant system in the global mobile world.

Hashtag. This simply means any word that begins with a hash (#) symbol. Hashtags have recently been popularized by Twitter because of Twitter's limited writing space of only 140 characters, as they help people to associate their tweets with an event, product or a piece of news without having to explain the full context.

HTML (Hypertext Mark up Language). This is a web development language used to structure text and multimedia documents and to set up hypertext links between documents on a website. In general most websites are either based on HTML and more recently on Flash.

IPAddress (Internet Protocol address). This is a unique address through which each computer that connects to the internet is identified.

IPR (Internet Penetration Rate). This is a matrix that is used to measure the effectiveness of the web referencing of a brand based on several keywords on different search engines. It allows these keywords to be controlled at any given time and is also used to benchmark the referencing of competitors.

iSmell. A personal scent synthesizer in the form of a computer peripheral device designed to emit smell when a user visited a website or opened an email. It functions through being connected on a computer via a USB port. The device contained a cartridge with over one hundred primary odors, which could be mixed to replicate natural and man-made odors.

iVillage. A website that is dedicated exclusively to connecting women at every stage of their lives. Its main features are news and content on health, beauty, style, fitness, entertainment, fashion, and so on. It also has interactive content such as message boards and social networking tools for sharing and collaborating.

Java. This is a programming language expressly designed for use on the Internet. It was originally designed to be implemented on every computer system in a standard way, which means running any software written in Java unmodified on any computer system. This didn't happen due to practical limitations (no need to go into that) which explains the mixed perceptions of this program by users.

Keywords. These are pre-identified words and phrases that are integrated in the background of websites and are used to optimize their visibility and referencing on search engines and editorial and media websites.

Landing Page. The page on which the user literally "lands" when they click on a link in an email, a blog post or a banner advert. The landing page is the starting point for the measurement of the result of the links.

Leaderboard. The format of an online banner advert that often appears on the top horizontal strip of a website. It is usually of 728 × 90 pixels.

Log. This contains files that provide the a trace of the activities of a website such as page visits, downloads, image and animation views and so on.

Luxemosphere. This is the strategy of reproducing a luxurious atmosphere in an environment both online and offline. It can be applied online through the integration of specific web elements that are directly linked to the five human senses. Luxemosphere is a concept developed by Luxe Corp.

M-commerce. This is simply the practice of commercial and transactional activities through mobile technologies and mobile phones. Although this is very popular in Japan, it is also gaining strong grounds in Europe and North America.

Menu/Menu Bar. This is a horizontal strip that contains lists of available sections and sub-sections for certain programs or websites. In Windows the menu bar resides at the top of each open window, while in Mac it is found at the top of the screen. The purpose of the menu bar is to provide access to options and items contained on the website or the program.

Microsite. This refers to an to an individual web page or a cluster of pages designed to function as an extension of a main website. It is used typically to add a specialized content that could be information or commercial-based. The main difference between a microsite and its parent website is its specific purpose and specialized content. It could have its own domain name or a subdomain linked to the parent website. Microsites are sometimes referred to as mini-sites.

Mixi. One of Japan's most prolific social networking websites with over 10 million users accounting for more than 80% of the Japanese social networking market in Japan.

Mlog. This is basically an online music log or the sound-based version of a blog.

ML. This is a programming language used in website creation. *Also see* HTML.

MMOG (Massive Multiplayer Online Game). This refers to online based 3-D multiplayer games often based on role playing in real time. If you happen to have a 15 year old nearby, they may probably give you a better definition.

MMS (Multi-media Messaging Service). This is enhanced form of SMS text messaging service that enables images, audio and video files to be transferred instantly through mobile phones.

MP3. This is a system used for storing and digitally transferring music on digital audio players over the internet.

Multi-channel. This is a term generally used to refer to online and offline channels in a company's business activities.

Myspace. An online social network that connects people and enables them to share content ranging from images, news, music, videos and all types of Internet transferrable files.

Navigation. The act of passing through a website's pages during a visit. It could also include charting a path on a website that will enable quicker future visits.

Newsletter. A regularly sent online news publication generally about a single or multiple related topics of interest to a specific group of people. Online newsletters are often sent by email to the subscribers of a website that have "opted in" to receive such newsletters from the website.

OLED (Organic Light Emitting Diode). This is a screen display technology that can also be used as a light source. It uses less power (LCD requires a backlight function which means a high energy requirement). OLED technology is emerging to be the next-generation technology for screen displays and will likely replace LCD displays used in such devices as Plasma TVs.

Offline. Simply put, the state of being disconnected from the internet.

Online. Simply put, the state of being connected to the internet.

Online Community. Well, a community online. *Also see* Social Network *and* Web 2.0.

Opt-in. This is a "Permission Marketing" term that means providing website visitors with the option of accepting an offer or a request from the website by checking a box through a click. This is often to confirm a web user's authorization for either a subscription (such as a newsletter) or the adoption of a service. It allows the visitor to express their intention to subscribe to the service rather than the service being imposed on them. *Also see* Permission Marketing.

Opt-out. This is the opposite of "opt-in" and is where website visitors are given the option of accepting an offer or a request from the website by un-checking a box through a click. In this case the selection has already been made for the user by the website, generally without the user's authorization, and they are given the option of withdrawing from the offer is desired. This practice is generally considered to be unethical as a majority of website visitors are generally aware of this choice made on their behalf. It is also one of the oldest tricks of the web for collecting and trading in email addresses. *Also see* Permission Marketing and Brokering.

Optimization. The process of improving the quality and volume of traffic on a website from search engines like Google, Yahoo! and Bing. It could be through natural search results or paid search results.

PC. Personal Computer, just in case for some reason you forgot.

PDF. Portable Document Format, just in case you never bothered to know.

Permission Marketing. The practice of providing consumers with the possibility to give their consent to be subscribed to offers from a website in advance. These offers could include newsletters, promotions, events and sales provided directly by the website or its partners. Permission marketing often takes the form of either checking a box to accept the propositions (opting in) or unchecking a box to reject the propositions (opting out). The former is considered to be ethical while the latter is viewed as unethical.

PHP. A widely used scripting language that produces dynamic web pages with rich content. It can be used on most web servers and operating system or platform.

Plug-in. The extension of a software to give it more functionalities.

Podcast. A series of digital media files in audio or video formats that are released episodically online.

Pop-up. Small windows that open automatically on a web page and often contain advertisements or promotions. They are generally considered as intrusive and may be blocked using several web options.

QQ/Qzone. A Chinese social networking website that permits users to connect and collaborate through writing blogs and diaries as well as sharing files such as photos, videos and news items.

QR code (Quick Response code). This is a code that allows the contents of a mobile phone to be decoded and downloaded at high speed.

Ranking. The position of a website in the results found on a search engine using specific associated keywords.

Redirect. A method of temporarily directing website visitors to a URL address different from the one they originally typed before landing them on their original intended page. This method is used to demonstrate a high level of website traffic even if the click on the re-directed website is not a real visit.

Referencing. The collective techniques of increasing the visibility of a website in search engines. These could include indexing, positioning, ranking and optimization.

Reporting. A report system that shows the returns on an online advert or email campaign in real time.

Rich Media. These are multi-media technologies such as videos, animations, sound, which could be included in websites, adverts or emails.

RSS Feed (Really Simple Syndication). This is a system that allows people to subscribe to a website and permits them to receive the updates on the website in real time without having to visit the websites. This is particularly useful for websites whose contents change frequently, such as media websites and blogs.

Sample Sale. The practice of selling products on line at marked-down prices generally significantly lower than their original prices. These websites use a concept of exclusivity (members only) and short sale periods (between 24 and 72 hours) to entice online shoppers.

Search Engine. A web search tool that automatically references web pages and classifies them according to their popularity and frequency of visits. The search results are based on keywords or key phrases and are found by what is known as a "robot" or a "spider" (which by the way is not visible on the page, in case you're wondering)

Search Engine Marketing. A marketing approach that uses the search engine as its main activity field, mainly through regrouping sponsored links and natural references and identifying ways for higher visibility in this context.

Search Engine Optimization. *See* Optimization.

Second Life. A fully integrated virtual world where the users exist through personal avatars that perform nearly all human functions and activities as in the physical world.

Skin. This is a graphic tool that allows the alteration of the appearance of a web page. It is often used in the context of advertisements or brand identity reinforcement.

Smart Phone. A mobile phone that offers advanced capabilities and functions similar to the ones found on a computer. These functions could include an integrated operating system, email, internet access, e-book reader, USB port or VGA connector.

SMS (Short Message Service). This is a system that allows sending short text-bsed messages through a mobile phone.

Social Network. An online community that thrives on congregating thousands of users at a time to connect, exchange, collaborate, converse, share and influence one another in multiple ways. The communities may be based on a specific interest area or otherwise.

Social Web. *See* Social Network.

Software. An system-based application that enables the performance of specific functions in the digital and electronic contexts. It may be based on a computer, the Internet, a mobile phone or other devices.

Spam. An email sent to recipients on a database with the motive of promoting or advertising products and services, mostly undesired by the reiepients. The email addresses are often obtained in a fraudulent manner and are often traded with other companies. In other words as soon as an email address gets in the hands of a "spammer", it is most likely already on its way to hundreds of other databases. Thank God for spam blockers.

Tag. A bookmark or ticket in the form of a code that is used to provide the information about a website needed for its referencing in search engines.

Tag Marketing. This is a code placed on web pages to record visits to the pages. Its purpose is to measure the rate of activity on the pages, the level of interest of the contents and the rate of transformation from a simple visit to a transaction.

TiVo. An electronic television programming that features the possibility of recording multiple TV programs both present and past, according to their title, actor, director, category, or keyword. It also provides other benefits such as downloads, advanced search, personal photo viewing, music offerings, and online scheduling.

Twitter. A social website that provides the possibility of staying connected with people and informing them of events in real time. It permits communications through text characters, web links and images. Contrary to popular belief, this is not a disease but an important phenomenon in the current web evolution.

UNIX. This is an operating system that functions in much the same way as other operating systems such as Windows and MAC, although it has lost its popularity over the years.

URL (Uniform Resource Locator). This is a chain of codes and characters that allow the identification of the address of a website in the World Wide Web that is typed in the internet navigation bar.

Viral Marketing. The practice of using sending and forwarding the links to web pages to others directly from the website. It is the equivalent of word-of-mouth publicity and is sometimes referred to as "word-of-mouse".

Virtual Immersive World. A digital-based simulated environment intended for its users to inhabit and interact through personal avatars. These avatars are often in three-dimensional form and are able to perform several human-like functions. See also Second Life and MMOG.

Virtual Reality. A technology that allows a user to interact with a computer-simulated environment both in the real and imaginary worlds. They are often visual-based experiences linked to computer screens or through other display types and are focused on stimulating the senses. Pilots use this technology for flight simulations and it is becoming more accepted in other sectors including luxury.

Vlog. A video-based web log. *Also see* Blog *and* Mlog.

WAP (Wireless Application Protocol). This is an open network communications system used in a wireless environment to provide access to content and services similar to that of a web browser. WAP is mainly used for accessing mobile websites from a mobile phone or a PDA.

Web 2.0. A term that is generally used to refer to the current phenomenon of the social web, driven by social networks and collaborative platforms controlled by user content. These platforms include blogs, online communities, discussion platform and all associated elements found in mainstream websites. *See also* Social Network *and* Social Web.

Webmosphere. The atmosphere or ambience on a website. It is created using specific web elements that are linked to the five human senses and its goal is to appeal to the mind rather than the eyes. *Also see* Luxemosphere.

Web Page. A document on the World Wide Web, consisting of an HTML file and any related files for scripts and graphics, and often hyperlinked to other documents on the Web.

Website. A set of interconnected webpages, usually including a homepage and a welcome page located on the same server. They are often created and maintained as a collection of information and content by a person, group or company.

Window. A term used to refer to a website or a web page.

World Wide Web. This is the network of all the websites and contents of the digital world and their interconnection to one another.

XML (Extensible Mark-Up Language). This is a programming language used for encoding documents electronically and integrated in the creation of websites. *Also see* HTML *and* ML.

YouTube A video-sharing website on which users can upload and share videos. Most of its content has been uploaded by individuals and it has become a major online destination for video-sharing.

Index